In Pursuit of Gender

Worldwide Archaeological Approaches

EDITED BY
SARAH MILLEDGE NELSON
AND MYRIAM ROSEN-AYALON

ALTAMIRA
PRESS

A Division of
ROWMAN & LITTLEFIELD PUBLISHERS, INC.
Walnut Creek • Lanham • New York • Oxford

ALTAMIRA PRESS
A Division of Rowman & Littlefield Publishers, Inc.
1630 North Main Street, #367
Walnut Creek, CA 94596
www.altamirapress.com

Rowman & Littlefield Publishers, Inc.
4720 Boston Way
Lanham, MD 20706

12 Hid's Copse Road
Cumnor Hill, Oxford OX2 9JJ, England

British Library Cataloguing in Publication Information Available

Library of Congress Cataloging-in-Publication Data
   In pursuit of gender : worldwide archaeological approaches / edited by Sarah Milledge Nelson and Myriam Rosen-Ayalon.
        p. cm. — (Gender and archaeology series ; v. 1)
   Includes bibliographical references and index.
   ISBN 0-7591-0086-1 (cloth : alk. paper) — ISBN 0-7591-0087-X (pbk. : alk. paper)
     1. Social archaeology. 2. Sex role—History. 3. Man-woman relationships—History. 4. Women—History. 5. Women, Prehistoric. 6. Feminist archaeology. I. Nelson, Sarah M., 1931– . II. Rosen-Ayalon, Myriam. III. Series.
   CC72.4.I5 2002
   305.3909—dc21   00-049598

Printed in the United States of America

∞ ™ The paper used in this publication meets the minimum requirements of American National Standard for Information Sciences—Permanence of Paper for Printed Library Materials, ANSI/NISO Z39.48-1992.

Contents

Preface and Acknowledgments

This book is the fruit of a conference at the Rockefeller Study and Conference Center in Bellagio, Italy, in October 1998. We thank both the Rockefeller Foundation for the conference support and the wonderful ambience and the Wenner-Gren Foundation for providing overseas transportation for participants. We, the organizers of the conference, met in 1996 at this beautiful place for scholars, and before our month was over we had decided to apply to hold an international meeting that we called "Worldwide Archaeological Perspectives on Women and Gender."

The conference was based on the expectation that archaeologists from around the world would have important contributions to make to the study of gender in archaeology. Even participants who had never thought about the topic before would, we expected, illuminate gender in the past from the perspective of their own regional tradition. We reasoned that we could all learn from one another and expand method and theory in gender archaeology and extend its reach. We wanted to expose all the participants to one another's different archaeological traditions; to see what we could mutually learn; and, however much or little experience we each had with gender in archaeology up to that point, to learn to approach gender in the past with new perspectives. We firmly believed that neophytes and experts could learn from each other. In addition, we did not wish to discourage thinking about women (instead of gender) in the past because that is an important place to begin, and often a place to return to, when thinking about gender. Thus, gender may be approached through looking for women and their activities, especially in areas where women's roles or tasks have been either ignored or taken for granted. Specifically focusing on women is often a way to refresh thinking about gender. This book is evidence that our beliefs were well founded.

Accordingly, participants in the conference came from Thailand, India, South Africa, New Zealand, and Israel as well as Europe, Canada, and the United States. We invited active and well-published field archaeologists who would be aware of the pitfalls of overinterpreting the data. Not every archaeologist who attended the conference does fieldwork in his or her home region, a fact that also gives a wider spread to the kind of data presented. The chapters in this book represent archaeological work in China, Japan, Thailand, the Philippines, Andaman Islands, Egypt, South Africa, southwestern Asia, Italy, Germany, France, Argentina, Brazil, Central America, and eastern and western North America. Time periods range from the Lower Paleolithic to the early historic Philippines. Societies represented include hunter-gatherers, early horticulturalists, incipient and well-developed states, and historic communities as well as ethnoarchaeological explorations and primate studies.

While this menu may appear to be rather wide ranging for a single book, the chapters are united by a common determination to take seriously a gendered past, a social archaeology that considers the agency of men and women beyond their purported artifacts. Both method and theory are weighed in various chapters. The chapters thus gathered in this book are characterized by advances in theory, greater specificity in methods, and generally impatience with old categories that obscure rather than illuminate gender relationships. Some chapters note that a gendered past is not in itself a given. Each chapter includes background for readers unfamiliar with its region and time and sketches the problems that are locally on the archaeological agenda. The chapters present the best, most current scholarship on their topics and in their regions.

1

Introduction

Sarah Milledge Nelson and Myriam Rosen-Ayalon

The study of gender in archaeology is experiencing growing pains. While at times it seems to be coming of age with the more sophisticated theories and methods, at other times the practitioners disagree profoundly with one another on questions such as whether gender has some biological basis or in what ways sex may be socially constructed. Thus, there are not only multiple ways to seek indications of gendered lives in the past but also multiple notions about what gender is. While all the authors in this volume would agree that pursuing gender in the past is a worthwhile endeavor, they set forth to accomplish this in various ways. Many archaeologists, men and women, would agree that the endeavor is justified. The surface has been surveyed, but more "digging" into the topic is warranted, and the deeper the exploration, the more vexing the issues become.

The chapters in this volume demonstrate some of the many fruitful avenues to explore in pursuit of gender. They also contain a plethora of data from individual sites and cultures that have been interpreted or reinterpreted from the perspective of gender. The topic has gone well beyond the task of "finding the women" who were overlooked in archaeological interpretations for so long, as having timeless and invariable roles and to be of little interest because change was minimal. However, in many places and times in the past, women need to be foregrounded in order to create a new perspective. These chapters explode old assumptions that women in the past had timeless and invariable roles. Essentialist ideas of "woman" are also put to rest. Women may differ even within a single culture by age, class, marital status, presence or absence of children, and the kinds of work they do.

At the meeting at Bellagio, we struggled with words. Even the distinction between sex and gender, once so productive in reducing the essentialism inherent in the notion of "women," is perceived on further inspection to produce its own traps. If sex is based on biology and gender is based on culture, there are many gray areas where the distinction is not so clear, and what about other genders not so clearly tied to biological sex? How to recognize other genders in the archaeological record is tricky, given that we often cannot perceive them under our own noses in the present.

In using the word "gender," we knowingly venture onto untrodden paths and rickety causeways. Donna Haraway (1991: 127–48) shows just how unclear the "sex/gender system" is, although it made good sense in English. This was highlighted for her when she needed to translate the term into multiple languages for an encyclopedia and found that some languages lacked words for the concepts. Most of the authors in this volume are native English speakers, but for several authors English is a second language. One participant in the symposium explained that the concept of gender is absent in her native tongue and therefore had no analog in archaeology in her country. The concepts we dispute in English may not even approximate equivalents in other languages, and it is wise to be aware of the extent to which language shapes our concepts. However, because we are using English, we will stick with the term "gender."

While pursuing gender in archaeology is far from a simple endeavor, the attempt does change the discipline. When gender becomes a focus of explanation, the possibilities for expanding archaeological interpretation with both rigor and imagination open up new territory. In the past, one of us has made the bold assertion that pursuing the topic of gender can improve archaeology (Nelson 1997: 13). The chapters in this volume, and the discussions at the conference on which they are based, demonstrate some of the ways that inserting the topic of gender into the heart of a research project can be accomplished and, more important, how considering gender seriously exposes weaknesses previously unnoticed and demands greater attention to detail.

These chapters show the increasing sophistication of archaeological explanation as we continue to dig more deeply into understanding gender. However, despite the many researchers who have paved the way, using gender as a research tool in archaeology does not provide a single obvious path, and it is far from a grand boulevard leading to new "truth." There are roads that branch in several directions and many byways that remain to be explored. Gender in archaeology should not be considered a new subdiscipline; rather, it should infuse the entire field and charge it.

Many years ago, Alfred Kidder divided archaeologists into the "hairy chested"—by which he meant dirt archaeologists—and the "hairy chinned"—

thinkers—who espouse grand theory. These expressions have been used to expose the unconscious assumption that archaeologists are male (Nelson 1997), but here we want to make a different point. Gender research moves between field observations and grand theory without regard to the placement of hair or the gender of the archaeologist. It can correct for both overtheorizing without regard to data and for too narrowly focusing on a single site or region. Focusing on gender creates more sophistication in using archaeological data. These chapters are attuned more to discovering differences than to finding sweeping evolutionary trends—a tendency in archaeology that has previously hindered the movement toward this increasing sophistication. Grand theory has been declared the most important part of archaeology, replacing moving dirt (by the "hairy chested") as the test of a real archaeologist (the "hairy chinned"). Gender archaeology moves back to a dialogue and does not polarize method and theory.

THE ROOTS OF GENDER ARCHAEOLOGY

What has now become most frequently called "gender archaeology" began in several ways. The first was recovering women in an archaeological discourse that largely assumed only males as actors. At the same time, androcentric assumptions were aired, questioned, and reassessed. In North America, cultural anthropology led the way. These were tasks begun in the 1970s, and they are not yet completed, although a great deal has been accomplished. Inequalities between men and women in the field (in both senses) were described, quantified, and analyzed in the 1980s. The 1990s turned to inclusiveness. Archaeology lagged behind cultural anthropology, but its potential to shed important light on gender in the past is beginning to be reached.

While some early attempts at adding women to prehistory are now seen to have been rudimentary and perhaps to have reached dead ends, they were a necessary beginning, a product of their time. The pursuit of gender in the past is perhaps more like a spiral than a straight line. The literature on the subject is unruly but lively, and that vitality, and the capacity to indicate new paths for archaeology, is important even beyond gender studies.

The development of gender studies in archaeology illuminates the chapters in this volume in various ways. First, the traditional anthropological concept of an "egalitarian" society clearly has as an underlying assumption the notion that women are never equal to men at any time and in any society. Furthermore, this interpretation not only uses inequality between men and women as a given but also considers it of no interest. In contrast, the earliest feminist discussions of women and gender (e.g., Rosaldo and Lamphere 1974; Reiter 1975). Rosaldo

(1974) asked whether such a sweeping generalization could conceal some very interesting variations. She also wondered why such an imbalance might be universal and later began to question the truth of its universality (Rosaldo 1980). Division of labor by gender is not the whole question, and it does not have a yes or no answer. What, where, how, and when are at least as interesting as who is perceived to be the worker. and sometimes the emic perception differs strikingly from the etic one (Brumbach and Jarvenpa 1990).

In the earliest days, women archaeologists asked the perfectly reasonable question "Where are women in representations of the past?" This was necessary because of a pervasive androcentrism in our own culture, now becoming (to some extent) passé. This point of view placed men in the middle of cultures and cultural evolution. Women were peripheral, deviant if different, and rarely interesting. Like other disciplines, such as history and cultural anthropology, men's interests and activities were used to stand for the group as a whole. "Cultures" were seen as wholes, not as divided into groups by gender, class, and faction with competing and crosscutting interests. It was the general rule that whatever men did was used to define the culture. Women's "tasks" were presented as similar the world over. An awareness of this muting of women led first to the question of what women *were* doing while men were creating culture (Dahlberg 1981). Even in the 1970s, when women's work was acknowledged, it was usually simply stereotyped as baby and child care and household maintenance along with some "crafts." These attitudes are rooted in biological essentialism. The only absolute universal is that women give birth to the babies. However, even that is not true of all women and certainly is not true of any woman all her life. Thus, the fact that women, not men, give birth cannot explain everything about gender differences and cannot explain anything about differences among women.

The more the female side of the past was explored, the more evident it became that the formulations of what archaeologists study, from gathering to the origins of agriculture to the formation of the state, needed to be retheorized. When attention is paid to what women did, pronouncements that had seemed "obvious" before are exposed as androcentric or essentialist, requiring further exploration of the subject.

Also impinging on archaeological explanations was the use of the past by feminists who had newly encountered their common interests as women. This was the "me too" era, when goddesses, priestesses, women warriors, queens, and huntresses were discovered. On the other side, women in their "usual" roles could be construed as heroes of the evolutionary story. Gathering could be the foundation of culture, mothers were the center of society, and women's "natural" peacefulness was the glue that held society together. Digging sticks were just as important as throwing sticks.

Thus, three themes, equally essentialist although contradictory, can be found in the early feminist literature. One is that women can do everything men can do—that men and women are just alike. Another is that women are different and that they are better. The third is that women's activities are as important to study as men's activities and that the relationship between them is critical to describe in order to really understand a particular society. It is this last theme, followed in this volume's chapters, that does not essentialize men or women, that has led to far more sophisticated archaeology. As women archaeologists began to make their voices heard, the analyses of women in the past became more subtle and more varied. Men in archaeology began to perceive the analysis of gender in archaeology as important as well and contributed other perspectives.

As new volumes on gender in archaeology appear, some issues become more cloudy, but the available data expand, and new methodologies enrich the study of gender. Some regional books that have appeared recently look at South Africa (Wadley 1997), Italy (Whitehouse 1998), Africa in general (Kent 1998), and North and Meso-America (Claassen and Joyce 1997).

One branch of gender theory in archaeology is moving toward biologizing gender (Gilchrist 1999). They have failed to note that the original distinction made between sex and gender was a conceptual one: Sex refers to biological differences between men and women, and gender applies to the cultural difference. While the distinction may become blurred, on an archaeological level the distinction between sex and gender is still a useful heuristic device. We may know that a table is made up of molecules, but at one level of analysis it is the solid wood rather than the moving molecules that needs to be the center of attention. Nelson and Kehoe (1990) showed that the "powers" of observation need to be adjusted to the task at hand. The task of engendering archaeology needs the sex/gender distinction to "see" gender as it played out in specific cultures in the past. The danger of biologizing the sex/gender system is that it can explain differences between humans and other species but not between human groups.

METHODS FOR STUDYING GENDER

Multiple lines of evidence are one of the most secure ways to study gender in archaeology, and these chapters reflect that choice. Methodologies for studying the sex/gender system in these chapters include such widely diverse types of data as ethnohistoric documents and prehistoric DNA. Ethnographic analogy and the direct historical approach (to use a term from North American anthropology) are used to good effect. Domestic uses of space are a possible road into understanding gendered spaces in the past but can be a danger to be skirted in some circumstances. Ritual space, including caves, and other places where ceremonial objects are found can be fruitful places to seek gender.

Burials and their contents and contexts are another rich source of data for researching gender in the past. Because burials can be sexed (with varying degrees of certainty), they can be compared to apparently gendered grave offerings, noting both conformity and nonconformity with expectations according to sex. Unusual combinations may reveal additional genders or non-gendered roles or other life circumstances that may enhance or diminish the expression of sex or gender in death.

Depictions of men and women are an important source to reveal facets of gender not approachable with other data, especially when people are shown engaged in a specific activity or marked in various ways by indications such as hairstyles, clothing, or artifacts. Rock art is particularly prolific in gendered images, which can be made to tell several kinds of stories. In these chapters, different kinds of inferences are drawn from rock art in South Africa, Thailand, and Italy, demonstrating the rich possibilities of this type of data.

Questions of how women are perceived (by males?) occur in several of the chapters. An attempt is made not to project these beliefs into universal truths but to suggest rather the variety of possibilities. Fekri Hassan and Shelley Smith (chapter 3) suggest that in predynastic Egypt, the figurines emphasize fertility rather than sexuality, but Ruth Whitehouse (chapter 2) makes the case that fertility is not germane to Italian figurines. The "pretty lady" figurines of formative Meso-America may be emphasizing youth, beauty, and sexuality, according to Rosemary Joyce's analysis in chapter 6, rather than fertility per se. Thus, the contexts of the data are vitally important to richly textured interpretations. Generalizing about sexuality or fertility is not the point—understanding particular gender arrangements is the goal.

One of the most gratifying characteristics of these chapters is that nothing about gender is taken for granted. It was understood not only by those who had spent years studying gender in archaeology but also by the novices that it is necessary to question even (or perhaps especially) the aspects of gender differentiation that seem most "natural" to us. We all learned a great deal from one another.

CHAPTER ARRANGEMENT

Deeper processes than sources of data were at issue in our discussion at Bellagio. Thus, these chapters are grouped to reflect themes that arose during the conference: *gender ideology, gender roles,* and *gender relations.*

Gender ideology considers what people think about gender and how gender can be an organizing principle in a culture. This is clearly true of American culture, which until the 1970s divided even help-wanted ads into male and female categories. Gender ideology asks, What is believed about women and men? How are differences between the sexes naturalized, or polarized, or projected on objects or ideas that have no inherent gender?

Gender roles take us in another direction, reflecting the economics of gender—what women and men are expected to do in their daily lives, how and where they do these things, and with what tools. The archaeological tools that have already been used in household archaeology are expanded to include gender distinctions.

Considering gender relations is a way to approach the politics of gender—men and women in their negotiations of power. Power seems to be gendered male in Western culture but may be otherwise gendered or ungendered in other times and places.

Using these topics as guidelines, we begin with gender ideology, follow with gender roles, and end with gender relations. These are permeable categories, and emphasis on any one of them still requires some attention to the other. However, this division serves to put similar chapters near each other for easier reading and allows the reader to think about these topics in a comparative perspective.

SUMMARY

These chapters ask gendered questions and question gender attributions. They agree that the interpretation of gender in archaeological contexts is difficult but that it is an important endeavor. The contexts are varied, the methods differ, and the underlying assumptions are not always completely congruent. However, interacting with one another, these chapters advance the archaeological study of gender with detailed data and carefully reasoned conclusions that move into new territory with both the confidence of seasoned archaeologists and thoughtful grounding in gender-based theory.

I

GENDER IDEOLOGY

SARAH MILLEDGE NELSON

The definition of gender ideology used by Hays-Gilpin and Whitley (1998: 4) is relevant here: "Meanings and values attributed to gender categories in a given culture, and assignment of gender to non-sexed phenomena or ideas (for example moon/sun, earth/sky, soft/hard, domestic/public), on the basis of these meanings and values."

Variations in beliefs about gender in different cultures have been well documented, starting at least with Margaret Mead (1963, 1975). Gender ideology includes the ways that gender is conceptualized by the society as a whole and the ways that various subsets of the society understand gender. Women and men may be seen as substantially the same or as polar opposites. Men and women may have different gender ideologies or may share them. Thus, some women may have different beliefs than men about their own abilities, whereas other women may subscribe to the masculine view current in their culture. Such variations are often created by class differences, but other divisions, such as race or faction, can contribute to variations in gender beliefs as well.

Gender ideology is often expressed in activities, objects, or features of the landscape that have no inherent sex. These clues can be teased out archaeologically in several ways. An obvious beginning includes depictions of gendered people and their attire, artifacts, or actions. Habitual activities of men and women can take on gendered meanings that seem to be "natural." Symbolic representations may also indicate gendered objects or metaphors. Cows can stand for adult women and oxen for men (Hassan and Smith, chapter 3), or men can be related to elands in ways similar to their relationship to women (Parkington, chapter 7).

Thus, the rubric of gender ideology subsumes both gender identity—how individuals perceive their own gender—and societal correlates of possible gender identifications. Each chapter in this part addresses some facet of gender ideology. They address diverse subjects, such as beauty, hunting, birth, death, and nurturing. In each case, the author relates the discussion directly to the details of the archaeological record. While other sources may be also used—from folk tales to ethnohistory—the emphasis is on local, not global, meanings. Universal truth is not sought but, rather, nuanced local meanings. In some cases, changes in meanings are emphasized (Joyce, chapter 6; Hassan and Smith, chapter 3).

Archaeologists can draw on work by cultural anthropologists and others to find solid ground for their interpretations. For example, Peggy Sanday (1981) has explored the assignment of gender to deities and demonstrates that a culture's origin myths, insofar as they are gendered, are "scripts for social action." Myths codify gender ideology by attributing them to the beginning of time. On the other hand, generalizations about the interpretation of art as shamanic visions may be too sweeping to represent all possible art, and other kinds of data may provide alternative understandings (Parkington, chapter 7).

In chapter 2, Whitehouse concentrates on southern Italy in the Neolithic period, from about 7000 to 5000 B.C. Using a combination of types of evidence: burials, cult caves with paintings, anthropomorphic figurines, and architecture and space, she explores gender relationships in ways that have not been attempted before in Italian archaeology. The placement of gendered depictions in the caves suggests that the caves are the locus of male rituals. She argues that, since the paintings deep in the caves depict men hunting, it was not a major part of the economy when the paintings were made. Hunting had become part of the ritual sphere instead, perhaps emphasizing masculinity.

Whitehouse reasons that this exclusivity of male ritual suggests antagonism between the sexes. She uses ethnographic analogy to bolster her interpretation, citing Melanesia as an example of small-scale societies where gender categories are antagonistic rather than complementary. Reasoning that it is likely that women had their own rituals in other locations, she considers women's work, combined with depictions of women. Anthropomorphic figurines, which are generally referred to as "mother goddesses" in Italy, provide one source of information. These figurines are rare and are found in cult caves as well as in settlements. Those placed in caves are of uncertain gender, while those found in settlements are clearly female. Another distinction is that figurines in settlements are all made of clay, in contrast to the stone figures in caves. Therefore, Whitehouse argues, the settlement figurines were made by women, for women's rituals. She raises the question of affective space and suggests that men and women may have experienced the same space in different ways. She posits that ritual activities include rites of passage that involve shifting statuses and possible shifting genders.

In chapter 3, Hassan and Smith write about women in predynastic Egypt, centering around 3000 B.C. Their concern is to discover how gender iconography, especially images of women, reflects changes in the formative period of Egypt. Women, they suggest, were the prototype of the supernatural, as shown by female figurines that have aspects of birds and cows. They also use burial data, especially types of objects buried with women and men, and the changes through time of appropriate gendered burial goods.

By 3000 B.C., Egyptian polities had become small states based on long-established agriculture, craft production in precious materials, and long-distance trade. While Hassan and Smith perceive changes in gender patterns through time, they also note that some iconographic features are persistent, especially those relating to cattle. Throughout several thousand years, cows are identified with women and bulls with men. The well-known cow goddesses of Egypt may be reflected even earlier in the raised arms in female figurines, imitating longhorned cows. Hassan and Smith suggest that the underlying cosmogeny is based on a female principle of birth and nurturing. These images were particularly important in mortuary contexts from which the dead were believed to be reborn. Identification of spirits with birds is Hassan and Smith's explanation for the beaklike noses on predynastic female figurines, connecting women to birds and souls. The use of the color green more often with women than with men is a reflection of the connection of women with plants, again a kind of life-affirming role.

These authors find that women and men at this time period were social equals. Women were different from men in having the power to transform in a generative way. Sexuality per se is not emphasized in the figurines or in the grave goods. Like Parkington and Whitehouse, they perceive, on the basis of deposits of projectile points and animal skins that occur more often with men, that hunting was an important male identifier, even though this was a fully agricultural society. Rulers in the protodynastic period were mainly male, but they still needed the protection of female goddesses, still associated with cows and the color green.

In chapter 4, Rubinson tackles the theory question of the meanings of mirrors in central Asia, about 5000 B.C. By carefully examining the distribution of mirrors in graves, she shows that mirrors cannot have the same meanings or functions throughout this vast territory despite the fact that people share many traits, including dependence on horses and a nomadic way of life. Thus, mirrors cannot automatically be equated with "priestesses," nor are they always found with women or even with adults. Meanings of mirrors are specific to each culture and need to be treated accordingly. Similarly, Nelson in chapter 4 considers the meanings of jade in burials.

In chapter 6, Joyce relies on both images and documents to discuss what she calls "appearance cues," ways that clothing, ornaments, artifacts, and body modifications mark and even call attention to various significant aspects of a person chosen to mark significance in a given culture. Joyce's approach to these markers is to consider how a person's changes in status in Aztec society were inscribed on the body itself. The importance of these identifiers is underscored by ceremonies that accompanied body piercing or scarification as well as changes in ornaments and clothing. Most elaborate of all was treatment of the hair. It is interesting that unbound hair was typical of the prostitute in Aztec society, as it is in many other cultures (Hiltbeitel and Miller 1998; Nelson 1997).

Joyce links data from postconquest Aztec with earlier times, noting abundant evidence that costume, hair, and the body were important in depictions as well as glyphs. Even Aztec burials can be used to make such comparisons since the use of ornaments of imperishable materials such as shell, pottery, and jade and other stone began in the early formative period. At that time, patterned use of ornaments was restricted, adults only having ear ornaments in early burials, while later sites had patterning by material and iconography. Joyce shows that some of the ornaments are gender specific, while others depict other characteristics.

Figurines enrich the interpretations afforded by the burial data since they depict perishable aspects of clothing and ornament that are missing in burials. The figurines exemplify gender as performance, as repeated action. Most of them represent richly arrayed young women portraying their sexuality.

In chapter 7, Parkington focuses on rock art in South Africa in which men and women are depicted doing different tasks in separate settings in order to relate the scenes to folktales of the San that were recorded by early European settlers. In the rock art of the Western Cape, people are shown clearly sexed, with distinctive ways of painting men and women. Most scenes of people are processional, and Parkington makes a case for interpreting these lines of humans as the depiction of ceremonies, including trancing and dancing. He does not, however, interpret them as individual shamans.

Parkington points out that a limited repertoire of animals was painted. Some likely game animals, such as elands, elephants, and small bovids, are present in abundance but are not often shown being hunted. However, hunting is important in some of the scenes. In these, men are shown with bows, which women never hold. Hunting is seen by Parkington as the "complete and pervasive experience," but he refers to bow hunting rather than net hunting, so surely this would be the case only for men. For women, perhaps for the "complete" experience might be childbirth or other events not depicted in rock art.

Parkington proposes that both oral stories recounting myths and rock depictions equate sex and food and therefore animals and women. This is a form of the direct historical approach, with an assumption that stories do not change their basic referents. In these stories, gender is achieved by hunting metaphors. The hunter is to the large meat animals as the husband is to the wife. Parkington finds in these myths and stories a metaphoric relationship between food and sex. The need to recover these distinctions from amorphous beginnings was, he believes, the driving force behind the myths and the images. He therefore suggests that the San, contrary to some studies that suggest fewer gender distinctions among hunter-gatherers, were almost obsessed with the need to emphasize differences. This is a useful cautionary example for the tendency to universalize hunter-gatherer gender relationships. It does not necessarily follow that men and women were unequal in perceived value to the group, but it does suggest that in some way gender differences were foundational in the culture.

Parkington is somewhat uncomfortable with the notion that women are equated with animals and suggests that in this context they would not mind being "prey" because they have equal status as childbearers and childrearers. The word, he says, does not carry the right connotations in English. Nevertheless, this formulation seems to reflect our own attitudes toward women as "merely" child producers and not producers of anything else. While it is somewhat troublesome that he finds "active and dominant roles of men and the passive roles of women," as Whitehouse says in chapter 2, it is not a requirement of gender archaeology that our results be politically correct—they do need to consider possible alternative explanations and to demonstrate that even given androcentric ethnographies in the past, the proposed explanation is the best available.

Similarities and differences of gender ideologies can thus be acknowledged in various cultures. Many of the chapters in this part use depictions of people for part of their argument. Written or oral sources contribute additional lines of evidence, as do artifacts.

2

Gender in the South Italian Neolithic: A Combinatory Approach

Ruth D. Whitehouse

INTRODUCTION

Gender archaeology is in its infancy in Italy. Work by Italian scholars has been directed at "finding" women in the archaeological record and on reconstructing women's roles and statuses in the past; such studies have concentrated on societies of later archaeological periods, such as that of the Etruscans, where material culture remains can be supplemented by textual references. Such "remedial" work is necessary, and it undoubtedly serves to focus archaeological attention on women in the past, at the same time showing up the androcentric biases of most mainstream archaeology. However, so far work in Italian archaeology has failed to address gender as a classificatory system in any society, involving both female and male classes (and allowing the possibility of third and further genders). Nor has it considered gender roles and relations as aspects of social structure that are dynamic and subject to negotiation and change. Work of this kind in Italy has so far been carried out by only a few scholars, all from the United Kingdom or the United States (see contributions in Whitehouse 1998); this situation reflects current research trends in those countries that differ from those that dominate in Italy.

Of this small body of recent scholarship on gender in Italian archaeology, several papers have concentrated on Iron Age societies and have used as their starting point the abundant funerary record of this period, which offers, in theory at least, the possibility of comparing "sexed" bodies with "gendered" grave goods, to provide an entry point into the study of gender ideology as well as gender roles and relations. Moreover, this period (the first millennium B.C.) is chronologically closer to times for which we have some textual evidence, from classical writers, that may perhaps be brought to bear on Iron Age societies. Perhaps surprisingly, several other papers have focused on an earlier period, the Neolithic, which lacks any conceivably relevant historical or ethnoarchaeological evidence, leaving us with the archaeological record alone. Moreover, the Neolithic also lacks the rather clearly differentiated burials of the Iron Age, but it does offer other types of evidence that can perhaps be used to cast light on some aspects of gender. This period forms the subject of the present chapter, which represents a synthesis of the work of various scholars on the subject and aims to present a more complete and balanced picture than I have offered in my earlier forays on this topic (Whitehouse 1992a, 1992b).

THE NEOLITHIC OF SOUTHERN ITALY

The geographic scope of this chapter is mainland southern Italy, with a concentration on southeast Italy (the modern region of Puglia and adjacent parts of Basilicata), which has produced most of the evidence (fig. 2.1). From about 7000 B.C. (calibrated), this area was populated by Neolithic groups living in farmsteads and small villages and practicing a mixed farming economy based on the cultivation of wheat, barley, and pulses, and the rearing of sheep, goats, cattle, and pigs. Hunting made only a very minor contribution to the diet, although it may have played an important role in ritual. Social organization is assumed to be of generically tribal type, and there is no evidence of any institutionalized hierarchy. This rather stable lifestyle survived without major disruption (through a series of changing pottery styles) until the late fifth millennium B.C. It was followed by a period of increasingly radical change in the early fourth millennium (Final Neolithic) and later in the fourth to third millennium B.C. (Eneolithic, or Copper, Age).

The archaeological record for this period includes settlements, burials, cult sites in natural caves and artificial rock-cut structures, and some extraction and working sites for stone tools of various sorts (flint and obsidian for chipped stone tools and a range of hard rocks for ground stone axes).

SOURCES FOR STUDYING GENDER IN THE NEOLITHIC OF SOUTHERN ITALY

The sources of evidence potentially available for studying gender in the societies of Neolithic southern Italy are multiple, providing the opportunity, in theory at least, to assemble a composite picture. This has to be a more satisfactory situation than when aspects of gender are reconstructed from one source only, such as burial data. Unfortunately, however, all the potential sources of

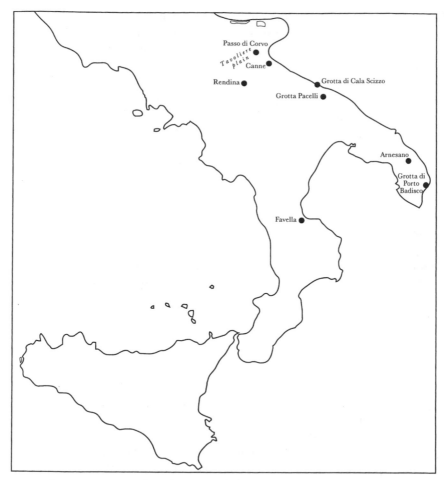

Figure 2.1.   Map of southern Italy showing sites mentioned in the text.

evidence in southern Italy have their own problems that constrain interpretation. Some of these problems affect all types of sites, for instance, the poor quality of many past excavations that has resulted in the loss of vital contextual information and the nonretrieval of many classes of evidence collected routinely in modern excavations. One particular problem is poor chronological control of the data, with few sites or contexts dated by carbon 14 and many assigned to inadequately defined ceramic phases. Other problems are specific to particular types of sites. For instance, many parts of southern Italy have suffered severe damage from deep plowing: In the Tavoliere plain, where many ditched Neolithic settlements are recorded, the entire topsoil has been removed over large areas, with the result that archaeological features survive only where they were dug into the underlying subsoil. Thus, the lower parts of ditches, pits, and postholes survive, but we have usually lost all ground-level features, depriving us of potential information about how buildings were subdivided and for what purposes spaces, both internal and external, may have been used. In the case of the funerary data, the problem of poor recording during archaeological excavation is compounded in some cases by the subsequent loss of the skeletal material, which can no longer be traced. These examples should suffice to illustrate the very imperfect nature of the data sets available to us, which impose quite severe restrictions on our interpretative possibilities. These qualifications need to be borne in mind during consideration of the studies to be discussed in this chapter.

The sources of evidence that have been used up to now in discussions of gender in this area and period include burials (Pluciennik 1994, 1998; Robb 1994a); cult caves (Whitehouse 1992a, 1992b; Skeates 1994), anthropomorphic figurines (Holmes and Whitehouse 1998), and architecture and space (Morter and Robb 1998). Some of these scholars have discussed more than one of these types of evidence (see, in particular, Robb 1994b; Pluciennik 1998). I first consider the work done under each of these headings separately and then attempt to combine and reassess them in the discussion section.

Burials

John Robb has made a major study of Neolithic burials from central and southern Italy and Sicily (Robb 1994a). This work gathers together a very disparate body of data and extracts from it some useful generalizations. The area covered by Robb's survey is larger than that of this chapter; however, of his 75 or so burial sites and minimum of 413 individuals buried, more than 75 percent fall within my area, and, since Robb does not record marked regional differences within his sample, it is reasonable to assume that his conclusions are valid for my area.

The burials occur in sites of various kinds: settlements, caves, and, especially in the Late to Final Neolithic, separate small cemeteries. There are many cases of disarticulated collective burials, but there are also many individual inhumations. The normal burial position is crouched or flexed, with a majority facing east (in the case of burials in the open) or facing the cave entrance (for cave burials). No cemetery or group of burials is adequate in size to provide useful information about an individual community, and Robb's generalizations refer to Neolithic burials as a whole, with chronological subdivisions in some cases. No burials have very elaborate grave structures, although there are a few cists made of stone slabs or boulders and at least one artificial rock-cut tomb. Most burials lack grave goods altogether, and where they do occur they are few in number and are usually simple pots, stone tools, and ornaments.

A few burials have a single elaborately painted drinking vessel, and one has a stone figurine; these are Late to Final Neolithic in date, as are most of the stone cists and the one rock-cut tomb.

Robb looked for patterning of various kinds in the data, including differences related to hierarchy, gender, and age. Only about 100 skeletons were sexed, and, of these, grave goods and other burial characteristics were known for only 62 (with a more or less equal sex ratio), and it is on this sample that his statistics are calculated. He found no differentiation, suggesting high individual status, which supports the widely held view that these were societies without institutionalized hierarchies (e.g., Whitehouse 1984). He did, however, find one statistically significant correlation related to gender: Males were more often buried on their right sides and females (and juveniles) on their left sides (fig. 2.2). This is in agreement with the situation widely recorded ethnographically, but in Neolithic southern Italy it does not represent a clear-cut binary division. As Pluciennik (1988: 66) points out, in this case 31 percent of

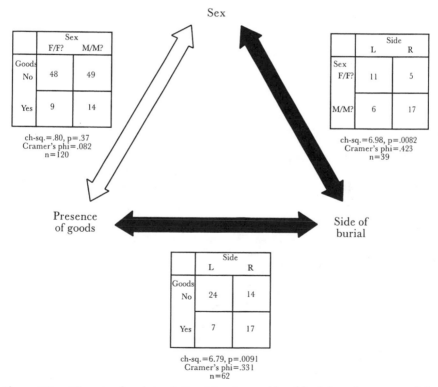

Figure 2.2.   Diagram showing relationship of sex, side of burial, and grave goods in Neolithic burials (after Robb 1994a).

females and 26 percent of males are buried on the "wrong" side. Robb offers one possible explanation for this, suggesting that what was marked by right-hand-side burial might have been male gender rather than biological sex and thus would not have applied to all biological males until they were socially recognized as full adult males, presumably after some specific ritual initiation and/or some specific social achievement. The problem with this suggestion, again indicated by Pluciennik (1998: 67), is that it fails to explain the 31 percent of women buried on their right-hand side. Did these have male gender, and, if so, what possible meaning does male gender have in this context? Robb himself indicates another possibility: "The formal distinction in rite may have corresponded not to gender as such, but rather to some culturally-ascribed attribute (for instance, social prominence) which was not identical with gender or sex, but which bore a statistical relationship to one or both of them" (Robb 1994a: 48). Pluciennik argues that a male–female dichotomy was not a basic system of categorization in these societies, which instead demonstrated both greater variability and greater fluidity in their structuring principles. My own view is that, statistically significant or not, it is difficult to place too much weight on a correlation to which between one-quarter and one-third of all cases are exceptions. However, pace Pluciennik, it does not follow that because gender was not clearly marked in death, it did not play an important role in life.

Cult Caves

I have argued that a number of natural caves, crevices, and rock shelters, as well as some artificial rock-cut structures, in peninsular Italy and Sicily were used for cult purposes during the Neolithic and Copper Age (Whitehouse 1992b). In particular, I have argued that some of the larger sites, and especially the Grotta di Porto Badisco (also known as the Grotta dei Cervi), were utilized for male initiation rites in a system used to create and reinforce control of men over women and older men over younger ones. The Grotta di Porto Badisco is a cave with three long narrow corridors or galleries, accessed through low tunnels that have to be negotiated on all fours (fig. 2.3). Each corridor is divided by natural features of the cave, sometimes enhanced by human efforts, into a number of distinct zones, almost all of which have wall paintings, executed either in red (ochre) or in dark brown (bat guano). The designs include figurative motifs ("matchstick" figures), often organized in scenes, handprints, and abstract designs (which may represent schematized versions of the figurative motifs). My detailed analysis of the distribution of the paintings (Whitehouse 1992b: chap. 5) showed that the figurative motifs and the most complex scenes are concentrated in the zones nearest the cave entrance, while, as one moves deeper into the cave, the abstract motifs come to dominate and, in one of the

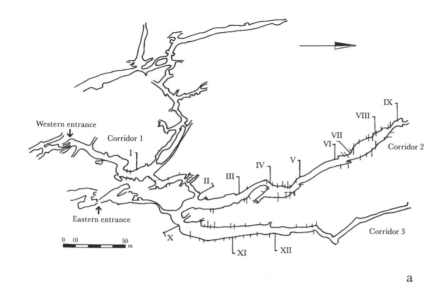

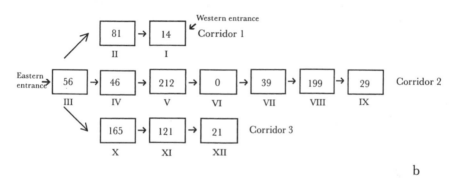

Figure 2.3. Grotta di Porto Badisco: (a) plan of cave, showing corridors, entrances, and zones of paintings (after Graziosi 1980); (b) schematic plan, showing corridors, entrances, and zones of paintings; the numbers inside the boxes represent the number of individual motifs in each zone.

corridors, the distinct separate motifs merge into large areas of overlapping pattern (fig. 2.4). My interpretation of this was that the most accessible and "readable" versions of sacred themes occur in the parts of the cave reached first, while the deepest zones have the most secret and difficult versions. I related this to a system of secret ritual knowledge, achieved through a series of initiations, the stages of which were mapped onto the natural topography of the cave.

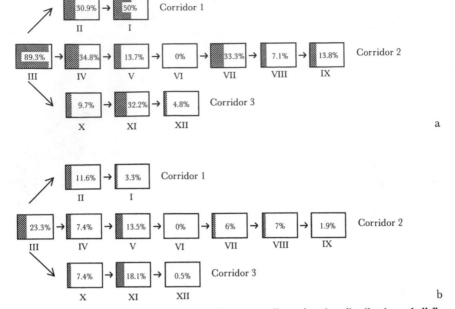

Figure 2.4A. Schematic plan of Grotta di Porto Badisco showing distribution of all figurative motifs: (a) percentage of paintings in each zone; (b) percentage of all paintings of this type.

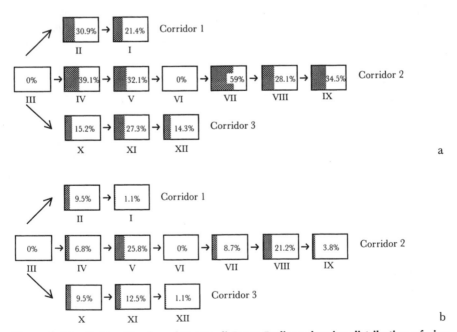

Figure 2.4B. Schematic plan of Grotta di Porto Badisco showing distribution of nine main abstract motifs: (a) percentage of paintings in each zone; (b) percentage of all paintings of this type.

I was able to introduce gender into this analysis since in the first zone of the cave to be entered (Zone III of the excavators' designation), which has only figurative designs arranged in a number of scenes, it is possible to distinguish clearly between some definitely male figures (shown with penis) and some definitely female ones (executed in red with a blob of brown paint in the pubic area). From these figures, I was able to extend the analysis by identifying gendered arm positions: a female position with one arm in the air, the other curved downward, as though with hand on hip, and a male position with arms extended in front of the body, either actually holding a bow or as though holding one; another possible male position has both arms in the air (fig. 2.5). With this additional information, I was able to assign gender to all the clearest human figures and to make comparisons using these identifications. What emerges is that male and female images occur in almost equal numbers in the entrance zone, but further into the cave only male figures occur (fig. 2.6). I suggested that this might indicate that women participated in only the initial, more public stages of ritual at the site and that initiation into the more difficult and secret (literally "deeper" in this case) aspects of the cult would have been restricted to males. I used ethnographic analogy, particularly the rich record

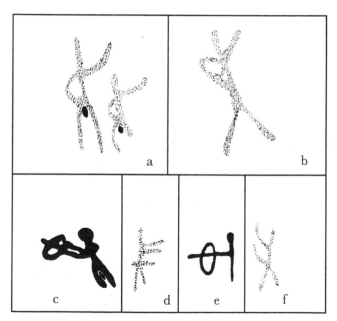

Figure 2.5. Painted figures in the Grotta di Porto Badisco (after Graziosi 1980; not to scale): (a) definite females (zone III); (b) probable female (zone III); (c) definite male (zone VII); (d) definite male (zone III); (e) probable male (zone IV); (f) probable male (zone III).

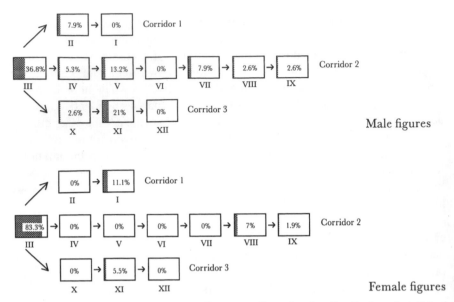

Figure 2.6. Schematic plan of Grotta di Porto Badisco showing distribution of gendered human figurative motifs. Percentages are of all male figures and all female figures, respectively, including probables.

from New Guinea, to suggest that the rites in question were initiation rites into a secret male cult used by the ritual elders as a power system to control both women (by exclusion from the cult or at least from all but the early stages of initiation) and younger men (through control of the rituals themselves and of the sacred knowledge that was slowly and in piecemeal fashion imparted to them during initiation). The nature of the ritual knowledge cannot be reconstructed in any detail, but we do have some clues as to its general nature. Almost all the scenes in the Grotta di Porto Badisco paintings are concerned with hunting (of larger and smaller animals depicted with antlers or horns, which I have suggested represent red deer and roe deer, respectively) with bows and arrows (and possibly in one case a bolas), and hunting is exclusively associated with male figures (fig. 2.7). Since the food remains from settlement sites of this period show little sign of consumption of wild foods, it seems possible that the importance of hunting had been transferred to the ritual sphere and was being exploited as a source of esoteric male knowledge and power. I argued furthermore, on the basis of the ethnographic analogy, that this was a society in which there might have been a high degree of gender conflict and opposition.

My interpretation has been criticized by several scholars, most comprehensively by Robin Skeates (1994). His critique has both an archaeological and

Figure 2.7. Hunting scenes in the Grotta di Porto Badisco (after Graziosi 1980; not to scale) (a, b) zone II; (c, d) zone VII; (e) zone VI; (f) zone IV; (g) zone X. For purposes of illustration, the hunting scenes have been extracted from their contexts and associations with other motifs.

an anthropological axis. On the archaeology, he argues that my analysis is insufficiently contextualized and too general and that I thereby miss differences in ritual use between different sites as well as changes through time. On this, I plead guilty, though I would claim in mitigation that my analysis was a first foray into this field and was bound to be somewhat crude and oversimplified. Skeates's anthropological criticism is based on the fact that ethnographic studies suggest that small-scale agrarian societies usually have gender ideologies characterized by complementarity, mutuality, and cooperation and not by hierarchy and conflict. Here I think that Skeates is guilty of exactly the kind of generalization he criticizes me for in my archaeological interpretation and that he is ignoring well-recorded differences in gender ideologies and arrangements documented ethnographically for different small-scale societies. Other scholars have produced critiques that parallel those of Skeates in some respects. Robb (1994b) agrees in general with my interpretation of Grotta di Porto Badisco but argues that the gender system indicated there should be dated to the Late or Final Neolithic or even the Copper Age and thus heralds a later phase when gender complementarity, which in Robb's view character- ized most of the Neolithic, was transformed into a gender hierarchy with a dominant male ideology based on hunting and warfare. This chronology for Grotta di Porto Badisco is certainly possible since the archaeological deposits show that the cave was used throughout the Neolithic and Copper Age and the paintings cannot be assigned firmly to any particular phase. Pluciennik (1998) argues as much for regional differences as for chronological ones and suggests that even if a particular activity was strongly gendered in one area and used as a source of prestige and power (e.g., hunting in Puglia), the same may not have been true in other areas. Finally, Morter and Robb suggest that while my inter- pretation of Grotta di Porto Badisco might well be correct, it may not have been very relevant to society as a whole: "The remote, peripheral locations of sites such as Porto Badisco could be understood equally well either as males controlling important secret knowledge in secret places, or as males being rel- egated to performing unimportant rites in isolated, shabby caves. In the former view, the rites are taken at face value; in the latter, their displacement from the central scenes of social life makes them appear almost as a futile form of resis- tance" (Morter and Robb 1998: 91). They go on to suggest that there may have existed complementary female and male worldviews, with complementary rit- ual systems and symbolism. All these points will be considered in the discus- sion later in this chapter.

Anthropomorphic Figurines

Italy has produced anthropomorphic figurines from Neolithic sites, although in far lower numbers than other parts of southern and southeast Europe. They are usually described in the Italian literature within a familiar interpretative framework as "fertility figurines" or "mother goddesses." Surprisingly, the fig- urines have not normally been studied collectively, and the work of Holmes and Whitehouse (1998) represents the first attempt to collect the information on these figurines systematically. Our catalog, although certainly incomplete and in need of supplementation, includes, we believe, a high proportion of the known material and provides a reasonable basis for discussion. We covered a larger area than that of the present chapter (the whole of mainland Italy and Sicily) and a longer period (including the Copper Age as well as the Neolithic), and we documented only 60 figurines. If we count only Neolithic examples from mainland southern Italy, we are reduced to 10 examples. Although this is clearly not a sample on which we can ground statistically validated conclusions, most of the 10 come from known contexts in recent excavations, and some interesting patterns emerge from the data. Of the 10, four come from definite settlement sites and a further three from presumed settlements. Of the remaining three, two were found in cult caves and one in a tomb. Although very varied in form, all the figurines from settlement contexts are made of clay and represent female figures, with sex indicated either by breasts (four examples) or by the pubic area (three examples, shown in different ways but each apparently indicating female genitalia) (figs. 2.8, 2.9). With one possible exception, from Favella, which is described by the excavator as in the birthing

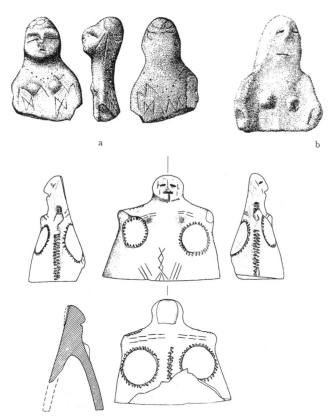

Figure 2.8. Figurines from Passo di Corvo (a, b) and Canne (c). Scale 1:2. (a) and (b) after Tinè (1983); (c) after Radina (1992).

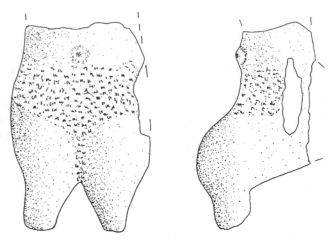

Figure 2.9.   Figurine from Rendina (after Cipolloni Sampò 1983).

position (Tinè 1996), the figurines do not seem to emphasize fertility in particular, and we are reminded of Collier and Rosaldo's (1981) discussion,
which showed that in small-scale societies women are often valued as much
for their sexuality as for their fertility and/or their roles as mothers. The two
figures from cult caves are also made of clay but are quite different from those
from the settlement sites in that they consist only of heads—one complete in
itself, one apparently broken off at the neck—but deliberately deposited in a
significant location in the cave as a head on its own. Although both heads look
vaguely female and are often described in the literature as women's heads, this
impression is probably the result of our ethnocentric perceptions of hairstyles
and should be ignored. They display no clear sexual features, although one,
from Grotta di Cala Scizzo (fig. 2.10), is interpreted by the excavators as combining both female and male symbolism. The female symbolism is found in
the mouth (which mimics the vulva and the division between the legs), while
male symbolism occurs in the nose and eyebrows, executed as a single feature
(which takes the form of a stylized bull's head, often thought to represent masculinity) (Geniola and Tunzi 1980). The other head, from Grotta Pacelli (fig.
2.11), provides no indications of sex or gender; either in terms of portrayal of
sexual characteristics or in terms of symbolism; it is carefully executed and
shows hair topped by what appears to be an elaborate headdress. The last figurine, from the rock-cut tomb of Arnesano, is quite different from all the others (fig. 2.12). First, it is made of limestone rather than clay and is quite large
(35 centimeters long, compared with a range of 6 to 22 centimeters in the other
figurines). Only the head is carved, with eyebrows and nose shown in relief
and with an incised triple V-shaped "necklace" beneath. The lower part is

Figure 2.10.   Figurine from Grotta di Cala Scizzo (after Geniola and Tunzi 1980).

Figure 2.11.   Figurine from Grotta Pacelli (after Striccoli 1980).

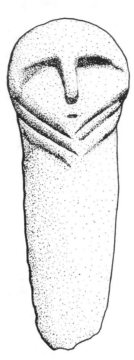

Figure 2.12.   Stone figurine from Arnesano (after Lo Porto 1972).

rounded and descends to a rough point; it might have been made either to stand in the ground or to be held in the hand. No sexual characteristics are portrayed, but the "necklace" may indicate female gender: Similar necklaces are shown on Neolithic figurines elsewhere in Italy, some of which have breasts and therefore seem to portray females. Moreover, necklaces also appear quite commonly on life-size anthropomorphic stone figures of the Copper Age (statue menhirs and statue stelae), where they occur on statues with breasts, presumed to be females, and on ones without breasts (unsexed) but never occur on statues depicting weapons, which are thought to indicate male gender. However, the Arnesano figurine is phallic in shape, so this may represent another example of mixed male and female symbolism (although taking a very different form from the Grotta di Cala Scizzo head).

   Of the figurines from settlement sites, some are unstratified surface finds, while others come from occupation deposits or pits where they may represent secondary depositions; none have specific associations with buildings or other features. Where associated with other material, they are of Early and Middle Neolithic date. The heads from the cult caves, however, come from primary depositions in significant locations. The Grotta di Cala Scizzo head had been placed in the corner of an artificial stone enclosure at the back of this small cave (fig. 2.13), while that from the Grotta Pacelli was placed face downward on a hearth inside a structure made of stone slabs. These are both associated with pottery of Late Neolithic type, that from Cala Scizzo being typologically slightly later (and carbon-14 dated to the later fifth to early fourth millennium B.C.). Unfortunately, the Arnesano tomb was not excavated by archaeologists, who arrived to find the tomb largely destroyed and the skeletal remains already reburied in the local cemetery. However, the tomb is thought to have been that of a single individual, identified as a young adult on the basis of a single tooth, buried with the figurine and three vessels of Final Neolithic type (fig. 2.14). This dating makes it the latest of the Neolithic figurines, and it could plausibly be interpreted as representing a transition to the Copper Age, which would explain the use of stone, the relatively large size, and the similarities to the

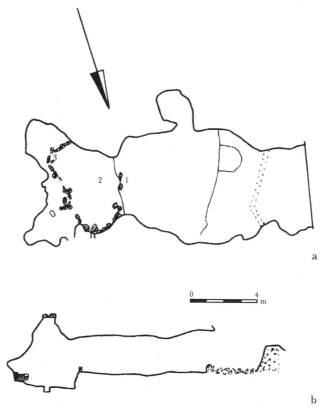

a

0   4 m

b

Figure 2.13. Plan of Grotta di Cala Scizzo (after Geniola and Tunzi 1980): (a) plan; (b) section. Numbers 1 and 2 mark the find spots of painted pebbles, 3 of the figurine.

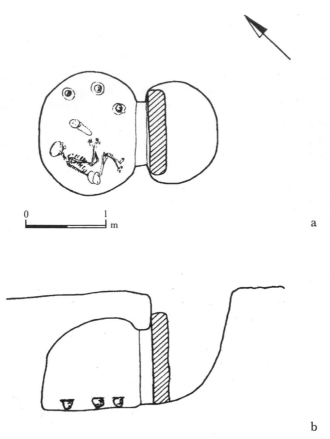

0 _____ 1
                m

a

b

Figure 2.14.   Rock-cut tomb at Arnesano, as reconstructed from eyewitness accounts (after Lo Porto 1972): (a) plan; (b) section.

Copper Age statue menhirs (one rather similar stone figurine from a tomb in northern Italy is also Late to Final Neolithic in date).

It is difficult to say very much about the use of the figurines from settlement sites, although their small number tends to suggest that they were for special rather than quotidian purposes. The incised motifs found on two of the figurines might also indicate special status. For the cult cave heads, we have suggested that—because of their careful manufacture and deliberate deposition in special locations—they were *sacra:* actual objects of worship, containing within themselves supernatural powers. The Arnesano tomb figurine we interpreted as possibly belonging to a ritual specialist of some sort (a shaman or a sorcerer) and representing an agent or familiar (Holmes and Whitehouse 1998: 113–14). Interestingly, although the Arnesano skeleton was not available for study and so could not be sexed, the reconstruction (based on eyewitness accounts of its discovery) indicated that it was lying on its left side. On one of Robb's possible interpretations, this would make the individual either a female or a juvenile male. While the evidence does not allow us to take this any further, we do here have at least a hint of a possible female ritual specialist.

In our article, we noted another interesting pattern relating to gender. Although we must obviously be cautious in our interpretations because of the very small number of figurines involved and because chronological differences may be confusing other patterns, there is nonetheless a very striking contrast apparent in the data. Settlement sites are producing unequivocally female images, while cult caves and tombs are producing ambiguously gendered figures, lacking clear sexual characteristics but sometimes with combined female and male symbolism. In the larger sample considered in our earlier paper, we found similar distinctions in other parts of Italy, although there were interesting variations. For instance, in northern Italy, one type of ambiguous female/male figurine does occur on settlement sites, as well as unambiguous female ones, while in Sicily there are examples of human/bird hybrids not found on the mainland (Holmes and Whitehouse 1998: 115). In our paper, we suggested one possible interpretation of the southern Italian pattern: a distinction between domains appropriate for same-sex manifestations (domestic) and for cross-sex or combined-sex manifestations (burial and other cult contexts). This is considered further in the discussion in this chapter.

In our paper, we did not discuss who might have made the figurines because we lacked any direct evidence. However, this is clearly relevant information, and in the context of the present chapter, I feel I might be justified in speculating a little. Most of the figurines—and all those from settlement sites—are of clay; they are normally made from fabric similar to that of contemporary pottery vessels and have similar surface treatment (some have incised or impressed decoration, some traces of a slip or painted decoration). If, as is commonly assumed on the basis of ethnographic analogy, women were the potters in small-scale societies, then it seems likely that they also made the figurines, at least those that show close technological similarities to pottery vessels, which coincide with those found on settlement sites. Karen Vitelli (1993) has made the same point in connection with the Greek Neolithic sites of Franchthi cave and Lerna, arguing that the pottery vessels and the figurines were made by the same people and that these were probably women.

Architecture and Space

Although there are many Neolithic settlement sites known in southern Italy, for the reasons outlined earlier we have few examples of well-excavated domestic structures and fewer still that preserve floor-level features. For this reason, Morter and Robb's (1998) analysis focuses on the use of space at a macro level rather than on individual buildings or settlements. They start from the assumption that the bounded (ditched or occasionally walled) village was the modal point in the Neolithic cultural landscape and that the world beyond the village would have been understood in terms of concentric zones at increasing distances from the settlement. They recognize at least five kinds of space that may have corresponded to nested social identities (fig. 2.15). Zone 1 is the innermost zone, formed by the domestic house and its immediate space, presumably occupied by small kin units. Zone 2 is constituted by the village and includes areas for communal activities, including burial and other ritual. This space is often bounded, especially in southeastern Italy, with one

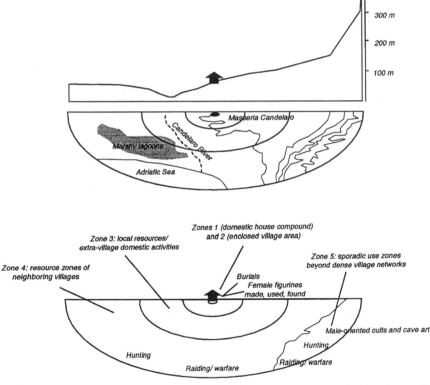

Figure 2.15. Diagram showing the spatial distribution of gender symbols in the southern Italian Early to Middle Neolithic (after Morter and Robb 1998). Spatial zones are illustrated using Masseria Candelaro (Cassano and Manfredini 1983; Cassano et al. 1987); the location of gender symbols is generalized from various sites.

function of the boundary being the separation of the coresident community from outsiders. Zone 3 is the one- to three-kilometer "catchment zone" around the village, exploited for subsistence activities and probably recognized as belonging to the village, in the sense of rights of access or usage. Zone 4 is the intervillage zone, usually ecologically different from zone 3, often unsuitable for agriculture. It would be exploited for raw materials, such as flint and salt, and also be used for hunting and gathering; it might be thought of as belonging loosely to a number of related villages. Zone 5 is at the margins of societies, sometimes topographically difficult terrain, occupied by strange and possibly hostile peoples; where they coincide with ecological boundaries, they may offer exotic resources, such as obsidian and possibly foodstuffs derived from different altitudinal systems.

Morter and Robb go on to assess the evidence for gender–space associations and consider both gendered behavior and gender symbolism (they recognize that there are difficulties in separating the two since symbolic evidence must be evoked to link an activity to either females or males before the behavioral data can be assessed). The best-documented link of this sort is that between men and hunting, based on the Grotta di Porto Badisco paintings described previously. As we have seen, hunting was not of major economic significance in these societies, and it may have been culturally important because it was part of male gender ideology. Spatially, it would have taken place in zones where game could be found (zones 4 and 5), and it is in these zones that many of the "secret" cult caves, which I have argued were the loci of male initiation cults, are located. As Morter and Robb say, "Both ideologically important male activities and the cults celebrating them took place far from villages." If warfare was also a male activity (undocumented but plausible), this too would have been carried out in peripheral zones (at least in attack mode). Whether women used these outer zones as well is unclear: As described previously, the Grotta di Porto Badisco paintings include female figures in the front part of the cave, and I suggested that women took part in the initial stages of ritual. If this is correct, then some women must have entered these peripheral zones on some occasions. Alternatively, as Morter and Robb point out, the marginal positioning of the female images may have served to signal to the male participants the theoretical exclusion of women from the rituals and not reflect their actual presence there.

Morter and Robb also discuss the anthropomorphic figurines and note the association of female imagery with settlement sites (although they do not make the specific comparison with the figurines from cult and burial sites discussed in the previous section). Their overall conclusion is that both in terms of gendered behavior and in terms of gender symbolism, there might have been a gradient from a female-associated domestic center to a male-associated periphery.

The virtue of Morter and Robb's paper is that it discusses gender in terms of space, which no other study has yet done for prehistoric Italy. However, their approach can be criticized from a number of perspectives, including those of feminism and phenomenology. Feminist analysis has shown that the concepts and models of modern geography, of various different kinds, are androcentric constructions that generalize unchallenged assumptions about what is in reality white, bourgeois, heterosexual masculine space (e.g., Rose 1993). Morter and Robb's concentric circles drawn around Neolithic settlement sites seem to me to have this flavor. However informed their analysis may be by ethnography, it seems too formal and too geometric (too masculine?) to model the prehistoric situation with any sensitivity. From a phenomenological point of view as well, a formal geometric model fails to represent even schematically the "intimate and affective" relationships between peoples and landscapes recorded in the ethnographic record and postulated for prehistoric peoples (e.g., Tilley 1994: 71). Recent archaeological studies, particularly in northwestern Europe, have tended to emphasize *paths through* rather than *control over* landscapes (e.g., Barrett 1994; Tilley 1994). Whereas both phenomenological and (some) feminist approaches would emphasize the *experience* of space over its *use,* phenomenology has not yet, in its archaeological manifestations at least, built gender into its interpretations, as feminism does. Feminist geographers have demonstrated that in our own society women and men experience space differently, and it seems likely that this may be true for many, if not all, societies. While I do not have the space to develop the topic here, I think that one direction for future research would be to identify a category of "affective" space. Affective space is space as experienced emotionally, and its analysis would involve distinctions between, for instance, comfortable space and dangerous space, approved space and forbidden space. In the case study, while it seems likely that Morter and Robb may have correctly identified some of the gendered aspects of space in Neolithic southern Italy, they have neglected what may have been crucial emotional factors. For instance, in terms of affective space, the house and the village (their zones 1 and 2) might have been comfortable spaces for both genders, made familiar by habitual use, where both women and men knew how to be in the world, although they might have utilized the spaces in quite different ways. At the other extreme, some locales in zone 5, the cult caves (but probably not the whole zone), might have been experienced quite differently by men and women. For both, the areas might have been dangerous and visits to them accompanied by apprehension and fear. However, for the men the locales would have been sources of initiation into ritual knowledge and therefore places from which they derived power, creating mixed negative and positive feelings. For the women, by contrast, the experience might have been entirely negative: If these were forbidden spaces for the women, the dangers they feared, however conceptualized (as malevolent spirits, monsters, or whatever), might have been real enough. Ethnographers have recorded cases of women being punished in various ways, even killed, for entering forbidden male spaces. It is not possible to develop this theme further here, and many scholars would regard it as beyond the reach of archaeology in any case; however, at the very least we should recognize that emotional experience would always have been an important part of the ways in which landscapes were understood, and in this context, as in so many others, it is probable that gender mattered.

DISCUSSION

As we have seen, a number of different types of evidence have been used by scholars to approach the study of gender in Neolithic southern Italy. Can we now bring these together to create a composite picture? All the studies offer more information on gender ideology (by which I mean the cultural construction of femaleness and maleness) than about gender roles (the work of women and men) or gender relations (issues of power, dominance and hierarchy between the genders), although some light is cast on these, too. Ultimately, we may hope to reconstruct aspects of gender identity and gender experience as well, although little work has been done on these as yet.

Gender Ideology

My first point is to recognize the unbalanced nature of my previous interpretation based on the Grotta di Porto Badisco. Embarrassing though it is to admit, I think I was seduced by the ideology of the male cult and accepted it unquestioningly as representing the views and values of society at large. Having said that, I feel that many anthropologists have been guilty of the same error in their accounts of living societies, an error that reflects the generally ethnocentric and androcentric nature of Western academe.

I still think it likely that the Badisco cave, and probably some others, were used for rituals of initiation into a secret male cult. I also think that the creation of masculinity, which was the function of the rites, involved the construction of men as hunters and as guardians of a tradition of secret sacred knowledge; it also involved separation from the world of women. What was lacking from my account was any consideration of female ritual and female ideology to complement or challenge that from the male point of view. We do not have the evidence to reconstruct this in the same way as we do for the male view, but we do have a few pointers. Using the gendered space model of Morter and

Robb, it seems likely that female ideology would have been based on the village, and this is probably where female rites took place. Female ideology and ritual may have focused on traditionally "domestic" concerns involving care of people, crops, and animals, but we have no indicators of anything specific on this subject. If the suggestion that the figurines were made by women is correct, we may take the figurines to represent women's own views of themselves. Since they show sexual characteristics (primary or secondary) but do not indicate pregnancy or childbirth (except in one doubtful case), we might argue that women were conscious of, and gave importance to, their sexed bodies but did not emphasize either fertility or maternity. The incised motifs on the figurines from Canne and one from Passo di Corvo may have had relevance to female cult, although they cannot easily be interpreted. The extent to which women knew about, participated in, or gave value to the men's rituals in their faraway secret caves is unknowable on present evidence.

One other aspect of gender ideology relates to my suggestion, derived from the study of the figurines, that there were different domains appropriate for same-sex manifestations (domestic) and for cross-sex or combined-sex manifestations (burial and other cult contexts). This suggestion borrows from Marilyn Strathern's work on models of gender in Melanesian societies (Strathern 1988, 1993). Her work brought to my attention the fact that in many small-scale societies, gender is not a question of identity attached to individuals, as it is in the modern West, but is rather an essence or attribute that can be extracted, reproduced, and exchanged. The types of gender transaction documented for Melanesia by Strathern are essentially transitory and thus not readily accessible to archaeological reconstruction, if they occurred in past societies. However, if there were fixed places for such transactions, the situation becomes more hopeful because repeated transitory events carried out in a specific locale might be traceable archaeologically; for instance, we might hope to find indications in the iconography. Changes of status and identity, including facets that relate to gender, are, of course, what rites of passage are about, and we might expect this to be reflected in the places where such rituals were carried out. This is what I suggest we have in Neolithic southern Italy. The ambiguous or combined-sex figurines occur in cult caves and burials, which are precisely the sites where rites of passage would have been performed. Of course, this applies only to the images represented by the anthropomorphic figurines (which as we have seen are few in number); the painted images on the walls of the Grotta di Porto Badisco show separate males and females and no combined-sex figures (although, interestingly, there are a few combined human–animal figures). I do not think this undermines my argument since the different types of images may have been used for different purposes. One possibility, for instance, is that the painted figures represent humans, while the figurines represent supernatural beings. This is, I believe, a direction of inquiry that could profitably be pursued in the future.

Gender Roles

We have very little evidence to help us reconstruct gender roles. The clearest association we have is that of men and hunting, as indicated by the Grotta di Porto Badisco paintings. This fits with what is indicated by ethnographic analogy, and I think we need have no difficulty in accepting it. However, as we have seen, hunting was of little economic importance and seems to have had value mainly in the ritual sphere. We may assume that the economically important subsistence activities would have been carried out by both women and men, but how such work may have been divided up we do not know. If Morter and Robb's spatial model is accepted, it might suggest that women's subsistence activities were those practiced in and close to the village, while men's activities were those that involved movements farther away. In this case, women might have been responsible for the cultivation of plants and for looking after animals that stayed within the village enclosure (possibly the young), while men would have been responsible for the herding of livestock that needed to be taken farther afield for pasture. Again this is supported by ethnographic analogy (see Pluciennik 1998: 175 and references). In terms of tool manufacture and use, we get no help from the associations of the very small number of recorded grave goods with sexed individuals: Pottery vessels and simple stone tools occur with both sexes. The Morter/Robb spatial model would suggest that men were responsible at least for the extraction and long-distance-exchange aspects of stone tool manufacture since the sources of these materials were in the peripheral zones. Ethnographic analogy would suggest that men were probably responsible also for making the stone tools, while women may well have made pottery and textiles.

I always feel uncomfortable when I come up with accounts that seem to support traditional gender stereotypes, and I find myself wondering whether I am still wearing ethnocentric blinders (on the other hand, I need to remind myself that I do not actually have a moral obligation to prove that prehistoric societies were politically correct!). In fact, the indications that we have on these matters are very flimsy; the suggestions made here are offered as working hypotheses for future investigation.

Another area where we lack information is the link between gender roles and ideology. Even if we assume the gendered division of labor suggested previously, we have few indications as to how the different activities were valued in society and whether they were differentially valued by women and men. I think we may assume that men thought hunting was important, but, as Morter and Robb indicate in the previously quoted passage, we can only speculate as to whether women accepted the importance for society of the men's ritual activities or whether they regarded these as irrelevant, serving simply to keep the men out of mischief in the village for a while. Another activity that may have been valued highly is pottery making. Vitelli (1993, 1995) has suggested that in Early Neolithic Greece, pottery may have been connected with (female) shamans, sorcerers, and healers and associated with the production of medicines, poisons, and the use of mind-altering drugs, all derived from plants, which may well have been women's concerns in these societies. This might also apply to southern Italy, and in this context we might remember the possibly female shaman or sorcerer buried with a figurine in the Arnesano tomb (see the previous discussion). Pluciennik (1997, 1998) has pointed out that in southern Italy, Neolithic pottery is rather different from that of Greece, with abundant coarse wares present from the beginning (in Greece they occur commonly only in the Late Neolithic), coexisting with various fine decorated wares. However, he has argued that even the "everyday" uses of pottery would have been highly valued as "new foods and/or ways of food preparation and consumption were important in themselves, (recursively) embedded in changing social roles and practices" (Pluciennik 1998: 74).

Since exploring concepts of value has long been a concern of archaeology and a number of approaches to the subject have been developed, this would seem a promising line of inquiry to develop. If we can attribute particular activities to one gender or the other *and* if we can assess how they were valued in society (both big "ifs," I appreciate), it would open up new avenues to understanding gender in these societies.

Gender Relations

In my 1992 analysis, I proposed a model of gender relations in Neolithic southern Italy characterized by a high degree of gender conflict and hierarchy. This was based largely on the interpretation of the cult cave sites as associated with initiation into male secret cults and with the analogy of the New Guinea societies where such cults are used as a basis of control by older men over both women and younger males. It was supported by one other line of argument, related to long-distance exchange, for which we have good evidence in our area. For instance, obsidian from sources in Lipari and Sardinia reached Apulia in southeastern Italy; as did hard rocks for axes from Campanian and Calabrian outcrops, while fine painted wares, probably made in southeastern Italy, were distributed widely in Sicily and southwestern Italy, with occasional appearances as far afield as northern Italy and Malta. Although we have no direct evidence for the social contexts within which exchanges of these materials and goods took place, it is quite likely that marriage alliances and kinship obligations were involved; one possibility is bridewealth transactions. Thus, it seems possible that the Neolithic societies of southern Italy were based on exogamous descent groups that imported wives, in some cases from considerable distances. In such systems, there is often antagonism between the genders since the women arrive as strangers who, although necessary for the continuation of the descent group, are suspected of not having its interests at heart and, in the worst cases, of actively plotting against it.

As discussed previously, this interpretation has been criticized by several scholars who favor models involving either gender complementarity and cooperation or much greater variability and complexity, with chronological, regional, and intrasocietal differences all possible. I think these views, especially the latter ones, have much to recommend them, and I am not inclined to defend my original argument with any vigor. I am attracted in particular to one idea outlined by Morter and Robb that suggests that in the Neolithic there may have been diverse views about roles and statuses held by different groups within society (obviously women and men, but perhaps also different age-groups and kinship groups) who would nonetheless have shared a broad understanding of cosmology and, I would add, root symbols. In this interpretation, the changes that occurred in the Late Neolithic and Copper Age, which saw the development of a male warrior ideology, may have arisen gradually and almost accidentally, as "increasingly important external community relations—channelled, of necessity, through male dominated spheres of activity—led to a distortion (or modification) of the existing gender arrangements, favouring the hand of one set of players—by happenstance, the males" (Morter and Robb 1998: 92). While I like this argument in general, I have to take issue with the "by happenstance." In European prehistory at least, and perhaps much more widely, it was *always* the male ideology—and the male people—that dominated in the societies of the metal ages. In my opinion, we need to look for structural reasons for the widespread, if not universal, occurrence of male domination—which returns us to one of the major themes of feminist research, well beyond the scope of this chapter.

CONCLUDING REMARKS

My survey of the work on gender in Neolithic southern Italy has led me simultaneously to two apparently contradictory conclusions. One is that there has been a fair amount of work done on the subject; the other is that we have still established remarkably little about gender in these societies. Both are true, I think, because they are relative statements. The work done on gender in this area seems quite a lot only by comparison with other parts of the world and with other periods and areas in Italy. In terms of numbers of people working on the subject or numbers of articles written, the output is tiny. No wonder, then, that we have gained very little information. However, I think we can feel some optimism about the future. I hope that the discussion here has demonstrated that there are a number of routes by which we can approach gender in prehistory, even in areas and periods that lack obviously promising sources of data, such as a rich funerary record. In my opinion, we have not got very far with our interpretations, not because of the deficiencies of the archaeological record but because we are still at the very beginning of gender studies in Italian archaeology. We have only just begun to ask the interesting questions; it will be some time before we can hope to get interesting answers.

3

Soul Birds and Heavenly Cows: Transforming Gender in Predynastic Egypt

Fekri A. Hassan and Shelley J. Smith

INTRODUCTION

This chapter explores issues of sex and gender in predynastic Egypt as may be discerned from grave goods, figurines, palettes, and iconography. Each of these categories provides a dimension to the multidimensional space occupied by each sex as a gendered category. The predynastic is a period pre-dating the emergence of the first Egyptian dynasties, around 3200 B.C., and is subdivided by ceramic assemblages into Nagada I (Amratian), Nagada II (Gerzean), and Nagada III on the basis of a system of sequence dating developed by Petrie (1900) and refined by Kaiser (1957). Radiocarbon chronology of these predynastic units is established by Hassan (1985). The ceramic zones of the predynastic are identified by reference to ceramics from the Nagada region between Luxor and Qena on the west bank of the Nile and at Armant (Petrie and Quibell 1896; Hassan 1988; Ginter and Kozlowski 1994). Sites with Nagada-like ceramics are known from many parts of Upper Egypt (fig. 3.1). Late Nagada II ceramics appear in the Nile delta following the widespread occurrence of a ceramic assemblage zone known as the Maadian. In Upper Egypt, the Badarian (Brunton 1937, 1948; Brunton and Caton-Thompson 1928; Holmes and Friedman 1994) pre-dates the Nagada ceramics.

We approach gender in predynastic Egypt with no favored statement of the identity of men or women. We chose the subject because we became aware of the lack of a systematic analysis of the role, position, status, or identity of women in predynastic Egypt, excepting Ucko's (1968) opus on anthropogenic figurines of Predynastic Egypt. Except for sundry statements on the prominence of women in predynastic Egypt based on cursory impressions of the

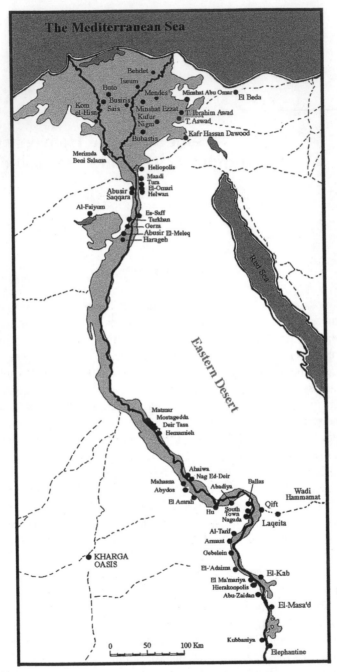

Figure 3.1. Location map of predynastic sites.

sizes of tombs and grave goods of certain women (Baumgartel 1947, 1970), the subject has not been approached in the systematic manner it deserves. Recently, a series of studies of grave goods, focused primarily on an examination of social inequality, pursue the approaches to mortuary studies developed in mainstream American archaeology since the early 1970s (for an exhaustive review and critique, see Carr 1995). Among such studies (Castillos 1979, 1982; Bard 1987, 1988, 1989; Anderson 1989, 1992; Griswald 1992), a study by Ellis (1992) focuses specifically on gender issues. His analysis of protodynastic burials (Nagada IIIa2—late First Dynasty, sequence dates 77–82) at Tarkhan showed that women's graves contained more types and more artifacts than men's graves. By contrast, men's graves were more voluminous and more variable. Slate palettes and beads were more common in female graves. These items were regarded by Ellis as adornments. Another contribution by Nordström (1996) on burials from the A-Group (contemporaneous with the terminal predynastic/protodynastic period revealed that relative to male burials, more female burials contained beads and pendants, amulets, bracelets, mortars, grinders, copper awls, and collections of pebbles. More male burials than those of females contained copper adzes, decorated bowls, feather fans, leather caps and bags, and wooden objects. Both showed a similar frequency of graves containing ordinary cups, bowls, and jars; imported Egyptian pots and wine jars; mollusk shells; and stone palettes. The significance of these differences cannot be easily explained in terms of stereotypical views of male and female domains informed by our current social conceptions and master narratives. The formulation of differences, a function of our criteria and statistical tests, specifies phenomenal forms. As such, it may mask unconceptualizable differences (cf. Derrida 1967) and obscures the implications of such differences. The differences as detected do not constitute *the* identity of women or define *the* difference between the *identity* of men and women but only point to certain dimensions of males and females and the potential (symbolic) significance(s) of these differences. Our analysis aims not to distract from or silence many other aspects of women or to define immutable qualities, no matter how such qualities are perpetuated cross-culturally and throughout history; rather, it aims to explore the momentary concretization of a collective construction of gender: a moment in the fluid process of making and unmaking the self. Neither do we claim here that we can single out individual experiences, convey the emotional intensity of death, or discuss the unspeakable experiences (Kristeva 1991). These are the domains of poetry and art requiring no systematic investigation or intersubjective validation, except inasmuch as we may validate and acknowledge the feelings of others.

We speak of "females" and "males" not as contrastive gender categories but as heuristic "sex" categories for analysis much as we would speak of "age" or "occupational" categories. The sex of an individual is not regarded here as the most outstanding social identifier, but it is the subject of our inquiry. Unfortunately, we cannot refine our analysis to deal with age differences since none are available.

In exploring sex-specific differences, we hope to define domains of differences and *deférences* and to confront the results that cannot be anticipated in advance, for example, whether grave goods of females are totally different from those of men, whether there is an emphasis on certain goods, and whether the differences between male and female mortuary goods are continuous or dichotomous. Our analysis is, of course, guided by our specifically stated variables and analytical methods. Our interpretations are not based on preconceived notions of differences but are tethered to results that are generated through exploratory devices open to all (assuming a certain computational literacy).

Inasmuch as gender is a social construct (sometimes independent of biological sex), the differences generated from our analysis are those of gender as constructed by us from the material remains and iconography associated with sexed males and females. We face the difficulty of not knowing who was responsible for selecting the goods and producing the iconography. We presume, perhaps erroneously, that it was a result of common, social (male and female) discourse and practice. Whether social practices and narratives are dominated by (biological) men or women is also difficult to ascertain for the predynastic period. We may be constructing a social male-dominated fantasy of women or a female-informed vision of predynastic gender. The extent to which men embody female visions and females encode and internalize males' images of them is hard to discern even today. We cannot exclude the possibility of a dialogue between the sexes, perhaps one between unequals, but both women and men must be considered within a context broader than the contrastive, if not conflictual, determinative domain of sex, power, and political equality (a domain important and necessary for a politics of gender). Women and men as selves in process within historical/cultural flux may not be narrowly viewed from the vantage point of "identity" as an essentialist construction. Gender as a category subverts women into becoming grounded and tethered to sex, an inescapable vector. As individuals, women or men may be identified primarily by criteria that are not grounded in the size of their hips or the function of their wombs inasmuch as a man's identity may not be a function primarily of the width of his shoulders or the hair on his chest. To the extent that anatomy is employed in iconography, it cannot be ignored, but the challenge is not to assume a universality of gendered sex or sexed gender but to explore the spectrum and ambiguity by which sex is gendered and gender is sexed.

The ventures into the domain of the hermetic meanings attempted here are based on a study of a variety of material remains from predynastic graves.

These include grave goods, figurines, palettes, and iconographic depictions on pots. We do not presume that we fully capture the meanings of women in predynastic Egypt, but we are prepared to posit certain queries that we can set for examination. Our queries may be regarded as hypotheses, but there is no attempt to test, if by that is meant to ascertain an inviolable truth. Testing by statistical means is a test of statistical significance bound with certain assumptions and subject to the vagaries of data. Nevertheless, we utilize statistics as a means to constrain our subjectivity and place explicit limits on what we can say or cannot say. Barring a philosophical treatise on "truth," we are content to deal with ideas that a collective body of investigators can examine using common canons and standardized measures. The beacon of light we throw on the past highlights certain domains and thus draws our attention to our results as a substitute for the past. We are aware of this limitation but submit that it is unavoidable. However, this does not lead us to embrace promiscuous subjectivity. Our ideas and fantasies remain uncommunicable and shut off from the public domain, as long as we do not espouse certain canons of methodology and inference that permit public examination, cross-examination, replication, and interrogation. It is only within the narrow and restrictive framework of simplistic dualism that dogmatism can be replaced with unbridled intellectual licentiousness. It would be also shortsighted to confuse science with positivism or empiricism, two philosophical traditions that crossed paths with science. What is germane here is that we can neither toss our experiences of materiality nor dispense with public dialogue without suffering a severe case of solipsism.

SEXING GOODS

One major source of information used here is the statistical examination of grave goods from five predynastic cemeteries: the Main Cemetery, the B Cemetery, and the T Cemetery at Nagada, and the cemeteries at Matmar and Mostagedda in the Badari region. Grave goods from these cemeteries (Baumgartel 1970) have been recently examined for evidence of social hierarchy (Bard 1987, 1989; Anderson 1989, 1992). The sample consists of all graves associated with a skeleton that was sexed, a total of 426 skeletons (209 females and 217 males). Sex determinations were made on samples of 400 skulls or skeletons from Nagada sent by Petrie to England to be studied (Fawcett and Lee 1902). Crania from excavations in the Badari region (including Matmar and Mostagedda) were measured and sex determinations made by D. E. Derry and B. N. Stoessiger (Morant 1935).

Predynastic cemeteries were adjacent to settlements. The Main Cemetery at Nagada covered more than 17 acres and consisted of more than 2,100 graves

(Petrie and Quibell 1896). At Badari, no segregation of burials by sex was observed (Brunton 1937: 48). Occasional burials, especially of children, occurred in the settlement. The bodies were typically placed in a contacted position with head pointing south and facing west. The hands are often near the face. Graves were dug as pits and occasionally roofed over with a few interwoven branches and then covered with earth. Wood remains are occasionally present and suggest that in some cases wood was used for roofing, biers, or pit lining. Body wrapping was not reported for the Nagada cemeteries, except for a mention of traces of cloth. One male skeleton was wrapped in skin. At Matmar and Mostagedda, matting was placed under and above the body and is nearly universal in occurrence during the Badarian, Nagada I, and Nagada II periods. It declines in use through time. Cloth remnants are occasionally present, but never in a condition that would allow to determine its use. Skins of gazelle and goat are frequent during the Badarian at Mostagedda, less so at Matmar, and likely represent a local practice. By Nagada III, only one skin was found at each cemetery. The hair side of the skins was placed next to the body and then wrapped in matting. Some of the burials (4 percent) show evidence of preinterment mutilation or secondary burial practices. In these cases, the head is often missing. In others, it is misplaced or buried separately. Ribs, vertebrae, forearms, or hands are also occasionally misarranged.

Although burial rituals are unknown, Petrie suggested that funeral feasts were probably held at graveside, where offerings were burned and the ashes with the sand beneath them placed in the grave (Petrie and Quibell 1896: 19).

STATISTICAL ANALYSES OF GRAVE GOODS

Fifty-three variables were coded for each of the 426 graves. The variables include counts of ceramic types, stone vases, palettes, baskets, jewelry, toiletries (spatulas, spoons, hairpins, and so on), cosmetic substances, figurines, fishing tools, textile-working tools, shell or woodworking tools, projectile points, grinding stones, mace heads, amulets, skins, and organic substances. Counts of the remains or depictions of fish, birds, hippopotamuses, gazelles, plants, cattle, or other animals were also recorded. We also coded the frequency of different colors. A category of highly valuable materials, mostly imports (obsidian, jade?, turquoise, silver, and lapis lazuli), were counted as a separate category from other valuable materials available locally (alabaster, malachite, resin, gold, quartz, coral, garnet, breccia, slate, shell, amethyst, hematite, galena, steatite, copper, carnelian, feldspar, diorite-gabbro, marble, ivory, and ostrich eggshell). Rare and unusual objects or conditions were regarded as a special category. They included a leather bag with a vegetable substance; human skull fragments with hair; a perforated, painted stone disk; cones of leather and clay; miniature rough pot; cylinder seal; weights; papyrus; a pointed bone spike; a dog in a coffin; four female figurines in a box; a small cake of organic matter; a pregnant woman; a belt of 5,000 beads; a cat-skin wrapping; a dwarf; and a bone shaft with perforated bone.

To avoid splitting the sample unnecessarily into small samples, a discriminant analysis to test for variability was performed using the SAS procedure DISCRIM, which allows a study of the differences between two or more groups of objects with respect to several variables simultaneously. Sixty-nine percent of the observations were correctly reclassified with respect to chronology, mainly Nagada II, and were correctly reclassified by cemetery 46 percent of the time. The categories "Nagada II" and "Mostagedda" each contain the largest number of actual observations and contain much of the variability of the sample as a whole. However, Nagada Cemetery T has a higher correct classification than would be expected by chance. Seven out of 10 graves were correctly classified. This confirms the special status of these graves and was thus removed from this analysis. Accordingly, excluding Cemetery T, the sample as a whole is homogeneous, and further analyses were applied to all cases regardless of period or location.

In order to interpret the source of differences in the categories designated in our analysis, we resorted to factor analysis. This technique is a multivariate technique used to reveal underlying source variables (factors) that account for observed variability and thus provide an economical means to discern a few key variables (factors) that account for sets of observed variables. Using this method, we could then gain information on the "themes" that lead to variations in grave goods *within* each sex group. We can also determine the relative importance of each of the themes (factors). Since the occurrence of cases with no categories undermines factor analysis, graves with no artifacts were excluded. This reduced the sample to 291 cases: 170 females and 177 males. Count variables were also considered if they occurred in at least 4 percent of the graves. A higher limit was not used since it may obscure meaningful variation (O'Shea 1984: 66). This led to the retention of 10 variables: utilitarian ceramics (combined), special ceramics, vases, palettes, jewelry, toiletries, lithics (combined), cosmetics, amulets, and the color green.

The results (table 3.1) reveal that variability for females can be accounted for by three factors. Factor 1 is most strongly defined by the color green and cosmetics. Factor 2 is defined mostly by amulets and palettes, while factor 3 is determined by utilitarian and special ceramics. By contrast, factor 1 for males is defined primarily by special and utilitarian ceramics and to a lesser extent by vases. Factor 2 is defined by the color green and jewelry, and factor 3 by toiletries and palettes. In addition, male factors are more equitable in the

Table 3.1.   Factor Structure Correlations

Variable	Factor 1	Factor 2	Factor 3
Female			
Green	.757	.263	.425
Cosmetics	.551	.027	.098
Jewelry	.406	.126	.176
Vase	.445	.410	.180
Amulet	.148	.507	.085
Palette	.183	.525	.179
Toiletries	.285	.400	.142
Utilitarian ceramics	.260	.168	.639
Special ceramics	.298	.169	.600
Lithics	.030	.004	2.084
Male			
Special ceramics	.745	2.063	2.033
Utilitarian ceramics	.710	2.067	2.087
Vase	.376	.008	.227
Jewelry	2.083	.752	.182
Green	2.036	.735	.094
Lithics	2.020	.095	2.005
Toiletries	2.015	.039	.601
Palette	2.050	.099	.579
Cosmetics	.047	.124	.204
Amulet	2.042	2.025	2.076

amount of variance explained (table 3.2), whereas the female factors show a distinct spread from the first, strongest factor to the other two. This indicates that male contents of male graves are distinctly, perhaps hierarchically, arrayed. By contrast, the contents of female graves, having much of their variance explained by one factor, are a more homogeneous group.

The results of factor analysis are supplemented by an analysis of the ratios of special items or conditions as listed previously (SG) and what was provisionally classified as "utilitarian" (UG): common ceramics, baskets, fishing tools, textile, woodworking and shell-working tools, and so-called ornamental objects (OG), which include palettes, jewelry, toiletries, and cosmetics. The results (table 3.3) reveal that there is an overall similarity in the ratios, except for the category of "special objects to ornamental objects" (SG/OG), which for females is almost twice that for males. In addition, corroborating the results of factor analysis, the coefficient of variation (standard deviation divided by mean) is greater for males than for females by about 30 percent.

A *t*-statistic for each variable and ratio was also computed to test the hypothesis that the means for each variable for males and females are equal. Differences in variances were taken into account by the SAS procedure TTEST.

Table 3.2. Factor Summary

Factor Number	Percentage Variance	Diagnostic Loading	
Female			
1	75	Green	0.72
		Cosmetics	0.64
		Jewelry	0.41
		Vase	0.35
2	25	Amulet	0.53
		Palette	0.53
		Toiletries	0.34
		Vase	0.28
3	22	Utilitarian ceramics	0.64
		Special ceramics	0.58
Male			
1	50	Special ceramics	0.75
		Utilitarian ceramics	0.71
		Vase	0.35
2	45	Jewelry	0.74
		Green	0.74
3	29	Toiletries	0.61
		Palette	0.58

Equality of *t*-test was tested by the *F*-statistic. Of the 53 *t*-tests, 12 variables and one ratio had a *t*-value exceeding that allowable for a null hypothesis, that is, no difference between variable means for males and females, at the 0.10 significance level. The results reveal that females had a significantly greater mean for toiletries, amulets, ornaments, polished red and rough ceramics, high-value items, cattle icons, and the special/ornamental artifact ratio. For males, statistically significant greater means consist of projectile points, lithics, and skins.

A combination of variables was also employed to interrogate the data for parameters that may be connected to social status, secular political power, and religious power. If the volume of a tomb and the number of objects are taken as indicators of rank or status, then there is in general no significant difference

Table 3.3. Mean (M), Standard Deviation (SD), Maximum Value (MV), Coefficient of Variation (CV)

	Female					Male				
Ratio	Number	Mean	SD	MV	CV	Number	Mean	SD	MV	CV
UG/SG	48	3.08	2.97	13	0.96	39	2.53	3.23	16	1.27
SG/OG	80	0.44	0.84	4	191.0	63	0.23	0.57	3	2.48
UG/OG	80	1.84	2.56	13	139.0	63	1.93	2.80	16	1.45

between males and females. Mean total number of artifacts is not significantly different between the sexes. Average tomb volume is greater for males as a result of one grave that is exceptionally large. The distribution of tomb volume for males and females is similar; all graves are 4.6 cubic meters or less.

Power symbols, such as mace heads, also revealed no significant difference, contrary to what one would expect if mace heads were linked with warfare and males. By contrast, out of 12 mace heads, eight of them were with women. However, projectile points show a significant difference, showing a greater mean in the case of males.

An analysis of the representations of items related to humans, gazelles, fish, birds, plants, cattle, other animals, and the colors red, black, green, and white was undertaken to discern any significant differences. The use of t-statistics revealed no significant differences at the 0.10 level of significance. Low frequencies contribute to nonnormal distributions and unequal variances, weakening the robustness of the t-test. The Shannon-Weaver test of diversity also showed that the distribution of these items in both males and females shows an equally high degree of diversity.

FIGURING SEX

The analysis of grave goods provides one dimension of women as a social phenomenon; anthropomorphic figurines (fig. 3.2) give us another. The treatise by Ucko (1968) provides drawings (from more than one angle) of 70 figurines and photographs of 36 as well as a descriptive catalog of 226. In the present study, 94 figurines from published illustrations were analyzed. Sixty-eight come from mortuary contexts, two come from the settlements at Badari, and 24 are of unknown provenances. The figurines come from the cemeteries at Badari, Nagada, Ballas, Mahasna, Dispolis Parva, Abydos, Mostagedda, Matmar, Mameriaya, Alawniyeh, and Kom El-Ahmar. Forty-four are from Nagada I, four are from Nagada II, and 46 cannot be assigned to a specific predynastic stage. Assignments of sex were based on genitals, breasts, and beards as biological sex identifiers. No contradiction with other characteristics were encountered by this assignment. The hip-to-waist ratio, following Ucko (1968: 174), differentiates between females with a ratio of 1.9 to 1 by comparison to 1.4 to 1 for men, with very little overlap. Among the figurines, 72 percent were females and 28 percent males (28 specimens). Thirty-two variables were coded for each figurine. Five of these are qualitative, and the rest are quantitative. Discriminant analysis revealed that female figurines were more stylized, have a normal distribution of variables, and are more consistent in their combinations of head height, body height, width, and number of facial features. Regression

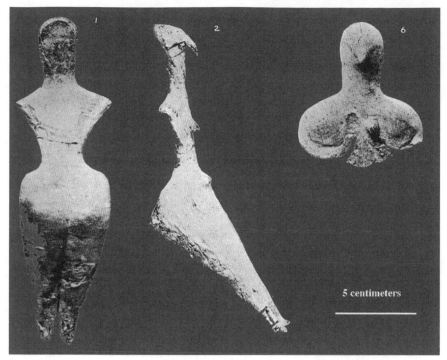

Figure 3.2. Predynastic anthropomorphic figurines.

analysis revealed that head height and body height showed little deviation from the "norm" for females, with greater deviation for male figurines. This may be a function of the absolute size of the body. As female bodies approached that of males (modality 16 to 18 centimeters), the head height of female figurines became as unpredictable as that of males. The association between certain features and the presumed sex (based on one criteria but not necessarily the others) using Cramer's V-value suggests a strong association between what is identified as a figurine's sex with genitals, breasts, and body shape. The next relatively strong associations are head, ear, mouth, and chin shape—features related to the face. One hundred percent of cone-shaped heads and 85 percent of no-neck head type are on female figurines. Spool-shaped ears are more common in male figurines. Leg position, presence of hair, presence of a navel, presence of hands, shape of brows, or presence of a necklace were not significant in distinguishing the sex of a figurine. However, only female figurines have arms that are long and curved overhead or curved under the breasts. Of the four males who have arms, three of them have them in an ordinary position, long and down at the sides. Twenty-eight percent of the figurines have no eyes. Eyeless females accounted for 82 percent of the eyeless figurines. When they had eyes, the eyes were round, by comparison to male figurines with "realistic" almond-shaped eyes or with pupils and/or eyebrows.

Characteristically, female noses were unrealistically large and beak shaped. Fourteen (93.3 percent) of 15 figurines with beaked noses were female figurines. Of 47 percent of faces with mouths, 83 percent were on female figurines. Males have long, pointed incised (bearded) chins. Thirty percent of the female figurines lacked breasts. Sixty-two percent of those with breasts displayed small breasts, and one had nipples. Only 14 percent have exaggerated large or pendulous breasts. Genitals are depicted on 30 figurines. Those with genitals were mostly males (65 percent). Some of the male figurines are shown with a penis sheath suspended from a belt at the waist. The females are shown either with a "V" carved at the upper-leg juncture or with incised dot pubic hair. The pubic dots are arranged in a crescent shape and extend over much of the abdomen. Females are more likely to be shown with a navel than are males; however, most figurines do not have a navel.

Two categories are more dominant among male figurines: full-length clothing (either painted, linen traces, or carved folds) and short skirts. Clothed figurines are 75 percent male. Exclusively female categories are abdominal or hip decoration. Five figurines have a girdle or apron depicted, and 14 have horizontal line between the waist and the pubic area, alone or in combination with short incised horizontal lines on the sides of the thighs. Black line designs, mostly geometric, co-occur on four female figurines. These could be cicatrices or tattoos. Three of these are heavy thighed; two of them are seated or bent at the waist, and one heavy-thighed and one narrow-legged figurine have blunt tapered bases. Raised linear horizontal bumps are shown across the abdomens of two figurines. Ucko (1968: 433) identifies these as umbilical hernias. The most common motif on the "tattooed" female figurines is a wavy line or a line of "V"s. On one, three almond shapes (mouths) are next to the wavy line (water). A patch of dots on the right breast could be akin to the hieroglyphic sign for grain. Their arrangement in threes suggests plurality. Cross lines on the right back may denote irrigation runnels or canals. One of the figures has "water" symbols between the breasts and on the thighs. A branchlike element is drawn on the left shoulder. Another female figurine has water signs on the thighs, zigzag lines on the chest, and rhomboid-leafed plants on the left thigh. Another tattooed figure shows a quadruped with a stick in its side. Near this, on the figurine's back, are parallel short lines.

We note that in the analysis of grave goods, two female graves contained two figurines each, while one male grave was placed in a box containing four figurines. Thirteen of the figurines fashioned from mud and vegetable paste modeled over a stick included 11 (90 percent) female figurines. Other substances used were ivory, clay (fired or unfired), and wood. A higher percentage of male figurines are made of ivory, whereas female figurines are commonly made of clay (78 percent).

DISCUSSION AND INTERPRETATION: MATERIALITY, EMBODIMENT, AND MEANING

An interpretation of the imagery of women as constituted from objects in a grave or the figuration of female bodies is entangled with the way we approach issues of gender and sex. Our preliminary observations in the introductory notes provide an orientation of our methodological and interpretative strategy. However, to delineate clearly our theoretical domain, we will provide additional signposts.

The objects in a grave and the anthropomorphic figurines are *proxies* of embodiment and materiality. The figurines provide clues of the female body *in a mortuary context*. The objects placed in the graves of females are *material supplements* that augment, modify, and contextualize the dead body in a social milieu at a specific social mode: death and burial. Lacking comparable data from settlements on female activities and social practices, we are likely to provide a partial view of a certain dimension of gender in predynastic Egypt.

The material figuration of the body and the placement of grave goods with a dead body are forms of embodiment. We distinguish between what may be perceived as the (biological) "body" and "embodiment," the latter defined here as the experience and social presence, presentation, engagement, and construction of the material body; embodiment is not the raw body but rather the nexus of discourse and practice entangled with the materiality of being (cf. Csordas 1994: 12). We cannot negate that the distinction is, in a sense, wanton since to speak of the "body" as a biological entity is to situate it within a nexus of cultural discourse and practice (cf. Quinn's 1991 critique of Lakoff and Johnson concerning the priority of culture over the body). This is again unavoidable because speaking and thinking are cultural and socially situated. The distinction thus is no more than an analytical device that carries no ontological weight. However, we are concerned here not with defining the biological body but with the difference between our construction of the body and those from predynastic Egypt in the hope of gaining insights, by analogy and contrast with our conceptions, into the ideational and social nexus in which women lived at a time when a major cultural transformation was under way.

The transformation apparently began in the Egyptian Sahara with the emergence of cow herding during the ninth millennium radiocarbon years before present (bp hereafter), possibly in response to climatic oscillations, and eventually the emigration of the herders into the Nile valley in the wake of severe droughts about 7,200 bp. At about that time, sheep and goat herders moved into the Nile valley from the Levant. They are also likely to have introduced domesticated wheat and barely. The local inhabitants of the valley from the 10th to the 8th millennium bp were fishers, foragers, and hunters. There is no evidence before 6,000 bp of any domesticated plants or animals in the Nile valley (Hassan 1988). Villages and hamlets were established in various parts of the valley, and by 3800 B.C. (5,000 bp), agrarian communities subsisting primarily on the cultivation of wheat and barley and keeping cattle, sheep, goats, and pigs, in addition to fishing, became widespread. The countryside was transformed; farming replaced foraging, and a new cultural stage was in the making. By 3500 B.C., towns, local trade, and trade with the outside world (as far as Afghanistan) through Levantine trade connections were established. Exquisite craft goods were manufactured from stone, gold, slate, and ivory. The changes appear to have been associated with the emergence of a multitiered hierarchical society. In another analysis of grave goods focusing on social hierarchy (Hassan 1996), the data support a model of political evolution from village polities at 4200/4000 B.C. (the Badarian) to petty states by 3800 and provincial regional states by 3500 B.C., leading by 3300/3200 B.C. to the emergence of great kingdoms prior to the "unification" of Egypt into a "nation-state" by 3000 B.C. (cf. Kemp 1989). Soon thereafter, within the span of 200 to 300 years, great pyramids were constructed as mortuary edifices of divine kings. Funerary rituals and royal cosmogony of this early stage in Egyptian civilization are known primarily from the Pyramid Texts from the Fifth Dynasty (beginning 2350 B.C.) to the Eighth Dynasty. By 3000 B.C., the king was already a great personage identified with icons associated in later texts with Horus, a falcon-god "represented" by the Living King, and a cow goddess. In a master narrative of cosmogony , the Heliopolitan Theology (Troy 1994), Horus is the son of a dead king (Osiris) and a cow goddess (Isis). Isis and Osiris, sister and brother, along with Seth and Nephtys, were the children of Geb (Earth) and Nut (sky), who in turn were begotten by Shu (air, with connotations of dry and empty) and Tefnut (moisture/spittle?), a couple created from a single divine entity, the androgynous Atum, who created them by either masturbating or spitting (Troy 1994).

Egyptian religion and its close links with monarchy in early dynastic times is essential in contextualizing gender in predynastic times. Funerary rituals and materiality already evident in early predynastic times became and remain the substantiation of Egyptian monarchy and religious beliefs. The grave was the locus of the world, the node between the living and the dead unified in a single world. The grave was the spatial launching pad for ascent, a beginning of a journey to where the living resume life in a transformed state of being (for an introduction to ancient Egyptian religion, see Quirke 1992).

Figure 3.3.   Narmer's palette (blowup of cow head).

It is from this historical context, directly and continuously connected with the predynastic past, that we can begin to grasp some of the dimensions of gender associated with funerary goods and iconography. We can hardly expect a persistence of the *same* configuration of gender from the early predynastic to the Heliopolitan theology, but we can expect transformations and developments grounded in previous rituals, beliefs, narratives, and practices. We propose thus to work backward and forward, confronting the evidence from textual contexts and materiality from historical sources with the iconography and archaeology of the predynastic past.

One of our first threads is that of the identification of cows with women. This is manifestly the case in dynastic Egypt. Isis, the mother of Horus, is a depicted either as an anthropomorphic figure with cow horns or as a cow. Hathor, who may also be portrayed as a woman with cow horns, is also depicted as a cow. The same applies to Nut, the sky goddess, who may be shown as a woman or a cow. The list includes other cow goddesses, such as Mehetwertet, Hesat/Mehetwetett, Bat, Hathor/Mehetwertet, and Neith. A face with cow ears, an icon later associated with Hathor, appears at the top of the Narmer's palette (fig. 3.3). These goddesses recall the figurines with long hands raised above the body as horns, exclusively associated with female figurines and depicted with what appears to be "deities" or divine figures on

Nagada II (Gerzean) pots. The king, regarded as a "Bull" and the "Bull-of-his-Mother" in historical texts, is portrayed on Narmer's palette (fig. 3.4) as a bull destroying an enemy fort. A bull also appears on another palette as a powerful warrior. The cult of the bull continues as an element in Egyptian religion, becoming especially prominent in later times. Bulls were sacred animals and represented Ptah at Memphis (the Apis bull) and the Theban falcon god Mont at Armant (Buchis bull), and served as the "herald of Re" at Iunu (Mnvesi bull). Cows and bulls were apparently sacred animals even before the predynastic period, as revealed recently by megalithic burials of cattle in the Egyptian Sahara dating to about 7,000 bp (F. Wendorf, personal communication).

The variety of cow goddesses and bull gods reveals a "prototypical" concept that may be embedded and embodied in various forms. This is not a concept taking form but rather a form giving rise to a concept and the concept extended and disseminated to include other concepts using the form as the anchor for a certain primary qualities. The bull as male and the female as cow are complementary opposites, antiphons as verses sung in response in alternate parts. This complementary is reflected in the coupling of gods and goddesses in the Heliopolitan theology (on the generative interaction of complementary elements, see also Troy 1986, 1994). The connectivity is through a marital relationship (or a sexual union) and progeny. These schema, joined with the transmutative schema by which a cow goddess may be interchangeable with another and the transubstantiative schema by which concepts are concretized, provide a means of comprehending certain cognitive operations behind Egyptian thought. Lateral thinking and analogical transfers employed in these schemata are indispensable for making sense of the plethora of Egyptian religious images and iconography.

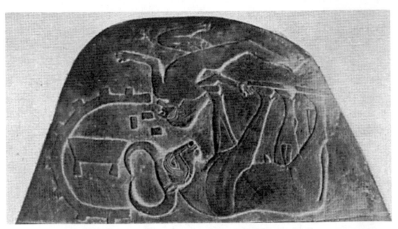

Figure 3.4.   Narmer's palette: the king as bull.

The identification of women with cows is further corroborated by an analysis of Nagada II (Gerzean rock art) from Nag Kolordana, Nubia (Hassan 1993), which is interpreted as a manifestation of a schema of maternity, nurture, and birth in which cows and calves were interchangeable with those of ostrich and chick ostrich and to a lesser extent elephant and baby elephant and giraffe and baby giraffe. The cow was occasionally shown with an udder. The motif of cow nursing a calf is later used as an icon of maternity and nursing in the depiction of Horus and his mother, Isis, and the king as a nursing child. A cult of the mother goddess was at the center of ritual and religious activity, as evident in the Coffin Texts. At Dandera, the worship of the archetypal cow goddess Hathor became an established cult. Hathor, a cow, was also the face of the sky, the face of the deep, and the lady who dwells in a grove at the end of the world (Clark 1959: 87). Her son, Ihy, is a child who emerges from his mother every day at dawn as the new sun. Hathor was the sky as well as the primordial mother combining both nun as the sky and the primeval ocean. Noteworthy here is the derivation of Nut's name from the *nun*, the dark, watery, chaotic, formless water abyss that surrounded Atum at the moment of creation. It is from this primeval water (the Nile flood) that a mound emerges as the place on which creation takes place, the place where light is born in the form of the sun.

The conflation of sky and water and the association of these cosmogonies' elements with a cow goddess can be traced back to the iconography of Gerzean pottery and tattooed figurines (fig. 3.5). The female figurines were exclusively

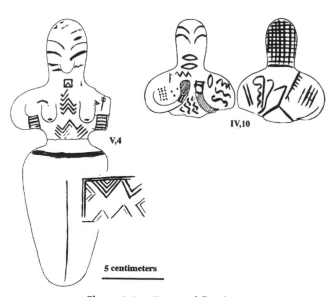

Figure 3.5.   Tattooed figurines.

tattooed with signs that can be interpreted as water signs. There were also signs of plants and grain. The Gerzean pots with wavy handles resemble the sign of water. The zigzag lines, again recalling the signs of water, establish a link between funerary beliefs and water.

We can thus present as a working hypothesis a model of a predynastic cosmogony that anticipates later cosmogonies by its emphasis on a female principle that operates as a medium of birth (life giving) and nurture (nursing) in association with water and plants as symbols of life. The association of these motifs with funerary contexts suggests that through the agency of the goddess or divine female principle, the dead were reborn, a reenactment of the act of giving birth in this world.

The isomorphism between life and death demanded a means of continuity through a transitional event situated at the grave. The Egyptians believed in a spiritual constituent that gods represented (*Ba*, plural *Bau*), as may be gleaned from the earliest texts. It applied to the king and later to all people (Wilkinson 1992: 99). The *ba* was represented by a bird and often loosely translated as "soul" or "spirit." The exclusive portrayal of beaks as noses in female figurines establishes a connection between women and "souls" in their form as birds. It is important to recall here that in the Nag Kolordana rock art, the iconography of cow and calf is paralleled by the iconography of the ostrich and a chick ostrich. As a bird, the ostrich may be linked with the idea of the "soul." The ostrich is not as prominent in subsequent textual narratives as the cow, but her traces remain in the form of the ostrich feather, the symbol of Maat, and the feather hieroglyph associated with the breath of life (DuQuesne 1995: 109). The ostrich is a bird that cannot fly and thus serves a manifestation of the soul of earth-bound creatures, like us, capable of magical flight (DuQuesne 1995: 109). Ostrich eggshell beads are common in terminal Paleolithic and Neolithic sites of the Egyptian Sahara and might have thus been a very ancient symbol of life. Not only does the ostrich move the air with her wings (note the importance of fans from ostrich feathers in later texts), but her eggs are used as containers for water in the barren (lifeless, sterile) desert. Ostriches are also depicted on Gerzean pottery as a common motif and are depicted as well on palettes. Of special importance here is the figure with a bird head and ostriches (fig. 3.6). There is also the shaping of palettes in the form of birds and the use of bird heads as a principal elements in the design of palettes (fig. 3.7). The use of ostrich eggshell beads as bird eyes is particularly significant as a link between beads and palettes.

The transformation from death back to life is a magical act that might have been linked with women as life givers. Sustaining the living after death is also achieved through the role of women as (wet) nurses. The connections between women and cows may be thus based on the importance of cows for

Figure 3.6.   Palette (figure with bird head and ostriches).

the sustenance of the life of herders during the frequent desert droughts and their milk as nourishment. In an agrarian context on the banks of the Nile, women became more closely linked with plants as cultivation gained more prominence as a source of life. The use of green pigment and green slate palettes to paint around the eye may be viewed in this context as a transformative life-giving, health-promoting, and healing act. It is for this reason that we must reexamine our notion of palettes as elements of "ornament" or "toiletry," as certain objects were initially categorized in our analysis. Such objects are, from the perspective gained from our analysis and interpretation, elements of a *vivi*-fying cosmic ritual (hence *cosm*-etics). This would also

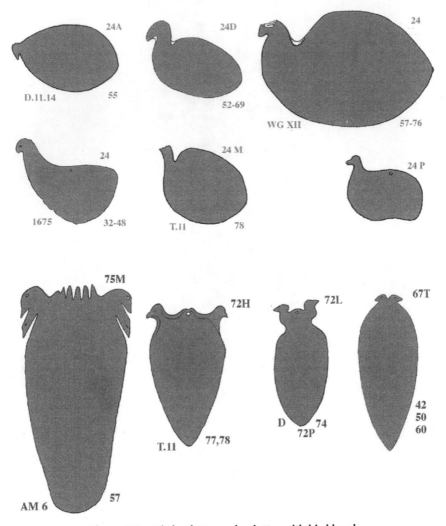

Figure 3.7.   Bird palettes and palettes with bird heads.

explain why palettes were used as power icons in a royal context, as in the case of Narmer's palette and other palettes with bird and cow heads. In fact, we can see a florescence of forms in the shape of birds, as well as fish and turtles, both related to water, before the emergence of terminal predynastic abstract forms (mostly rectangular) and commemorative or ceremonial palettes. Cosmetics are media for metamorphosis, for a transformation of self into bird, eye, plants, blood, or earth. Cosmetics are acts of masking that reveal the hidden connection in a metaphor of ritual using the body as its medium of transformation.

We thus posit that funerary rituals and beliefs in predynastic Egypt involved notions of women as agents of transformation and rebirth: The tomb was the womb in which human beings returned reconfigured into a contracted, fetal position to reenact birthing. The heavy loading (factors 1 and 2) in factor analysis (see the previous discussion) with green, cosmetics, amulets, and "toiletries" substantiates this position.

The overlap between men and women in a vast array of categories demonstrates that women, at least in the segments of the population interred in cemeteries, were on equal footing with men. They were differentiated from men, within the set of data and domains discussed here, by their transformative magic. There is no emphasis on their identity as "sex(-ual) objects" since they are not identified primarily by genitals or breasts. Evidently, they were not sex toys for the deceased, especially because they also occur in women's graves. The emphasis in the fashioning of a figurine that can be discerned as exclusively feminine is on cow horns, bird beaklike noses, and iconography of water and grain hieroglyphic-like signs placed on the areas of the female body close to the hips, pelvis, and breasts. Their association with plants and earth is reinforced by a preference for using mud or a mixture of vegetable paste and mud to make female figurines. Association with plants is also strengthened by a significant factor loading with the color green in grave goods. Wealth and prestige were not beyond their grasp, as we show no significant difference in variables that may be used as measures of these domains. In fact, the prevalence of mace heads with women (eight out of 12 in female graves) may denote that they might have held powerful political positions or that mace heads were symbols of protection not restricted to men considering that Nekhbet (a vulture goddess), Sekhmet (a lioness), and Wadjet (a cobra goddess) protected the king. By Nagada III, male graves began to outpace those of women (note Neithhotep's tomb), although during the First Dynasty the tomb of a queen, Merneith (Beloved of Neith), was quite substantial.

The greater association of men with projectile points, lithics, and animal skins in predynastic graves flags hunting as one of the defining roles of men. This is corroborated with the identification of a male schema in the Nag Kolordana rock art in which men, in opposition to women, were portrayed as hunters pursuing gazelles or antelopes accompanied by hunting dogs. Scenes of men as warriors on the protohistoric palettes also link men with warfare. However, the goddess Neith is associated in textual evidence with bows and arrows as a goddess of warfare.

The divergence between the religious domains of men and women is likely to have been linked in terminal predynastic/protodynastic times with the emergence of male kings who might have initially been legitimized by their association with female goddesses. For example, the name of Osiris, the mythical first king of Egypt, is a composite of female elements (Troy 1986: 32ff). The

Scorpion-King incorporates the identity of a goddess later identified with Selket. The Hathor-like heads with cow ears on Narmer's palettes hint to the elevated role of a female deity. The establishment of a royal cosmogony to legitimate male kingship and justify hereditary rule by male offspring might have been the reasons for developing a male-dominated view of creation. However, even that cosmogonic theology was a syncretic synthesis, patching together male and female goddess from different administrative districts (nomes) and time periods into a kaleidoscope unified by a genealogical account of royal descent. The falcon, Horus, flying high as the living god, was still the son and consort of his mother. Nut in the sky gave birth to Re, a sun god, who emerged in a solar theology (Heliopolis) to become the supreme deity supplanting androgynous Osiris with his dependency on the proactive Isis. Yet even Re was not beyond the magic of Isis, as related in a "tale" from the Ramesside period, when Isis learns the name of Re (thus acquiring his power) by her sorcery. In another story, The Book of Cow from Heaven, dated to the 18th and 19th dynasties (ca. 1350–1240 B.C.), Re, following an episode in which Hathor, the daughter and eye of Re, comes to his defense against rebellious mankind, relinquishes kingship, and returns to his mother the Cow of Heaven.

The relationship between Re and his eye, Hathor, as manifest in a story that persisted into Greek times, highlights the role of Hathor in maintaining peace and order in Egypt. Hathor is temperamental. She abandons her father in a fit of anger and wanders beyond the borders of Egypt into the "chaotic" territory of the Nubian Desert. Cajoled into coming back, her return was celebrated in a wild and drunken festival at her temple in Dendera in Greco-Roman times (Troy 1994). Even though there are many reversals and inversions in the role of Hathor, she was still venerated and worshiped.

EPILOGUE

A cow with a soul was not just a matter of defining gender; it was a domain of thought and mythogenesis that laid the foundation for millennia of Egyptian worldview and cosmic order. Deep in the marshes of the Nile delta, surrounded by the water of chaos, a protector of her brother, who was betrayed by his evil brother, takes matters in her hand and conceives, creating the future king of Egypt. As a bird, she shades Osiris with her feathers and gives him air with her wings as narrated in a hymn from the New Kingdom (Clark 1959: 105ff).

The search for eternal life and the manipulation of access to eternal life by kings is perhaps not exclusive to ancient Egypt, nor is Egypt in that sense unique in placing the body as its cognitive fulcrum. It is from the vantage point of our analogous experience that we can gain a sure-footed access to the past, not as a statistical table but as a lived experience. Nevertheless, it is only through systematic and disciplined thinking, well displayed in the recent investigation of the social and religious significance of mortuary practices by Carr (1995), that we may begin to have a well-founded basis for symbolic and semiotic interpretations. Carr's meticulous cross-cultural analysis reveals, contrary to current mainstream archaeological mortuary theory, that social organization is not the primary determinant of mortuary practices. Beliefs in the soul, the afterlife, and the nature of the soul's journey to the afterlife; the cause of illness and death of the deceased; and responsibilities to and punishment of the deceased's soul are the most common religious/philosophical determinants of mortuary practices. Although Carr's conclusions resonate with our interpretation, we concur with him that we cannot simply operate by superimposing generalizations. As we have attempted to do here, data analysis and exploration provide a means to discern the inner logical fabric of particular cultures; their bundles of symbols, meanings, metaphors, and tropes; their ways of structuring thought and transforming it into bodily experiences.

ACKNOWLEDGMENTS

We are most grateful to T. Kohler for assistance with the statistical analysis and valuable comments. Linda Stone guided us through many of the gender issues discussed here. Both served as committee members of Smith's (1984) thesis. Shelley Smith undertook all the statistical analyses and data collection and entry and participated in the initial analysis and interpretation. Fekri A. Hassan, however, is solely responsible for any interpretative errors or theoretical blunders despite having had enlightening and instructive discussion with Jeannette Mageo. Lana Troy shared her vast knowledge of the secrets of Egyptian goddesses and queens. Her insights were invaluable.

4

Through the Looking Glass: Reflections on Mirrors, Gender, and Use among Nomads

Karen Rubinson

Mirror, mirror, on the wall
Who is the fairest one of all?

> —*Snow White and the Seven Dwarfs,* The Brothers Grimm

The surviving past's most essential and pervasive benefit is to render the present familiar. Its traces on the ground and in our minds let us make sense of the present. Without habit and the memory of past experience, no sight or sound would mean anything; we can perceive only what we are accustomed to. Environmental features and patterns are recognized as features and patterns because we share a history with them. Every object, every grouping, every view is intelligible largely because previous encounters and tales heard, books read, pictures seen, have made them already familiar. Only habituation enables us to understand what lies around us. "If you saw a slab of chocolate for the first time," suggests John Wyndham, "you might think it was for mending shoes, lighting the fire, or building houses." The perceived identity of each scene and object stems from past acts and expectations, from a history of involvements. In Hannah Arendt's words, "the reality and reliability of the human world rest primarily on the fact that we are surrounded by things more permanent than the activity by which they were produced."

> —David Lowenthal (1985: 39)

In the middle and later first millennium B.C., metal mirrors, made primarily of bronze, are ubiquitous among burials of horse-riding nomads of the Eurasian steppe, a vast territory extending from the northern borders of China westward to the Ukraine (Komarova 1952: 42; Chlenova 1994: 500–501). The populations on the steppe shared a lifestyle that involved herding as the economic base, and they had perfected very effective means of warfare from horseback.

Many elements of the material culture employed in this lifeway were shared across the steppe, although variations of material and style were customary (Rubinson 1975; Chlenova 1994: 500–501; Bashilov and Yablonsky 1995: xii–xiv; Jacobson 1995: 2). Although the steppe populations themselves did not have writing, contemporary and slightly later texts from Near Eastern, Greek, and Chinese sources do exist that, when used judiciously, can provide some information on the intangible elements of the nomadic life that cannot be captured archaeologically (Bunker 1970: 14; Rolle 1989: 13–14; Jacobson 1995: 16–18; Ivanchik 1996: 167–289).

Recently, Davis-Kimball has suggested that among the female burials of the Sauromatians and Sarmatians she excavated at Pokrovka in the Orenburg region of Russia, the mirror, when found together with a shell, low table, or other "ritual" artifact, is a mark of the status "priestess," following categories established by Soviet scholars (Davis-Kimball 1997/98: 6, 8, 28, 35; see also Yablonsky 1995: 218). Davis-Kimball notes that complete mirrors found in male burials identify "priests," although she does not ascribe meaning to fragmentary bronze mirrors, such as those found in the male burial, Pokrovka cemetery 2, kurgan 16, burial 1 (Davis-Kimball 1997/98: 6; see also Davis-Kimball 1995: 17, fig. 5).

If the mirror in fact symbolizes "priestess" among female burials of the Sauromatians and Sarmatians, can that meaning be extended to mirrors found among other groups of nomads on the steppe and in central Asia, in areas and time periods beyond those excavated by Davis-Kimball, given the general similarity of the material culture of the groups? A review of some contexts in which mirrors are found, where the sex of the deceased is known, suggests that the meaning of mirrors as grave goods can be arrived at only by studying the complete context in each case and assessing the evidence on its own terms.[1]

It is important to note that although nomadic burials have been excavated for more than a century, data available for this kind of analysis are limited. In general, the sex of an individual has been determined by the nature of the accompanying grave goods rather than by an anthropological investigation of the skeletal remains.

There are, however, some excavations that allow for such an investigation, where the skeleton is sexed independently of the nature of the burial goods, as was done at Pokrovka (Davis-Kimball 1997/98: 6). Roman Kenk reanalyzed 150 burials of the nomadic period (ca. eighth century B.C. through ca. third century B.C.) from central and western Tuva that had been compiled from 40 years of excavations and studied by A. D. Grach (1980; Kenk 1986). Of these burials, 24, from five different kurgan groups, contained mirrors. Eight of these burials had no gender or age information available, and seven were adults of undetermined sex. Of the remaining nine burials, five were males and four females. Thus, where the sex is securely identified in this group of burials with mirrors, a total of nine burials, the male-female distribution is roughly 50–50. Additionally, the male burial of Sagly-Bazi II, kurgan 3, and the female burial from Sagly-Bazi II, kurgan 9, were accompanied by similar grave inventories, including, in addition to mirrors, wooden cups with pierced handles, bone arrowheads, bronze ax heads, and bits of gold foil decoration, presumably demonstrating a similar status and/or societal position. The ages of the adult males were as follows: one of undetermined age, one 30 years old, two 50 years old, and one 50 to 55 years old. Of the four female skeletons, one is designated "young," one aged 50, one 50 to 55, and one 50 to 60 (Kenk 1986: liste 3).[2] The fact that both men and women were buried with mirrors and that most of the individuals who could be aged were 50 or older raises the question whether the mirrors were used in the same way by both males and females in this population and whether the younger individuals, the "young" woman and the 30-year-old male, were employing mirrors (or were buried with them) for the same reasons as those who were older.

In the Altai, during the Pazyryk period (ca. fifth century B.C. through ca. third century B.C.), mirrors are found in many graves, of all three social levels defined by N. V. Polosmak (1994: 353): elite, midlevel nobility, and common people.[3] Certainly in the elite and common burials, mirrors are found with both male and female burials. At Pazyryk itself, in tomb 2, two mirrors were found. An undecorated tanged bronze mirror had a handle wrapped in leather and was placed in a case of leopard skin decorated with a gold disk and rings of blue and black beads. Rudenko, the excavator, associated it with the tattooed male burial in this tomb. The second mirror, of silver, was not found in situ, but, because it was in a bag with toilet articles, Rudenko (1970: 114, plate 70) suggested that it belonged to the woman in the tomb. A tomb of a woman from the Ak Alakh 3 burial ground has been ascribed by Polosmak to the same high-status group. Identified as a "possessor of special knowledge" by the excavator, the body, which had been tattooed, was found with a mirror by her left thigh; the mirror was formed from a piece of silver cut down from another object and set in a wooden frame with handle and carved back decorated with the image of deer with oversize antlers. The mirror had been placed in a felt pouch decorated with appliqué. Other grave goods found in the woman's sarcophagus included beads, bronze pendants, horsehair tassels, and a stone dish containing coriander (Polosmak 1998: 150, 152–55, 163, fig. 12).[4]

Another tomb at Ak Alakh contained bodies of both a male and a female. In this burial of "'middle-level' nobility," only the female had a mirror, which was found in a leather case near her waist. She was accompanied by an iron pick ax with a wooden handle, an iron dagger in a wooden scabbard, a wooden quiver, bone arrowheads, and remains of a bow (Polosmak 1991: 8–9; 1994:

351, 353). Perhaps of the same social level is a tomb from the Sayan Mountains of Siberia, where the male in the burial contemporary with those in the Altai was accompanied by a mirror with incised animal decoration on the back, illustrating a wolf, a horse, and a wild boar. Other grave goods found with the deceased included an iron pick ax and an iron knife in a wooden scabbard as well as small gold ornaments. It is possible that, in fact, this individual is of higher-ranking status, as suggested by the excavator, but appears to be "midlevel" because of the extensive robbing of the tomb (Borkovenko 1994: 48, 50–51, fig. 3:3).

At the site of less rich Altayan burials at Ulandryk, virtually all graves, whether of adult males or females or of children, contained either bronze mirrors or wooden copies of mirrors; in the related site of Yustyd, almost three-quarters of the tombs also contained mirrors (Kubarev 1987: 25; 1991: 98). The mirrors were both disk shaped with handles on the back and disk shaped with small handles in the same plane, generally simple flat loops, although sometimes decorated with animals (Kubarev 1991: 99–106).[5] In addition to mirrors, these burials contained, among other objects, wooden ornaments, bronze knives and daggers (sometimes in wooden scabbards), and ceramic and wooden vessels. The importance of the mirror to this population—at least in death—is underscored by the presence of wooden mirror models in the absence of metal mirrors in some of the tombs.

The cemeteries and burials described here are but a small part of the excavated nomadic burials of the first millennium B.C. in Eurasia, but they provide good evidence for a consideration of the distribution of mirrors among these populations. In all three areas discussed, mirrors are associated both with males and with females and, in the Altai, with both adults and children. Although this evidence is clear, what the mirrors are markers of is not easy to explain. Presumably, like the mirror in the painting *The Arnolfini Wedding* by Jan van Eyck, where the mirror is not only a symbol of purity and a mark of Arnolfini's wealth but also the literal witness of the ceremony, through the reflection it contains, mirrors among the inhabitants of the Eurasian steppe and central Asia had multiple meanings (Janson 1985: 51).[6]

However, ways to get at meaning are difficult in areas without written records, especially when the objects are undecorated. Nevertheless, many scholars have tried. Anatoly I. Martynov argues that mirrors probably symbolized light and/or the sun as well as fertility and that, because of their power, they were used as talismans. He suggests that this talismanic use is seen in the fact that in the Tagar culture (sixth to third centuries B.C.), the mirror was worn around a deceased person's neck (Martynov 1991: 69–70). Certainly, where the mirror was hung from the neck, it is hard to ignore the possibility of an amuletic function. Mirrors have been worn in this manner, at least in death, in much of the area under consideration beginning from the late third or early second millennium B.C. (Linduff 1998: 625–27).

I have suggested previously that the occurrence of mirrors in kurgan 2 at Pazyryk was as part of a shamanic assemblage because they were found together with a drum, a bronze brazier containing stones and hemp seeds, and a tripod of sticks that could have supported a felt enclosure—elements of the historic shaman's tools (Lewis 1984; Rubinson 1989).[7] Certainly shamanism was long-lived in historical times in Siberia and ethnographers have recorded useful details which may bear on the past, such as costumes hung with mirrors (e.g., Basilov and Zhukovskaya 1989: 161–69).

Ethnographic data from the recent past indicate that shamanism was practiced among many horse-riding nomadic groups in central Asia and Siberia (Basilov 1984: 46–63; 1989b: 161–69). I do not mean to suggest that all mirrors among early nomads were shamanic. Unless the entire population of Ulandryk were shamans, there must have been another use or meaning at a site where all graves, including those of children, contained mirrors or wooden copies of them. Mircea Eliade has recorded that copper mirrors were important among all northern Manchurian Tungusic shamans but that their actual meaning and interpretation varied from tribe to tribe (Eliade 1972: 153–54). If, in recent recorded history, the same object has multiple meanings even among a single ethnolinguistic group, it is much more difficult to get at the meanings of this object in the past.

In fact, it is likely that, despite the widespread occurrence and similarity of form of the mirrors discussed previously, that the meanings and uses were not the same in all areas. Esther Jacobson, discussing the Scythians, notes that mirrors occur in the burials of "males and females, both rich and poor, from the 7th through the late 4th century B.C." She adds that "while a few mirrors are distinguished by unusual ornamentation, in most cases the object type does not reflect the kind of concern for craftsmanship that one finds in respect to jewelry or vessels. This circumstance suggests that the mirror had limited and practical functions within the lifetime of the owner and within the burial ritual; in the latter context, it may have been thought to have protective properties" (Jacobson 1995: 182).

The tools that an archaeologist has to get at those limited and practical functions in life are especially circumscribed in interpreting cultures where most of the archaeological information is mortuary data. Ethnographic analogy, used judiciously, may be useful—not only the substantial data collected among tribal peoples in 19th- and early 20th-century Eurasia but also the data from the Native American groups who, on the Great Plains, were similarly dependent on horses (Anthony 1986; Basilov 1989b: 8). Further, the ancient texts of the adjacent settled populations can provide insight, but care must be taken. As Lowenthal has said, "Only habituation enables us to understand what lies around us. . . . The perceived identity of each scene and object stems from past acts and expectations, from a history of involvements" (Lowenthal 1985: 39). It is perhaps such habituation that moved Renate Rolle to describe the mirrors as a marker of "femininity" in the graves of the nomadic women she classifies as Amazons, without considering what that might imply for male burials with mirrors in the same cultural groups (Rolle 1989: 91). The examples given here of the burials from Tuva and the Altai demonstrate that, at least when interpreting mirror occurrence in Eurasia, the context of the object is more than the immediate context of the grave from which it is excavated. It is necessary to look at the entire archaeological/cultural group, not a single grave and not a single sex, to understand the function or functions of the mirror among the Eurasian nomads.

NOTES

1. For context, see, for example, Hodder (1982a: 217).
2. All five identifiable males with mirrors were from the kurgan group Sagly-Bazi II, as was one female. Two of the women were buried in the same kurgan in Kjuzlengi I; the young woman was from kurgan 5 of Sagly-Bazi I, group 2 (nos. 1, 2, 6, 14, 17, 21, 29, 30, 38, 44, 46, 61, 63, 70, 75, 87, 88, 93, 139, 144, 145, 149, 172, and 173).
3. Note that in the Altai, all elite and midlevel kurgans contained horses or horse gear, which is not described or discussed here. A few of the "low-level" burials were accompanied by horse burials as well.
4. Davis-Kimball (1998: 143–44) considers the Pazyryk female a tribal priestess as well as the woman from Ak Alakh 3 (or Ukok).
5. See Kubarev (1991: plate LXIV, 4, 7, 8) for the range of types, which includes a few examples with longer handles in the same plane.
6. Jan Van Eyck, *The Arnolfini Marriage,* 1434. See also Robert Baldwin (1985: 68) on mirror meanings from the 15th to the 17th century.
7. Rudenko (1970: 284–85) thinks that the hemp-smoking equipment was for purification purposes, as described by Herodotus, as well as part of ordinary life.

5

Ideology, Power, and Gender: Emergent Complex Society in Northeastern China

Sarah Milledge Nelson

Gender is a relatively new topic in Asian archaeology, although enough has been written about the topic in other regions to merit entire books dedicated to the subject (e.g., Claassen and Joyce [1997] for North America and Meso-America and Kent [1998] for Africa). Gender is increasingly recognized as a legitimate, if understudied, focus of archaeological research (Nelson 1997). Some relevant examples of mainstream notice of gender topics in archaeology include books on ancient civilizations (Scarre and Fagan 1997), on the archaeology of rank (Wason 1994), and on the role of ideology in early state formation (Claessen and Oosten 1996). Scarre and Fagan mostly note women's roles in various civilizations rather than engaging in any gender analysis, while Wason pays attention to a portion of the gender literature that relates to rank. Claessen and Oosten included two chapters that specifically address gender issues in the early state.

Gender studies in archaeology have moved considerably beyond the question of "where are the women in these analyses of the past," the question that was the first to be addressed; instead, newer studies consider gender relationships as a part of the social structure and as a dynamic that allows us to penetrate further into the cognitive domains of the archaeological past. In addition, a focus on gender requires that we eschew the "totalizing, stereotypical views of women and men developed and perpetuated within the Judeo-Christian-Islamic tradition and the commercial-industrial experience" (Hassan 1998) and consider ways that gender might be expressed and materialized in our archaeological sites that are not embedded in Western tradition.

A focus on ideology is also becoming more commonplace, with more emphasis on interpretations that are contingent on context (Hodder 1982b) as well as critiques of colonialist and nationalist interpretations of the past (Kohl and Fawcett 1995). For example, all the chapters in *Ideology and the Formation of Early States* approach the topic of ideology as "the organization of ideas and values in a society" (Claessen and Oosten 1996: 359). At least part of the ideas and values is frequently related to gender.

In terms of power, although much has been written, power has traditionally been defined from an androcentric perspective, which is to say from the perspective of the powerful. The very definitions of the cultural evolutionary stages of bands, tribes, chiefdoms, and states relate to power and its expression. In this evolutionary view, as political structure becomes more complex, power is increasingly placed in the hands of fewer and fewer people. On the other hand, feminist perspectives on power tend to emphasize the more complex interplays of differently constituted power. Studies of heterarchy (e.g., Ehrenreich, Crumley, and Levy 1995) are one new and effective way to address these issues. Another approach is to ask how and why people acquiesce to domination or how they are convinced to cede some of their autonomy to government power. Alison Wylie (1992) points out that all power is granted and is negotiated continuously. Power is not a thing but a process, and any power inhering in a group or individual is temporary. Elman Service addressed some of these issues by suggesting that "civilization" rather than "the state" was the topic that should be addressed; the organization of leadership rather than the beginnings of repressive force (Service 1975: xiii).

How, then, does an elite group lay claim to power, or leadership in Service's terms? How does it maintain its power and keep its symbols of power exclusive so that their symbolic force is not attenuated? What are the material expressions of that power? What role does ideology play? The Hongshan culture in northeastern China is a particular instance of this phenomenon and has data with which to approach these problems.

HONGSHAN CULTURE

The Hongshan culture does not have a plethora of dates, but those radiocarbon dates that have been calculated range from 4000 to 2500 B.C., calibrated. Most sites consist of small to medium-size villages (Torii and Torii 1904; Hamada and Mizuno 1938). These are mostly quite unremarkable, but at least one of them (Hutougou) contains a large stone cairn covering individual burials in stone slab coffins, each individual accompanied by well-carved jades (Fang and Liu 1984). In addition, there are two known ceremonial centers that seem to be the heart of Hongshan rituals (Lei 1996).

The two ceremonial centers are only 25 kilometers apart, but they are quite different and must have been used for different purposes as well as expressing different facets of the ideology. Dongshanzui consists of platforms and stone alignments that are interpreted as "altars" and "walls." Both round and square platforms are called altars; in later times, these shapes represented heaven and earth, respectively.

Dongshanzui's most notable artifacts are small and medium-size female figurines. The small ones are nude. One of them is clearly pregnant, and another held some broken-off object to one breast. Among the medium-size figures, portions of seated female statues are also found. One of them wears a belt made of two strands of rope, knotted in the front (Guo and Zhang 1984). This site seems to emphasize life, in contrast to death in the tomb areas of Niuheliang.

The site of Niuheliang covers an area of at least 80 square kilometers. Thirteen areas of stone-mounded tombs have been identified, each with several separate mounds. In some of them, the stones were very carefully laid and dressed on the outside edges. In the excavated mounds, most had rows of bottomless painted pots placed on the periphery of the mound (Fang and Wei 1986a, 1986b). Guo Dashun (1995) has estimated that as many as 10,000 such pots were made for placement in the tombs.

Individual burials within the mounds are delineated with stone slabs or piled cobbles, whether there is a single burial or multiple ones within the mound. Individuals are buried mostly extended and supine, although bundle burials are known as well.

Up to 13 jades have been found with a single individual. These jades vary in type and in shape, but all of them fall within a limited range of shapes. Annular shapes are the most common, including bracelets and a tubular shape that is thought to function as both headdress and a device to contain the hair, as a kind of ponytail holder. Multiple overlapping rings are often carved of jade as well. One example of three rings has a pig head on each end, and the common object called a *zhulong,* or pig-dragon, is an open ring with a pig head on one end. This type of jade object is perforated for suspension, as are most of the other jades that have been found. They have either a hole drilled through from both sides or an "ox nose" perforation that goes in and out from the back and cannot be seen from the face of the object. Other shapes include turtles, birds, squared spirals designated as "clouds," insects, and an object with teeth that could be seen as the upper part of a monster face, although it is generally referred to as a comb (Guo 1997). Whether or not there are dragons is a matter of interpretation (Sun 1984; Sun and Guo 1984), but the curved shape of the pig-dragon is echoed in the oracle-bone character for dragon (Childs-Johnson 1991: 93).

All but one of the tomb groups at Niuheliang were constructed on a hill, and most of the tombs are in visual line of sight from one another as well as the Goddess Temple. Another feature is an artificial hill that was constructed at what might have been the entrance to the ceremonial complex. This mound, known as the "earth pyramid," contains three concentric circles of stones, each higher than the other, covered over with a mound of earth. Despite extensive trenching, no burial site has been found within. In addition to the stone rings, the only feature within the hill is a layer of crude sherds near the top of the mound that are interpreted as crucibles. The only metal discovered at the site, however, is a single earring made of copper wire and a lump of unpolished jade (Han 1993).

The most unusual discovery at Niuheliang was a long narrow building of irregular shape that contained fragments of life-size and larger statues. Most of the statues represent humans, and some breast and shoulder pieces indicate that they depict women. A smiling face with inset green jade eyes is the most striking fragment found on the floor of the building (Sun and Guo 1986). For this reason, the building has been dubbed Nushen Miao, the "goddess temple."

Parts of animal statues were also recovered, including a pig's jaw and trotters and a claw that might represent a dragon or a large bird. Some statues seem to have been fixed to the wall of the structure. A short footing of the wall shows that it was painted with geometric designs (LPARI 1986).

A final feature of interest at Niuheliang is a flat area near the Nushen Miao that is faced with stones. It is known as the "platform." Little work has been accomplished in this area as yet, but one pit yielded a large painted jar with a lid. This seems to be a likely area for workshops or domestic structures.

HONGSHAN ECONOMY AND POLITICAL STRUCTURE

The subsistence base of the Hongshan culture consists of millets and pigs, a combination that was domesticated in northern China as long ago as the seventh millennium B.C. The earliest dated site is Xinglongwa, which has houses in rows and is encircled by a ditch (Wang 1999). These features indicate that it is likely that the site marks the first agriculture in the region. Even earlier pottery has been found in his region, which may turn out to be associated with yet earlier experiments with domestication. The stone tool inventory is unimpressive for the most part, with more chipped stone tools than implement types made of ground stone. However, one kind of large ground stone implement is interpreted as a plow, and a jade figurine of an ox has recently been discovered in Inner Mongolia. These objects suggest intensive agriculture that could support an elite and full-time artisans (Nelson 1995, 1996b).

At least three kinds of skilled crafts were practiced: constructing life-size statues of unbaked clay, making thin-walled painted pottery vessels, and carving jades. Other labor was expended on constructing the stone mounded tombs and other features of the sites as well as possible metallurgy.

The jades are of a very high level of artistry, with traces of the use of a rotary blade (Teng 1997). Jade carving has deep roots in northeastern China, with the first known jade artifacts found at the site of Chahai, which is slightly later than Xinglongwa (LPARI 1986; Nelson 1990). Pottery vessels also have a long history in the region, but those prior to Hongshan are incised or impressed and tend to be made in simple shapes, especially tall, wide-mouthed pots. Painted Hongshan pottery is made in many shapes and is neatly and elegantly painted with curvilinear geometric designs. Unpainted pottery vessels continue the previous shapes and designs.

The realistic large statues of unbaked clay are unlike anything else in China (Nelson 1991). They are made on armatures of wood and bone, with a layer of coarse clay, a layer of fine clay, and paint on the surface (Yang 1988). The Nushen Miao building is another unique feature of the Hongshan, having lobed "rooms" and a separate smaller associated building. No superstructure has survived, but the excavators believe that the building might have been made of wattle and daub and plastered with fine clay both inside and out. The interior shows signs of painted designs.

While the possible crucibles suggest a metal industry, there is little so far to corroborate that inference. A small clay mold fragment was found at another Hongshan site (Renmin Ribao 1988), but the evidence is thin. Weaving was likely practiced since spindle whorls have been found (Hamada and Mizuno 1938), and sheep bones suggest that it was wool that was produced. The organization of these crafts is unknown, but at least the production of the painted cylinders that were placed in the graves must have taken place somewhere near where the graves were constructed.

Some sources of local jades are known, so there need not have been extensive long-distance travel or trade to acquire the jade stone, but turquoise, which has no local source, is also used.

Both the jades and the size of the burial mounds suggest that only the elite received burial. The tombs suggest at least a three-tier elite, with in some cases a central burial and subsidiary burials in one tomb, and some elite who were buried in village sites (Nelson 1996a). The functions of the elite may have been to regulate the crafts and the rituals that supported their elite status.

IDEOLOGY OF THE HONGSHAN CULTURE

Two possible approaches to ideology in the Hongshan culture will be explored in this chapter. The first uses the material culture to determine how it may guide or limit the interpretation of the ideology. This involves considering the manufacture of these objects and the way they arrived at their place of deposition as well as how they are likely to have functioned within the culture. The second uses later Chinese writings and the "root metaphors" within them (Allan 1997) to ascertain whether they are congruent with the evidence of the Hongshan culture and might help to interpret it. While some features of Hongshan differ from other Chinese Neolithic cultures (e.g., Yangshao and Longshan) that are thought to be more directly ancestral to the three dynasties of Xia, Shang, and Zhou, other features of Hongshan do seem to be reflected in later Chinese thought and material constructs. Thus, it is not unreasonable to suppose that there is some continuity from Hongshan to later times when a written record exists.

The material culture, as already noted, contains a number of items that might be interpreted as part of ritual and symbol and that could lead to an understanding of Hongshan ideology. These include the shapes of the jades, the shapes of the ritual structures, and the nature of the large and small statues. It is also useful to consider the meaning of the portable items of material culture to determine whether any useful inferences can be drawn regarding who was eligible to wear them.

To begin with the large but fragile statues in the Nushen Miao, it seems that they must have been sculpted very close to where they were found. They could not have been moved from a village, for they would not have survived. They might have even been made in place, as part of the structure of the building. The pottery cylinders that were placed in the tombs in such large numbers must also have been made nearby, as the only way to transport them would have been by human portage from distant villages. The jades might have been made in villages, but it seems likely that they were created under elite supervision.

It is hard to understand what ceremonies occurred in the Nushen Miao and the tombs or even the unlikely crucibles on top of the artificial hill. Who constituted the audience for these rituals? What did they consist of? Since some of the statues may have been attached to the wall of the structure, they could not have been taken out and paraded around to impress the populace. The Nushen Miao is long but narrow—it was not intended for large groups of people to come and worship. Who, then, was allowed to enter? Perhaps the building was used only by the initiated. Perhaps, on the other hand, the building was a charnel house for the dead awaiting interment, for example, those that appear in the graves as bundle burials.

Similarly, the tomb mounds imply activities associated with the actual burial. After the construction of the slab-lined graves, was there a procession of people carrying the bodies? Was there a line of people, each carrying a ceramic vessel for the tomb? Perhaps the tomb was constructed and kept open long before the death of a ruler, with the painted cylinder already in place.

Another ritual that is difficult to understand is in the apparent pouring of hot metal into crucibles and presumably into molds on top of the artificial hill. Was this done to impress the populace with the transformational "magic" inherent in turning solid ore to liquid and back again? If so, where were the villagers placed to behold the events, and where and when and why did they assemble?

Root metaphors of China, to use Sarah Allan's (1997) felicitous phrase, include some that are well known and others that are more obscure. The division of the world into complementary sets of characteristics that are yin and yang is one of the more familiar. This concept underlies other dualisms, such as the symbolism of heaven and earth—heaven (or the sky) is round, and the earth is square (Allan 1991). The square and round altars at Dongshanzui suggest the possible antiquity of this symbolism.

However, the shapes of the jades may be the best window into the ideology of the Hongshan people. They consist of symbols of water and of the sky. Water is symbolized by turtles and dragons, clouds signify both water and the sky, and birds and circular forms may refer to heaven or the sky. Allan (1997) makes a case for water and plants representing virtue in Chinese philosophy. The designs painted on pottery, especially on the tomb cylinders, are plantlike. Earlier zigzag designs impressed into pottery could have been meant to represent water, although many other interpretations are possible.

We have not yet dealt with the ubiquitous pig symbolism. I have made an ecological argument for the importance of pigs in the Hongshan culture (Nelson 1996b, 1998), but this does not rule out pig symbolism. It seems that they must represent earth as they wallow in the mud. On the other hand, in later China and Manchuria, it is women who raise the pigs, and women were closely associated with that animal into the 20th century (Lattimore 1940). Since a pig statue is found in the Nushen Miao, perhaps it is their association with women that makes them important. Pigs were an animal of ritual sacrifice, and pig bones or even whole pigs were often included in northern Chinese Neolithic burials.

CONCLUSION

Joyce Linnekin (1990) demonstrates that symbolic and mythic associations of women in ancient Hawaii relate to their status according to rank. Allan (1991) finds "mythic thinking" reflected in early Chinese "cosmology, divination, art, and ritual." Allan points out, as Peggy Sanday (1981) has done before her, that myths are not independent of the social structure.

We cannot know exactly what symbolic meaning may have inhered in the jades, tombs, buildings, and ritual landscapes of the Hongshan culture, but we can expect that they made a coherent package and that they are likely to be reflected, if dimly, in later Chinese constructs. For example, the presence of yin symbolism, which prominently includes the female principle, seems to be a strong suggestion that women were symbolically important. Add to this the female images, and the case is yet stronger. Furthermore, there are hints of goddesses in the distant past in later Chinese writings. The Queen Mother of the West had a counterpart in the East (Chang 1983), and Nuwa seems to be a very ancient female deity (Wu 1982: 4). There is no reason not to think that women had stature as well as statues in Hongshan culture. While there is not enough evidence to insist that women had high status in Hongshan, there is no reason at all to deny it. K. C. Chang (1983) notes that female shamans are mentioned in early China, and Lei Congyun (1996) makes a similar point. One goddess who may be a reflection of the Nushen Miao statues is Xihe, who makes light and darkness by controlling the sun and moon (Allan 1991). The calendar and the heavens are ruled by her, according to the Yaodian. There is also a thunder ancestress. These manifestations, or something like them, are probably reflected in the ideology of the Hongshan culture.

More explorations of this sort are needed for a gendered archaeology as well as to move ahead with context and cognition, agency and values (Nelson 1997). Although these are only first attempts, it is important to begin thinking along these lines, to "flesh out" with men and women the prehistoric past.

6

Beauty, Sexuality, Body Ornamentation, and Gender in Ancient Meso-America

Rosemary Joyce

BODILY CUES AS MEDIA OF SOCIAL IDENTITY IN MESO-AMERICA

Documentary sources, both text and pictorial, from the 16th-century colonization of the central Mexican Aztec state by the Spanish, provide ample illustration of the way that appearance cues were used to cumulatively mark individuals for gender, age, achievement, and social status. Generally recognized as forms of "sumptuary laws" by European observers (and subsequent scholars), strict controls over clothing, ornaments, hairstyles, and other body modifications were recorded as applying to elites and nonelites; men, women, and children of different ages; and those who gained status in warfare or long-distance trade. By examining these controlled appearance cues not as markers of a preexisting category but as media through which Aztec bodies were gradually given specific social form, I have identified the manipulation of the body, its preparation for use of specific ornaments, and the adoption of different bodily cues as central actions in a sequence of life cycle rituals that produced adult men and women from the undifferentiated substrate of newborn Aztec infants (Joyce 2000b).

In rituals that began at birth and continued at least to first childbirth (for women) or the first capture of a prisoner (for men), clothing and ornaments served to mark transitions from one status to another. In infancy, transformations were foreshadowed symbolically and rhetorically by presentation of specific items of clothing and reference to specific hairstyles that were not to be adopted until years had passed. However, consistent with rhetorical imagery of infants as raw materials (feathers and jade) that needed to be worked into social forms, during these early years the bodies of children were directly manipulated and altered in appearance. The lips of boys destined to training for war were pierced to prepare them to receive the lip plugs that would signify their successful capture of different numbers of prisoners as young adults. Children dedicated to serve in the temple (and thus not be trained for warfare) lacked this piercing and instead were ritually scarred on their hips and chests. For infants with both destinies, these direct body modifications marked not only their intended adult work but also their sexual status: Children who entered the temples would be celibate, while boys who trained in war enjoyed sexual liaisons with special groups of young women and eventually might contract permanent marriages.

Children's bodies were thus marked for distinct experiences of adult sexuality in ways that could not be changed as easily as setting aside one form of clothing in favor of another. At a slightly later age, all children's bodies were further distinguished by ear piercing, again in anticipation of the eventual use of specific adult ornaments. Unlike the earlier body modifications, ear piercing did not distinguish adult sexual status or gender but rather prepared the setting for a form of ornament worn by all adults, regardless of status. In pictorial documents showing year-by-year depictions of the training of boys and girls, adult ornaments are worn by teenage boys on their entry into the temple or after their first capture of prisoners and by girls and boys in their marriage ceremony and related postmarital rituals.

By the time the ears were pierced, gendering of the initially formless infants was being marked by clothing. Not yet the full adult dress, distinctive upper garments from men's and women's costume are shown worn by the boys and girls undergoing instruction in adult work. The shift to adding layers of social signifiers rather than continuing the direct modification of the body suggests that transformation of the bodily substance of children from its initial nonhuman state into a substance like that of adults had been accomplished.

The final type of appearance cue to take full social form in the rich Aztec data was hair treatment. Hair presents an interesting paradox: Attached to the body, it can nonetheless be removed without pain and loss of blood. More like a manufactured substance than a body part, hair was the focus of an exceptionally elaborate set of treatments providing the richest communication of dimensions of social status recorded for the Aztec in a single kind of appearance cue. Children, both boys and girls, had their hair trimmed short—not quite shaved but left so short that it followed the shape of their heads—until around age 10 to 12. For both boys and girls, the first change was letting the hair grow long in back. Young boys who captured captives in war had various locks of hair cut and let grow as signs of each new capture. Those dedicated to the temple kept their hair in the long lock of youths. For young men, then, the contrast between long, flowing hair and elaborate combinations of long locks and shaved areas marked different forms of adult labor but also the differences that these implied in accepted sexuality. The flowing hair of young men was paralleled by that of young women, whose transition to adult status (described as marked by the delivery of a child) resulted in the adoption of a style of hair bound up into two horns. Controlling hair marked control of adult sexuality, and it is not coincidental that the negative stereotype of the female prostitute described for Spanish clerics singled out long, unbound hair as one of the signs of this practice (see Arvey 1988).

Hair provided an important site for the continuing modification of the body, and indeed the fact that hair grows continually required that it be a constant focus of attention to maintain the necessary social form. As a body part that grew out of shape, hair resisted static formalizations of appearance. It became the site where Aztec adults continually reenacted the social creation of bodily appearance out of the nonhuman material that infant bodies had represented.

A MESO-AMERICAN HISTORY FOR AZTEC PRACTICES

The circumstances of the Spanish conquest have left us with much richer material on relations among gender, age, status, and bodily appearance than are available for any earlier society in Meso-America (or even for any society contemporary with the Aztec). With this material as a guide, earlier societies that were historical antecedents in the Meso-American tradition can be reexamined in a new light. The prominence of particular kinds of elaborate costume ornaments that is a distinctive feature of the Meso-American tradition takes on new significance, as media through which other Meso-American societies shaped their own particular "social skins" (Turner 1980). The degree of attention devoted to costume and ornament throughout Meso-American history can be seen as an outgrowth of the social focus on costume as the site of creation of specific social identity. In those Meso-American societies that employed writing, signs representing individual names and titles of personages could be placed directly in costume, for example, when the name signs of the Maya ruler Stormy Sky were depicted in his headdress on Tikal Stela 31 or when a string of titles of a noble woman from Calakmul were lightly incised on the edge of her robe. This sort of incorporation of the signs for personal identity in costume further illustrates the way that individual costume in effect constituted a text documenting the formation of specific social personae into which could be inserted the signs of individual identity.

These features are evident already in the first archaeological sites that can be identified as part of the Meso-American tradition, in the early and middle formative periods (ca. 1500–500 B.C.). Although there is earlier evidence of sedentary populations in Mexico and Guatemala, it is during this millennium that, at multiple places extending from central Mexico to Honduras, a series of linked practices that characterize Meso-American cultures become visible (Joyce and Grove 1999). These include the first use for costume ornaments of materials sufficiently durable to preserve indefinitely (various kinds of stone, shell, and pottery) and the simultaneous adoption of fired clay as a medium for hand-modeled figurines depicting distinct, individual forms of body ornamentation and costume.

In studies of burial assemblages from the village sites Playa de los Muertos in Honduras and Tlatilco in central Mexico, I documented generally unstandardized practices of body ornamentation using highly formalized ornaments executed in a narrow range of materials that continued to be highly valued through to the 16th century (Joyce 1992, 1996b, 1999). The only characteristic that was constant in over 400 burials was the restriction of ear ornaments to adult burials.

In an analysis of a similar assemblage from the Pacific coast of Guatemala, John Clark (1983) observed the same pattern of use of ear ornaments only by adults. However, in these sites Clark also noted other kinds of patterned variation in costume within the burial population. Unlike Playa de los Muertos and Tlatilco, where there was no evidence of distinctive spatial arenas formed by architecture, the sites Clark examined included clusters of raised platform mounds, or pyramids, and other areas without these features. He found regular differences in the iconography and materials of ornaments used by individuals buried in or near pyramids and those in cemeteries away from the pyramids, which he suggested might distinguish religious and secular elites.

Examining a much smaller sample of burials from areas with platform mounds at La Venta, on the Mexican Gulf coast, I found the same correlation of ear ornaments with adult status, along with the use of costumes that were so strongly patterned that they were duplicated at contemporary sites with similar architectural precincts from central Mexico to Honduras (Joyce 1986, 1999, 2000a). The specific costuming practices documented for La Venta were duplicated at Chalcatzingo, Morelos, and Los Naranjos, Honduras, and may also have been evident, although poorly recorded, at the contemporary site of Zumpango del Rio, Guerrero. In general, they also match features of one set of burials distinguished by Clark (1983) at Chiapa de Corzo. In these more strongly stereotyped costumes from what appear to be more stratified societies of the formative period, both Clark and I found elements that appear to represent distinct ornaments of males and females. In particular, males often wore beaded belts and had elaborate pendants with distinctive iconographic elements attached to their ear ornaments. Women, in addition to lacking these items, sometimes wore pendants in the form of effigies of bivalve shells. While there are no strong trends by sex for costumes in the large groups of burials at Tlatilco (over 200 in the statistical sample), there is a weak association of beaded belts with males that may reflect the presence of the same kind of costuming in this less stratified society.

Together, the data from the examination of these different burial populations suggest that in the earliest days of the Meso-American tradition, costume was already a major medium for the marking of standardized social status. In less stratified social settings, the major distinction marked was that between adult and nonadult, achieved through the display of ear ornaments. Data from Tlatilco hint at the possibility that distinctions in gender were also present, as they were in the stratified societies, although less strongly represented in the imperishable medium of stone ornaments. This possibility is given further support by the evidence of distinctive costume on figurines from Tlatilco and sites like it.

Figurines testify to a much broader range of bodily appearance cues than are preserved in burials. The provision of ear ornaments and elaborate, individualized hair treatments suggests that these figurines depict individuals already of adult age, using the criteria identified from late Meso-American data. Depiction of total or partial nudity provides some basis to identify the probable sex and thus the likely gender being represented, although it is intriguing that a proportion of figurines at many sites appear to avoid distinctive depiction of sex or sexually specific genders, cautioning against presuming the universal salience of sexual identity in these figurines. Among the major indicators that have been used to identify male and female figurines, the provision of loincloths for males stands out. These garments conform in every way to the continuing depiction in later Meso-America of the item of male garment that comes to stand not only for maleness but, through its ornamentation and length, for specific male status as well, as when Aztec and Maya elites are described as wearing exceptionally long, ornamented loincloths.

Clothing on figurines provided with female sexual characteristics, on the other hand, is wholly unlike that depicted and described in images and texts from later Meso-American societies. Shown nude or with short skirts or kilts, formative-period female figurines lack the distinctive blouses and long skirts whose names in later Meso-American societies were so ubiquitous that they served as metaphors for adult women. At the same time, the use of ear ornaments and elaboration of hair treatments on these semiclothed female figurines reinforces the details of physical characteristics that suggest that these images depict mature individuals. The disjunction between the costumes of formative-period female figurines and later female subjects in Meso-American art raises the possibility that some or all of these figurines are meant to illustrate not fully adult women but another status: that of the young, newly sexually mature girl.

Richard Lesure (1997), in an analysis of formative figurines from one site on the Pacific coast of Mexico, has suggested that armless, nude figurines with explicit female sexual characteristics found there reflect the objectification of young women deprived of agency as objects of marriage negotiations controlled by elders, represented visually at the same sites by seated, fleshy male and female figurines shown wearing masks and other items of ritual regalia. Anne Cyphers (1993) argues that figurines from the central Mexican Chalcatzingo site, perhaps used in life cycle rituals, depict nubile young women and other women in various stages of pregnancy. More generally, I would suggest that formative Meso-American female figurines, with their elaboration of hair and jewelry and the use of costumes that reveal female bodies represent a record of practices of beautification linked intimately with the expression of sexuality.

BEAUTIFICATION, PERSUASIVENESS, AND PERFORMATIVE GENDER

Nancy Munn (1986: 96–97, 101–2) describes specific social practices in an Oceanian society through which individual bodies were made more attractive and desirable and the person more "persuasive" to others. She shows that in Gawa, the sensory attraction of the body is deliberately increased by the addition of skillfully worked materials that distinguish one person from others and calls these practices "beautification." Beautification, as a process, draws specific attention to an individual and contributes to the relative social assessment of that person, resulting in a quality of renown of great significance in this small-scale society. The identity built up through beautification and, in particular, the evaluations that other people make of it become grounds for differential perceptions of effectiveness and hence of different patterns of action toward people perceived as more "persuasive" or "potent."

Munn's analysis can be applied to similar statements in other ethnographies, for example, Amazonian societies where use of feather ornamentation distinguishes individual costume. The Cashinahua describe feather ornamentation as promoting *dua,* a quality of health and attractiveness, by acting as "medicine" (*dau*) and by making externally visible the inherent aura of each individual (Kensinger 1991: 43, 47–48). The Amazonian Waiwai regard the beautification produced by wearing feather costume as "a profoundly political matter" in which individual attractiveness provides grounds for interpersonal competition: "the efforts put into beautification are one of several means of displaying one's suitability as a good candidate for marriage, a kind of visual persuasiveness" (Howard 1991: 62).

Western observers tend to see shell ornaments, feather costume, and the like as inherently beautiful, but analysis of practices of beautification does not require agreement about what is attractive. Evidence of efforts expended within any society to distinguish personal appearance through modification of the body is potential ground to consider the possibility of beautification and its relative evaluation. For example, the wearing of palm leaf skirts in the Trobriands is described by Annette Weiner (1976) in terms similar to Munn's discussion of beautification on Gawa, even though the aesthetic dimensions of differences in these skirts are not as immediately evident to Western sensibilities as those of shell valuables. Significantly, Weiner shows that, as among the Waiwai, the Cashinahua, and in Gawa, one of the most important social settings for such bodily distinction in the Trobriands is ceremonies when newly sexually active girls and boys perform in public dances and displays, leading (as in each of the other cases) to the identification of desired sexual or marital partners.

Can these dimensions of the ethnographic studies be extended to the archaeological record? I would suggest that they can and that they provide a means to reunite research on gender in archaeology with aspects of contemporary gender theory. Judith Butler (1990, 1993) argues that gender is most profitably viewed as performance, taking shape through gesture, costuming, and setting, "an incessant and repeated action of some sort." Butler (1990: 112) makes this suggestion as part of a complex argument about the radical separation of gender from sex, where sex cannot determine gender, and the equally radical embedding of gender in sexuality, the ways that culturally interpreted bodies are sites for relations between gendered persons:

> If sex and gender are radically distinct, then it does not follow that to be a given sex is to become a given gender; in other words, "woman" need not be the cultural construction of the female body, and "man" need not interpret male bodies. This radical formulation of the sex/gender distinction suggests that sexed bodies can be the occasion for a number of different genders, and further, that gender itself need not be restricted to the usual two. If sex does not limit gender, then perhaps there are genders, ways of culturally interpreting the sexed body, that are in no way restricted by the apparent duality of sex. Consider the further consequence that if gender is something one becomes—but can never be—then gender itself is a kind of becoming or activity, and that gender ought not to be conceived as a noun or a substantial thing or a static cultural marker, but rather as an incessant and repeated action of some sort.

Butler's analysis suggests that there will be occasions and settings where the performance of gender is highlighted, specifically those occasions and settings involving the display of sexuality.

BODY ORNAMENTATION, BEAUTY, AND
SEXUALITY IN MESO-AMERICA

In formative Meso-America, the contemporaneous appearance of figurines as a medium depicting individualized appearance cues at the same time that burials incorporate elaborate imperishable costume ornaments, I argue, marks the initiation or foregrounding of gendered performance as a socially significant set of practices. The employment of costume ornaments, hair treatment, and clothing as constituents of the performance of adult male and female experience, I suggest, was not random but reflected the interpenetration of gendered performance and the enactment of competitive sexuality. Personal appearance was subject to beautification, that is, modification by addition of materials that enhanced the body or were themselves objects of admiration. Beautification was particularly important to newly sexually mature young adults, especially young women, the preferred subjects of most formative-period figurines, the possible objects of the rituals in which such figurines were employed, and the individuals who retained the most elaborate costumes when they died untimely deaths.

One way the focus on beautification and youth is evident is in the differential elaboration of costume of the young in burials. In my analysis of burials at the formative Mexican site, Tlatilco (Joyce 1999, based on data from Garcia Moll et al. 1991), I found that out of a sample of 212 burials, of which 86 (41 percent) were sexed female, 16 (7 percent) were buried wearing imperishable costume ornaments. Half of these were female ($N = 8$, 50 percent), and slightly fewer were male ($N = 6$, 37 percent); the remainder were juveniles too young to be identified in terms of adult sex. Elaborate costume was worn by young women between ages 15 and 25, who were also accompanied by the largest number of other materials in their burials, including up to 11 figurines. Small ceramic masks in two of these burials may have been additional parts of the fancy costumes these young women wore, while ceramic stamps appropriate for ornamenting the body included in three of these burials suggest a more perishable form of body modification.

Older women, between 30 and 45 years old, not only wore less jewelry (at most a single strand of beads at the neck or wrist) but had only simple bone or shell beads and lacked the jade, rock crystal, and polished iron ore beads and pendants of the younger women. The general simplification of costumes preserved with these slightly older women suggests a lessened emphasis on personal appearance, or beautification, at the ends of their lives. Unique to these older women, however, was a high frequency of ceramic rattle balls whose form and location in burials suggest that they may have been worn on the legs, and of whistles that could have served as pendants. Five burials of women aged

25 to 40, three with no other imperishable costume ornaments, were accompanied by up to five rattles or whistles.

The age range of men buried wearing costumes was slightly older than that of women, from 20 to 50, but again the most elaborate costumes were worn by younger men, those under 30. Among these were men who wore multiple strands of beads at the neck, arm, and ankle as well as ear spools and rings, incorporating jade, bone, shell, and iron ore. As with their young female counterparts, some males between 20 and 30 were buried with small ceramic masks and stamps that might be other media of beautification. Also like the women of Tlatilco, slightly older men, from age 25 to 35, were buried with up to three ceramic rattle balls. For the five youths with stamps and masks and the three with rattles, these ceramic objects were their only form of costume elaboration. In general, men buried wearing costume were accompanied by less diverse and numerous objects, including much smaller numbers of figurines, than were similarly costumed women, suggesting differential attention to women's graves at Tlatilco. More dramatic evidence of possible asymmetry in practices of beautification is presented by the incidence of modification of the shape of the skull. While 58 percent (124) of all adult burials showed evidence of such practices, 77 percent of female burials had been subjected to this body modification, which began in infancy and was evident in individuals as young as nine months.

The emphasis in burials on the ornamented bodies of youthful and young adult men and women, seen in patterns of distribution of imperishable ornaments, calls attention to the unrepresentative quality of figurines at the site. The abundant figurines recovered from burials at Tlatilco in general represent apparently youthful males and females. Figures identified as male have flat chests and uniformly wear loincloths and ear ornaments. Occasionally, they have necklaces or helmets with chin straps. Their hair may be worn in long tresses, shaved on top, or short. Female figurines share almost the same range of hair treatment, with the exception of shaved heads. They may wear distinctive headdresses: a band supporting one to three round disks, a beaded ornament, or a series of horns that may have been a hair treatment. Their female status is signaled by small modeled breasts, sometimes accompanied by clearly delineated genitalia and in a few cases a swollen belly. Unlike male figurines, ear ornaments are not always present, and in addition to necklaces, female figurines may wear bracelets. The most distinctive ornament of some female figurines is a real fragment of polished iron ore placed as a pendant at the neck. While most often provided with no clothing, some of the female figurines wear short, flaring skirts. Elaborate face and body painting is preserved on a few examples.

The costumes depicted on formative figurines revealed and accented rather than concealed the body. Contemporary depictions in large-scale political

monuments added a knee-length skirt to the costume of women and a kilt and
at times a cape to that of men. The body itself and its highlighting through the
use of painting, hair treatment, and ornaments are in effect the subject of formative figurines, a subject matter that presents moments of beautified, gendered performance. The inclusion of masks as part of the costume of some of
the individuals buried at Tlatilco and particularly of rattle balls whose sound
would have depended on rhythmic movement hints that the kinds of performances in which gendered beauty was on display in this formative society may
have been characterized by dancing.

THE PUBLIC PERFORMANCE OF GENDER IN
PRE-HISPANIC MESO-AMERICA

The primary context recorded in the rich data for the 16th-century Aztecs for
moments of beautified gendered performance is in fact the participation by
groups of young men and women in ceremonies marked by public processions,
singing, and dancing. On the occasions described in surviving sources, young
men were led out from the House of Youths, where they were living while
training for and first experiencing warfare, a place where they learned to dance
and sing. The young men danced with eagle down covering their heads,
adorned with flower garlands and a cape of flowers, wearing shell jewelry, and
the bells called *oyoalli* on their legs (e.g., Sahagún 1951: chaps. 21, 28).

Young women also took part in public dancing: "And when it was Hue
Tecuilhuitl, there was dancing which was the particular task of women; old
women, maidens, mature women, little girls. The maidens, who had looked
upon no man, were plastered with feathers; their faces were painted" (Sahagún
1951: chap. 27). These young women, with painted faces, pasted with red feathers reaching from ankle to thigh, from wrist to shoulder, and with garlands of
flowers on their heads, exchanged inflammatory comments with the boys in the
month of Hue Tozoztli (Sahagún 1951: chap. 23): "Thus the women could tor-
ment young men into war; thus they moved them; thus the women could prod
them into battle. Indeed we men said 'Bloody, painful are the words of the
women; bloody, penetrating are women's words.' . . . Indeed we have gone; we
have said that we shall not live."

That the lively exchanges between the young men and women were, as they
appear from the comments and descriptions, sexually charged is further inti-
mated by a riddle that asks, "What are the things that, at their dancing place,
they give stomachs, they make pregnant?" (Sahagún 1969: chap. 42; see also
Sullivan 1982; McCafferty and McCafferty 1991). This metaphor for the accumulation of thread on the spindle attests to the connection seen between the

dancing of young men and women and their sexual activity. Betty Ann Brown (1983) argues that Sahagún's texts actually describe *less* participation by women than their accompanying images depict, an observation that would strengthen the argument proposed here concerning the participation of young women in public ceremonies. Many authorities have assumed that the only women taking part in such dancing were ritual prostitutes, but both Brown's analysis and my own suggest that this is not the case.

The culmination of almost 3,000 years of Meso-American history, these late pre-Columbian public dances were opportunities for young men and women to display their sexual attractiveness and test their newly achieved adult status. The special costuming described in loving detail was an important part of these dances, a form of beautification directly descended from the costuming recorded on formative-period figurines, constructed from the ornaments laid to rest with their young owners. Performing beauty and sexuality, Aztec youths also ultimately performed their gender.

7

Men, Women, and Eland: Hunting and Gender among the San of Southern Africa

John Parkington

THEMES IN SAN EXPRESSIVE CULTURE

In the 1870s, //kabbo (fig. 7.1) was a middle-aged man serving a sentence at the Breakwater Prison in Cape Town and dictating his experiences to Lucy Lloyd and Wilhelm Bleek, the latter a leading philologist and linguist. //kabbo had been arrested in his home range in the Karoo interior of South Africa, where farmers were invading his lands, fencing them, and establishing small towns. At about the same time, Qing was a young horseman guiding the magistrate J. M. Orpen through the rugged valleys of the Maluti Mountains and conversing with him through interpreters around the campfire. Qing was a "bushman." In the 1970s, !Unn/obe was a ju/'hoansi mother recounting stories she had heard from her parents to Megan Biesele, an anthropologist and folklorist, in the small village of Kauri in the Kalahari. By the 1990s, all three, along with a few of their kinsmen and women, had become significant figures in the quest to interpret southern African rock art. What gave them this authority? The short answer is authenticity, membership of the long and now threatened tradition of San (otherwise "Bushman," or, in Botswana "Basarwa" and in Lesotho "Baroa") expressive culture. These three could comment from the inside.

Three thousand years ago, all people in southern Africa were hunter-gatherers. There is no evidence in the archaeological record of the remains of any domesticated plants and animals until at least that time. In fact, the earliest reliable evidence, in the form of the bones of domestic sheep and cattle or of preserved cereal grains, is no more than about 2,000 years old. This is important in the context of the rock art of southern Africa because the earliest evidence for both paintings and engravings far precedes that of domestication (in the

Figure 7.1.   //kabbo, one of Bleek and Lloyd's most important informants.

Western Cape, for example; see Yates and Jerardino 1996). The art traditions of the subcontinent certainly began among hunter-gatherer people. After 2,000 years ago, hunter-gatherer communities were gradually replaced by herding or farming people in a complex process that took almost the whole of these two millennia. There is some dispute as to whether farming and herding were introduced by large incoming populations of new people or were spread by transmission of domesticated plants and animals into hunting groups without much population movement. There are further disputes about how regularly or how easily people were able to move between the economic categories of hunter, herder, and farmer. Whatever the mechanisms, hunter-gatherer groups were incorporated, transformed, marginalized, and often decimated by the herders and farmers who came to dominate the southern African landscape. By the time European settlers arrived in the mid-17th century A.D., much, but by no means all, of the subcontinent was occupied by farmers or herders. In the long term, this transformation has been irreversible, people with domestic stock and crops replacing hunter-gatherers whenever and wherever they wished or were able to compete for land.

By the beginning of the 18th century, hunter-gatherers had been displaced from all but the extremely arid interior Karoo and Kalahari regions and the extremely rugged Drakensberg Mountains. White settlers began to move into the interior, hunting down groups of hunter-gatherers in organized raids and later establishing small towns in the Karoo. Remnant hunter-gatherers were incorporated as farm laborers and domestic servants, and many, such as //kabbo, were arrested for offenses such as murder or stock theft and sent to build the breakwater at the harbor in Cape Town. Lloyd and Bleek learned that the hunter-gatherers were the /Xam bushmen, or San, and began the process of recording their stories, songs, and cosmology. A little over 100 years later, similar hunter-gatherer communities in the Kalahari had been incorporated into the political economies of Namibia and Botswana, but not before anthropologists had recorded some of the ecological context and expressive culture of these residual foragers. As far as we know, neither //kabbo nor Qing nor !Unn/obe ever made a rock painting, but along with Lloyd, Orpen, and Biesele and now ourselves, they have become part of a network of thoughts and words linking paintings, engravings, songs, and stories into a web of ideas about San expressive themes. Bleek and Lloyd showed their /Xam informants copies of rock paintings made by the geologist George Stow. Lorna Marshall quoted published versions of /Xam stories to explain comments that her ju/'hoansi informants had made to her. David Lewis-Williams referred to personal communications from Megan Biesele from her Kalahari fieldwork to support his interpretation of rock painting panels.

Despite agreement on the source of insights, current writers differ substantially on the meaning of rock paintings. The dominant interpretation is unquestionably that of David Lewis-Williams and his colleagues (Lewis-Williams 1983, 1986; Lewis-Williams and Loubser 1986; Lewis-Williams and Dowson 1989; Dowson 1992; Dowson and Lewis-Williams 1994) who argue that the rock paintings and engravings of southern Africa are essentially shamanistic: the occasions of trance, the visions of altered states, and the experiences of shamans. Anne Solomon (1992, 1994, 1996) has challenged this hegemony recently and argued that issues of gender and the symbolism of death are more prominent than the shamanistic version allows. I will try to show here that many of the conventional themes of southern African rock paintings, especially in the Western Cape, reflect the tensions of social and sexual roles in the context of the unfolding life histories of men and women in a hunting-and-gathering society (Parkington 1996). The gendering of these societies is achieved through an extended hunting metaphor that juxtaposes and likens the relationship between a hunter and the large meat animals with that between a man and his wife. Because of the prominence of images of these large meat animals, I suggest that the paintings are a component in the gendering of San society, structuring practice and bolstering ideology. These views are not necessarily conflicting with those of Lewis-Williams or

Solomon, but they do locate the centrality of meaning in different parts of San experiences.

PEOPLE OF THE EARLY RACE

Many of the most revealing stories recorded by Wilhelm Bleek and Lucy Lloyd (see, e.g., Lloyd 1911) contain a phrase that they translated as "people of the early race." The key element in these stories is the fact that the cast of characters cannot easily be seen clearly as either people or animals. They are people with animal names and animals that behave like people, not unlike Peter Rabbit, Donald Duck, and many Gary Larson characters. This ambiguity is thoroughly exploited and allows the /Xam storyteller to play with notions of difference and similarity, to ignore or to highlight the incongruencies, and to moralize without being too direct. It is, however, as Hewitt (1986) has perceptively pointed out, important and informative to note which animals are present in this "primal time" and what roles they play. Prominent among people of the early race are porcupine, dassie, Egyptian mongoose, blue crane, baboon, meerkats, and, very importantly, the mantis. Larger carnivores, including lions, jackals, and hyenas, also appear regularly; elephant and rhino are often mentioned, but large game, such as gemsbok, hartebeest, kudu, and eland, are surprisingly rare.

A characteristic of people of the early race stories is the frequently catastrophic marriage between animal species: jackal and quagga, lynx and springbok, and rhino and various suitors. While this can be taken as a device to underline the dangers of marrying strangers and may well be intended as such, it also focuses on a crucial metaphoric relationship between food and sex. The absurdity of a lynx marrying a springbok is accentuated by the carnivore and herbivore identities. The suitors for the young rhino calf are the lynx, hyena, jackal, and leopard. Linked to this is another theme, namely, the transition from girl to woman, which in many stories proves to be the point of conflict, where the terms "marry," "grow up," and "suitors" are euphemisms to describe the onset of sexual availability. A final strand in this set of opposites and transformations is provided by the sudden transition from primal to modern times, which is brought about by the conflicts of food, sex, and adolescence but which also hinges on the relationship of hunter and prey. The intentional and repeated fusion of these themes leaves no room for doubt that here is a major underlying issue dealt with in the stories. The point is well illustrated in the many pages devoted to "the anteater's laws."

In this extensive and extended account, the anteater adopts a young female springbok and brings her up in the burrow. When she reaches adolescence ("is grown up"), the jackal courts and marries the springbok, stealing her from the anteater and precipitating a conflict that is variously described in several versions of the story. The end of the story is a listing of the "laws," wherein lynx and anteater establish and list whom every animal should marry and what every animal should eat. Henceforth, anteaters marry other anteaters and live in burrows, eat ants, and so on. It is quite clear that proper behavior means eating and marrying the right things, as good a focus on food and sex that it is possible to have. This listing signifies the end of primal time, the onset of the modern world when order is established. It has rightly been seen as a second creation, but the emphasis on the moment of adolescence, the opposition of carnivore and herbivore, the linking of food and sex, and the transition from absurdity to order needs to be recognized. People and animals are no longer the same, but what will be their relationship? This is partly clarified in other stories where the hunter-to-prey relationship is explained.

HUNTING AND ELAND

As noted earlier, the animals that comprise the people of the early race are mostly not particularly visually impressive and include many birds and small mammals. The choice of the anteater, an insectivore, to deal with incongruence of a marriage between a jackal and a quagga or a lynx and a springbok is surely intentional. However, there is one group of animals that appears only in a specific context, almost inadvertently causing the abrupt transition from primal to modern times. These are the large game animals, those hunted among recent hunter-gatherer communities only by men and always with the bow and arrow. The roles given to large game such as the eland, the gemsbok, and the hartebeest are unambiguous and extremely informative. There are no moralizing stories in which these impressive game play bit parts. Rather, they are described prominently as the favorite creations of /kaggen, the mantis, who gave them their markings by feeding them different kinds of honey. They also appear in stories that describe the appropriate behavior of a hunter who has successfully shot a large game animal. Especially on the occasion of a first kill, the hunter must battle against the influence of /kaggen, who is clearly the protector as well as the lover and creator of large game. Unless the hunter follows prescribed rules of behavior, the game will escape.

The role given to the eland is that of a critical element in the creation of the relationship between a hunter and his prey, a key player in the transition from primal to modern times, and the focus of another defining moment. In the several versions of the creation of the eland by /kaggen that have survived, including ones by both //kabbo (Bleek 1928) and Qing (Orpen 1974), the transitory nature of a verbal narrative, as well as some geographic variability, is apparent. Sometimes the story focuses on the creation of the moon, and often the complex nature of the mantis is thoroughly explored. One core event, however, is the seclusion of the newly created and growing eland in a remote part of the landscape and its discovery and killing by younger members of /kaggen's family while he is away. It is implied that /kaggen had some purpose in mind for the eland that was thwarted by the killing and cutting up of the animal by hunters who, critically, had not sought /kaggen's permission for the kill. The eland was a person while /kaggen was rearing it but was referred to as meat after its death, a shift that is probably extremely significant as the eland-person is the only plausible human in primal times. In many ways, this is the original kill, the event that creates the relationship between hunter and prey and an event that was unsanctioned. On discovering the eland kill, in Qing's version /kaggen announces that thereafter it is the hunters' job to chase and kill eland because they had been spoiled for his original purpose. The manner by which the hunters had discovered the eland is also significant. A young relative, usually the ichneumon or Egyptian mongoose, /kaggen's grandson and therefore on informal terms with him, discovers that /kaggen is taking honey to rub on the eland rather than bringing it back to his wife the dassie. Eating honey is a widely used metaphor for sex among recent southern African hunter-gatherers, which makes it clear that /kaggen's act is one of adultery. He is confusing food with sex and, more specifically, what should be hunted with what should be married, though the act of killing establishes the difference.

It is hardly surprising that after this traumatic event, /kaggen takes up the side of the large game he created and loves in their eternal conflict with the hunter. It seems likely that the initiation or first-kill ceremonies for young men described later make reference to this original event and deal with the question of permission and the role of /kaggen. We can see from the stories that /kaggen was the creator not of all animals but, specifically, of the large game, those that Megan Biesele (1993) calls the "great meat animals." We may also wonder why the mantis, a small and relatively insignificant animal, which seems almost never to have been painted, was singled out for this pivotal role. There are probably many reasons, but it might be significant that after copulation the female mantis eats the male, binding together sex and food in a particularly close and striking way.

HUNTING AND MARRIAGE

There is another story that illustrates the pervasive connection between hunting and sex, significant because it comes from northern Namibia, from an old man called Gaira, whose parents were !kung and Hei//om, and was recorded in the 1930s. This is the story of Heiseb and his gemsbok wife (Thomas 1950: 17–19; Guenther 1989: 94–95). Presumably because of the biogeography of large game distributions, the gemsbok replaces the eland but significantly adds to the relationship between marriage and the hunting of large game with the bow and arrow by men. Heiseb has a gemsbok wife as well as a human one. The (human) sons follow Heiseb and find him giving honey and, even more improbably, meat to the gemsbok in preference to their mother. In this version, the mother-in-law and wife kill the gemsbok wife but announce, as in the Qing version of the creation and killing of the eland, that "hereafter shall meat be meat, and men shall be men" and that "hereafter those finding Gemsbok in the plains shall hunt and slay them, for they are food to be eaten of men." This story explains, and so justifies, the killing of large, beautiful animals by men and links the spoiling of large game to the transition from tame to wild. Many animals are referred to in primal times as "pets" of other animals, a word that probably requires further attention.

Here, as in the Karoo half a century before and 2,000 kilometers away, the story illustrates the similarity of a man's relationship with his wife and his prey. Honey is again the metaphor, food and sex are again confused in the initial events, and the modern situation is brought about by a seminal kill. As in the Karoo, there is also a transition from the "primal" absurdity of a gemsbok enjoying meat and honey to the order of the predator-to-prey relations of modern times. The transfer of focus to the gemsbok reminds us that it is not any meat that is confused with wife but only that traditionally procured by men almost exclusively with the bow and poisoned arrow. Animals killed by women, or even by men with snares and pit traps (animals such as porcupines, dassies, tortoises, and small antelope or very large game such as elephant and rhino), are not covered by this metaphor. It will be clear later that the choice of large game successfully defines the male role in both sexual and hunting terms.

KALAHARI LIFE HISTORIES

The stories recorded in the Karoo and elsewhere are tantalizing traces of an extensive expressive vocabulary that must have shifted through time and been manipulated differently across space. A key element in the reconstruction of southern African hunter-gatherer metaphors is the more extensive ethnography from the Kalahari in the 20th century collected by professional anthropologists and folklorists. These more detailed descriptions allow the metaphors to be situated in the life histories of men and women, admittedly from times when hunting and gathering had been substantially augmented by other forms of economic activity. Only with this rich context can the different trajectories for men and women emerge as defining the choice of metaphor and the significance of

conflict. Quite obviously, men and women relate to one another in very different ways as they age and take up their prescribed but not immutable roles. It is
the prescription and mutability that presumably fuel the dialogue. In the Kalahari, men are first boys, then men and later old men; women are first girls, then
women and later old women. Roles and rules vary with age.

A good starting point is the pair of ritual events that define the transition
from boy to man and from girl to woman (Bleek 1928; Fourie 1928; Schapera
1933; Silberbauer 1981; Barnard 1992). When a boy kills his first large game
animal, preferably an eland, with the bow and arrow, he has reached the
moment to join the company of adult men, to become at once both hunter and
potential husband. When a girl experiences her first menstruation, she has
reached the moment to join the company of adult women, ready to assume the
duties of wife, although she may have been married for some time. Both
moments are signaled by the spilling of blood and in a sense the first such
spilling. Both events are marked by seclusion, by the withdrawal of food and
comforts, by dancing, and by the emphasis on adhering to strict rules of behavior, with grave consequences for infringement. As if to underline the similarity, the girl is said to have "shot an eland" and is rubbed with buchu, an aromatic plant favored by the eland.

Boys' first kill rituals are performed for several boys at one time, but girls'
rites are held for individuals. Large game are critical for both. At a girl's first
menstruation, the older ju/'oansi women perform the eland bull dance, an
occasion when they discard their clothes and dance suggestively as mature
members of the eland herd, welcoming a new fellow animal, a potential prey
item. Sexually active men are not present, but older men may play the part of
eland bulls to enhance the sexual tension of the occasion. Women are similarly
excluded from boys' first-kill rites. Among the Auni, the initiates begin as
boys; are deprived of fire, food, and clothes; and are then reintroduced, as men,
to plant foods, honey, and finally meat. A major component of the rites is a
lengthy period of exhausting dancing, led by senior men, probably healers or
trancers. After the rite, they can marry. These rites can also be described as
second creations, when boys and girls are ritually re-created as men and
women in contexts heavily laden with the metaphors of food and sex. They are
also occasions that sanction, establishing rules for hunting and marriage.
Blood, honey, and sweat figure prominently as indicators of events, as
euphemisms for other deeds, and as agents of potency.

As boys and girls, the lives of young hunter-gatherers are not severely constrained by rules, with much flexibility as to what can be done and what will
be tolerated. However, as adults, hunter-gatherers are either hunters or gatherers and should follow the rules that their roles demand or use whatever tools
they can to bring about change, although this is not easy because men and
women are clearly defined kinds of people. There is here, then, a parallel to

the transition from absurdity or incongruence to order that the stories reflect in the transition from primal to modern times. Proper behavior of the kind sanctioned and prescribed for modern people begins with the second creation. After this, men are hunters who hunt game and marry women, who, in turn, are gatherers but also game; this is seen as a parallel to the relationship between carnivores and herbivores (McCall 1970).

The tensions of relations between adult men and women are phrased in terms quite clear to people from a hunting society, but they do not last a lifetime. When men and women cease to engage in sexual relations, when men cease to hunt large game and women cease to menstruate, relations change and more flexible rules apply. Quite obviously, menstruation defines the adult woman and large game hunting the adult man, with the first and last spilling of blood selected as markers of changes in status. There are many rules that regulate these two processes, not least those that define menstruating women as dangerous for the hunt, that prescribe abstinence by men before a hunt, and that forbid women from touching certain equipment. None of these rules applies to a net that a woman may make and own and that her elderly husband may use to snare a steenbok or to an elephant caught in a pitfall trap.

KALAHARI TALK

As we might expect, the metaphors used in rituals have suffused everyday language and talk. Perhaps the best examples are McCall's (1970) "wolf courts girl" and Marshall's (1976) and later Biesele's (1993) "women like meat," both of which explore the pervasive use of a terminology that intentionally confuses sex with food and, more specifically, with hunted game. The conceptual linkage between this custom and the stories of Namibia, the Karoo, and the Drakensberg many decades earlier is extraordinarily clear. Biesele describes in full the conflation of woman and large game, or great meat animals, and links this to the widely used ju/'hoansi concept of n!ao, which may well have been understood by //kabbo but never articulated to Bleek or Lloyd in this way. N!ao is a metaphoric linking of women's procreational roles, men's hunting of large game, and the highly influential matter of the weather. N!ao is seen as good or bad as determined by conditions at the moment the blood of birth or the blood of a kill touches the ground. N!ao is a potency possessed by all people and by large game but not by smaller animals, trees and plants, or features of the landscape itself. This choice of potent things reminds us, as does Biesele, that men's hunting is not contrasted in this metaphoric language to women's gathering but rather to their childbearing role. The behavioral basis of the metaphor was clear to Silberbauer (1965) when women complained of their husbands' putting their poison in them and making them pregnant.

The impact of this balance is seen in the organization of bride service, when a man hunts for his parents-in-law for some years, providing meat for them as his wife provides children for him. What seems to be achieved by this contrasting of hunting and childbearing is a balance of authority, a pairing of responsibilities. Whereas childbearing would seem to be biologically defined as female, hunting is culturally defined as male by the network of justificatory stories. The physical parallel of inserting poison into animals and semen into women is exploited and extended, allowing men and women to take on the roles of bringing the resultant processes to successful conclusions—the first death, the second life. Women are present at a birth and determine the outcome; men are present at the kill and control the division of the choice parts. As a metaphoric framework, it has the advantage of allowing all people to find their place and use the language and does not appear to be simply an artifact of male control.

Marshall was told that pregnancies resulted from the mixing of semen and menstrual blood (M. Biesele, personal communication, 1993), which helps explain the connection among adulthood, childbirth, and menarche. It seems likely that with this system of thought, menstruation would appear as a failed kill, a spilling of blood without effect. It is hardly surprising that hunters would want to avoid contact with such an event as they prepared to embark on a strenuous eland hunt. One of the difficulties of the metaphor emerges, however, from the phrase "she has shot an eland" in that the young woman both is and has shot the eland. Similarly, the scarification markings that a young boy receives at his first-kill ceremony mark him as both eland and hunter. It seems that people are all eland in some sense.

ROCK PAINTINGS

If we accept that there is and has been a widespread theme in bushman or San expressive culture that links hunting to sexual relations between men and women as they age, it might be expected to emerge in rock paintings and engravings. Does it? Here I restrict my comments to the rock paintings of the Western Cape, though I think that they apply to some extent in most other regions of the subcontinent. The paintings show an almost total neglect of the landscape, of trees and rivers, and of any attempt at topography or environment. There is a strong preference for the side view for both people and animals and a use of multiple perspectives in the construction of compositions that turn three-dimensional reality into two-dimensional pictures. Each component in a composition is depicted in its most distinct aspect, supporting the idea of the principle of legibility, the notion that things should be painted in such a way as to eliminate ambiguity, unless ambiguity was the point being made (Garlake 1995). This aspective rather than perspective approach (Schafer 1974) is perhaps best seen in the net hunting scenes, where the net is folded out in such a way as to be readable as a barrier to the implied movement of the small bovids (fig. 7.2). No other solution works.

Paintings are repetitive but almost never identical, each panel making use of familiar conventions to create a new effect. The limited choice of subject material is extreme, with most kinds of animals never depicted. Human subjects outnumber animal images by at least two to one, the remainder being geometric images and hand prints. Intentional narratives involving more than one species are rare and restricted to those with humans and one kind of animal. No attempt is made to convey or even refer to anything like an ecosystem or a community of living forms. From this, we must conclude that the painting of an animal did not require visual contextualization but could easily be referenced by the viewer from experience in other aspects of expressive culture. This is precisely the value, for us as outsiders, of the comments of //kabbo and the ethnography of Biesele, where potentially such references can be found. As no painters can be interviewed, I assume that the most successful explanation is one that finds the most intertextual connections.

PAINTING ELAND AND HUNTING

It is almost a cliché, but one worth repeating, that the repertoire of painted living forms is neither a menu nor a checklist. There are no paintings of shellfish; almost none of plants; very few of insects, with the important exception of bees; and very few of reptiles or amphibians, with the important exception of snakes. In fact, if we compartmentalize the plants and animals of the landscape along

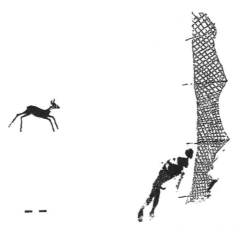

Figure 7.2.   A white net from the Bushmanskloof Wilderness Area.

social and symbolic dimensions, using the ethnography of southern African hunter-gatherers as a guide, some very clear selections and emphases emerge in the paintings. Women gather shellfish and collect tortoises and other small game but never actively hunt large game, such as eland or hartebeest, with the bow and arrow. Shellfish, tortoise, and dassies are too small to share, steenbok and porcupines may be shared with kin in the same camp, but an eland will provide enough meat to share with several camps of hunter-gatherers. Shellfish are brought into a camp in the thousands with no obvious emotional impact, a steenbok may elicit some expectations and cause some comment, but the occasion of an eland kill will bring the camp to a crescendo of excitement. Steenbok, grysbok, and ribbok can be snared, eland and hartebeest must be killed with the bow and poisoned arrow, while elephant or rhino could be taken only in large pitfall traps. Shellfish are sessile and easy to collect, steenbok are territorial and wary, but eland are mobile and extremely difficult to approach, let alone kill. Carnivores are competitors rather than food but share with elephant and rhino the connotation of danger. Baboons are visually like people, relatives too close to hunt. There is a dimension here whereon increasing size of food parcel is correlated with risk, sharing potential, excitement, technology employed, and male involvement.

The list of animals painted must be treated with some caution, not least because many images are difficult to ascribe to genus, whereas some can be identified from key residual traces. A further problem is the poor temporal resolution of images, which means that we are looking at a palimpsest that may mask great changes in image preference over time. In the Western Cape, though, as elsewhere in southern Africa, there are no paintings of plants or of shellfish, both of which are extremely common in the local archaeological record and both of which are presumed to have been gathered mainly by women. Paintings of tortoises, dassies, porcupines, hares, mole rats, and small carnivores, such as meerkats or mongooses, are very rare or nonexistent, although some of these are very common among archaeological bone assemblages. Small bovids are frequently painted but are often hard to identify as to genus. The most striking emphases are revealed by the very large numbers of paintings of eland and elephant, though hartebeest are fairly common as well. The absence of many forms is clearly ecological and biogeographic rather than intentional neglect, but this listing requires us to explain the abundance of eland, elephant, and small bovids.

Eland paintings in the Western Cape (fig. 7.3) are mostly bichrome, with the torso painted in one color, almost always red, and the neck, head, and lower legs in another, almost always white. In many eland, the nape and forehead are also in red. After some time, the more fugitive white paint disappears, leaving the distinctive red torso and nape and giving the impression of short legs. This distinctiveness almost certainly contributes to the large numbers of eland,

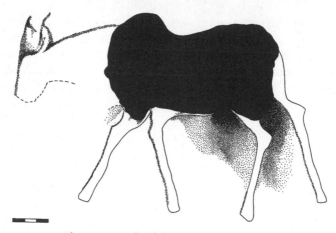

Figure 7.3.   Eland from the farm Keurbos.

many of which are strictly adiagnostic large bovids. George Stow probably misinterpreted this residual pattern in the southern Drakensberg when he identified eland as lions and copied them as such. Eland were painted singly or in lines or processions and include very few obvious calves. They are often the largest images in the shelters in which they occur but never, in our experience in the Western Cape, form part of any narrative association with people. We have seen no scene with people hunting eland.

Elephant paintings (fig. 7.4) are easy to recognize because of the animal's distinctive physiology, contributing to the high frequency in our records. We

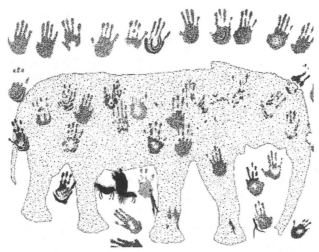

Figure 7.4.   An elephant surrounded and superimposed by handprints.

have recorded red and yellow elephants, very occasionally black, and always monochrome. White tusks are rare. The depictions are often very large but can also be extremely minute. Unlike paintings of eland, those of elephants, as also rhino, very often include young animals. There are some cases of people and elephants painted in what appear to be narrative scenes, though these are fairly rare, and elephant also occur in boxes or otherwise are circumscribed by crenellated lines. In two cases, we have found elephant-headed people, therianthropic conflations of elephant and people, and on another two occasions, we have seen elephants on the heads of people.

Small bovids are common and outnumber eland by several to one. These paintings are also sometimes bichrome but more often monochrome and usually red. The most distinctive pattern for small bovids is the association with nets in what we have taken to be net hunting scenes (Manhire et al. 1985). In these extremely interesting compositions, one or more small bovids are depicted facing a cross-hatched, vertically organized shape that, in the better-resolved paintings, is clearly meant to be a net (cf. Lewis-Williams and Dowson 1988). In some paintings, the sticks holding the net up and the arrangement at the ends of the net are clearly drawn. These scenes offer the repeated association of a small bovid species, probably steenbok, grysbok, or ribbok, with people, some of whom are located as beaters driving the animals toward the net. It has surprised us that these paintings almost always have the net at the right-hand side of the composition and are thus read from left to right. We have taken this as an example of the way that time is reproduced in the paintings because many compositions freeze action that was originally part of a sequence. It seems that beginnings are at the left, outcomes and destinations are at the right, and time is depicted from left to right.

PAINTING PEOPLE

Paintings of men and women are extremely common in the rock paintings of the Western Cape, as elsewhere in southern Africa. Although most of these images are residual and sometimes faint and may lack some of the original detail, we have pointed out that there is often no difficulty distinguishing men from women (Parkington 1989). This is partly because penises and breasts are frequently detectable (figs. 7.5, 7.6) but also reflects the distinct ways in which the physiological differences between men and women are painted. Although the necessary statistical work still needs to be done, there are differences in the depictions of calves, thighs, buttocks, waists, and shoulders of men and women that correlate well with particular sets of equipment; with specific bodily gestures, such as sitting and clapping; and with the intentional juxtaposition of

Figure 7.5. Men painted naked from Groothexrivier.

clear males and females with those less easily distinguished. Most views of people are side views, and a large proportion appear naked or very nearly so, both of which facilitate the easy identification of primary or secondary sexual characteristics. Some may disagree (e.g., Stevenson 1995; Lenssen-Erz 1997), but it is our opinion that almost all human figures painted in the Western Cape were meant originally to be unambiguously recognizable to the contemporary viewer as men or women, even particular categories of men or women.

Before discussing these categories of people, it is worth noting the important case where some ambiguity seems to have been specifically constructed in the painted images. This is the set of images usually referred to as "therianthropes," where human and animal characteristics are combined in a single figure (fig. 7.7).

Figure 7.6. Women painted nearly naked from the Bushmanskloof Wilderness Area.

In most cases, this takes the form of a human body with an animal head and some-times feet or hooves, although there are much rarer cases of an animal body with human legs. Significantly here, the intention is ambiguity not between male and female humans but between a human and some species of animal. We have found no examples of human figures with breasts and a penis, as we have no examples of breasts on a figure shooting a bow or of a penis on a figure carrying a weighted digging stick. The objective seems to have been to conflate the human and ani-mal by depicting the most characteristic features of each, the choice of animal head allowing maximum opportunity for the viewer to identify the animal intended.

There are several ethnographically recorded contexts in which people con-flate humans and animals and that may help to understand these therianthropes (Skotnes 1991, 1996). The people of the early race are an obvious conflation, where a humanlike person has an animal name. It is conceivable that the way to turn this verbal device into a painted equivalent is to paint a humanlike per-son with an animal head. A second possibility, and the one favored by David Lewis-Williams, is that therianthropic figures are painted expressions of the transformation of a trancer into animal form on entering an altered state of con-sciousness. Therianthropes would be interpreted as shamans in this view. A third possibility, and one that I favor in at least some cases, is the ethnograph-ically recorded use of language that intentionally confuses the hunting of game and the marrying of women, as in Biesele's (1993) *Women Like Meat*. These are not mutually exclusive, nor do they need to be universally applicable, and the issue becomes distinguishing when one reference is more important than another in each context. This we can hope to achieve by contrasting the metaphorical conflations reported ethnographically in these contexts and com-paring them with the details of particular paintings.

Figure 7.7.   Therianthropic figures from Horlosiekop.

   That issue aside, the frequent depiction of penises on men, along with the
regular emphasis on large thighs and buttocks on women, draws attention to
erotic potential at the expense of ethnographic reality. Men do not hunt without a breechclout in the Kalahari, and women do not expose their buttocks
except at the eland bull dance. Moreover, whereas men are almost never
painted without the bow and usually with the quiver and arrows, women are
much more rarely painted with the weighted digging sticks they would have
used to dig up corms and other roots. There is a clear parallel between this pattern and the contrasts between the roles of hunting and childbearing emphasized in the n!ao concept. In a parallel to the near absence of hunting scenes,
there are no copulation scenes that we know of, though a few paintings do
appear to be rather vulgar. The norm is for a procession of human figures to
comprise almost always only men or only women.

   Most of the paintings that might well be male, to judge from the quivers and
bows, but that have to be recorded as indeterminate, are rendered difficult to
sex because of the depiction of cloaks or karosses that mask the genital and
breast regions of the body (fig. 7.8). Although we are used to referring to the
painted shapes as karosses, we realize that they are conventionalized elements
and bear little resemblance to ethnographically photographed images of
kaross-clad or cloaked people. These kaross-clad figures are extremely interesting and are visually and conventionally similar to the bichrome eland paintings of the Western Cape, perhaps another kind of therianthrope. As with the
eland, these human figures take the form of a torso or kaross, usually in red,
from which neck and head and lower legs emerge in another color, often white
but sometimes black. The painters seem to have been extremely careful in both
cases never to allow any painted item to intrude onto the torso/kaross shape.
Equipment always hangs behind the shape of the kaross, often appearing at
both sides. Turn an eland through 90 degrees, and there is a kaross-clad human.
It is our opinion that the viewer has been explicitly encouraged to see and ponder on this use of similar conventions.

Figure 7.8.   Cloaked or kaross-clad men from Sevilla (detail).

It has been noted (Schapera 1930) that the kinds of first-kill ceremonies for groups of young men described earlier are not recorded among the southern San people, only among those of northern Namibia (Fourie 1928). One painting traced by us seems to imply that such events were held as far south as the Cederberg in precolonial times (fig. 7.9). This scene is an excellent example of the composition of an image from components that are used elsewhere to make quite different but related paintings. Two processions of men, though some would be recorded as indeterminate sex (none is clearly or even suggestively female), are painted facing right, along with an eland torso, also facing right. In the top line, the front eight figures are naked; the remainder have karosses and carry bags, quivers, and bows. In the lower line, all appear naked, and several have small lines painted from the head; some carry sticks. The upper line clearly contrasts the states of naked and clothed, emphasizing the difference by rigid placement in the line. Above the naked men, to the right at the implied destination of the line, is a series of eight or nine hunting bags and at least one bow. This is as near a painted version of the first-kill ceremony as we are likely to get. It allows us to see the clothed–naked contrast as a conventional distinction between initiated and initiate and uses the hanging hunting bags at the top right of the line as a symbolic destination or outcome for the ceremony. There are ethnographic references to young men taking up the wearing of a cloak or kaross when they begin to hunt seriously under instruction from a father or an older hunter (Dornan 1975; Bleek 1928).

It is ironic that many people believe the rock art of South Africa to consist largely of hunting scenes because they are very rare, certainly in the Western Cape. Most assemblages of human images are processional. Lines of exclusively female figures, often carrying short sticks (fig. 7.10), are good examples of the eland bull dances held at the first menstruation of a young woman. In some of the compositions, one or more male stick figures with bows are placed

Figure 7.9.   Lines of cloaked and naked men from Sevilla.

Figure 7.10. Women dancing with short sticks.

opposing the lines of women, perhaps older men playing the role of eland bull, active hunter, or both. Other lines of exclusively male figures are repetitively drawn, sometimes in repeated postures as if to be read as dancing steps (fig. 7.11). In some cases, the men walk along double lines of paint in contexts that evoke the long periods of dancing at first-kill ceremonies (fig. 7.12). These latter certainly depict trance in the form of short lines of paint from the nose as well as the frenzy of trancers who have entered an altered state. Yet other assemblages of human figures clearly depict scenes that are close to the healing dances performed in recent times in the Kalahari, with clapping figures and rows of dancers.

There certainly are a few paintings in which men are depicted shooting arrows from bows, but these are almost all better described as fights than hunts (Manhire et al. 1983). It is, indeed, quite extraordinary to have so many paintings of men, bows, and large game but so few where men are shown using the bows on the game. The fights are compositions where people,

Figure 7.11.   Two women and a group of men dancing, with repeated posture.

Figure 7.12. **Tracing scene from Groothexrivier.**

always men where distinctions can be made, shoot at one another, perhaps the most explicit and informative being the one popularly known as "veg' 'n' vlug," or fight and flight (fig. 7.13). In this painting, a shallow indentation in the roof of a low overhang has been painted in such a way as to render it as a rock shelter. Several human figures stand or sit in the shelter, and some shoot arrows out toward a second group of human figures who face right toward the shelter. These latter also shoot arrows and are drawn as if walking along a pair of finely rendered red parallel lines, at first sight a path. Other human figures are painted moving rapidly away from the shelter, also "running along double lines," completing the title of fight and flight. As if to dispose of this simple explanation, the artist has shown the double red lines, along which people approach the shelter, entering the bow stave of one bow, leaving the bowstring, and entering the mouth. Elsewhere in this painting, a human figure reels in one of the double red lines, one with an apparently supine male figure on the other end. This is an extremely complex and important painting and is an invaluable key to the unlocking of the conventions used by painters in the Western Cape. A close inspection of the central panel shows that there are, in fact, two kinds of arrows painted. Red ones are shown in midair and

Figure 7.13. **The central part of a scene from Sevilla.**

can be read as shot from the red bows that people on both sides of the fight carry. However, white residual arrows with small red dots of paint near the nock end are also visible, all of them striking the bodies of the group approaching the shelter, none of them in midair and with no obvious bow to have delivered them. These are almost certainly the invisible "shimmering, silvery arrows of misfortune" (M. Biesele, personal communication), which are more metaphoric than real and which almost certainly have played some role in the conflict depicted here. The red dots are presumably the harm, the hate, or the misfortune borne by the arrows.

A third kind of assemblage of human figures is what we have informally called "group scenes" (fig. 7.14), following the habit of Johnson et al. (1959); Maggs (1971); Yates, Golson, and Hall (1985); and Parkington and Manhire (1997). In these paintings, the key element is a set of hanging bags, sometimes including the pegs on which bags hang and under which people sit. Usually, one or more humans are seen to be clapping, one or many dance, and both men and women are recognizable by their physiology, their posture, or their equipment. In the most detailed cases, the variety of bags, and sometimes other hanging equipment, emphasizes the point that all members of the community are present, though children are hard to confirm. In rock shelters where we have found paintings, we have often also found small wooden pegs hammered into cracks in the wall. The hanging bags are, thus, almost certainly a conventional depiction of the home shelter, and the group scenes generally are close analogues for the healing dances held in the Kalahari. Interestingly, no therianthropes are included in these scenes, and no animals are persuasively shown to be associated.

Figure 7.14.   A group scene from Keurbos.

HUNTING AND GENDER

Although it is currently fashionable to speak of diversity among the hunter-gatherers of southern Africa (Barnard and Widlok 1996; Kent 1998), differences and similarities have to be measured on some scale and against some outside reference point. I argue here that there are some persuasive general patterns in expressive culture that emerge from ethnographic fragments recorded over two centuries and across many thousands of square kilometers in southern Africa. These patterns refer to the association of a particular set of "large meat animals" and women. Nowhere is it possible to replace these animals with others, and no fragment, however small or anecdotal, contains contradictory references. Consider the following set of observations, in which I use the word "eland" to stand for that or an equivalent large game animal.

A boy goes to his first-kill initiation school when he kills his first eland, a signal of his ability to hunt and, thereby, his transition to adulthood. A girl is said to have "shot an eland" when she first menstruates. At this point, older women dance an eland bull dance to welcome her into the company of adult women. She is said to be fat like an eland. Men clothe their wives in the skins of eland that they have shot and killed with the bow and poisoned arrows. They recognize the similarity between the insertion of poison and the insertion of semen and use this in metaphoric figures of speech. Only men hunt eland, and they do it only with the bow and poisoned arrows, which is the only recognized way to claim a first kill. At the first-kill ceremony, a boy becomes not only an adult hunter but also a potential husband. Men who do not make the kill and attend the ceremony do not marry. Large game animals, such as the eland, are n!ao animals said to possess a potency that affects the weather on their death. Men affect the weather at the moment the blood of the kill touches the ground. Women similarly affect the weather at the moment the blood of birth touches the ground. N!ao, thus, contrasts the killing of large game by men with the birthing of children by women, using, as at the first menstruation and first kill, the metaphoric significance of blood as a bridging mechanism. Ethnographers note the litany of respect names used for eland and the excitement caused by the returning of eland meat to a camp. In stories, the killing of the first eland was the moment the relationship between hunter and prey was established, to the distress of the eland's creator, who continues to take the side of the animal in its ongoing conflict with the hunter. All hunters, but particularly those who have made their first kill, must observe strict rules of behavior before and after hunting and killing eland. These observations include a prohibition on sex before a hunt, to note the similarity of, but clearly to distinguish between, the two linked processes of hunting and sex. This linkage is included as a component of many stories, including critical ones that mark the transition between primal time, before people and animals were distinguishable, and modern times, when men hunt and eat animals. In the earlier time, men married meat; in the later times, they married women and hunted meat. In some stories, a hunter's relationship with his eland or gemsbok prey is directly compared with that with his wife. Women like meat, but they are also like meat, particularly like the eland after their first menstruation.

It is important to note that men and women do none of these things to celebrate or mark their hunting of or attitudes toward any small animals, such as dassies, porcupines, tortoises, or fish, or even small game, such as steenbok or grysbok. In many parts of the subcontinent, we do not have information on parts of this system, but where we do there is always a concatenation of meanings and significances that links men's hunting behavior with women. The implication of this is that large meat animals have a particular and specific significance for both men and women and are used as a framework for conceptualizing the relations between them. The widespread prominence of eland and other equivalent large meat animals in the rock art of southern Africa clearly links the paintings to the verbal expressions of this set of values and ideas. Mapote, a man painting on the wall of an official's house in Lesotho in the 1920s (How 1970), expressed the need for eland blood as a binder for his pigment because the local hunter-gatherers were "of the eland." I believe that Vinnecombe's (1976) use of the phrase "People of the Eland" to imply a parallel between eland and people is essentially correct.

If southern African hunter-gatherer societies were gendered through an extended hunting metaphor linked to the n!ao concept, was the system an example of egalitarian thought, a framework embraced equally by men and women? This appears to be the case from the reports of both male and female ethnographers, though it may be asked how women could be content to see themselves as "prey." The key to this is surely the inadequacy of this word in English to capture the nature of the relationship between a hunter and the animal he sought to kill. There is ample evidence, both in southern Africa and elsewhere, to suggest that hunters respected, treasured, and even identified with the large meat animals, although clearly they dispatched smaller game, usually by methods other than the bow and poisoned arrow, with no ceremony or reflection. To kill an eland is to leave a big hole in the world and to take the life of another "person." It is also clear (D. Guthrie, unpublished manuscript) that hunting for a hunter-gatherer, gatherer as well as hunter, was so deeply entrenched and embedded in the minds of people that we who are not hunters can scarcely imagine its significance. It is abundantly clear from the ethnographies that the pursuit and killing with the bow and arrow of large game animals for food was a way of being, a complete and pervasive experience involving excitement, tension, identity, self-worth, and fulfillment. Under such circumstances, for a woman to be compared to the object of respect and the symbol of achievement was anything but demeaning. We perhaps need another word.

All ethnographers of 20th-century Kalahari hunter-gatherers make it clear that both men and women value meat more highly than plant food, rejoice over the occurrence of a big game kill, and see hunting as the behavior that charac-terizes maleness. It is also clear that hunting means bow-and-arrow hunting and that there are many ways of killing animals that do not qualify for this term. All those ethnographers also relate the parallel status and attitude toward women's contribution as childbearer and childrearer. The n!ao concept enshrines this, and all people live it. The effect of this pervasive and shared attitude is to allocate both authority and responsibility to the two complemen-tary categories of adult people—the one for production, the other for repro-duction. Whereas women are biologically identified as childbearers, men are culturally identified as hunters, and large game is culturally selected as the symbol of production. The fact that large game animals can be shared and can thus help build and maintain the interband linkages that create hunter-gatherer society beyond the family makes the choice of eland, gemsbok, or kudu logi-cal in these roles. The equivalence of the two spheres of responsibility is then underlined by a series of linked verbal and visual metaphors that stitch the two together, making women game and men lovers of women as well as hunters of game. In practice, bride service, where a man hunts for his new in-laws for some years until two or three children are born, gives material substance to this exchange of contributions.

The impact of these cultural and behavioral devices is, on the surface, the establishment of a metaphoric framework in which all people, both men and women, can find a place. The relationships do, however, establish the active and dominant roles of men and the more passive roles of women. The domi-nation of nature by people is linked to the domination of women by men. Because so much of this system is culturally determined, it is always, theoret-ically at least, open to challenge and modification. Biesele (1993) emphasizes that expressive culture in recent times in the Kalahari is generated not by authority but by continual reinforcement, endorsement, or manipulation by participating individuals. Because the equation of large game and women is so widespread, far beyond the world of southern African hunter-gatherers (Fid-des 1991; Cartmill 1993), in fact, interesting questions are those of how, when, and why such a system came about. My guess is that it has a Holocene time depth because before that time hunting equipment, movement patterns, groups sizes, and population distributions were arguably quite different (Parkington, in press). The formative context for the gendering of society through bow-and-arrow hunting of large game animals has to have included the nature of con-temporary hunting-and-gathering behavior. Whether earlier versions of gendering will be accessible beyond the reach of ethnographic accounts and without contemporary rock paintings is a key question.

ACKNOWLEDGMENTS

In October 1998, I was fortunate to be able to spend a week in Bellagio listening to, talking about, and thinking about archaeological perspectives on women and gender. I thank the participants for their companionship and stimulation, Sarah Nelson and Myriam Rosen-Ayalon for the invitation to attend, the Rockefeller Institute for its support, and the Wenner-Gren Foundation for travel. Yvonne Brink, as in the past, made very perceptive and helpful comments on an earlier draft. I thank Dale Guthrie for the stimulation of his as yet unpublished manuscript "Breaking the Code of Palaeolithic Art."

II

GENDER ROLES

SARAH MILLEDGE NELSON

Gender roles are "what men and women actually do in specific social contexts" (Hays-Gilpin and Whitley 1998), especially what they are expected to do or what they do most of the time. Gender roles emphasize the material side of gendered lives. To understand what women and men normally do in their daily lives is important for archaeological interpretations.

To this end, ethnoarchaeological studies have been useful in suggesting archaeological correlates for seeing gender roles. The spatial correlates of gendered activities can help interpret house floors as well as outdoor space. Are houses divided between male and female activities or perhaps activities performed by people of different ages? Do people do their outside tasks in gendered groups? Is the selection of a place to work dependent on gender or on extrinsic factors, such as shade or the location of a water source?

It is important to know whether and to what extent artifacts have gendered uses within particular cultures. If men do the hunting, to what extent are the tools of hunting theirs exclusively? Can they be used for other purposes? Can one gender "pollute" the spaces or artifacts of another? Where are artifacts kept when they are not in use, and do those storage places mark gendered spaces?

Time is another important issue for understanding gender roles. Within Western cultures, gender roles have shifted partly because of women flocking to the workplace, leaving household chores to be divided between adults who both work outside the home. In the same way, we can look at any newly introduced tasks that are to be performed within a culture, whether it is collecting shellfish (Claassen 1991), making pottery, or crafting textiles for market.

In chapter 8, Margaret Nelson, Donna Glowacki, and Annette Smith consider women's impact on household economies among the Maya. In this ethnoarchaeological study, they specifically sought material correlates of women's work that could be applied to archaeological sites. They point out that the standard discussions of economic status are based on men's productive activities. They look instead at women's contributions to households and the relative wealth of households as it relates to women's contributions. They also consider the extent to which craft labor impacts other activities that women perform within the domestic unit and in the larger culture. Focusing on residential space, they consider how much of it is committed to women's work. Within women's areas, they examine the organization, special facilities and tools, and whether work done there may have an impact on the rest of the material goods of the household.

A major result of this study is to show the archaeological invisibility of women's contributions to household income. Women tend to expand a particular facet of their usual activities rather than engaging in tasks that are entirely new. Thus, households in which women's products are created for sale cannot be distinguished from those in which the production is for use within the household. Nelson et al. suggest that, archaeologically, trash areas are a better resource for identifying women's overproduction of particular items than households themselves.

Chapter 9, by Joan Gero and Cristina Scattolin, is an archaeological expansion on the previous chapter. Using data from Yutopian, an early formative site in northwestern Argentina, Gero and Scattolin show that variability in gender relations can be teased from this apparently egalitarian culture. They take apart the categories that have been used to divide household activities from craft specialization and show that the processes of specialization are in fact occurring within the household. Production is occurring in two ways at the same time. Gero and Scattolin remind us that gender categories are not necessarily obvious and fixed. The simplistic notions of either gender hierarchy or gender complementarity, they argue, need to be deconstructed. In a single society, both modes may operate in different realms. Gender, these authors urge, is not a thing but a series of relationships—a process, a performance. Both gender complementarity and gender hierarchy could be read from the details, but Gero and Scattolin show that division of both labor and integrated household labor are present, as represented by food production and copper reduction at the same hearth. Both forms of labor serve to produce social cohesion.

In chapter 10, Zarine Cooper uses archaeology in the Andaman Islands to highlight the problem of asking gender questions where little else is known of the culture. Their living descendants were famously studied by Radcliffe-Brown (1922) and also by Man (1885). However, continuity between archaeological sites and later inhabitants is difficult to show. One continuity is the use of shells for a variety of tool functions. Cooper surveyed the islands, and found one cave site in addition to midden sites on all the major islands. These results showed that the islands have been inhabited for about 2,200 years. The cave and the contents of one midden are described.

She turns to ethnographic accounts of the Andaman Islands within the 19th century to consider gender in her sites. She points out that, despite a generally egalitarian society, division of labor by gender was marked. Because of the dominance of shells, she focuses on their uses and their distribution as artifacts according to the sexual division of labor. Women, ethnographically, were the collectors of the shellfish, which were used as food before the shells became raw material for tools or ornaments.

Pig bones represent the majority of fauna in the middens, extending an understanding of foods utilized. However, the disposition of shells, bones, and pottery in the middens fails to reveal the division of labor by gender.

In chapter 11, Rasmi Shoocongdej looks at three rock art sites in the late historic period (4,000–2,000 b.p., or 2000–0 B.C.) in western Thailand. Styles of clothing and ornament suggest that these rock paintings form a group. The art styles are also compatible with having been made by related people, and they seem to depict different facets of the same culture. She considers both the spatial distribution of the sites and the content of the scenes depicted. One scene seems to be a ritual procession, with dancing and drumming. The second includes animal and human figures in which some of the humans wear elaborate headdresses. Some are dancing, while others hold musical instruments. These have been interpreted as processional events perhaps leading to fertility rituals or associated with funerals. Since women and men are both depicted, as well as children, it can be assumed that rituals involved the entire community. Other scenes are of hunting and appear to depict men only, while some scenes with animals show both men and women.

In terms of gender roles, women are not passive but active participants in the scenes. Both sexes, as well as children, dance or play musical instruments. Both men and women are shown in the presence of animals. Women plow, and men hunt, so we know the gendered activities outside the home, but household activities are not depicted in these paintings. This suggests that rituals have more to do with extended roles. The most secure conclusions about women's roles is that they were participants in ceremonies. The scenes are painted at high points, which may have been the places of the ritual activities they depict. There is also some evidence of temporary camps, perhaps for the ritual participants, suggesting ceremonies lasting several days at least.

In chapter 12, Charles Higham selects a broader sweep of place and time in Southeast Asia and southern China. He principally presents data on cemeteries with excellent skeletal preservation. The site of Khok Phanom Di in Thailand is extremely unusual, with areas of a burial ground apparently allotted to

particular matrilineal families through time, allowing more detailed generational data than is usually possible. Higham infers that making beautiful and
exportable pottery brings high status to women because indications of the potters' trade are found in abundance in the rich female graves. The wealth that
accrues to their families, however, lasts only a generation or two.

Examining burials in various sites through time, he finds that Neolithic sites
with burials are rare. An analysis of Nong Nor, in the Bronze Age, shows that
wealth is a factor in the cemetery, but wealth is not distributed by age or sex.
It is interesting that grinding stones are associated with males. Other cemeteries likewise show men and women equally likely to be rich, containing exotic
goods and more grave goods in general. By the Iron Age, a change had
occurred, with gender clearly marked in burials by weapons with men and
weaving tools with women, but both are wealthy graves. Scenes on the tops of
cowry shell containers include warfare involving men, sometimes taking
women captive, but others show women in positions of power. Thus, the gender message is mixed.

In chapter 13, Cheryl Claassen discusses the time constraints of women's
work and therefore the likelihood that children's labor was called on to take
up the slack, especially for the care of younger children. Using data from the
Middle Woodland period in the American Midwest and bioarchaeological
data, she considers time management by women.

Bodies in cemeteries from Middle Woodland are marked by differential
tooth decay, hypoplasias, sex differences in muscle use, and sexual dimorphism in height. These all suggest marked differences in men's and women's
activities. Before the Woodland period, during a time known as Archaic, indications in skeletons of different workloads for men and women are found in
the location of arthritis—in the shoulders for men and in wrists for women.
More people were spread on the landscape in smaller groupings than in the
preceding Paleo-Indian period, and, Claassen suggests, each individual may
have had to perform a variety of tasks as a result of smaller groups and fewer
people.

Pottery, with its attendant tasks ranging from finding clay sources and processing clay to constructing and firing pots, appears in the Woodland period.
New sources of food and techniques for obtaining food, along with cooking
and storage, are also evident. Birth rates increased, requiring more child care.
All these tasks demanded women's time. They are accompanied by a notable
change in skeletons, most obviously in upper-arm muscles, showing more evidence of women working harder.

This greater workload for women had to be rearranged in some way.
Responsible children, especially girls, are called on in many societies to tend
younger siblings. Observations on children's skeletons suggest that they were

weaned earlier and probably were fed a mush made of starchy seeds, which would suggest that mothers needed time for other tasks and turned infant care over to older siblings.

Other archaeological indications of time saving, Claassen indicates, may be the shift from shell mounds to dirt mounds and the use of pottery (although its manufacture would have added tasks). Maize is first found in the Middle Woodland, but skeletal analysis does not show that it was important in the diet. These observations demonstrate how changes can be interpreted in the light of gender questions.

The search for gender roles thus can utilize a number of theoretical perspectives and many kinds of methods.

8

The Impact of Women on Household Economies:
A Maya Case Study

Margaret Nelson, Donna Glowacki, and Annette Smith

Women are integrally involved in the internal and external relationships of their households. They also substantially contribute to the economic well-being of their households through a range of activities, including gathering, hunting, producing goods, bartering, and working for wages, to name a few. In this chapter, we seek to examine the relationship between women's work and the economic status of their households within subsistence farming communities. We address the relationship between the scale of their work and how it is materialized in both the spatial organization within houses and the composition of household assemblages. We are particularly interested in material evidence for varied contributions by women to the economic conditions of their families because we wish to be able to extend the insights gained from this research to improve understanding of the economic contributions of women in small-scale, prehistoric communities.

The first goal, to obtain insights about the relationship between women's work and economic status, was stimulated by the limited extent to which household economic status is perceived among archaeologists to be related to the contributions of women. Studies of economic status commonly refer to the endeavors of men or are silent on the differential contributions of men and women to household economic status. We focus on the contribution that female craft production and wage labor make to the overall well-being of the household. In this sense, we are concerned with the roles women play in the economy of a household, how these vary within a community, and the extent to which they correlate with relative degrees of wealth. We expect, following Arnold (1985) and others, that craft production and wage labor in subsistence farming communities are diversifying strategies among households at the lowest end of the economic scale. We seek to identify this relationship between relative wealth and income-generating labor by women and then examine these diversifying strategies.

The second goal, to understand the relationship between the scale of craft production and the organization of households, is motivated by an interest in understanding the effects of craft labor on the range of activities and responsibilities of women. Among subsistence farmers, the roles of women within their household would rarely be restricted to producing crafts for external distribution (Arnold 1985). Instead, women and men balance a range of responsibilities. Those responsibilities centered within the residential space of the household are the focus of this research. We examine the extent to which residential space is committed specifically to women's work, and we explore the organization of that space, the use of special facilities and tools, and the impact of work on household material inventories. These analyses aid in understanding the ways that women's work is materialized and can be recognized archaeologically.

Our motivation for this research is initially archaeological. We wish to develop an understanding of how women's contribution to household economic status can be conceptualized, broadening our models of how variation within communities and differential status developed in the past. In small-scale societies with limited potential for accumulating or producing in excess of need, the scale of production beyond need might be so slight as to be invisible archaeologically regardless of how important it is to the economic status of the household and to understanding the diversifying strategies of household economies. Further, we wish to begin examining how women's work influences the organization of residential space and the materials used within household space. "Because of the increasingly critical importance of households in archaeological interpretation and theoretical advancement, especially in Mesoamerica, it has become essential to understand how material items relate to social, economic, and demographic characteristics of household inhabitants" (Hayden and Cannon 1984: 1).

We come to this study as archaeologists who specialize in the prehistory of the North American Southwest. Two aspects of southwestern prehistoric communities are relevant to our interest in this ethnoarchaeological analysis. First, prehistoric pueblo-dwelling people were subsistence farmers. They relied on rainfall to irrigate floodplain, alluvial fan, and mesa top fields. The Southwest is an arid to semiarid landscape; limited rainfall can vary temporally and spatially in unpredictable ways. In addition, well-watered, rich soils are in limited supply. Thus, farming in the Southwest is and was a risky proposition (e.g., Minnis 1985; Ahlstrom et al. 1995; Schlanger and Wilshusen 1993). Second, households were economically autonomous to a great degree, at least until the 14th century; people moved frequently among villages and between villages and small farmsteads (Nelson 1999; Varien 1999). We are interested in how households managed in this risky farming environment. Just as modern subsistence farmers diversify their economic strategies, we expect prehistoric households to have employed varied approaches to establishing secure economic bases. This study will provide insights for exploring women's roles in household economies and the visibility of diverse economic strategies of women. We return to a consideration of prehistoric farming households and communities at the end of this chapter.

Our ethnoarchaeological analysis focuses on a contemporary Maya village in which most household economies are based primarily on subsistence farming. Although collaboration in economic endeavors occurs among households (Hayden and Cannon 1982), much of the daily focus of work is within households, which are fairly autonomous. The village is San Mateo Ixtatan, a Maya settlement of about 700 families in the highlands of northwestern Guatemala (fig. 8.1). The village rests in the massive Cuchumatane Mountains at an elevation greater than 8,000 feet (2,800 meters) above sea level. Thus, agriculture is marginal, and households depend on a range of additional sources of sustenance. The socioeconomic relations within the community are not stratified or rigidly hierarchical (Hayden and Cannon 1984: 3). In this context, the contribution of craft production and wage labor by women is vital to their households. In this sense, the San Mateo example is excellent for examining variation and patterning in the contributions of women's work as well as the effects of craft production and wage labor on the other demands of women for space and time.

HOUSEHOLD ECONOMIES, WOMEN'S LABOR, AND HOUSEHOLD SPACE

Households have been defined and studied in myriad ways. This is related, in part, to the inherent complexity of households and the multiple factors influencing household functions and organizations. Our study focuses primarily on the economic aspects of household organization and the impact of women's income-generating labor, in the form of craft production and wage labor, on the household economy and on the house space. Therefore, the following background highlights aspects of the corpus of household research pertinent to our focus.

The Household Concept

Much research on households in anthropology over the past two decades has been inspired by the work of Richard Wilk and his mentor Robert Netting. In 1982, Wilk defined household as primarily the smallest cooperating economic

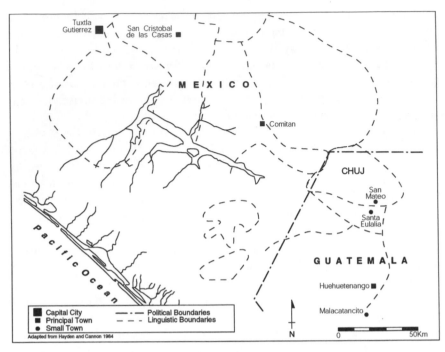

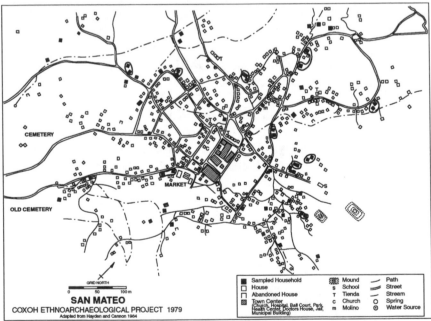

Figure 8.1. Maps of the study region and village of San Mateo Ixtatan (from Hayden and Cannon 1984).

entity of production, distribution, reproduction, and transmission (Wilk and Rathje 1982). A decade later, he differentiated the functional from the cultural aspects of households (Wilk 1991). The functional aspects include a list of features similar to those outlined in 1982, with the important addition of coresidence. Cultural aspects emphasize rules and strategies; the former are culturally sanctioned guidelines within which households operate, and the latter are household decisions made in the context of rules. Others find difficulty with the household concept (e.g., Horne 1982; Kramer 1982; Hammel 1984; Collins 1986); Hammel has stated simply that "a household, in fact, is the next bigger thing on the social map after an individual" (1984: 40–41).

Wilk's inclusion of coresidence is an important element for archaeologists in operationalizing the analytic unit "households" (Hirth 1993). Many have argued about the residential quality of households, but archaeologists have embraced the coresidential feature because it allows them to materialize the concept, recognizing spatially delimited units in the archaeological record that have parallel sets of rooms, features, and artifacts for the performance of a range of domestic activities. Because one goal of this chapter is to gain an understanding of women's contributions to household economies in ways that can be applied to archaeological research, we analyze households as coresidential units. We acknowledge that Hayden and Cannon (1982), in an analysis of Mayan data including the village used for this study, identified corporate groups that collaborate in important economic endeavors. Their work identifies economic dimensions that operate at a more communal level than those we seek to identify.

Household Economies

Researchers from many disciplines, including anthropology, sociology, and economics, are interested in the economic dynamics within and among households. In anthropology, attention has been paid to the organization of production within households. Sahlins's (1972) "domestic mode of production" characterizes household economics as reciprocal, emphasizing pooling and sharing, in small-scale societies. Wilk (1989) and Cheal (1989) recognize various other factors motivating household economic relations, including self-interest and domination. Cheal distinguishes two structures: the moral economy and the political economy. The former structure is governed by the characteristics described by Sahlins, the latter by self-interest, unequal relations, and exchange rather than sharing. Collins (1986) directs attention to the individual, rather than the household, but her perspective on economic strategies is enlightening for analysis at either scale (although Collins rejects the idea that household studies are useful). On the basis of her research in the Andes of southern Peru, she argues that "peasants participate in multiple economic activities because of the failure of any single activity to provide an adequate living" (Collins 1986: 665). She has described a "diversification strategy." Her argument is a classic ecological one: Diversification provides options under conditions of risk, in this case risk of shortfall from an ever changing economic climate. Arnold (1985) argues, in a similar vein, that households participate in ceramic production as a response to limited availability of adequate farmland. In short, families who cannot feed themselves from their land produce pottery (or other crafts) to generate "income." Thus, we would expect that subsistence farmers or peasants, especially those poorest in landholdings, would engage in a range of craft and wage labor activities, in addition to farming, as a strategy to ensure their future survival.

Diversification is a strategy for ameliorating risk of shortfall for individuals or any social unit, including the household. A diverse household economy allows it to change focus according to the vagaries of the broader economic climate. This is an especially useful strategy in contexts where household members have little control over the wider economy. Thus, economic diversity is a stabilizing force for households; it may not improve their status at any one point in time, but it improves their long-term well-being. Collins (1986) points out that diverse activities can be competing, especially if they are conducted in different productive spheres, as are subsistence farming and wage labor. Arnold (1985) discusses the importance of scheduling pottery production around the demands of agriculture. In a subsistence farming community, the farming is critical to sustaining each household.

Archaeologists are particularly interested in the development of unequal relations among households and have considered the development of craft production as one aspect of the emergence of ranked social relations. In small-scale societies, "the more limited the range of economic opportunities, the more homogeneous households will be in both size and structure" (Hirth 1993: 27). Hirth (1993) and Netting (1982) argue that access to land conditions the structure of households and variability among them. Nonelite households with limited access to land and resources are fairly homogeneous, but outside sources of "employment," such as craft production and wage labor, create variation. Craft activity, depending on the scale of production, Hirth (1993: 28) argues, can restructure households through growth in household size rather than interhousehold economic organizations such as craft guilds (1993: 27–31). Wilk's (1991) work among contemporary Maya households in Belize supports this generalization; household size increases with opportunity and declines as economic conditions decline. Hayden, however, has observed the reverse: Poverty associates with larger household size because married children cannot afford to move out and form independent households (B. Hayden, personal communication, 1998).

An important aspect of emerging rank is that it is not based on household production strategies but on development of differential access and control. Control over resources and labor is commonly perceived as the source of differences in rank among households (Blake and Clark 1989; Hirth 1993: 31; Hayden 1995; Arnold 1997). The difference is associated with ability to accumulate and hold greater wealth in the form of consumable resources and land. Differential access to and control of ritual knowledge has also been identified as a source of inequality and the basis of leadership in small-scale societies (Brandt and Spielmann 1998; Potter 1998). Stone, Johnson-Stone, and McNetting (1984) argue that development of inequality occurs in the context of population pressure on resources. However, the increases in household production of crafts do not appear to be a pathway to wealth (Wilk 1991); rather, they are a diversifying strategy used by those at the low end of the economic scale.

Discussions of resource control, surplus production, and diversification rarely assess the role of gendered production and labor, even when the focus is on individual strategies. Arnold (1985) has discussed the important role of women's ceramic production in supporting poor households, noting that ceramic production can compete with farming and other household and family obligations. Collins (1993) points out that members of a household do not all have common interests and goals governing their decisions. For example, men and women in some Andean communities take on different obligations to their affines at marriage that create competing interests. This view of conflicting interests within households differs from the pooling and sharing perspective on household economies (Wilk 1991).

Gender and Household Organization

Both men and women engage in production of surplus, including crafts, to support their household. Wright (1991) has pointed out that many studies of the development of craft production assume that women are the primary producers in household-based production, but men are assumed to be the important players when production is scaled up (for the latter argument, see Arnold 1985). Assumptions about women's roles in craft production are based on their assumed involvement in household activities that restrict their movement outside their homes (Hammond and Jablow 1973; Arnold 1985; Crown and Wills, n.d.), but Arnold and Santley (1993) note that task responsibilities shift in ways that require careful consideration of our assumptions about roles within households. At minimum, poor households rely heavily on the productive activities of females (Redclift 1985); Ehlers (1990) observes that the term *la lucha* is used in Maya villages to refer to the many of activities that women perform to keep their households afloat. Some have argued that women's labor is not recognized as a significant contribution because it falls within what are considered "normal" household responsibilities (Browner 1991). Women produce crafts for exchange and sale but are less involved in trading or selling them outside their communities (Hammond and Jablow 1973). In this study, we are concerned explicitly with the role of women's production and labor in the economic well-being of their household. We categorize all adult females as "women" and examine their income-generating labor in terms of both wealth-building and diversifying strategies. In addition, we examine the complexities of different mixes of income-generating activities and their visibility in the material aspects of the household space and assemblage composition. This approach unfortunately ignores the diversity of potential gender roles but examines variation in the roles of the category "women" (as we have defined it) within household economies. We recognize that other kinds of roles influence relationships within households in San Mateo Ixtatan, for example, generational categories (B. Hayden, personal communication, 1998), but focus on gender in this study.

One of our expressed interests in the study of women's labor is its materialization in the house and property of women. Hegmon, Ortman, and Mobley-Tanaka (1997) summarize literature on gender and household space and we draw a great deal from their work. Following from the work of others, they point out that "what people do—their practices—may reproduce but can also transform" structures of relationships and in turn the use of space. Variability or differences from the norm may be evident in the use of the places in which people live and work. Drawing on Hillier and Hanson (1984) and Goffman (1979), Hegmon et al. argue that architecture "structures social interactions and metaphorically reinforces social relationships" (1997: 2). If much of the variation in women's labor occurs within their household space, in their patios, houses, and kitchens, we should expect variation in their labor to be evident in the organization of space and the availability of space to women.

The organization of space within houses is influenced by a number of considerations, including the nature of gendered relations (status, power, and autonomy) within the household (Hegmon et al. 1997), as well as wealth, political and social status, agricultural intensity, activity diversity, and environment (Bawden 1982; Gilman 1987; Wilk 1988; Marshall 1989; Robben 1989; Arnold 1990; Blanton 1994; Matson 1996). For example, Wilk (1990) suggests, for the Kekchi Maya of southern Belize, that the form of the exterior of a house conforms to community standards indicating shared belief in equality among households and unity within the village. The interior of houses is more conditioned by functional considerations. Hegmon et al. (1997) argue that homogeneity and diversity in interior house features are indicative of levels of community integration and ideologies about conformity in the prehistoric North American Southwest.

Men's and women's roles and tasks within their house areas influence the organization of space use for activities as well as for storage (e.g., Ardener

1981; Lyons 1989; Hastorf 1991). Separation of work space along gender lines reinforces and naturalizes ideas about gender differences (Lyons 1989; Hastorf 1991; Hegmon et al. 1997). In the households analyzed in this study, women's space is fairly clearly separated from the rest of the household, sometimes by separate structures and other times by a division within a structure. In this context of delineated female space, we expect that the amount, organization, and accessibility of work space should be influenced by the kinds and diversity of tasks performed by women. For example, pottery production requires storage, preparation, and work areas (Arnold 1985; Wright 1991), although Arnold (1990) has noted that spatial limitations condition firing techniques and the location of pot firing. However, the space in buildings within a household compound may not be influenced by craft production when the settings of work include many contexts outside domestic architecture (Rapoport 1990). The positioning of facilities used by women is also indicative of their status and work demands within households. Bourdieu (1973) argues that the low position of women in Berber households is indicated by the marginal placement of cooking areas in houses. Hegmon et al. (1997) suggest that the central placement of facilities used by women is related to the degree to which they can participate in other ongoing activities as well as the degree to which they can be monitored by others (see also Lamphere 1993). We believe that the positioning of features is also related to the extent to which women need committed space for their work. Thus, we expect that the positioning of support facilities and commitment of space exclusively to women is in part related to the scale of production by women.

THE SAN MATEO CASE

San Mateo Ixtatan is a Maya community in the highlands of northwestern Guatemala (much of what follows is from Hayden and Cannon 1984 and from the senior author's personal experience in the village). Households for this study are defined as coresidents of a delineated compound area including kitchen and sleeping structures with a shared patio and adjacent farming plot. Fifty-one San Mateo households were part of the Coxoh Ethnoarchaeological Project in 1979. These are the cases examined in this chapter.

People in San Mateo Ixtatan generally have low incomes and depend on farming for basic subsistence, but this was not always the case. The traditional subsistence of the village was more commercial than today. Salt mines in and around San Mateo Ixtatan were controlled by the village and mined by community members. The salt water was gathered in vessels and boiled, then the salt was extracted. Salt was distributed widely in the region, forming the foundation of a strong regional economic position for the village. Historically, San

Mateo relied heavily on mining and exporting salt, almost to the exclusion of agriculture (Hayden and Cannon 1984: 10). However, in the 1960s, completion of the regional road system allowed commercial, low-cost salt to become easily accessible, eliminating the market for the San Mateo salt producers. Villagers turned to subsistence farming, investing primarily in maize cultivation.

San Mateo families live in plank and mud-walled houses with earthen floors, although a few families, primarily non-Maya, have wooden houses with wooden floors. Households may occupy a single structure in which all activities are performed or have multiple structures with kitchens separated from sleeping areas. The variation in composition of household structure area is presented in table 8.1.

Food is prepared in ceramic and occasionally metal vessels on an open fire on the earthen floor. Meals are comprised of maize and black beans. Eggs, greens, and small amounts of meat are eaten in varied quantities, depending on the economic well-being of the household. Maize is ground for a fee in mechanical grinders located centrally within the village and further processed with manos and metates by the women of each household.

Most households grow traditional crops (primarily maize) on which they depend for sustenance. Households maintain parcels of land adjacent to their homes in the village. Some of these are quite small; sustaining even a small family can be difficult, especially since the farmland is rocky, and, at an elevation of 8,000 feet, the growing season is short. Those with small plots or no land have a variety of ways to acquire food and other goods. Some have additional fields near the village, others farm distant plots in small isolated farmsteads or small farming settlements, some produce goods for sale or barter, and some perform wage labor. Both men and women engage in farming, produce or acquire goods for local and regional markets, and work as wage laborers, although the latter is more often a male activity.

Within San Mateo Ixtatan, women engage in a wide range of activities to raise money or have goods to barter (table 8.2). These goods are bartered or sold primarily within the village or in adjacent village markets. A few produce goods for sale in regional markets, such as the one in Huehuetanango. Women rarely leave the village to sell or barter their own goods; this is usually done

Table 8.1.   Types of structures and their frequency in each household compound

Household Number	Separate Kitchen	Separate Nonkitchen	Multiuse Dwelling, Kitchen and Habitation
1	1	1	0
2	0	1	1
3	0	1	1
4	0	0	1

continued

Table 8.1. Types of structures and their frequency in each household compound

Household Number	Separate Kitchen	Separate Nonkitchen	Multiuse Dwelling, Kitchen and Habitation
5	1	1	0
6	0	0	1
7	0	0	1
8	0	0	1
9	0	0	1
10	0	1	1
11	0	0	1
12	0	0	1
13	0	0	1
14	0	0	1
15	0	0	1
16	0	0	1
17	1	1	0
18	0	0	1
19	0	0	1
20	0	1	0
21	0	0	1
22	0	0	1
23	0	0	1
24	1	1	0
25	0	0	1
26	0	0	1
27	0	0	1
28	0	0	1
29	0	0	1
30	0	0	1
31	0	1	0
32	0	0	1
33	1	1	0
34	0	0	1
35	0	0	1
36	1	1	0
37	0	0	1
38	1	4	0
39	1	1	0
40	1	1	0
41	0	0	2
42	0	0	1
43	0	0	2
44	0	0	1
45	0	0	1
46	1	2	0
47	0	1	1
48	0	0	1
49	0	0	1
50	0	0	1
51	0	0	1

by men. However, women bartering and selling their crafts dominate the local marketplace in the village center.

Fifty-one households were visited by a team from the Coxoh Project. Information was gathered by talking with the adults in the household and by mapping all structures and items in the residential area and adjacent garden plot. The Coxoh Project interviewers were men because their Spanish was best. Custom dictates that women in households not speak at length with men, so most of our interviews were with the male heads of households; some, however, were with women. The native language of the community is Chuj, which is the dominant and sometimes only language spoken by women. Many men speak Spanish to some degree. Nevertheless, we worked through a village member who served as an interpreter. Mapping of the household compounds was as detailed as possible for each compound. An effort was made to record all items in use, in storage, and discarded, including their form, location (on a map), and condition. Data for this study are derived from the questionnaires, maps, and item inventories, generously made available in a coded data set by Brian Hayden. The senior author participated in making maps and inventories of all 51 households in 1979.

METHODS AND EXPECTED RESULTS

This study addresses two concerns: the role of women's production in the economic condition of their households and the impact of the scale of women's production on the organization of residential space and women's space in particular. We discuss the variables of importance for each of these concerns separately. All variables are listed in the appendix.

Household Economies and Women's Production

The economic condition of households should be influenced by contributions from women's production. We are interested in whether the households in best economic condition within this village achieved that condition because of a

Table 8.2. The range of income-generating activities by women

Income-Generating Activities	Number of Participating Households
Blouse embroidery	24
Pottery	5
Brooms	10
Food	6
Candles	2
Merchant	2
Wage labor	15

substantial contribution by women through production of goods for trade or barter or by their wage labor. This expectation is consistent with general models of craft production that explain its origins in terms of the ability of households to sponsor such activities. Alternatively, we expect that overproduction by women to generate needed income occurs in the poorest households, with the least land, as a way to sustain the household where farming is inadequate. This perspective is consistent with notions of craft production developing in the context of economic stress or uncertainty, as discussed earlier.

These alternatives imply different patterning. In the first case, the volume of crafts produced and the amount of income derived from this production and from wage labor should positively correlate with measures of the economic condition of the household. In the second case, craft production and wage labor income should negatively correlate with measures of economic well-being. To evaluate the extent of craft production, we use the income derived from the sale of craft items (income is expressed in pesos because other villages studied by the Coxoh team were in Mexico, where the peso is the currency). Income from craft production by women was originally recorded in craft categories (blouses, pottery, and so on). We examined income from each craft category and also combined the categories into one variable labeled FPESO to represent the total income generated by women in each household. Wage labor was evaluated by total yearly income derived from it.

Economic well-being was evaluated with several measures: economic interval scale, economic rank, total land, and the percentage of all purchased goods, as summarized by Hayden and Cannon (1984) (see appendix). Some heads of households reported a greater income than they actually had; therefore, the economic rank variable may not be fully representative of actual income (Hayden and Cannon 1984: 135–37). Households of a given rank may not have material possessions reflecting that rank because of differing values, preferences, or strategies. It is possible to validly interpret households with numerous indicators of wealth as having a high economic rank; however, not all households of high rank will be evident through their material possessions.

Household Spatial Organization and Women's Production

To use insights gained from ethnographic research as aids to understanding the past, we must examine how they influence material remains. How are items, features, and distributions within household space influenced by patterns of variation in women's labor? Craft production requires space. Pottery manufacture is probably the most space consuming of the craft activities by women in the village of San Mateo Ixtatan. Salt processing and food processing (grinding and cooking) are primarily indoor activities, while pottery manufacture and embroidery occur both inside and outside the house. The number of different tasks women perform should correlate with space committed to their work and the storage of their materials. Similarly, the larger the scale of production, the more space is needed within which to work and store finished pieces and raw materials. Although some portions of craft production can and do occur on patios, we expect the amount of interior space available to women to positively correlate with the diversity of their craft activities and the amount of craft production by them. In addition, we expect that the amount of patio space should correlate with the scale of pottery production. Vessel molding is conducted primarily in patios, although firing and temper grinding is more frequently done in the house.

In San Mateo Ixtatan, residential space is commonly divided, with the kitchen the domain of women and the remainder of the residential area shared or dominated by male activities. This is not a rigid pattern. Where the entire household occupies a single structure and the hearth is in the center, much of the house space is shared. We expect these to be households with little craft production by women. In other households, women have an entirely separate structure for their kitchen. This may be correlated with overall economic well-being, but we explore whether it also correlates with the investment of women in craft production. The organization and availability of space is evaluated using several variables: percentage of all structural area that is committed to women's labor (defined by us as kitchen), the construction of this space as separate or part of a multiuse structure, the presence of a hearth in this space not shared with general-use space, and the percentage of all women's space used for storage and open to work (see appendix). We also look at the size of the patio area, which, although undifferentiated physically, may offer space for women's craft production, especially ceramic production and storage. Production variables are the same as described in the preceding paragraph.

These spatial analyses may provide information for recognizing the involvement of women in craft production in archaeological contexts. If a greater percentage of space or a different arrangement of space or hearth features is produced as a way to accommodate the diversity or volume of women's production, we may be able to better understand such spatial variation in prehistoric small-scale social contexts. This analysis proceeds with an appreciation for the many variables that influence the amount and organization of household space, as discussed earlier in this chapter. We do not expect that craft production is the only factor influencing household space.

We also examine the extent to which the crafts produced by women would be evident in the material record of the household by looking for the tools, products, and facilities of those activities in the household compounds. Stark (Stark and Hall 1993; Roler and Stark, n.d.) argues that overproduction of ceramics is difficult to see in the inventories of specialists' households when the scale of production is limited and varies over time. We evaluate this concern.

ANALYSIS

The scale of women's production is assessed by combining all income derived from craft production within their households and wage labor. We refer to this as FPESO; it combines the following sources of income: sales of pottery, embroidered blouses, candles, baked goods and food, and brooms, and services such as merchants and wage laborers. Variation in women's income is presented in figure 8.2; a list of activities for income is presented in table 8.2. Five households (numbers 7, 10, 17, 18, and 35), 10 percent of those visited, have much higher income from women's labor than do the other 46 households. In 13 households (25 percent), women do not engage in craft production or wage labor for income. Women in most other households gain little income from craft production or wage labor.

The contribution that this income makes to the overall economic well-being of a household can be seen in the relationship between Economic Scale and FPESO. Economic Scale is the sum of the value of livestock, earnings, and land, and serves as one measure of the relative well-being of a household (Hayden and Cannon 1984). These data, however, were collected through interviews, where income levels can be under- and overestimated, although the Coxoh field

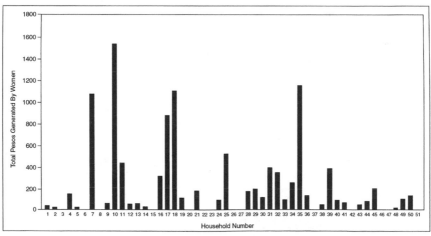

Figure 8.2. Bar graph showing the amount earned from women's craft production and wage labor in each household in San Mateo Ixtatan as reported during the fieldwork in 1979.

crew strove to check evident discrepancies (Hayden and Cannon 1984: 110). We find no correlation between Economic Scale and FPESO ($r = -.04$).[1] The large number of households in the lowest levels of the Economic Scale variable for this village may mask any correlation at higher income levels. In some households of low economic status, but not in all, women engage in craft production and wage labor. Women's labor does not contribute substantially to households of high or even middle-range economic status but appears to keep some poor households afloat.

Hayden and Cannon (1984) grouped income from women's production into four categories: pottery manufacture and sales; sales of embroidered blouses, or *huipils;* sales of all other crafts; and wage labor. We find that all but one of these categories has nearly a zero correlation coefficient in relation to economic scale. However, the correlation between blouse (*huipil*) sales and economic scale has an *r*-value of .14, which, although not statistically significant at the .05 level, is the only positive relationship. Blouse sales yield little income; thus, this activity does not have much impact on the economic status of the household.

Land is central to economic well-being among subsistence farmers, such as the Maya in San Mateo Ixtatan (Hayden and Cannon 1984: 142). Although at times residents of San Mateo Ixtatan have derived wealth from controlling access to salt mines, the villagers currently depend on household and corporate group-level subsistence farming. While land is included in the Economic Scale variable, we look separately at the relationship between the amount of milpa land held by each household and the involvement of women in craft production and wage labor. With the lack of correlation between economic scale and female income, we did not expect a correlation between female income

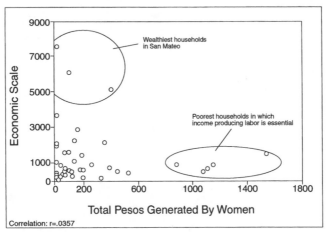

Figure 8.3.   Graph of the correlation between income generated by women and the economic scale of each interviewed household in San Mateo Ixtatan as reported in 1979.

and land. We were not disappointed ($r = .11$); the relationship is positive, but not significantly (fig. 8.4). A pattern of households, with limited land, engaging in activities that provide alternative sources of income is integral to views of the role of craft production in small-scale subsistence economies (Arnold 1985; Collins 1986). However, the pattern is more complex. Among those households with fewer than 100 cuerdas of land (1 cuerda = 25 by 25 meters), only four derive much income from craft production and wage labor by women. Hayden and Cannon (1984) discuss varied economic strategies in San Mateo Ixtatan; further research might explore the economic activities of these poorer households. We restrict our view to women's labor.

Another measure of economic well-being is the ability of households to purchase valued items (Hayden and Cannon 1984: 108–10), which include luxury items (as listed by Hayden and Cannon 1984), plastics, rubber, metal, musical instruments, rosaries, and horse gear. Hayden and Cannon (1984: table 35, 108–10) found significant association between luxury items and the number of crafts and services engaged in by households (the craft index and the service index) and note that specialists "are more likely to use their wealth to obtain imported exotica" (1984: 128).

For our analysis, the percentage of valued items in each household was calculated by summing the number of luxury items, plastics, rubber, metal, musical instruments, rosaries, and horse gear, all of which are purchased items, and dividing the sum by the total inventory for each household. FPESO (income from women's labor) does not correlate with the percentage of valued items within a domestic assemblage ($r = .06$). Valued items comprise from about 20 percent to about 65 percent of all household items (fig. 8.5). The households

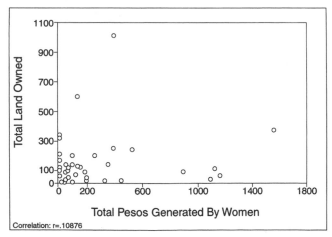

Figure 8.4. Graph of the correlation between income generated by women and total land owned by each interviewed household in San Mateo Ixtatan as reported in 1979.

with the most income from women's labor have from 30 percent to over 45 percent valued items in their inventories; they are in the middle range with regard to valued goods. Thus, although these are among the poorest households, they do not have the lowest percentages of valued items. One clue to this pattern may be in the correlation between a subset of women's income and a subset of valued items. Income from wage labor correlates significantly with the percentage of plastics and rubber items ($r = .38, p < .05$). Women engaged in wage labor may be better able to afford these luxuries or may have greater access to markets offering these goods. They may also have less time to produce traditional equivalents.

Women's labor in craft production and for wages does not replace their household obligations to work in their fields and care for their families and homes. One of the ways households manage to diversify or take advantage of new opportunities is to have a sizable adult labor pool (Wilk and Netting 1984; Wilk 1991; Hirth 1993; Blanton 1994). Interhousehold corporate groups accomplish this as well (Hayden and Cannon 1982). We find a positive correlation between the number of adult women in the household and their income from female labor ($r = .50, p < .05$) and a positive correlation between income and the diversity of tasks performed by women to generate that income ($r = .61, p < .05$). We also find that every household does *not* engage in all craft and labor tasks. There are two strategies in San Mateo Ixtatan: In some households, women produce and sell pottery and engage in wage labor; in other households, they make blouses and produce miscellaneous other crafts. Those households engaged in pottery production and wage labor have more women

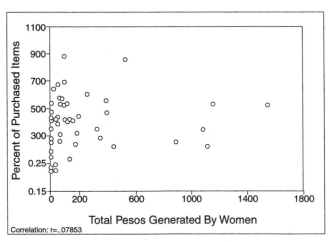

Figure 8.5.   Graph of the correlation between income generated by women and the percentage of all household items that were purchased.

than those engaged in other crafts (for pottery $r = .38$, for wage labor $r = .63$). Pottery production involves many more stages and much more labor in material acquisition than does embroidery, candle making, or baking; having more women in the household might make pottery production more viable, although Wright (1991) notes that men may participate in the range of activities supporting household-level pottery production. Wage labor frequently takes women away from their houses and families. If other adult women are available to care for the home and family in the absence of the wage laborers, this option may be more acceptable to the household and to the women.

Why is pottery production associated with wage labor as a source of income for households? Collins (1986) discusses the importance, for subsistence farmers, of having sources of income that are not responsive to the same market forces. Pottery production feeds both the local village demand for cooking, storage, and serving vessels and the regional-level tourist demand for native crafts. Wage labor is conditioned by agricultural demands primarily in lowland *fincas*. Thus, diversity is practiced among some San Mateo households, but the patterns of diversification are complex.

The second goal of our study was to examine how the scale of women's labor influences the organization of their households. This can be assessed most simply by examining whether engaging in income-generating labor results in more space allocated to women within their houses. Many of the craft tasks require room to work and to store raw materials and finished products. In the San Mateo Ixtatan houses, shared living space is fairly clearly divided between men and women, although they use some areas together. The division is accomplished in some households by building separate kitchen structures within which women do most of their work and store most of their items (figs. 8.6, 8.7). In households with kitchens at one end of a shared living room (figs. 8.8, 8.9), women's space is concentrated around the cooking and food preparation area, which is usually roughly half the room. Some households have separate kitchens and additional space for women in other structures. We calculated the indoor space dedicated to women within households by measuring kitchen structures, kitchen areas, and other places where women's items concentrated. This measure was converted to a percentage of all household interior space rather than expressed as area, recognizing that total household interior space and, by extension, total kitchen space may be influenced by economic status. (Hayden and Cannon [1984: 131] find it correlated with Economic Rank, a variable based on calculation of Economic Scale; Blanton [1994] discusses the relationship between wealth and overall house size.) There is no significant correlation ($r = -.07$) between the scale of women's income from craft production/wage labor and the percentage of household space committed to their use (kitchen), nor is there a correlation between this

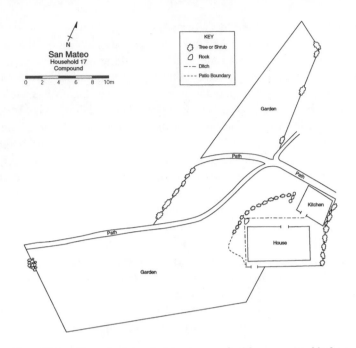

Figure 8.6.   Map of a household compound with a separate kitchen.

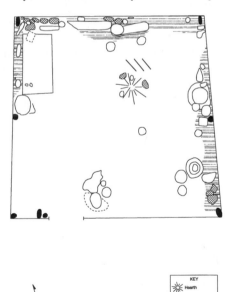

Figure 8.7.   Map of a kitchen as a separate structure.

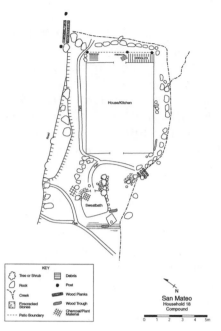

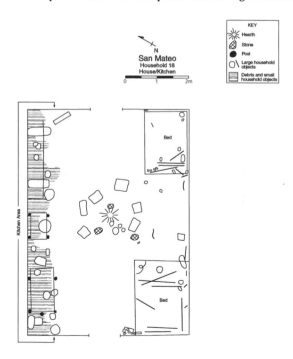

Figure 8.8.   Map of a household compound with a single multiuse structure.

Figure 8.9.   Map of a multiuse structure with the kitchen area at one end.

percentage of space and the number of adult females ($r = -.09$). We removed the wealthiest households from the analysis, thinking that they might be skewing results, but the lack of correlation remains ($r = .03$). If women worked on crafts primarily outside, especially pottery makers, patio area might correlate with the scale of production. However, there is no correlation between income from pottery sales (a proxy for scale of production) and patio area ($r = -.02$; we ran this with the wealthiest households removed). Among the five pottery-selling households, three (7, 18, and 19) have patio areas substantially below the mean for all households (mean = 49.9 square meters, household number 7's patio is 15 square meters, 18's is 12 square meters, and 19's is 18 square meters). Income from women's labor does not correlate with overall household area, either ($r = .03$). Thus, the scale of women's work in craft production and wage labor is not materialized in the size of the total household space or their portion of the household space. It would not be visible archaeologically in structure sizes and layout.

Within houses, we examine the use of interior space and its influence on the distribution of features and open space. First, we evaluate whether involvement in income-generating activities by women is associated with possession of kitchen spaces that are separate structures. Do women who generate income have their own kitchen buildings? Table 8.3 is a cross tabulation of the presence of kitchen structures and engagement in craft production for income; there is no significant association (chi-square = 1.52, d.f. = 1). Given this lack of relationship, we examined whether women whose work area is within a more generally used structure have exclusive control over the hearth area or share it with other family members (men and children). Exclusive use of the hearth was determined by its placement.[2] Hearths toward the center of a house are considered common access, while those integrated into the kitchen end of the room are considered the primary work area of women. Table 8.4 shows the relationship between hearth placement and engagement in income-generating labor for those households that lack a separate kitchen. There is no association at the .05 probability level (chi-square = 1.29, d.f. = 1). In fact, the pattern in

Table 8.3.   The relationship between women's labor and available space in their household compounds

	Women Not Producing Income	Women Producing Income	Total
No separate kitchen	11	27	38
Separate kitchen	1	9	10
Total	12	36	48

Note: Pearson's chi-square = 1.52, d.f. = 1.

the table is opposite of that expected. Most central hearths are in households where women engage in income-generating activities.

Second, we examine whether women who engage in income-generating activities maintain more open space or have more support facilities. Adding tasks to their household load without increasing the amount of space available for work might be compensated by keeping work areas open for a range of tasks. To evaluate open space, we calculated the total amount of women's interior space that is unavailable for work because it is occupied by built-in features or by artifacts. This was compared with the diversity of income-generating work within the household. We expected a negative correlation (the amount of space consumed by facilities and items and unavailable for work should decrease as the demand for work space increases), which we found ($r = -.16$), but the r-value is not significant at a probability level of .05. It is possible that women who engage in income-generating activities have more facilities to support their work. We identified wooden storage bins, cabinets, and tables within kitchen areas. The number of these does not correlate with diversity of income-generating activities ($r = -.16$). In addition, we looked for specific facilities that would identify craft production. Pottery hearths are the only facility specific to a craft. Two of these are present in the households studied, both in a household where women produce ceramic vessels for sale. Among the many women who make blouses for sale, none have fixed looms or weaving equipment; most blouse manufacture involves embroidery, not weaving. Similarly, among those who sell food, there are no special support facilities. Thus, women's income-generating labor is not materialized in greater separation of women's space, more open space, or more support facilities, although some pottery production is evident in the presence of pottery hearths.

Finally, we consider whether women's income-generating activities are evident in their material inventories. Hayden and Cannon (1984) observed, for San Mateo Ixtatan, that variable frequencies of artifacts in households are influenced by a range of factors, including economic and social roles, strategies of poor families and newcomers, and strategies for building and maintaining power. We wished to pursue women's roles in economic strategies as they

Table 8.4.   The relationship between women's labor and the isolation of their cooking hearth area

	Women Not Producing Income	Women Producing Income	Total
Hearth in kitchen	9	17	26
Hearth centrally placed	2	10	12
Total	11	27	38

Note: Pearson's chi-square = 1.29, d.f. = 1.

might be materialized in the household inventories. Pottery making requires a few wooden, metal, and plastic implements; many items that could be used by potters are found in household inventories, but no potter's tool kit was recorded. Stark and Hall (1993) noted that the specialized tool kits of potters are difficult to identify archaeologically when the scale of production is small or variable, as it is in San Mateo Ixtatan. We expected that production of ceramics for sale might yield inventories of vessels that were of superior quality. However, the households that sell pottery do not make vessels that are of the highest decorative or technical quality (for definition of quality variables, see Hayden and Cannon 1984). Blouse embroidery requires thread, needles, and embroidery hoops. Thread and needles were ubiquitous in households. Nearly everyone does some embroidery, as all women wear embroidered *huipils* that they make at home. Embroidery hoops were recorded in two households, both of which produce blouses for sale. However, the other 22 blouse-selling households had no embroidery hoop evident, although these and needles were probably stored in places not examined during fieldwork. Candle making was part of the income-generating craft activities of two households; one of these had candle-making frames. Making and selling food might have been supported with tortilla presses; these were found in six households, none of which sold food. As noted earlier, wage labor correlates with high percentages of plastic and rubber items, but these are present in all households. As with other material indices, the craft activities by women that generate household income are not unambiguously evident in their households. We suspect that the tools from craft production and discarded products might be most evident in trash, but this context was not systematically examined. In San Mateo, some trash is placed in community dumps (e.g., ceramics) and some cast into gardens.

DISCUSSION

Our exploration of women's labor, household economic condition, and household spatial organization has reinforced standing notions about small-scale subsistence-based economies but has also identified more complexity in household-level production in those economies. We found that women who engaged in income-generating activities, including craft production and wage labor, were in the households at the lowest end on the economic scale for the village. This pattern has been noted by many other anthropologists. However, we found that the diversifying strategy of adding income-generating activities or of expanding activities to generate income was accomplished in two ways in this village: either primarily pottery production combined with wage labor or primarily blouse sales combined with a range of other minor activities. The households engaged primarily in pottery production and wage labor had more adult women than the other households in which women generated income. These are also the households that produced the most income from women's labor. Collins (1986) noted the value of diversifying into different economic spheres, especially for peasants who lack influence over those spheres. As we have discussed, pottery production and wage labor address quite different spheres. We also found that although the households in which women engaged in crafts and wage labor to generate income are at the lower end of the economic scale in the village, they are not consistently the smallest households with the smallest houses, nor do they have the most limited material inventories. Women's labor may contribute subtly to the economic improvement of their household.

Woman's income-generating labor is not materially visible in the household compounds at San Mateo Ixtatan. They do not have more space or separate structures that support their income-generating work. The lack of correlation between labor and space may result from several factors in this village. First, women who produce crafts for sale generate relatively little income. At the time of the fieldwork, we noted that women spent no more than about 10 percent of their time on crafts for sale (B. Nelson, personal communication). Women may not need much space to store their products and materials. Second, women do so much in their household space that craft production, for the most part, may be worked into downtime in other activities and not require much committed space; ceramic production may be an exception. Third, men also engage in a range of craft activities that require work space. The division of space by gender and the definition of shared space must be a compromise among many competing factors.

As with other material indices, the craft activities by women that generate household income are not unambiguously evident in their households. Support facilities and materials do not identify particular crafts that are made for sale. This invisibility of women's labor for income results from the nature of production in this village. Every household produces most of the materials it needs. Those women who engage in income-generating craft production simply produce more of some items: pots, blouses, brooms, candles, and food. Nearly everyone in the village has limited resources and does not produce substantial inventory for sale. Thus, women's craft production is an extension of their usual household work and does not result in a particular material inventory or special facilities. Only wage labor is outside the usual range of household tasks for women, and this produces an inventory richer in plastics and rubber. Systematic examination of trash deposits might, however, yield differential frequencies and volumes of materials used to produce crafts and discarded products in those households that produce crafts to generate income, even at a small scale.

Men engage in a wide range of activities that generate income. We have not considered these in this study but believe that a detailed analysis of the relationship between men's and women's labor within households would further expand our understanding of the complexity of household economics and the materialization of diverse economic strategies.

Women's labor was the focus of this study. We sought to identify how women contribute to their households beyond the daily labors of caring for land and family. Their contributions are complex and, we have found, somewhat invisible in the material evidence of their lives. This is because in San Mateo Ixtatan, women garner income by expanding their usual domestic activities to generate income rather than moving beyond their usual activities, for the most part. We suspect that this is true for many small-scale societies in the past, making it difficult to recognize the diverse strategies of households in sustaining and improving their lives.

Returning to the prehistoric context with which we are most familiar, the North American Southwest, what has been learned that can apply to understanding women's roles in household economies and the development of overproduction of craft items? What issues are raised from this ethnographic research that enrich the questions we ask about the past? We believe that overproduction of various items (pottery, textiles, and ornaments) was used as a diversifying strategy by farming households in the North American Southwest, in much the same way that it was in the 20th-century Maya community of San Mateo Ixtatan; some women made some extra crafts for exchange to others for needed household items. The diversity among households, however, may not be visible archaeologically in the artifact and feature content within houses. The richness of household strategies seems to be invisible to us among small-scale societies. However, as many archaeologists already know, trash may be a richer source of information for variation in small-scale production, but the variations between households may be slight and may require neighborhood-level analysis. Overproduction may be visible primarily in contexts of neighborhood or village specialization, where some households in a village overproduce the same item and distribute it to other communities. The contrast would be between the accumulated middens of groups of households rather than single households. Here we are not referring to a pattern, such as that among the Inka, in which villages of specialists are formed for the nearly sole purpose of producing great volumes of material. Rather, some households produce in excess of need and exchange to other communities; the pattern of small-scale overproduction may be visible in the concentration of types at some villages and the distribution of compositional evidence of source indicators. In the Southwest, as in some modern Meso-American subsistence farming communities, there are several cases of village specialization in ceramic production beginning as early as A.D. 700 (Hegmon 1995), when villages rarely exceeded a few dozen families, and extending into the A.D. 1400s (Spielmann 1998), when villages housed hundreds of families (see papers in Mills and Crown 1995). Of particular interest is village specialization in production of utilitarian ceramics. If women were the primary producers of ceramic vessels, in particular the utilitarian vessels used in domestic contexts, they may have been the initiators of exchange networks that integrated farming communities during several decades. We suspect that the initial development of this production and exchange by a few isolated households is not going to be visible to us as archaeologists, as evident in this ethnographic study, but that as craft production and exchange within a village became focused on a single product and extended beyond the village, small-scale craft production will be visible and can be studied with attention to the organization of the household and the role of women in this endeavor. Such issues need further examination.

NOTES

1. All correlation coefficients are evaluated as statistically significant at a probability level of 0.05.

2. We have no interview data or observations on hearth sharing or exclusive use, so placement was our best proxy.

APPENDIX: VARIABLES CODED FOR THE
CASE STUDY ANALYSIS

Variable Number	Code	Description
1	HH	Household
2	TOTSTRUC	No. structures per compound
3	TOTKITCH	No. kitchens per compound
4	HSEPRKIT	No. single house–kitchen structures per compound
5	MAIZBINS	Maize bins (1, none; 2, outside; 3, inside; 4, in and out; 5, rafters)
6	KTCHAREA	Kitchen floor area (m^2)
7	TOTAREA	Total enclosed floor area, dwellings (m^2)
8	%KITCHEN	Kitchen area/total area converted to a percentage
9	%USEDK	Amount of kitchen area taken up by fixed facilities and stored items
10	PATAREA	Patio area (m^2)
11	KTCHHRTH	Location of hearth within the house space 1—Closer to kitchen area inside the structure 2—Centrally located in structure, regardless of structure use 3—Kitchen area only 4—Not applicable
14	FACILITI	Total no. support facilities available 1—Grinding Area 2—Salt Box 3—Grinding area and salt box 4—Salt box and maize box 5—Maize box 6—Maize box and grinding area 7—Grinding area and maize box 8—Not applicable
15	ELECTRIC	Electricity (1, absent; 2, present)
16	WATER	Water (1, absent; 2, present)
19	ECONOFEM	No. of economic females (14 and over)
20	TOTECONO	Total economic adults
21	AGEOFHHH	Age of head of household (or if deceased, wife) 1 = 0–19, 2 = 20–29, 3 = 30–39, 4 = 40–49, 5 = 50–59, etc.
24	WYRSSCH	Head of household's wife years in school
25	SOCRANK	Social ranking (Cumulative for all members in household): based on lineage position, age, cargo positions, and miscellaneous factors, such as making or selling trago (negative), lack of respect for authorities, being drunk all the time, etc. (1 = lowest, e.g., widow)
26	HHPOTERS	No. of potters
27	LOCBAXGR	Location of bax (calcite) grinding (0 = N/A)
28	LOCMODLG	Location of modeling activities (0 = N/A)

continued

Variable Number	Code	Description
29	LOCFIRG	Location of firing (0 = N/A)
30	AMTPROD	Quantity produced/year (maximum)
31	TECHQUAL	Technical quality of workmanship (0 = N/A)
32	DECOQUAL	Decorative quality of workmanship (0 = N/A)
33	POTSALES	Profit from sales/year (pesos)
34	FWAGELAB	No. female wage laborers in household (finca workers, etc.)
35	FWGEPESO	Pesos gained/year from female contributions
37	NMKBLOUS	No. in household that make blouses
38	BLOUSOLD	No. sold/year for whole household
39	BLSPESO	Pesos gained from the sale of blouses
40	SELLBAX	Sell or trade bax (calcite): 1 = grind bax 2= bax pieces (non–potter households only) 9 = don't grind or collect bax
41	CNDLMAKR	Candle makers (present/absent)
42	BAKER	Baker (present/absent)
43	BRMSMADE	Brooms made by women (1 = used to make, 2 = still make, 9 = don't make)
44	SELLFOOD	Food sold from house (present/absent)
45	MERCHANT	Merchant (present/absent)
46	TAILORS	Tailors (present/absent): male or female
47	MIDWIFE	Midwife (present/absent)
48	ESPCPESO	Pesos gained from activities (41–47) and any other female specializations not mentioned
49	FPESO	Total pesos derived by income generating labor of women (10s of pesos)
50	LABORDIV	Labor diversity—the number of different income-generating activities
51	ECOSCALE	Economics interval scale The sum of the following in 10s of pesos: Value of all livestock Earnings/year from finca and other wage labor, specializations (including potters), and other activities (stores, cantinas, etc.) Milpa surplus sales, egg/honey sales, garden sales Hunted sales, contributions from others
52	ECORANK	Economic ranking, 1–6
53	CRFTINDX	Craft index

blouses	bax	candles	bone needle
carpenter	baskets	hats	weaving (loom)
pita fiber	redes	cacho	capal
skin preparation	flute	musical instruments	moral
tabla	tejamanil	spinning	blowgun
salt	masks	ritual objects	baker
brooms	leatherwork		adobe

continued

Variable Number	Code	Description
54	TOTMILPA	Total land owned both planted and not planted
56	SERVINDX	Service/entrepreneur index

midwife	curandero	nurse	fiador
tendero	cantina	maize mill	restaurant
merchant	muleteer	trago vendor	butcher
tailor	catequista	salt merchant	food seller
cargador	shoe repair	posada owner	
	industrial machine repair		

Variable Number	Code	Description
57	TOTINV	Total no. of items in household
58	TOTVAL	Total no. of valuables (all nontraditional purchased items)
59	%VAL	TOTVAL/TOTINV converted to a percentage
60	METAL	No. of metal items in household
61	%METAL	METAL/TOTINV converted to a percentage
62	PLASRUB	No. of plastic and rubber items in household
63	%PL_RUB	PLASRUB/TOTINV converted to a percentage
64	LUXURY	No. of luxury items in household
65	EMBRDYHP	No. of embroidery hoops in household
66	CART	No. of carts or cart related materials (e.g., wheels)
69	LOOMBACK	No. of backstrap looms in household
71	PACKFRAME	No. of pack frames in household
72	PNTBRUSH	No. of paint brushes in household
73	SALTBOX	No. of salt boxes in household
74	LRGTABLE	No. of large tables in household
75	TORPRESS	No. of tortilla presses in household
76	WOOLCOMB	No. of wool carding boards/combs in household
77	CNDLFRAM	No. of candle-making frames in household
78	MISCWEAV	No. of weaving tools in household

9

Beyond Complementarity and Hierarchy: New Definitions for Archaeological Gender Relations

Joan M. Gero and M. Cristina Scattolin

INTRODUCTION: THE BINARY WORLD OF GENDER SYSTEMS

It sometimes seems that archaeologists, enthusiastic about recovering aspects of the gendered human experience from prehistoric contexts, have launched an "archaeology of gender" without examining the assumptions that underpin their conclusions. Possibly because each of us has a gender (at least one gender), we assume that gender categories are obvious, that what follows from gender categories is straightforward and unproblematic, and that we understand how gender works in social and economic life. In contrast to the obviously unfamiliar aspects of prehistory, such as technologies for bronze casting or Pleistocene weather patterns—things that we have never experienced in our own lifetimes—there is something reassuring about ancient gender systems that ties "them," ancient women and men, more or less straightforwardly to "us," modern inhabitants of Western industrial societies.

It is this seemingly transparent and naturalized aspect of knowing about ancient gender systems that we want to address in this chapter. More specifically, we draw attention to the implicit classification of gender systems that has emerged in the gender and archaeology literature based on unexamined assumptions about what gender is and how it works. Although it is never put forward as a unified and inclusive scheme for considering all gender systems within its terms, a typology of gender systems is nevertheless in general usage today, and because no other "types" of broadly inclusive gender systems are available to generalize differences among gender systems, we are left with a much reduced, binary set of two "types" that is used frequently in the archaeological literature.

That is, we find common references to (1) gender hierarchy, in which one gender (the male gender) is said to dominate, oppress, control, or set the agenda of the other (female) gender, and (2) gender complementarity, a notion that not only includes the idea of an equality of the genders but that also emphasizes the interdependence of males' and females' economic activities: Each gender needs the other to complete itself and its work. Let's consider each of these.

Gender Complementarity

Gender complementarity as one means of organizing and coordinating gender difference is well illustrated and discussed in Bodenhorn's (1990) article "I'm Not the Great Hunter, My Wife Is," about the Alaskan North Slope Iñupiaq. "In precontact Iñupiaq society, there was no institutionalized way to live as an adult outside of marriage" (Bodenhorn 1990: 62); indeed, the division of labor and interdependent tasks by men and women were essential to the social and economic well-being of the society. Not only does "the women's needle make the hunter" (62), but success in whale hunting is shown to be dependent both symbolically and energetically on the collaborative activities and gendered characteristics of men and women possessing complementary attributes. Bodenhorn skillfully points out the central belief that "the whale comes to the whaling captain's wife" (61), and while women depend on whale meat as a basic component of their diet, without the spiritual advantage of a "generous" woman, even an accomplished male hunter will not enjoy success or, indeed, be able to survive.

Others have also observed the pronounced gender complementarity for the Iñupiaq (Bodenhorn 1990: 62–63), and a particularly rich description of the conceptual features of complementarity comes from Rainey (1947). Bodenhorn summarizes several mutual responsibilities that were carried out by whalers/whaling couples in the early 20th century:

> The husband hired a skilled craftsman to make the special wooden pot from which the wife would offer a welcoming drink of water to any whales caught by him. The wife hired an old woman to make special mittens to be worn when carrying the pot and she made the whale-hunting boots to be worn by her husband during the whaling season. She played an important role during the launching of the umiaq (whaleboat) and then returned home, placing the special pot and her husband's drum by the entrance of their house. He, in turn, wore her belt and kept her left-handed mitten in the boat. She provided the drink of water to the whale [demanded in respect to an animal that gives itself to a hunter]; then, after butchering, offered her husband a drink from the same pot. (Bodenhorn 1990: 62–63)

An important point to emerge from this example is that all the activities described in the quote (and others) are considered integral parts of the process of Iñupiaq hunting. What is specifically included under "hunting activities" as defined by the Iñupiaq is much broader than what we would consider "hunting" and in fact specifically includes both men's and women's activities, illustrating how gender complementarity "works": It provides inclusive conceptualizations of the world that emphasize gender interdependence. Complementary gendered individuals, in turn, provide central units of symbolic as well as functional importance.

In another important discussion of gender complementarity, Joyce (1996a) shows how the pairing of representations of male and female Maya elites on Classic period public monuments accentuates the duality and interrelationality of gender. The Maya frequently displayed gender as paired in "right" and "left" images at the same time that they emphasized "up" and "down" relationships. Joyce cogently observes that in both representational dimensions, right/left and up/down, the spatial axes incorporate an inherent quality of pairing that is absent from other organizational possibilities; the paired representations also contrast with representations of distinctly and exclusively male or female spaces (Joyce 1996a: 175–76). Moreover, many representations incorporate aspects of both male and female costume in the same image, "blur[ring] the boundary between the dichotomous gender poles they represented": "The combined costumes themselves represented images of the total natural universe: the horizontal plane of the earth's surface and the vertical axis of the central world tree" (182). Thus, here too, the power of the Maya elite is shown to depend not on their individual and bounded gender identities but on the complementarity they embodied and the power that derived from possessing aspects of both genders. The reiterated cosmological order in spatial and symbolic elements underscores an ideology of gender complementarity where power derives from wholeness, which in turn is achieved by combining the male and females aspects of being. Joyce goes on to enumerate contemporary Mayan ritual practices in which gender complementarity provides the essential dynamic for coordinating male and female labor and value.

Gender Hierarchy

Gender hierarchy is much more commonly attributed to social groups than is gender complementarity; indeed, the universality of male dominance was among the first subjects of a feminist discourse in anthropology (Nelson 1997: 115–16ff). In most class- or kin-based (ranked) societies, men are seen and/or assumed to control and hold authority over some or most of the critical resources, the means of production, public offices, symbolic and ritual currencies, and, of course, over the women. In fact, the evolutionary generalizations that state-level society produces an inevitable restructuring of gender relations and gender roles toward increasingly hierarchical and patriarchal gender systems (Silverblatt 1988; see also Conkey and Gero 1997) and that the undercutting of women's sources of power is a common strategy and product of state formation are widely accepted conditions—even where accompanied by a cautionary note that the form and degree of women's subjugation are hardly uniform in case to case (Pollock 1991; Gero 2001) or that the meanings of hierarchical gender systems are disputed and under revision (Cohen and Bennett 1998: 311). It is hardly surprising that an overwhelming proportion of archaeological studies of "women's status" conclude that the gender system under study was hierarchically organized and that women had lower status than males.

Thus, gender systems are generally characterized as either complementary or hierarchical, and one theme in the gender/archaeology literature has been to portray the movement from one condition (complementarity) to the other (hierarchy). Only occasionally have researchers been able to conceive of, and thus note, the coexistence of both gender modes, as in Joyce's studies where representations of ruling Mayan women and men are seen to represent "woman as complement to man in ritual and political action, as part of a single elite class with unitary interests" (Joyce 1993: 263). Much more often, the two gender modes are differentiated and opposed.

CRITIQUE AND ALTERNATIVES TO BINARY GENDERS AND BINARY GENDER SYSTEMS

There are many grounds to critique or discredit or dismiss this simple dichotomous classification. First, we suggest that the categories of "hierarchical" and "complementary" are of little use because they are too generalized. The two archetypes of named gender systems in this classification scheme are invalid by reason that each "kind" of gender system lumps together too much variability. Classifying gender systems or gender relations as hierarchical or complementary fails to specify exactly what is it that is hierarchical or complementary, implying perhaps that all relations and all aspects of a gendered ideology will be either hierarchical or complementary. There is no further indication of where these ordered relations reside: within everyday domestic activities? Or productive tasks? Or interpersonal exchanges? In the symbolic meanings attached to individuals or to ceremonial occasions? What in fact would mark gender relations in these instances as "hierarchical" or "complementary"?

Instead of such monolithic sets of relations, women and men more often have distinct areas of autonomy, authority, and power and are clearly more powerful, directive, and "dominant" in some areas of cultural performance than in others. Henrietta Moore (1988: chap. 3) has pointed out the forceful control that women can assert over "the larder" and stored agricultural products in many sociohistoric arrangements, even within "hierarchical" gendered situations. Spiritual authority has been noted in many societies as relating to women's realms. If we observe a wide range of gendered activities in our constructions and characterizations of societies' gender systems, we often find areas of women's authority and independence operating alongside areas of men's authority and independence. Observing whether men or women occupy public, authorized roles as rulers or as hereditary officials hardly covers the infinite numbers of social occasions in which gender roles are called up and acted on, nor does this situation predict what other areas of intergendered interactions will also be hierarchically ordered. Taking this point seriously, we must conclude that the only way that many societies can be considered to operate as gender hierarchies is by a subtle and presupposed prioritizing of exactly which activities will count as significant indicators of hierarchy, arguing against overly simplified categories of gender systems.

A second problem for the overly simple dichotomous classification system that has slipped into usage for all gender relations is the amount of messy overlap between the two supposedly discrete and oppositional classes of relations. There are many instances where gender relations might be "complementary" within a circumscribed group of women and men but would be termed "hierarchical" between that group and others; we also note that some areas of interaction are often set apart and operate under different gender rules from the more general gendered arrangements and violate the overarching typological terms. We have yet to see discussion in the gender-in-archaeology literature that emphasizes variation in how and in what realms gender systems are organized "hierarchically" or "complementarily," and we are losing descriptive accuracy and nuance here. The exaggerated simplicity of this binary classification fails to recognize the subtle, nuanced patterns of gendered interactions that would occupy the middle ground in this reductionist scheme, that mix characteristics of hierarchical and complementary gender schemes, or that make any separation of characteristics illogical. For instance, the very notions of interdependence of genders, central in "complementary" gender systems, may also be seen to reside in purportedly hierarchical gender systems, insofar as the "dominant" gender "needs" the "subordinate" gender. An example of simultaneously interdependent and hierarchical gender systems might adhere in how Algonquin languages distinguish gender categories: Women are identified with a "lower" realm and men with a "higher" realm—clearly, you cannot have "higher" without "lower," although these categories refer to a supposedly hierarchical gender system.

Third, and perhaps more important, the implicit classification of (all) gender systems as "hierarchical" or "complementary" deeply misrepresents what gender is and how gender roles work to organize social settings. It has been said often before that gender and especially gender relations are not "things" that individuals or social systems "have" — gender is not a bounded, static phenomenon but is rather a constructed set of relationships embedded in other cultural and historic institutions and ideologies, such as status, class, age, ethnicity, and race (Conkey and Gero 1991: 9; Nelson 1997: 30). Gender and gender relations are a process—some call this a "performance"—that individuals undertake in different ways during different periods of their lives, in different ways with different individuals of their own or of other genders, and in different ways in different contexts. Individuals vary enormously in the expressions of their sexuality and in their "genderhood," from moment to moment, person to person, and context to context, at different points in their lives; indeed, the stability of individuals' performances of gender is hardly consistent, not only from one person to the next within a given social system but even within a given individual's performance of gender from moment to moment. Yet such an idea of gender is utterly erased in the gross generalizations of "complementary" versus "hierarchical."

Finally, reconsiderations (or "problematizing") gender system categories must also consider how the simplified binary "hierarchical" and "complementary" categories can accommodate the fact that many social systems admit "third" (and higher numbers of) genders. Such notions as "two-spirit people" (for American Indians) proliferate because sufficient numbers of people fall outside the dominant culture's definitions of prescribed cultural behavior to defy simple "male" or "female" appellations and include not only transsexuals, transvestites, homosexuals, and hermaphrodites but also people who generally feel uncomfortable with the social identity ascribed to other adults sharing their sex markers. Even in ordinary English parlance, we have words that hedge on gender categories with terminology that makes finer distinctions, such as "tomboy" or "sissy." Other cultures regularly admit roles and rules for gender variance, by now richly described in the gender literature (e.g., Herdt 1994; Jacobs, Thomas, and Lang 1997; Kehoe 1998; Arnold, chapter 14 in this volume). Such studies show, for instance, that traditional two-spirit roles among North American native peoples such as the *nádleehé* (Navajo), the *winkte* (Lakota), the *hwame* (Mohave), or the *tainna wa'ippe* (Shoshoni) are defined not in terms of sexual preference but in terms of individuals choosing to undertake, on a permanent basis, the occupational work associated with the other gender: men doing beadwork, pottery making, and basketry or women who compete in rodeos, work with cowboys, and generally hang out with the men (Lang 1997: 109), sometimes also dressing in styles appropriate to the other gender and at times entering either same- or opposite-sex sexual relations.

Other conceptualizations of gender recorded in Amazonian South America emphasize a duality of simultaneous and equally acceptable male and female aspects within every individual; these are sometimes conceptualized as an "inner" female core and an "outer" male aspect (regardless of the shape of the genitalia, all humans are considered "female" internally, but the external, operative agent of action is called "male") (S.-E. Isaksson, personal communication). Saladin d'Anglure (1994) describes gender concepts among the central Arctic Iglulik as unstable and malleable, with transformations of gender possible in two directions; at birth, the gender of a newborn infant is fixed by means of specific rituals, but nevertheless an individual's gender is vulnerable to change by choice under some external conditions (Saladin d'Anglure 1994: 84–88). Other reports of gender concepts emphasize a changing of gender over a life span, such that individuals may start off demonstrating mainly "female" characteristics, enter a middle phase of life in which "maleness" is accentuated, and ultimately grow old in another female aspect. In some cultures, gender is seen as competing male and female aspects within any single person.

The point here is not only that many nondichotomous, nonbinary gender categories are formally recognized in ethnographic and ethnohistoric accounts but also that they undermine the essentialism implicit in our binary gender categories on which "hierarchy" and "complementarity" are erected. Whether or not archaeological authors intend this reductionism, it is inescapable that broad characterizations across large numbers of separate sociohistoric groups and an averaging of behaviors across many discrete contexts within each must also homogenize "women" and "men" to the same crude essences of gender roles and gender ideologies. Nor is the point whether we can recognize variants of the dominant gender categories in archaeology; rather, it is important at least that we conceptualize our subject matter in ways that honor how gender performances and gender ideologies actually operate in the real world.

What, then, are we to do with the broad characterizations of gender that we inherit as folk categories in everyday life? We must admit that the actions taken by individuals in their performance of gender accords with, is guided by, and is "taught" through existing cultural norms, constraints, and advice. Individuals perform gender in some ways and not in others in part because gender norms do exist, and it becomes a shortcut in social science to generalize and give concrete form to these constrained, encouraged, and normalized performances as "gender roles" and "gender ideology." However, the variability in gender performances of individuals in any given social system is not predicted by gender norms, just as disbursement around a mean is not predicted from the value of that mean, and categorizing entire cultural systems by simple binary designations risks a distortion of the very nature of gender performance. While there may be some utility to classifications, it also behooves us to probe alternative ways to get beyond the problems general to all categorization schemes and to all lumping strategies in social science.

ALTERNATIVE NONCATEGORICAL SCHEMES
FOR STUDYING GENDER:
STUDIES FROM YUTOPIAN

If we reject the focus on broad comparative characterizations of "systems," another tack that is frequently adopted in "engendering" the archaeological record is to generalize about women's status relative to men's status within specific gender systems; indeed, this approach is taken in many studies of prehistoric social contexts. Theoretically, this approach avoids the problems of lumping together too much variability under classes of gender systems called "hierarchical" or "complementary" and focuses more immediately on female and male access to power within a single sociohistoric instance. As tempting as this tack may be, it unfortunately embodies many of the same failures that we just reviewed in relation to the use of a binary classification of gender systems. Elsewhere (Gero 2001), one of us has argued that even within local gender systems, we are on a wrong track to collapse the many gendered activities and gendered spaces represented in specific archaeological instances into such variables as "status," determining whether women's "status" is higher or lower than men's. Neither status nor power are best understood as homogenized, monolithic notions that can be read like degrees of heat from a thermometer for different sociohistoric moments; such abstracted notions ignore the complex, sometimes contradictory areas of authority, autonomy, and control that women and men hold within any single society, a situation that is better described as the mosaic quality of gendered status and power.

We want to argue, then, that our most satisfying results may come from concentrating on local manifestations of prehistoric gender, disentangling the various ways that gender organizes social life. Because gender is such a central organizational feature of all societies, it will be manifest in many areas; these might include, but are certainly not exhausted by, the following:

1. The public roles or offices that must be filled, sometimes by single genders but always with more or less well-defined gender boundaries for these, with even strong gender tendencies sometimes violated by opportunistic recruitment for such offices and roles based on nongender criteria, such as birthright, kin relations, and experience.
2. The symbolic valuing of activities, as in what work is considered important and central, critical to the ongoing success of social/political/ economic/"meaningful" life as opposed to undertakings that are routine, "fail-safe," or taken for granted.
3. The on-the-ground organization of work that focuses on caloric output or material production by gender or that asks where gender activities are

segregated by task or, alternatively, integrated across gender lines—the degree to which specific tasks require gender integration/segregation.

4. The use of gendered representations or images in public and private contexts, inquiring how closely the represented images match social realities, where and in what directions distortions are introduced (and why), and under whose control is the production of gendered images.

5. Mortuary practices (a popular research direction because skeletons can be sexed and relatively easily associated with material and expressive cultural artifacts), where subtle investigations of the intersections of age, class, and gender can be discerned.

Any of these would yield a continuum of gender expressions and meanings rather than a dichotomy of classes of types of systems.

We propose that the archaeological study of gender is best served by moving in this direction. In the remainder of this chapter, we build on our research in Argentina, rejecting generalizations about male or female "status" (although the data could be used to construct such arguments) and avoiding making the data speak to "complementary" or "hierarchical" gender relations. Instead, we take up the question of gendered labor required by specific household undertakings. Since much of the analysis for these materials has yet to be undertaken, we offer this example of noncategorical analysis in still rather general terms.

LOCATING GENDER AT YUTOPIAN

In the chronology of northwestern Argentina, early formative society (600 B.C.–A.D. 600) is characterized as being made up of segmentary, egalitarian, self-sufficient groups, always in low densities, with strong regional or microregional characteristics. Settlements are idealized as replicative, dispersed individual or clustered domestic structures, either freestanding or with walled agricultural fields adjoining them, although only a few examples of these have been excavated (Berberian et al. 1989; Scattolin 1990; Nuñez Regueiro 1998; Albeck, in press). In the central area of northwestern Argentina, the circulation of exotic goods, including complex ceramics such as Condorhuasi polychrome and Candelaria modeled wares, copper and gold adornments, and bronze bracelets and bells, is well known for the early formative period, although often these elaborated goods lack excavated provenience (Tarragó and Scattolin 1999).

In 1994, 1996, and 1998, we undertook excavations at the early agricultural site of Yutopian located 3,000 meters above sea level in the Valle del Cajón, province of Catamarca, in northwestern Argentina (fig. 9.1). Yutopian is located in the south of the valley on its western margin, situated on a sharply defined ridge that stands out against a gently sloping plain. The variable stone constructions on the hilltop and upper slopes of the site cover an area of some 300 by 100 meters and appear to represent 10 more or less distinct clusters of aggregated structures and enclosures. The eastern side of the ridge has been modified to a series of elongated agricultural terraces. Dense surface concentrations of decorated sherds correspond to various recognized regional types of pottery of early and late periods, and lithic materials, including tools, flakes, and debitage, are especially abundant and varied.

A series of test pits laid across the site revealed stratigraphic differences and allowed us to propose that the most recent occupations had been located in the extreme south of the site, that the central area of the site represented the superimposition of late occupations on top of earlier ones, and that the extreme northern end of the site was occupied exclusively by early formative households without subsequent reoccupation by later peoples. When the bottom of

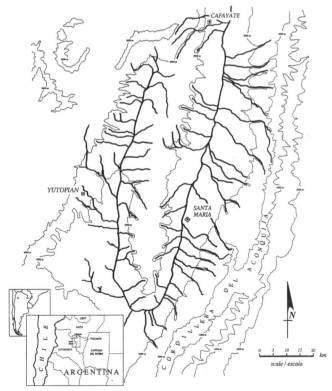

Figure 9.1.   Location of the site of Yutopian, province of Catamarca, northwestern Argentina.

a test pit in the northern portion of the site revealed a large grinding stone (*conana*) with a ground stone pestle (mano) still resting in its concavity as though it had just been used, we began to focus our excavations in a northern cluster of related enclosures that we call Sector III (fig. 9.2).

By now, five years later, we have excavated four well-preserved, abandoned early formative period (200 B.C.–A.D. 500) semisubterranean house floors from which we can read a range of gendered activities (Gero and Scattolin, in press). Three structures (structures 1, 2, and 3) are clustered together, sharing a common patio area, while the fourth structure, farthest north, is apparently without other adjacent structures, although it exhibits a well-defined, partially enclosed patio area where many activities were evidently carried out. For the

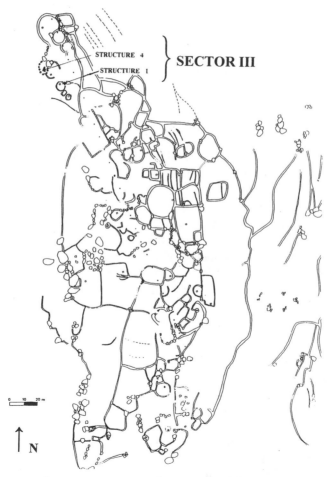

Figure 9.2. Yutopian site map, showing Sector III.

purposes of this chapter, we will not report fully on the frequency and distributions of the many classes of artifacts that relate to activities within the Yutopian early formative houses; rather, we will concentrate on two distinctive classes of features that suggest contrasting gendered arrangements.

From structure 1, a cluster of four *conana* grinding stones was recovered, concentrated in the northwestern sector of the structure, one with its mano still within it (visible in our first test pits) while other manos were close by. These are distinguished from a fifth grinding stone, not only by location but also by form and size: The concentrated *conanas* are larger and oval in form, and their central concavity presents a larger grinding surface, while the fifth grinding stone is smaller, round, and removed from the others in its position near the entrance to the structure. Among the concentrated *conanas,* differences can be noted in size, area of grinding surface, and degree of use. It seems evident that this area is related to food preparation, most likely the grinding of corn, which is the most profusely represented botanical remain in our collections (Meldem 1995; Rossen 1998), although some of the largest bone remains from the living floor were also recovered from this northwestern sector of structure 1.

In many interpretations of gendered activities, the four clustered conanas would be associated with the work of women, and their concentrated location on the same occupation floor would also suggest that they were in use simultaneously. These interpretations are well within the confidence range that we expect in archaeology, given the worldwide association between women and the grinding of grains and given the interpretive conventions that govern spatial associations among artifacts. Thus, we recognize here a communal mode of food production, where several women apparently worked together to feed several households or to feed an extended household; the alternative explanation—that the clustered grinding stones represent more "specialized" preparation of food, with a single woman grinding different foods in each of the different conanas but all intended for a single and smaller consumption unit—is less likely, given the overarching similarities among the four conanas. Although we assign this work to a group of women without questioning the internal relations among them, we know that within the traditionally recognized binary gender categories, much internal diversity exists. Weismantel's (1989) ethnography of the domestic cycle of Andean households, for instance, illustrates young married daughters and/or daughters-in-law sharing hearths and grinding stones with their mothers or mothers-in-law and demonstrates distinctions among the women of a single household, showing the interplays of generational differentiation, power, positioning, and status between them.

In addition to the clustered grinding stones, we have also located two raised, ringed hearths of fire-hardened clay in the central areas of structures 1 and 4, each with upright stones firmly fixed in their centers to support a cook pot (fig. 9.3). Associated with these well-preserved features were fragments of heavily

Figure 9.3.   Yutopian, structure 1, with central hearth.

burnt bone and other vegetative food remains: The area around the structure 1 hearth was associated with carbonized corn and beans (Meldem 1995), while the structure 4 hearth was associated with beans and considerable quantities of rinds from the chañar fruit (Rossen 1998), suggesting the preparation of a brewed and fermented beverage, which is primarily how this plant is consumed today. It can be expected that the stages of food preparation represented at and around the hearth also might be gendered as female spaces and might again refer us back to the segregation of gender tasks in household labor.

However, the hearth in structure 1 was also associated with a more remarkable find: an appreciable quantity of lightweight, glassy bubbles of scoria, analyzed as clay-soil particles that had been vitrified at 1,000 degrees Celsius (1,800 degrees Fahrenheit), a temperature significantly above that reached in normal cooking fires. To achieve this intense localized heat, the hearth fire would have had to have been blown at its center, underscoring the significance of the associated fragments of ceramic tubes, also recovered in association with the hearth levels in structure 4. Significantly, small samples of raw copper silicates embedded in an impure, quartz-containing parent rock (Vandiver and Gero, in press) were also recovered from the structure 1 hearth area, and from the neighboring structure 2 came two fragmented polished stone laminating hammers. Thus, we are able to suggest that at least the structure 1 hearth, already recognized as having been used for food preparation, also represents some stage of pyrotechnical processing to produce copper artifacts. Metal production sites for the early formative are rare and occur in other known cases near sources of copper, apparently on a larger scale of production. In fact, metal-working specialists have been proposed for the early formative period (González 1994), and metallurgical workshops have at least tentatively been identified (Nuñez Regueiro 1998: 223–28).

Thus, Yutopian's domestic structures yield evidence of two distinct productive activities undertaken in household contexts: first, the grinding of grains as an aspect of food production, seemingly undertaken by aggregate women for an indeterminate number of other, non–grain-preparing persons, and, second, metallurgy, seemingly intended for circulation and consumption outside Yutopian and not undertaken uniformly by all households but rather only in certain prominently situated and especially well constructed structures.

GENDER AS AN ORGANIZING PRINCIPLE IN YUTOPIAN EARLY FORMATIVE HOUSEHOLDS: WHICH CATEGORIES, IF ANY?

Avoiding questions about status or hierarchy, we are still interested in knowing how gender organizes—and is organized by—these distinct productive activities. That is, we start by looking at how gendered people of different ages and ranks are segregated and "specialized" by specific activities (such as corn grinding) and how, at the same time, gendered individuals of different ages and ranks are integrated by activities that crosscut gendered categories. In this way, we get closer to understanding not only the gendered domestic arrangements at a site such as Yutopian but also to what exactly gender is and how it functions. Moreover, we can continue to observe how conventional, supposedly gender-neutral categories (even beyond the categories of "status," "hierarchy," and "complementarity") risk obscuring these dynamics.

Let us consider how the work at Yutopian is preconfigured by the particular set of concepts known as "specialization." It is interesting to note that in associating women with corn grinding, we might argue that women specialize in this domestic work, that women "specialists" undertake the task of preparing grains for household food consumption. However, classic definitions of specialization preclude this by positing a basic categorical opposition between "domestic" labor and "specialist" labor. Household food production ("domestic" labor) is not specialized, however intensified and spatially segregated it might be and however delimited the production personnel might be (composed, for example, solely of older, married individuals of a single gender). Metallurgy, on the other hand, undertaken to produce a product that circulates outside the household, does qualify as "specialist," even though work may involve nonsegregated household personnel and even though production overlaps in space and indeed uses the same built facilities as "nonspecialized" tasks. Costin (1991: 4) is quite clear on this point: "Division of labor by sex and age within the household is basic to all human societies and must be excluded from the definition of specialization." Even more emphatically, Clark and Parry (1990: 297) tell us, "Craft specialization is production of alienable, durable goods for *nondependent* consumption [emphasis added]. . . . We consider production specialized only if the consumers are not members of the producer's household; if the consumers and producers are members of the same household, production is not considered specialized."

Thus, the notion of "craft specialization," derived and defined for examining stratified societies, dismisses household divisions of labor as irrelevant and relegates such labor to ongoing background work that varies only in uninteresting ways. The household itself, taken for granted as persistent, stable, and static, becomes a "black box" (Weismantel 1989: 55) in the socioeconomic landscape of specialized labor. By posing "domestic" production as a binary opposite to "specialized" production, the two kinds of productive systems become noncomparable.

However, in fact, if we take Costin's widely cited definition of specialization and merely omit the "extrahousehold" requirement, we find a perfectly fine description of food provisioning by (some) women to the rest of the resident group: "Specialization is a differentiated, regularized, permanent and perhaps institutionalized production system in which producers depend on . . . exchange relationships at least in part for their livelihood, and consumers depend on them for acquisition of goods they do not produce themselves" (Costin 1991: 4). Food-preparing labor is indeed differentiated, regularized, permanent, and institutionalized; producers make their livelihoods doing it (quite literally), and consumers depend on this system to acquire goods that they themselves do not produce. Opposing a "sexual division of labor" to "specialized" labor is achieved entirely and merely by arbitrarily closing the unit of analysis at or above the level of the household, effectively precluding full-time "women food preparers" from being specialists. Yet the social dynamics of dependency and exchange and the fulfilling of specific and regularized labor tasks by prescribed personnel are strongly parallel in intra- and extrahousehold production relationships.

Ultimately, what is fascinating about Yutopian, then, is that the dynamics of dependency and exchange seem to operate in two distinct patterns of productive household activity. The grinding of corn, a task that is carried out by individual adult married women (who may work together), segregates the household work group by age, sex, and space; it distinguishes, marks, and fixes interdependent "difference" within households and thus creates and sustains intergenerational and intergender dependencies within households.

The dynamics of intrahousehold dependency for copper working, however, are different. Copper working is not a uniform activity carried out by replicative individual specialists who are specially marked by or for this one activity. Instead, copper working involves a nonlinear series of tasks, including the location and transport of primary materials, the grinding of minerals, the manufacture of crucibles and molds, the collection of firewood, the maintenance of an intensified fire, the elaboration of final forms, the adding of decorative elements, and so on, which together imply the cooperative, integrated participation of interdependent individuals across age and sex lines. While we cannot know for sure which household individuals participated in these chores, the nature of the tasks involved makes it logical to suppose that the labor of different age and sex groups was involved and combined, a supposition that is supported by the lack of spatial segregation of these activities. Indeed, the focusing of this work in the center of the structure as opposed to its isolation in one delimited area of the structure, as well as its dependency on facilities used in other productive activities, again argues for an integration of copper work into other household activities and personnel. Copper working thus blends "difference" within productive households and enmeshes a given household into a larger system of dependencies with other households.

CONCLUSIONS

In this chapter, we have argued that binary classifications of gender systems into "complementary" and "hierarchical" classes and the recognition of "male dominance" or greater male status within hierarchical systems neglect critical areas of gender arrangements where authority and autonomy, control and knowledge, are distributed in a more fine-grained manner among gendered participants. Crosscutting, sometimes contradicting, the ideologies of prestige, power, and status are practical arrangements taken on by gendered personnel that often give significant control over resources and independence of action to the "dominated" gender. Not only do we fail to see how action and responsibilities are distributed across genders in such analyses, but characterizations of sociocultural systems in such gross, generalizing manners fail to illuminate how gender arrangements are integral to, underpin, and substantiate basic social structures. The analysis of gendered household activities at Yutopian was undertaken to illustrate such fundamental structural principles at work.

When we examine gendered arrangements at the household level at Yutopian, we find that production can be broadly outlined to operate on (at least) two very distinct dynamic principles. On the one hand, household labor is segregated or divided by gender (i.e., a division of labor) to create separate, marked, and specialized workforces that are interdependent for some vital needs. On the other hand, household labor is integrated by gender to bind personnel into a larger operating body vis-à-vis other similar coordinated household units. Both forms of productive organization, a "division of gendered labor" and an "integration of gendered labor," share a single primary social product at the household level: the creation of mutual ties and obligations along crosscutting axes of social integration. These distinct and interdependent processes are obscured or obliterated by defining away domestic labor as nonspecialized, just as they are obscured by characterizing gender relations as "complementary" or nonhierarchical.

That divided labor and integrative labor operate at different levels of society is a familiar observation, even where the household has been considered an indivisible social unit: Food "sharing" integrates the household, while producing and circulating copper artifacts integrates the larger community of dispersed households. However, at Yutopian we observe that both systems of production act together to intensify household cohesion, importantly along different axes of age, gender, and kin. Household forms and household work are explained and illuminated rather than assumed and obscured under generality, and it is the close attention to gender that reveals how social structures are organized, maintained, and reproduced.

ACKNOWLEDGMENTS

Warmest thanks to Sarah Nelson and Myriam Rosen-Ayalon for the opportunity afforded to Gero to participate in the Bellagio conference in its magnificent setting and to all the participants, especially Cheryl Claassen and Peggy Nelson, for their constructive commentary. Dr. Pamela Vandiver of the Conservation Analytical Laboratory at the Smithsonian Institution performed the remarkable analysis of the scoria and related materials from the hearth in structure 1, for which we are especially grateful. Floor plans for all structures were done by Josh Fletcher.

10

The Enigma of Gender in the Archaeological Record of the Andaman Islands

Zarine Cooper

INTRODUCTION

Among hunter-gatherer communities, few have generated as much debate and interest as the Andaman Islanders. In order to elucidate their origins, archaeological investigations were undertaken in the Andamans by Cooper (1985, 1987). As a result, numerous shell middens were brought to light, as well as a cave site, thereby attesting to the existence of human habitation in all the major islands (Cooper 1990, 1993a). The Andaman middens, which do not exceed 2,200 years in age, are constituted of molluscan and vertebrate remains and are rich in pottery as well as in artifacts of shell, bone, and stone. Such accumulations are associated with long-term occupation in the form of either a communal hut or a cluster of shelters. The locations of these encampments are primarily determined by the availability of freshwater (for further details on the functional attributes of middens, see Cooper 1994).

Thus, midden archaeology is essentially the investigation of refuse or discard and not of the area of habitation per se. In the absence of meaningful artifact associations on a three-dimensional scale, the densely packed matrix of the Andaman middens is only amenable to the analysis, on a temporal scale, of morphological and other changes within individual artifact categories. There is no doubt that while such sites can yield valuable information on subsistence patterns and local ecological factors, evidence of social organization, mythological beliefs, and linguistic groupings would not survive.

Keeping these limitations in mind, any attempt to explore an archaeological perspective on the role of women and the issue of gender relevant to the society of the Andaman Islanders would have to rely on the available anthropological literature, including recent observations of Onge encampments (Cooper 1994, 1997a). As these records can enhance archaeological interpretation, they will be used to define the functions of certain artifacts from archaeological contexts in relation to the sexual division of labor and to their symbolic value, if any.

In this connection, I am well aware of the epistemological pitfall of viewing gender as a static category of analysis wherein the socioeconomic milieu in which specific genders are associated with artifacts or technologies is not explained (Dobres 1995: 42). Instead, objects imbued with gendered symbolism will be highlighted with a view to understanding the characteristics of gender relationships among the Andaman Islanders and their perceptions of the remnants of their past. As "gender processes concern dynamic strategies of social identity, whether consciously or tacitly negotiated," the past can be engendered (Dobres 1995: 42).

The data reviewed in this presentation have been recovered from two excavated sites, namely, the midden at Chauldari in South Andaman Island and Hava Beel cave on Baratang Island.

CHAULDARI

The shell midden at Chauldari is 4.5 meters high and is located about 300 meters away from the mangrove-fringed shore of Flat Bay (Cooper 1987, 1990). During the earlier phase of occupation (2.2 to 4.5 m), species belonging to rocky shores and estuaries, such as *Saccostrea cucullata, Nerita lineata,* and *Thais luteostoma,* are dominant, while during the later occupational period, the mudflats seem to have been increasingly exploited for bivalves such as *Marcia recens, Anadara granosa, Anadara antiquata,* and *Scapharca (Cunearca) congrua.* The lowest deposit has been dated to 2,280 ± 90 years b.p.

There is a distinct break in the sequence of occupation at a depth of 2.1 meters (2,070± 100 years b.p.), probably as a result of exposure and pedogenic change. This is supported by the chemical and mineral analysis of the soil as well as by X-ray diffraction studies of shells that indicate that aragonite dominates in all the layers, except at 2.1 meters, wherein the presence of calcite has been detected.

SHELL ARTIFACTS FROM CHAULDARI

As shell is the principal visible constituent of this and other middens, its economic and social significance will be discussed first. Regarding artifacts, only 177 shells exhibited evidence of deliberate modification and/or use. Although these specimens comprise a mere 2.18 percent of the mollusk collection from Chauldari, current knowledge of the indigenous economy suggests that shell constituted one of the most important raw materials for the manufacture of tools and ornaments (Cooper 1988).

The present review will focus on two principal artifact categories from this site: first, bivalves with use wear on their margins and, second, perforated shells. For the sake of convenience, the pieces used as ornaments have also been classified as artifacts.

Bivalves with Use Wear

Dominant among these is the *Polymesoda coaxans* (Gmelin), which is identified by Man (1883: 376) and Radcliffe-Brown (1922: 447) as Cyrena. The shell functioned as a knife, scraper, and spoon and formed an essential part of men's hunting gear (Man 1883: 363). Small wonder then that it was always "to be found lying about their [Andaman Islanders'] encampments" (Radcliffe-Brown 1922: 447). The bivalve appears to have been primarily utilized for a wide range of woodworking activities, inspiring Man (1883: 376) to observe "that among their savage arts there is probably nothing so calculated to surprise and interest a stranger as the many and clever uses to which necessity has taught them to put this simple but highly effective tool."

As a spoon, the use of the *Polymesoda* was not restricted to either sex. However, tasks such as the cutting of thatching leaves, shredding *Tetranthera* wood, butchering animals, making bows and arrows, and sharpening bamboo knives and the inner edge of a boar's tusk in order to use it as a spokeshave were generally undertaken by men. The ubiquity of this bivalve is best reflected in the pleasure it afforded young men when testing their powers in throwing long distances to send shells of *P. coaxans* "skimming through the air," the convex side being held uppermost (Man 1883: 387).

With regard to activities that were performed exclusively by women, using the *P. coaxans,* they involved severing the umbilical cord after the birth of a child, cleaning newly born infants, and preparing the fiber of the *Gnetum edule* for the manufacture of fishing nets and sleeping mats. As these items were made only by women, the collection and processing of the trailers of *G. edule* were entirely their responsibility. On the other hand, it was the duty of the male members of a group to procure branches of the *Melochia velutina,* the fibers of which were utilized in making cinctures, harpoon lines, and turtle nets.

There are two noteworthy aspects of the value in which *P. coaxans* was regarded. First, important though it was as a tool, it was nevertheless expendable, as this species is a mud and mangrove dweller and would have been easily available since a major part of the coastline of the Andamans is fringed by mangroves. In areas where this mollusk was not readily accessible, it was usually obtained through trade. This probably explains its presence throughout the sequence at Chauldari, albeit in negligible quantities, which is significant, especially in regard to the consistent occurrence of differential wear patterns on the margins of the specimens in question.

Second, in terms of its symbolic value, a *Polymesoda* shell was required to be placed in one of the hands of a dead person at the time of burial, presumably to help the deceased in the afterlife; the bivalve was replaced by a steel knife after the establishment of the British penal settlement in 1858, when metal was easily available (Radcliffe-Brown 1922: 106). One of these bivalves was also supposed to be held by a male dancer during the performance of certain ritual dances (Radcliffe-Brown 1922: 165). In addition, we are informed that when people were swimming in shark-infested waters, shells of this species were attached to belts with fibers of the *Anadendron paniculatum* in the belief that they frightened sharks away (Man 1883: 384). Even medicinal properties were attributed to the *Polymesoda,* the heated shell of which was used to cauterize a wound caused by a thorn, stone, or shell.

It is interesting to note that although the society of the Andaman Islanders is by and large egalitarian economically, there is a marked sexual division of labor, about which more will be said later. In light of this, it appears that subsistence activities, the undertaking of which were determined by the sex of the persons concerned, came to be associated with the tools specific to the their execution. This in turn extended to the raw materials involved and the procurement and processing of the same.

As in the case of the *P. coaxans,* an item of economic significance assumed symbolic value that in turn acquired overtones of gender by virtue of its relation to the sexually determined allocation of certain tasks. This apparently did not apply to artifacts such as clay pots, which were made by both men and women (Man 1883: 399; Radcliffe-Brown 1922: 473). Moreover, the *Polymesoda* seems exceptional in that its collection was not restricted to either sex, although its use as a knife and scraper was restricted largely to men. Perhaps this accounts for its use by male dancers and the superstition concerning sharks. With respect to the latter, it was the men who undertook fishing and turtling in deep waters, whereas the women specialized in the collection of mollusks for food purposes and in fishing with hand nets in shallow water, either in the sea or in streams.

Perforated Shells

In this category, the deposits after the break in occupation yielded mostly bivalves, while gastropods dominate in the lower half of the midden. The bivalves are characterized by holes on or near the umbo that resulted from scratching away the surface prior to or in the process of gouging it.

Among the 29 gastropods, all except one belong to *Nerita lineata*. Most of these are represented by apertures, necklaces of which are still worn by Jarawa men and women, as corroborated by photographic records and personal observations. It is important to note that most of the *N. lineata* shells were recovered from the lower part of the Chauldari midden, which accounts for the preponderance of the perforated specimens in this section. This is the only instance, in this site, where the total number of shells of a particular mollusk, which are concentrated within certain archaeological deposits, seems to have influenced the percentage and distribution of artifacts that were made from them (*Saccostrea cucullata* and *N. lineata* comprise 76.34 percent of the sample from the lower levels). On the whole, however, all the bivalves and gastropods, with the exception of *P. coaxans,* were primarily exploited for food, and some of the shells were used as artifacts only after the removal and consumption of the flesh. In this connection, it may be noted that the collection of shellfish for food was undertaken by women, as was the manufacture of ornaments of shell, fiber, or any other material (Man 1883: 330; Radcliffe-Brown 1922: 44).

BONE TOOLS

Out of the 197 bones from the Chauldari midden, 168 (85 percent) are of *Sus scrofa*. Among these, 118 (73.24 percent) were recovered from the lower levels (2 to 4.5 meters). These included 32 charred bones of *S. scrofa,* which accords well with the preponderance of charred shells in the lower horizons. The remaining bones belong to a variety of animals, including dog, monitor lizard, and rodents.

As with the molluscan remains, the artifacts of bone are by-products resulting from the processing of various faunal species that contributed to the local diet. Teeth constitute the most commonly occurring elements among the bones of *S. scrofa*.

The 12 artifacts (6.09 percent of the total bone collection) are evenly distributed throughout the sequence. Six of these are barbs and have been chiseled out of pig and rodent incisors as well as long-bone fragments. The others are pointed tools or gouges that represent pieces of the ulna, tibia, radius, and femur of *S. scrofa*.

The barbs were in all likelihood fashioned by men for their arrows. The gouging tools may have been shaped by men as well as women. Just as incisors could function as barbs, a boar's tusk made an effective spokeshave, especially for the purpose of planing bows and paddles (Radcliffe-Brown 1922: 448). In this connection, mention may be made of a partly broken, but much used, upper-right canine of *S. scrofa* that was found in an exposed section of the midden near Beehive Hill on Middle Andaman Island (Cooper 1987: 90). Interestingly, such teeth were sharpened with a quartz flake or a *Polymesoda* shell.

Among the other bones from Chauldari is the vertebra of a monitor lizard (*Varanus* sp.) from a depth of 1.1 meters. Not only did these reptiles form a part of the local diet, but their vertebrae were strung into necklaces.

Although shaving and scarification were carried out by women, the cuts down a man's back were always made by a male friend with the help of an arrow meant for hunting pig (Man 1883: 332). In this case, the arrowhead would have been of iron, as are those made by the Jarawa, Sentinalese, and Onge today. Formerly, however, bone or stone arrowheads may have been used.

Other "Functions" of Bone

It was, and still is, customary to preserve the skulls of pigs and turtles as trophies. These are suspended from the roofs of shelters but would eventually end up in a midden. Perhaps this explains the presence of numerous pigs' teeth mentioned previously. In regard to the part of the skull that was to be preserved, traditions varied among different groups. For example, the Onge are known to have preserved only the mandibles of pigs, while the Great Andamanese preferred to keep the skulls. The Jarawa, on the other hand, were accustomed to binding both the skull and the mandible with strips of cane (Cipriani 1953: 74). The survival of traditions in this regard, despite contact with outsiders, was proved by the recent observation of six pig mandibles suspended from the roof of an Onge communal hut that was meant to be reoccupied (Cooper 1994: 252). In addition, three turtle skulls were stored in a basket. Similar trophies were absent from the temporary encampment that was in use during my visit.

The fact that middens actually reflected prowess in hunting and that these perceptions changed over time is indicated by Man (1885: 269): "Whereas in the olden days they [the Andaman Islanders] were able to regard the slowly increasing heap with pride as witnessing to the success and skill in hunting and fishing of the community near whose encampment it was situated, nowadays all cause for boasting regarding their achievements is considered at an end in consequence of the material assistance they receive from the dogs we have given them, and the superiority of the weapons they have been able to manufacture from iron obtained from the Homes."

Apart from faunal remains, it is not unusual to find human bones in a midden (Cipriani 1966: 76), although none were found at Chauldari. In Little Andaman, burials generally took place within a hut, whereas elsewhere in the Archipelago this practice was carried out away from the camp, which was abandoned only in the event of the death of an adult (Radcliffe-Brown 1922: 107). In fact, Man (1883: 144) asserted that "none save infants are buried within the encampment."

What is even more interesting is the practice of exhuming the bones of the dead a few months after burial. The skull would then be cleaned and decorated with ochre as well as strings of shell and would be worn around the neck of the nearest relative of the deceased (Man 1883: 143). This honor was accorded to any person who had died, regardless of sex or age. The other bones were converted into necklaces by the female relatives and distributed among friends who treasured them for their curative properties and to ward off evil spirits (Man 1883: 86). "Like all their other possessions these relics are lent or exchanged, passing from one person to another, until sometimes a skull may be found in the possession of a man who does not know to whom it belonged" (Radcliffe-Brown 1922: 113). It is only natural that, with the passing of time and memories, a bone necklace would lose its value and be discarded, perhaps to be replaced with one representing a recently deceased person.

It is indeed ironic that whereas faunal remains would be associated with a particular encampment, the human skeletal parts in a midden may belong to members of other groups. Moreover, their variable occurrence would not be determined by the modes of disposing of the dead but by the fragmentation and distribution of the bones of people, regardless of sex or age, from diverse locales.

Thus, faunal remains resulting from hunting expeditions were differentially modified and manipulated, as was the case with mollusks. Artifacts such as barbs, points, and necklaces or belts of animal bone were related to subsistence activities and, in respect of personal decoration, to the social sphere. From the practical point of view, tasks were divided between men and women; the latter being responsible largely for ornamentation, including body paint.

Hunting trophies notwithstanding, an ever-growing pile of bones was a source of pride for the entire community. However, as a repository of the remnants of ancestors, a midden constituted a direct link with the past (Cooper 1993b: 265). The Andaman Islanders therefore perceived a midden not merely as a heap of waste but as an ancient encampment (*bud l'artam*) (Man 1883: 78). This perception was that of the group as a whole, whereas the process of discarding waste entailed collective effort in which the issue of gender simply did not arise.

STONE TOOLS

The 12 stone tools from Chauldari are representative of almost all the deposits and include one hammerstone of porphyritic diorite, five flaked quartz pebbles, two pointed artifacts (one on jasper and the other on serpentine), and four quartz chips. The reliance on shell artifacts, as well as on those made of bamboo and hardwoods, probably explains the paucity of stone implements on this site.

An analysis of these as well as of similar collections from other sites supports the view that the industry as a whole is amorphous. Flakes with sharp edges were generally used for shaving purposes, cutting fingernails, and sharpening boar's tusks, while those that were naturally pointed served as implements for scarification (Man 1883: 380; Radcliffe-Brown 1922: 445). Tattooing and scarification were practiced by the Great Andamanese, though not by the Onge. However, stone flakes and chips were used for shaving by all the Andaman Islanders, and this was a task that was undertaken generally by women, who were also responsible for removing the hair of a newborn child (Man 1883: 334–35, 380).

Interestingly enough, one chert flake and one on quartz showed positive indications of the presence of human haemoglobin (T. Loy, personal communication). Another chert flake appeared to be coated with a protein film and bore striations having subparallel inner striae. Although the source of these residues is yet to be determined, the implications of such research in determining the functions of artifacts are far-reaching.

Stone was not only easily expendable but was readily substituted by flakes derived from the thick bases of beer and wine bottles, which became abundantly available after 1858 (Cooper and Bowdler 1998).

Considering that stone was relatively insignificant in the technological repertoire of the Andaman Islanders, one can understand why it could be so easily replaced throughout the archipelago. This raises the question as to whether it would be possible to relinquish the bow and arrow, of which there are several kinds, if a more effective weapon were available, especially in light of the fact that archery was, and is, regarded as belonging to a man's domain through which his manhood or adulthood could be proven. This query assumes significance given an Onge hunter's statement "that in some cases when a pack of dogs cornered a pig, the latter could easily be dispatched with a *dhou* [large chopping knife], thus rendering the bow and arrow quite redundant" (Cooper 1994: 242).

It is interesting that customs relating to the socioreligious sphere, such as the preservation of animal skulls, as witness to successful hunts, have continued up to the present day, whereas objects concerned purely with subsistence strategies, such as clay pots (see Cooper and Raghavan 1989) and stone tools, were unhesitatingly dropped despite having survived in the economy for over two millennia.

In this regard, the archaeological data from the Andamans reflect "the readiness with which ideas and innovations can be adopted, while others are eschewed or ignored. . . . The utilitarian value of any object would probably be measured in terms of the prevalent social, religious and economic concepts of a society. . . . Thus, society as a whole was characterized by an insular structure which was, however, versatile enough to permit the infiltration of certain introductions such as canoes and pottery, though probably through widely different channels of communication, and at different periods in the course of history" (Cooper 1989: 144).

HAVA BEEL CAVE

This large limestone cave (42 meters long, 9.3 meters wide) is named after the *hava beel* (white-nest swiftlet [*Collocalia fuciphaga inexpectata* Hume]). As the nests constitute a highly valued delicacy in Southeast Asia, the Andaman Islands have always attracted Malays, Burmese, and Chinese visitors who are known to have been well acquainted with Hava Beel. It was also reported to be a Jarawa encampment until as recently as the 1950s. The basal date of 1,540 ± 110 years b.p. for Hava Beel cave compares well with the ages of the middens at Wot-a-emi as well as at Beehive Hill and Yerata Nala in Middle Andaman Island (Cooper 1993a).

A 2-meter-wide and 4.4-meter-deep trench exposed lenses of dark organic matter deposited on a clay pellet matrix to a depth of 3.5 meters. A piece of bamboo was recovered from a layer 58 centimeters below the surface of the cave floor and uncharred wood fragments from 78 centimeters. In addition, sieved soil samples yielded microscopic plant remains that have yet to be identified (Cooper and Raghavan 1988).

Lumps of resin from the first meter of deposit below the surface were tentatively identified by Fourier-transform infrared spectroscopy as from a tree of the genus *Dipterocarp* (Cooper 1993a). However, it is possible that the sample is of the tree *Canarium euphyllum,* the resin of which is used by the Andaman Islanders to make torches.

The absence from the deposits of pottery, faunal remains, or stone and bone tools suggests that the main Jarawa encampment was located outside the cave, as attested by the scatter of mollusk shells outside the entrance and the location of a shell midden about 100 meters away. While it is possible that the Jarawa occupied the cave for short periods of time, one cannot rule out the possibility that it was frequently visited by Malay and Burmese collectors of swiftlets' nests.

The contents of this cave contrast sharply with those of middens in that it is associated with a transient Jarawa camp, albeit one that was also used by outsiders for another purpose. The midden, which is small, suggests that a few Jarawa women accompanied the men, and while the latter were out hunting, the former collected mollusks and crabs in addition to catching small fish in the mangrove-fringed creek nearby. Foraging in the shallow waters of the mangroves and along the seashore was primarily the women's responsibility. Thus, division of labor in such a situation would once again be reflected through the distinction between the remains, in this case of large terrestrial fauna and those of aquatic species outside the cave. The plant material in the cave, however, cannot be entirely attributed to the Jarawa for the reasons already given.

With regard to subsistence, the economic contribution of women was on par with that of men in terms of the daily haul of aquatic fauna and plant foods. With reference to the Onge, Sarkar (1974: 586) observes that "when unfavourable weather prevents open sea fishing, the Onge for aquatic food are to depend only on the catches made by the females in the coastal belt. Thus by introducing the clear cut division of labour between the sexes and also their distinct operational zones, the Onge have ensured the regular supply of fish for their daily diet."

DISCUSSION

These data demonstrate the inherent flexibility in the organizational characteristics of hunter-gatherers. This is further exemplified by the Agta of eastern Luzon in the Philippines, among whom the division of labor is subject to individual needs and preferences whereby women adjust hunting and childrearing to each other and to their other subsistence efforts (Estioko-Griffin and Griffin 1981). In this system, hunting techniques are not determined by the sex of the hunter.

Research among the Kuruk fishermen of the Indravati valley in central India revealed that despite each family member having his or her share of household chores, there are no rigid rules that bind a person to a particular task in life, nor is there any well-defined hierarchy of economic organization within a community. Hence, work is divided among family members to suit their daily requirements in the most practical way, so that spontaneous cooperation in domestic and economic life becomes essential (Cooper 1997b: 88).

As a rule, however, important activities do entail a certain amount of division of labor between the sexes. Thus, the collection of edible plants is done mostly by women and children, while the men usually undertake the heavier tasks of setting drift nets, building weirs and traps, and hunting. This dichotomy in the allocation of vital tasks according to sex and age is apparently in the interests of achieving the highest level of efficiency and productivity, highlighting, as a result, the element of expediency underlying forager subsistence, in this case a subsection of the Maria Gonds of Bastar district (Cooper 1997b).

Whether it is among the Gonds or the Andaman Islanders, the contribution of random foraging, especially by children, is significant enough to warrant mention here. Time and again I have been amazed at the ability of young boys and girls to procure birds, fish, and other food. Some of these activities demand considerable skill, a fact that the adults seem to take for granted as being part of their daily routine. This "very real" contribution by children to a forager economy has often been overlooked, as pointed out by Gregg (1979–80: 130) with reference to the Semang of Malaysia. With respect to the Hill Pandaram of South India, "a major proportion of the animals captured or killed are secured during random foragings" by both men and boys (Morris 1982: 78). These factors need to be taken into consideration when attempting to correlate tool kits in an archaeological context with supposed male and female economic roles.

THE POSITION OF WOMEN AMONG THE ANDAMAN ISLANDERS

Despite the sexual division of labor, which also prevails among other hunter-gatherers, there was a generalized female involvement in ritual and political activities. In fact, women were never excluded from any of the rituals described by Man and Radcliffe-Brown,. The roles they played in these ceremonies suggest that they were equally important to and participated fully in the symbolic activities.

In the absence of institutionalized leadership, there were persons of influence who lacked enforceable authority and maintained their status through personal achievement, for example, hunting success, experience, and wisdom. An equivalent status position existed among women. In this connection, Radcliffe-Brown (1922: 134) records an instance when arrangements to end hostilities between groups were made by women. This was followed by a ceremonial dance in which the women of the visiting group not only participated but also gave the men of the other group a good shaking, perhaps as a reminder of their displeasure.

Although kinship was the basis of social organization, terms of address emphasized status and respect rather than denoting consanguinity. Moreover, status was strictly age related and was accorded to all senior persons, regardless of gender. Thus, generation grading, not gender distinctions, determined social differentiation among the Andaman Islanders.

Women played a particularly important role in two symbolic activities: scarification and other corporal decoration. Young girls and boys submitted to scarification from their early childhood. The most conspicuous gender distinction was manifest during the ceremony marking the end of the abstention from eating pork. During this occasion, a boar was killed for a young man and a sow for a girl; it was not necessary for both to undergo these rituals simultaneously. At the time of scarification, the cuts down a boy's back had to be made by a man with the sharp blade of a pig arrow, as mentioned earlier.

Clay decoration and patterns were executed during extremely elaborate ceremonies that intervened at intervals during the entire human cycle. These ceremonies included initiation at puberty for both boys and girls, marriage, end of mourning, and communal peacemaking. In addition, there were special occasions that required body painting and dancing, such as during illness, at meetings of different local groups, during the death of a relative, before burial, and after hunts and large meals of animal meat. Once again, women had the monopoly of this symbolic representation.

This suggests that women were not only included in the ritual human cycle but also directly concerned in fundamental activities. Since little is known about the values of the Andaman Islanders, my purpose is not so much to prove that the Andaman situation reflects one of male and female equality as to show that, within the scope of the information that was gathered, women created links of cooperation between persons, families, and even local groups. By their economic and specific ritual and political functions, they were major contributors to the economic/social life of the group.

Regarding sex roles, it must be emphasized that among the Andaman Islanders, both male and female roles, if differentiated, were essential to the whole group and mutually supportive. Every member of a group not only controlled his or her production of food and manufacture of goods but was equally responsible for ritual cooperation and peace. In this society, differentiation did not give way to demonstrations of superiority or prestige. For example, the husbands of Andamanese women are known to have shared with their wives the same prohibitions of food during pregnancy and to have attended the delivery of their children.

Public/familial spheres are often said to be universal opposites: Women are confined to childbearing, and men take care of political affairs and extracommunal problems. However, as we have just seen, among elders, decision making about production, distribution, settlements, disputes, and ritual feasts was often collective. Men individually made decisions about the activities for which they were responsible, and so did the women. At the ritual, political, and ideological levels, women performed the function of mediator and participated in public life, which apparently did not seem to lead to any conflicts between the sexes. The place of women in the society of the Andaman Islanders thus reflects the relations of equality, cooperation, and solidarity that foraging societies require.

In this respect, the position of women in the Andamans seems rather different from that of all other hunting-and-gathering societies in South and Southeast Asia. Although among communities such as the Birhor, Paliyan, Maria and Muria Gond, Semang, and Agta there appears to be an absence of systems indicating the control of men over women's labor and reproduction, there is no rigorous separation of men and women, and nowhere is there to be found such a specific inclusion of women in political as well as ritual life.

Why is this so? At this stage, it would be difficult to find a convincing answer, given the lack of a simple relationship between foraging as a subsistence mode and a specific pattern of social organization.

CONCLUDING REMARKS

Without referring to anthropological sources and recent surveys, it is impossible to discern sexual division of labor, particularly when the rough distinction between men's hunting and women's gathering technologies would be confounded with the variable tool emphases of the seasonal cycle.

However, subsistence strategy and local environmental adaptation are, to a great degree, preserved. Thus, the interpretable portion of the archaeological record is inherently skewed toward a representation of the general processes of cultural interaction with the environment and away from aspects of specific cultural idiosyncrasies less directly connected with the adaptive function.

To conclude, the Andaman midden deposits embody the culmination of collective effort in which gender is inherently indistinguishable, having been obfuscated through variable archaeological visibility and a socioreligious system wherein such distinctions are not fostered.

11

Gender Roles Depicted in Rock Art: A Case from Western Thailand

Rasmi Shoocongdej

INTRODUCTION

The study of gender has been recognized as an important part of anthropological research for many years. The study of gender roles has been of particular interest and has contributed to our understanding of broad anthropological questions such as the development of inequality and social complexity (e.g., Dahlberg 1981; Conkey and Spector 1984; Bacus et al. 1993). Cross-cultural comparative studies show that gender roles vary in groups with different environments, economies, and levels of social complexity (e.g., Johnson and Earle 1991). Generally, the study of gender roles has centered on identifying the characteristics of each gender and examining the dynamic interrelations of these in response to different conditions in their social and natural environments.

Unfortunately, it is not always easy to identify gender roles in the archaeological record. Besides mortuary evidence, rock art can assist archaeologists to understand social relationships between women and men in the past (e.g., Lewis-Williams 1983). Over the past three decades, numerous attempts have been made to study rock art in Thailand (e.g., Kanchanakom 1972; You-Di 1974; Na Nakorn Panom et al. 1979). However, this rock art research has focused mostly on typology, artistic technique, and design. In this research, very little attention has been paid to the study of gender roles.

This chapter attempts to examine gender roles in past societies through the examination of rock art in the late prehistoric period (4,000–2,000 years b.p.) in western Thailand. It will analyze the spatial distribution of rock art sites and will consider the designs themselves, allowing an investigation of the evidence for group-specific ritual performances. The rock art provides insights concerning the participation of women and men in a variety of activities.

Rasmi Shoocongdej

This chapter is organized in the following manner. First, I will review the general concept of gender roles from an anthropological perspective. Second, I will present an overview of three rock art sites from western Thailand. Third, I will examine what can be learned about gender roles from this rock art. In this study, three questions will be considered: What tasks were performed by each gender, what was the relative status of women within the society, and what are the spatial relationships between the gender representations at these rock art sites?

DEFINITIONS OF TERMS

Before examining the depiction of gender roles in rock art, I will begin by briefly defining the terms used in this chapter. *Sex* is a biological difference between females and males. *Gender* is a cultural construct defining women and men. *Gender roles* are "the differential participation of men and women in social, economic, political, and religious institutions within a specific cultural setting. Gender roles describe what people do and what activities and behaviors are deemed appropriate for the gender category" (Conkey and Spector 1984: 15).

Gender Roles

In the past decade, the simplistic characterization of foraging "Paleolithic" societies as based on male domination in contrast to the agricultural "Neolithic" societies as based on female domination has been reevaluated (e.g., Dahlberg 1981; Leacock and Lee 1987). It is no longer valid to make these kinds of sweeping generalizations since variability in the division of labor and in gender roles has been observed ethnographically.

Generally, a division of labor linked to gender roles has been documented in all cultures. However, the particular tasks assigned to women and men do not always reflect differences in strength, status, and power.

Among non–food producing societies, women contribute about as much to the subsistence economy as do men. In the particular case of tropical environments, women play an important role in production (e.g., Murdock 1949; Eder 1984). The nature of work varies among cultures. Often, gathering is women's work; men usually hunt and fish. However, in some cases, women participate in all the subsistence activities that men do. For example, among the Agta of the Philippines, women do hunt and participate in trade (Griffin and Estioko-Griffin 1985). However, when there are differences in participation, the dominance of one gender in one sphere does not necessarily lead to dominance in another since women and men do different things. This division of labor by gender is not visibly inequitable; both genders contribute to production in a complementary way. Children also assist adults in various activities.

In the political sphere, men participate more than women (e.g., Leacock and Lee 1987: 37). In non–food-producing societies, social roles are based on age; old people, especially males, often lead the groups. For example, among the Semang of Malaysia, a shaman, or medicine man, is "the most influential individual in the band. He wears a distinctive costume, observes special food taboos, carries an emblematic wand, and often receives a special burial" (Murdock 1949: 101). Social relations are egalitarian. Both women and men can play important roles in ritual performances (e.g., Griffin and Estioko-Griffin 1985). Furthermore, women as well as men participate in ritual ceremonies when large groups aggregate. Ceremonialism involves group ritual that serves to bring people together into larger aggregation (Tonkinson 1991: 155–62).

The development of food production may have led to changes in the division of labor by sex. However, foraging and hunting can still be widely practiced. In the tropics, for example, the Batek of the Philippines, men usually herd animals, clear fields, collect rattan, hunt, and fish, whereas women generally gather plants, cook, take care of children, and collect firewood and water (e.g., Eder 1984). In other words, men's tasks often relate to external activities, and women tend spend more time in household activities. Among food-producing groups, economic exchange or trade is a common phenomenon; for example, the Isabela Agta men often engage in trade with outsiders. Men increasingly spend a certain amount of time away from home (Rai 1990). A division of domestic and public sphere is gradually developed. However, some activities, such as cultivation, collecting rattan, and clearing garden (e.g., Kunstadter, Chapman, and Sabhasri 1978), are cooperatively carried by women and men.

Among food-producing societies, group ritual is associated with larger communities. Ceremonialism serves to define local groups and to maintain regional intergroup relations (Johnson and Earle 1991: 196). Generally, social relations are kin-based societies that have village headmen with limited authority. As was the case in foraging societies, elders, often males, are respected for their experiences and practical knowledge and diplomatic skills. Male leadership varies from headmen to bigmen. Men also lead ritual ceremonies (Rachman 1991: 311–31). However, in some cases, women also perform roles in ritual. For example, among the Kalinga, Abba, and Apayao of the Philippines, women perform the roles of shaman in sacrifice rituals (De Raedt 1991: 360).

In sum, variation in gender roles is generally found in nonstratified societies. There are differences in gender roles among groups, and in some groups, women do the same things that men do. Among non–food-producing and food-producing societies, the tasks and activities seem to overlap one another. Gender roles vary, depending on economy, social structure, and degree of interaction with the outsiders (e.g., exchange or trade).

ROCK ART DISTRIBUTION IN
WESTERN THAILAND

In this section, I will provide a general description of the rock art from three sites in western Thailand: Tham Ta Duang and Khao Plara in Kanchanaburi province and Khao Plara in Uthai Thani province (fig. 11.1). In order to analyze the paintings, the conventions of depicting humans are applied to

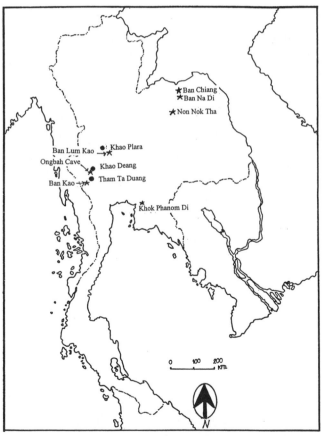

Figure 11.1.   Location of rock art and archaeological sites in Thailand mentioned in text.

classify a male and a female, including a sexual organ and styles of hair and clothing.

Tham Ta Duang

Tham Ta Duang is a cave located within a limestone mountain about two kilometers from Khwae Yai River, Kanchanaburi province. Its altitude is 300 meters above sea level. Besides rock art, the site contains artifacts including flaked stone tools, waste flakes, animal bones, and sherds inside the cave (Fine Arts Department 1986, 1988b). The rock art consists of pictographs painted on the cave wall with red ochre that are located approximately two to four meters above the cave floor. The paintings include mostly human figures in silhouette representing a narrative story of a local group. A total of 51 figures are documented (Supakijwilekakarn 1990). The paintings range in size from 30 to 45 centimeters.

Human figures are the dominant motif at Tham Ta Duang. There are three painted areas in the cave (figs. 11.2 and 11.3). The presence of two styles suggests that different groups created these paintings.

One style found in the first area is a group of 18 human figures, shown in profile, including men and women, walking in line and carrying two objects, possibly drums (Sangvichien 1974). Most of the figures are in dynamic postures as if they are walking in procession. Interestingly, two male figures are wearing headdresses. Below the previous painting, there are three groups of human figures in silhouette. First, there are human figures standing in line, wearing headdresses and loin clothes. Next to these figures, there are stick figures of men,

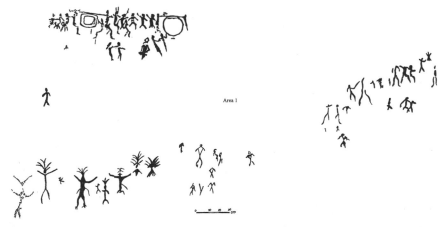

Figure 11.2.   Pictographs at Tham Ta Duang, Kanchanaburi province, western Thailand (adapted from Srisuchat 1989; Supakijwilekakarn 1990).

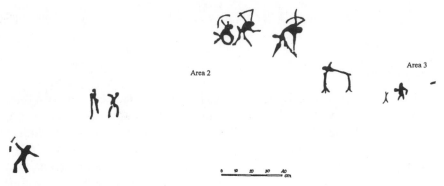

Figure 11.3.   Pictographs at Khao Deang, Kanchanaburi province, western Thailand (adapted from Srisuchat 1989; Supakijwilekakarn 1990).

and in the last group there are human figures standing in line and these are in a bad state of preservation. Another style of painting is seen in the second area. Here, there are the poorly preserved human figures and three male figures shooting arrows. Finally, in the third area, there are a human figure, possibly a woman, with decorated shoulder, and fragmentary figures, also poorly preserved, that are possibly human.

Thai scholars suggest that the paintings at Tham Ta Duang depict a ritual procession; dancing possibly was a part of the ritual. Two interpretations of the rituals depicted have been suggested (Sangvichien 1974; Supakijwilekakarn 1990: 50). One idea is that this was a funeral ritual in which drums were used as part of the ceremony. The second suggestion is that this was a fertility ritual. Based on relative dating with Ban Kao and Ongbah caves in western Thailand (Sorensen 1974, 1988), this site dates to between 4,000 and 2,000 years b.p. (Supakijwilekakarn 1990).

Khao Deang

Khao Deang is a cave situated in limestone near the Khwae Yai River, Kanchanaburi province, and is approximately 50 kilometers from Tham Ta Duang. Its altitude is 450 meters above sea level. The rock art consists of pictographs painted on the cave wall with red ochre, located at a height of approximately 3 to 25 meters above the floor. There is a grinding stone made of sandstone found near the painted area (Fine Arts Department 1986; Srisuchat 1989). The rock paintings range in size from 10 to 60 centimeters. The painted forms include human and animal figures in silhouette, human and animal figures in partial silhouette, human and animal figures in outline, and nonfigures. They seem to be narrative. Out of a total of 75 figures, 11 human figures wore clothes, mostly shown in a front view (Supakijwilekakarn 1990: 54).

There are four painted areas along the wall (figs. 11.4. 11.5, and 11.6). The first location contains three human figures in dancing postures and poorly preserved figures.

The second location is the most outstanding rock art feature at Khao Deang. It is a group of people in dancing postures with elaborate dresses, playing musical instruments. This possibly represents a ritual ceremony. In addition, women and men have the long lines extending from the tops of their heads that might be headdresses. There are scenes in rock painting depicting possible family units. For example, women, men, and children have their hands raised as if participating in dancing ritual. Above these figures, in the second of the four main

Area 1

Figure 11.4. Pictographs at Khao Plara, Uthai Thani province, western Thailand (redrawn from Srisuchat 1990).

Area 2

Figure 11.5. Pictographs at Khao Deang, Kanchanaburi province, western Thailand (adapted from Srisuchat 1989; Supakijwilekakarn 1990)

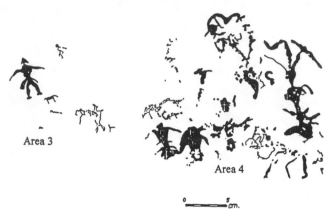

Figure 11.6. Pictographs at Khao Deang, Kanchanaburi province, western Thailand (redrawn from Srisuchat 1989)

areas, there is a figure of a man throwing a spear at a single head of cattle or buffalo. The panel next to the hunting scene contains approximately three individual figures standing separately. There is a larger human figure, possibly a man, who is elaborately dressed. On both sides of this larger figure is a smaller-size person, possibly a child, holding a musical instrument. On the left side, the figure, possibly a girl, is holding a musical instrument in one hand. On the right side, a boy also holds a musical instrument. Below these paintings is a human figure, possibly a woman. Finally, the right end of this location is composed of human figures. Only one can be identified as a female figure wearing loin clothing and her left hand holding a musical instrument.

The third location consists of a group of human figures. Two standing figures are each associated with an animal. A possible female is with a dog, and a male is with a single head of cattle or buffalo. The fourth location is in a bad state of preservation, which makes it difficult to identify.

The majority of the scenes in the rock art at Khao Deang are depicting dancing in ritual ceremony. It is believed that the paintings were part of fertility rituals (Srisuchat 1989: 73). Based on style and subject matter, the paintings at this site possibly were created at the same time by the same groups. Certain styles of loin clothing and headdress in the rock art at Khao Deang are similar to those at Tham Ta Duang, suggesting a relationship between these two sites.

Recently, based on evidence from bronze drums found at Ongbah cave (Sorensen 1974, 1988), Wongthes (1994) suggested that the ritual processions at Tham Ta Duang and Khao Deang might relate to the "Dong Son" culture, an Iron Age culture in Southeast Asia, dated approximately to 500 B.C. He proposed that the objects found in the scene at Tham Ta Duang cave could possibly be Dong-Son drums, and the depictions of humans with elaborate dresses and headdresses are similar to the decorations on Dong-Son drums.

The figure of the dog suggests this might be a food-producing society since dogs are often found in archaeological sites associated with agriculture (e.g., Fine Arts Department 1986, 1988a). In addition, the picture of a man throwing a spear at a head of cattle depicts hunting. It is important to keep in mind that hunting was a part of the subsistence economy in food-producing societies in this region. Based on relative dating from Ban Kao, the site dates to between 4,000 and 2,000 years b.p. (Srisuchat 1989: 73).

Khao Plara

Khao Plara is located in a limestone mountain range in Uthai Thani province, which is north of Kanchanaburi province about 180 kilometers and about 100 kilometers from Khao Deang. Its altitude is about 597 meters above sea level. The rock art consists of pictographs painted on a cliff wall with red ochre or hematite. There is a polished stone adze found at the site. The pictures are located at a height of four to seven meters above the floor and are arranged in a horizontal line. The paintings range in size from 10 to 100 centimeters. The painted forms include human and animal figures in silhouette, human and animal figures in partial silhouette, human and animal figures in outline, stick figures, sketched figures, and nonfigures. The paintings appear to be a narrative story. Out of a total of 40 figures, 30 are human figures. Animal figures include dogs, cocks, a turtle, a frog, deer, and cattle or buffalo (Srisuchat 1990).

There are 12 sets of paintings along the same cliff wall (figs. 11.7 and 11.8). This description of paintings starts from the left and moves to the right. The first is a single human bending forward. The second is composed of three human figures in dancing postures. The third is a single head of cattle in X-ray style. The fourth includes two human figures in dancing postures. The fifth consists of two human figures. One, possibly female, is wearing loin clothing and a headdress. The other is a male figure in X-ray style wearing loin clothing, associated with two dogs, undoubtedly domesticated. This male figure is much larger than the female figure. The sixth area includes a human figure, possibly a woman with elaborate loin clothing and a headdress, pulling a string over an animal, possibly a head of domesticated cattle. The seventh area contains a group of three human figures associated with animals. The left figure is a possible male, wearing elaborate loin clothing and a headdress, bending forward. The middle figure is a person with a chicken on an arm. The third is seated and is possibly a pregnant woman. This figure is associated with a frog and a turtle. The eighth area is composed of possibly a male figure, with loin clothing and elaborate headdress, in a dancing position. The ninth contains two male and animal figures, including possibly a deer or a dog with a headdress and a domesticated dog superimposed, on sketchy human stick figures. One figure of a man is in a dancing pose, raising two hands, whereas another figure is a man, elaborately dressed and with

Figure 11.7. Pictographs at Khao Plara, Uthai Thani province, western Thailand (redrawn from Srisuchat 1990)

Figure 11.8. Pictographs at Khao Plara, Uthai Thani province, western Thailand (redrawn from Srisuchat 1990)

a headdress, pulling a head of cattle that is depicted in X-ray style. The 10th set of figures consists of four outline and abstract figures of possible men; one of these figures is giant sized and superimposes on an X-ray figure of cattle that superimposes on sketchy abstract figures. The 11th contains pictures of a man fighting with a bull, a male figure wearing loin clothing and an elaborate headdress in dancing pose, possibly three male figures, and animal figures of cattle drawn in outline form. Finally, the last set of paintings includes a man drawn in outline form wearing loin clothing and a headdress in a bending-forward position and abstract figures drawn in outline form.

The painting at Khao Plara records important events occurring in the past. According to Srisuchat (1990: 84), the scenes represent ritual performances and hunting expeditions. She suggests that the paintings represent communal art for ritual purposes. Further, this was a fertility ritual that occurred in an agricultural context, based on the depictions of cattle. Hunting scenes record successful hunting activities. The figures of humans with elaborate headdresses and loin clothes are similar to the paintings at Khao Deang by the same prehistoric groups. The many superimposed figures and differing scenes depicted indicate that this site was visited on many occasions over a period of time. Based on relative dating from Ban Lum Kao in Uthai Thani province, central Thailand, the site dates to 2,000 years b.p. (Napintu 1988).

ANALYSIS

I now turn to the questions posed earlier: What tasks were performed by each gender, what was the relative status of women within the society, and what are the spatial relationships between the gender representations at these rock art sites? To address these questions, the chronological relationships among these sites must be sorted out. Once a basic chronological framework has been established, I will analyze the rock art data in terms of style, the activities associated with genders, and gender roles in ritual ceremonies. Finally, I will consider site function.

Chronology

In western Thailand, there is evidence of continuous human occupation beginning in the Late Pleistocene (e.g., Shoocongdej 1996). Because of the lack of absolute dates, it is difficult to determine the age of any particular group of paintings from these three sites. Archaeological excavation has not yet been undertaken at any of these sites. Here, dating is based on the dates associated with surrounding sites and the depictions of domesticated animals and people wearing clothing among the rock art figures. These lines of evidence suggest that these sites date to between the Middle and Late Holocene (or "Neolithic" to "Metal" ages) from 4,000 to

2,000 years b.p., the period when animal husbandry was adopted (Sangvichien 1974; Srisuchat 1989, 1990, 1991; Supakijwilekakarn 1990).

In western Thailand, the earliest evidence of domesticated dogs, pigs, and chickens is reported from the Ban Kao site, based on carbon-14 dates, which dates to approximately 4,000 to 3,000 years b.p. (Sorensen and Hatting 1967: 160). Domesticated cattle and dogs were found at Ban Lum Kao in Uthai Thani province, which dates to 2,000 years b.p. (Napintu 1988) and at Non Nok Tha in northeastern Thailand, dating to 3,000 years b.p. Buffalo were found at Ban Chiang and Ban Na Di in northeastern Thailand in a later period, dating to approximately 2,500 years b.p., when iron was introduced (Fine Arts Department 1986, 1988a). Although animals were already domesticated, prehistoric people continued to hunt wild animals, such as deer, wild pig, and fowl (e.g., Sorensen and Hatting 1967; Fine Arts Department 1988a; Napintu 1988).

Domesticated cereals have not yet been discovered in situ from the archaeological sites in western Thailand from this time period. However, evidence of rice was found at Khok Phanom Di, a contemporaneous coastal site in eastern Thailand (Higham and Maloney 1989; Higham and Thosarat 1994). As for clothing, evidence of prehistoric textiles is found from Ban Chiang, dating to 4,000 to 3,500 years b.p. A fragment of fabric attached to bronze bracelets has been identified as silk and hemp (Aranyanak 1985: 47–54). From the rich archaeological evidence, it is reasonable to assume that during the Middle Holocene, prehistoric people in Thailand had a knowledge of plant and animal domestication.

Furthermore, a relative rock art sequence can be developed on the basis of the superposition of figures, spatial associations suggesting that figures were part of the same scene or painting episode, similarities in style in the rock art, and associated material culture (Srisuchat 1989, 1990). There seems to be a strong link between the three sites; it is clear that the rock art designs might have been part of a continuous tradition. Based on subject content and spatial association. Tham Ta Duang and Khao Deang might have been occupied concurrently, while Khao Plara might date to a slightly later period.

Style

Here, style is used in a broad sense to refer to any aspect of the rock art that conveys information relating to group identity (Hegmon 1992). The style of the rock art includes the form of the painted figures, such as silhouette, partial silhouette, outline, stick figure, and sketched figure. Other aspects of the figures, such as the ways in which loin clothing and headdresses are represented, are also included as a part of the style. Particular styles can be associated with individuals or social groups.

The representations in this rock art are more or less abstract (table 11.1). Admittedly, it is frequently very difficult to determine the sex of the human figures when they are poorly preserved or if there is insufficient detail. Despite the fact that human figures cannot clearly be sexed biologically, they can still be assigned to gender categories on the basis of particular styles in a given context, such as styles of hair or clothing. For instance, in the rock paintings at Khao Deang, figures of women have a very distinctive head style that is triangular in shape, and dresses. At Khao Plara, figures of women appear to be fatter than figures of men. Children can be identified by the size of the figure in any given context.

In general, figures of both men and women are commonly found at all three sites. Animal figures, found at two of the sites, include dogs, turtles, cattle, buffalo, possibly deer, and chickens. Table 11.2 shows the numbers of figures of humans, animals, and others at the three sites. Because of the poor preservation of most of figures, the number of unidentified figures is quite high.

Table 11.3 shows that the human and animal figures of red color in the form of silhouettes, outline, sticklike figures, and sketched figures are found only at all three sites. The X-ray style and superimposed paintings are only found at Khao Plara. The paintings from these three sites included the repetitive use of simple design elements. The X-ray style found at Khao Plara seems to be more elaborate than the others. However, it is possible that the use of any particular style had particular symbolic meanings.

Table 11.4 shows that three distinct views of the figures are found in the rock art; they appear in profile, in frontal view, and in a twisted perspective. It should be emphasized that the twisted perspective is found only at Khao Plara.

A characteristic feature of the human figures is large legs and elaborate decoration or dress, especially headdresses with feathers. These features are found in rock art throughout the northwestern mountains in Thailand during late prehistory, suggesting that this was a regional style of prehistoric groups at this time.

There are many variations in the postures and actions of the human figures, including sitting, jumping, playing musical instruments, dancing, shooting arrows, plowing, herding, and standing. Movement is emphasized; in the typical representation of dancing, the figure is standing straight with arms up and hands raised or with arms extended to the side.

Additional types of human figures include (1) women and men with elaborate headdresses and wearing loin clothes resembling skirts with an end falling down in the back and sides, (2) women and men wearing loin clothes like skirts

Table 11.1.   Types of Figures Found at Three Rock Art Sites

Site	Female	Male	Animal	Unidentified Human and Other Figures	Total
Tham Ta Duang	9	14	—	28	51
Khao Deang	12	5	3	55	75
Khao Plara	6	12	11	11	40
Total	27	31	14	94	166

Table 11.2. Stylistic Variation in Figures

Site	Women	Men	Children	Animal
Tham Ta Duang				
Khao Deang				
Khao Plara				

Table 11.3. Painting Techniques at Three Rock Art Sites

Site	Silhouettes		Outline		Sticklike		X-ray	
	Female	Male	Female	Male	Female	Male	Female	Male
Tham Ta Duang	3	6	—	—	6	8	—	—
Khao Deang	12	5	—	—	—	—	—	—
Khao Plara	6	4	—	6	—	—	—	2

Note: Unidentified sex is excluded.

Table 11.4. Painting Views Depicted in Rock Art

	Profile		Frontal View		Twisted Perspectives	
Site	Female	Male	Female	Male	Female	Male
Tham Ta Duang	6	8	3	6	—	—
Khao Deang	2	2	10	3	—	—
Khao Plara	1	2	1	2	4	8

Note: Unidentified sex is excluded.

with an end falling down in the back and side, (3) women and men with headdresses, and (4) nude men and women. Types I, II, and IV were found at all three sites. Type III was found only at Tham Ta Duang (table 11.5).

At Khao Plara, figures of women and men are depicted wearing dresses and ornaments, and various animals are associated with them, such as dogs, cattle or buffalo, a frog, a turtle, a deer, and a cock. Cattle or buffalo and dogs outnumber the other types of animals. It should be noted that dressed figures of women and men are found in dancing contexts, while nude figures appear mostly in hunting scenes. At Tham Ta Daung, sticklike figures of types I and III are found together in a procession; those of type IV are depicted shooting arrows. Finally, at Khao Deang, the three types (types I, II, and IV) of human figures outlined previously are found in a dancing context. A nude figure of man is found in a hunting scene.

Activities Associated with Genders

The major subsistence activities depicted in the rock paintings are hunting, fighting with wild buffalo or bulls, pulling a head of cattle or buffalo, possibly plowing, and possibly herding. Nonsubsistence activities include walking, dancing, and participating in ritual ceremonies.

Table 11.6 shows various activities that are associated with figures of men and women. Women, men, and children are depicted in a variety of activities. Men are represented in more diverse activities than are women. Hunting is the most frequently depicted. Other activities involving men include shooting arrows, holding cattle or buffalo, fighting a bull, carrying objects, and dancing. Women were not depicted in hunting scenes. Women figures frequently are shown associated with men. Women engage in various activities, such as

Table 11.5. Types of Human Figures Found at Three Rock Art Sites

	Type I		Type II		Type III		Type IV	
Site	Female	Male	Female	Male	Female	Male	Female	Male
Tham Ta Duang	—	—	—	—	3	5	7	10
Khao Deang	1	1	8	1	—	—	2	3
Khao Plara	3	6	3	2	—	—	—	3

Note: Unidentifed sex is excluded.

Table 11.6. Activities Associated with Genders

Site	Women's Activities	Men's Activities
Tham Ta Duang	Walking in line Dancing	Walking in line Carrying objects Shooting arrows Dancing
Khao Deang	Dancing Playing musical instruments Sitting	Dancing Hunting a wild buffalo or cow
Khao Plara	Dancing Sitting Plowing with one head of cattle	Dancing Pulling with a buffalo or cow

sitting, walking, dancing, plowing, and playing an instrument. Children also participate in playing musical instruments and dancing at Khao Deang.

Table 11.7 shows that there seems to be a very complex association between cattle or buffalo as well as dogs and humans, which might be related to the subsistence economy. In general, the animal figures depicted were part of the local fauna in the region that was contemporaneous with the prehistoric artists. These animals are commonly found in archaeological sites (e.g., Sorensen and Hatting 1967; Napintu 1988; Pookajorn 1984). Interestingly, animals are shown not in herds but as individuals. It is important to note that cattle or wild buffalo and dogs seem to play major roles in the region's ritual and symbolic animism. Cross-cultural data show that cattle or buffalo and chickens are commonly sacrificed in various ritual ceremonies. For instance, for the Lua of northwestern Thailand, buffalo are sacrificed for rituals of the major earth spirit, for communal agricultural ceremonies, for the funerals of important persons, for curing a serious illness, and for a guardian spirit of the village. In addition, the Lua eat dogs on ceremonial occasions, and chickens are sacrificed in combination with larger animals during the major agricultural and communal ceremonies (Kunstadter et al. 1978: 101–2). Among the Zhuang of southern China today, frogs are sacrificed in rainmaking ceremonies accompanied by the beating of bronze drums similar to the "Dong Son drum" in order to warrant sufficient rainfall and fertility (Wongthes 1994).

Table 11.7. Associations between Genders and Animals

Site	Women	Men
Tham Ta Duang	None	None
Khao Deang	Dog	Cattle or buffalo Dog
Khao Plara	Turtle Cock Frog	Cattle Buffalo or bull Dog Deer

Figures of men are often associated with dogs, cattle, wild buffalo, and weapons, while figures of women are associated with dogs, turtles, chickens, and frogs. Chickens and turtles appear to be associated only with women. Wild animals, such as buffalo and deer, seem to be associated with men. Dogs and cattle are found with both women and men. In the prehistoric food-producing societies in Southeast Asia, cattle played an important role in the subsistence economy since they were used for preparing fields, for a food source, and for transport. Unfortunately, there has been no analysis done on the use of cattle or buffalo from surrounding archaeological sites in the region.

The data indicate that both genders as well as children are equally involved in the ritual ceremonies; this is was not a predominantly male activity. Interestingly, domestic activities are not shown at the three sites, suggesting that these paintings were made for ritual purposes. Here, domestic activity means work carried out within the camp or household.

Gender Roles in Ritual Ceremonies

The different sizes of the human figures wearing loin clothes that end falling down in the back and sides with highly elaborate feathered headdresses and ornaments imply status, authority, or position within the society. At Khao Plara, a figure of a man was depicted in a twisted perspective with two dogs, one on each side (fig. 11.8), possibly symbolizing authority or high status. This man might have been a headman. A figure of a woman with an elaborate headdress and loin clothes is dancing next to him. In addition, there are figures of men and women, painted in X-ray style, wearing bracelets or ornaments, and pulling cattle. These could have symbolized important roles in ritual performances.

At Tham Ta Duang, the figures of men wearing headdresses in the middle of a procession might represent people with authority in the ritual ceremony. In this procession scene, men carried both drums and women walked along in line. Following the first group, another group appears in which all have elaborate headdresses and loin clothes, possibly including both women and men who also played important roles in the procession. They are in dancing postures. The last group appears in nude style and played the least roles in the performance, also in dancing postures.

At Khao Deang, the human figures involved in ritual performances include (1) larger-size figures with highly elaborated dresses and headdresses, indicating that they played important roles in the ritual, especially a larger-size figure of a woman standing in the front; (2) smaller-size figures of men and women with highly elaborate dresses and headdresses, indicating that they played less prominent roles; and (3) nude figures of men and women, implying that they played the least-significant roles.

There is some other evidence that these kinds of social distinctions existed at this time in this region. At Ban Kao site in Kanchanaburi province, there was a burial of an old man with elaborate and distinctive grave goods compared to others from the site, suggesting that he held a position of high status, possibly a shaman (Sorensen and Hatting 1967: 142).

In addition, there are a few symbolic human figures with animal heads and human bodies, possibly of men, found at Khao Plara. In addition, human figures of undetermined sex with animal feet are documented at Tham Ta Duang. These figures might symbolize a form of shaman who merged with the animals.

Site Function

Based on archaeological evidence found at these three rock art sites, the sites were used occasionally for the performance of communal ritual activities and as temporary camps by prehistoric people. Interestingly, these three sites are located at prominent vantage points that could have contributed to their value as sacred places for specific ceremonies.

Most of the pictographs are on the plain rock surface of the cliff or cave walls. The height of painted locations at Khao Deang and Khao Plara is selected for painting the ritual events. These sites might have been used only for ritual purposes, though the sites might have been visited several times in the past. Tham Ta Duang is more suitable for use both as a temporary camp by foraging populations, as indicated by the presence of pebble tools, and as a ritual site by a food-producing population, as suggested by the presence of pottery and the presence of the painting of the procession.

DISCUSSION

This chapter has explored gender roles in late prehistoric societies in Thailand by examining the depictions of roles and relative status of women and men in rock art. Similarities in style in the paintings at these sites suggest that there was a relationship among these rock art sites. This is especially seen in the identical human figures with elaborate dresses and headdresses, possibly of feathers, found at all three sites. Technically, red is used throughout the western region. Figures were commonly shown as silhouettes, outlines, stick figures, and sketched figures.

The three sites are distributed in a line running in a north-to-south direction. The paintings at Tham Ta Duang and Khao Deang might be contemporaneous. The paintings at Khao Plara appear to have been made during a later period. However, they probably are in the same tradition since the rock paintings share similarities in style and composition, including figures of men, women, and animals, such as dog and cattle.

Clearly, these rock paintings may be generalized representations of the kinds of rituals and other activities that occurred in the past. The paintings from these sites appear to be narrative stories. All three sites were possibly used for temporary camps and for ritual purposes, and they appear to have been related, as indicated by the similarities in style in the rock art.

The rituals perhaps served the social function of promoting solidarity among groups. They also could have helped to symbolize ethnic identity among local groups who were brought together to participate in the same ceremonies.

The scenes seem to be formal, stylized, and repetitive. Two identical rituals are found: a ritual procession at Tham Ta Duang and ritual dancing at Tham Ta Duang, Khao Deang, and Khao Plara. One interpretation is that these are fertility rituals (possibly related to rainmaking), which are commonly observed in food-producing societies. Rain brings fertility to crops and other agricultural products. The presence of depictions of cattle, buffalo, chickens, fowl, and turtles might support this interpretation (Srisuchat 1989, 1990; Supakijwilekakarn 1990). In particular, the figures of a frog and a turtle are associated with a pregnant woman. In Thailand today, fertility rituals are usually practiced during times of crisis, for example, a drought. This ritual incorporates song, music, and dance (Vallibhotama 1993: 153–63). Furthermore, buffalo is the most important animal for subsistence economy and affects social status in the food-producing societies in Southeast Asia today, and it is often killed in important ritual ceremonies, such as funerals and communal rituals (e.g., Condominas 1977). However, the nature of rituals in late prehistoric Thailand needs to be investigated further through the archaeological study of sites in the region.

In terms of activities associated with genders, there is no archaeological evidence of associations between particular artifacts and individuals of specific genders from these sites because of the limited nature of the archaeological evidence. However, the rock art provides evidence of activities being performed by individuals of each gender, although domestic activities are rarely depicted at these sites. The most common scenes depict hunting associated with men, indicating that men's roles were still closely associated with this activity. Herding was also a man's activity. Plowing appears to have been associated with women, suggesting that women played a prominent role in subsistence economy. Communal rituals such as dancing are well represented in the rock art paintings, which indicate that both women and men participate in rituals such as dancing and playing music. In certain ritual performances, women would play major roles, while men would have important positions in other ritual ceremonies, as is commonly observed in food-producing societies.

CONCLUSION

This chapter has examined the roles of women and men through the study of rock art from three sites in western Thailand. General conclusions can be drawn from the analysis.

First, there is very little available and reliable archaeological evidence related directly to these rock art sites. Therefore, we have poor chronological control and little information regarding subsistence and settlement. Consequently, it is extremely difficult to place these sites into an absolute time frame and to understand the past cultural system. However, various lines of evidence suggest that the rock paintings were probably created by food-producing populations. Based on relative dating from Ban Kao, Ongbah, and Ban Lum Kao from the same region, these sites could possibly date to between the Middle and Late Holocene, or 4,000 to 2,000 years b.p. AMS (accelerated mass spectrometry) dating technique might be used in the future to define the chronology more accurately. For the present, relative dating has provided a chronological baseline for studying the rock art.

Second, from an economic perspective, men's activities appear to relate to hunting large animals, such as wild buffalo or bulls, and herding cattle. Women might possibly participate in agricultural activities, such as plowing and herding activities. Among other activities, women and men as well as children participated in dancing in ritual performances.

Third, regarding the relative status of women in these societies, women played important roles in ritual performances and the subsistence economy. In these early food-producing societies, there was not a sharp division between the domestic and the public sphere. Women's roles and status were equal to men's, and they could participate equally in ritual ceremonies, although the lack of representations of the domestic sphere makes it difficult to know how much men participated in this realm. Furthermore, children participated in dancing and playing instruments in ritual performances.

Fourth, cattle and dogs possibly had a symbolic meaning in fertility rituals in food-producing communities since they are important animals in subsistence economies. Finally, the nature and variability of gender role should be further investigated archaeologically in Southeast Asia. In particular, it would be interesting to examine the relationships between the genders and various animals in mortuary ritual.

ACKNOWLEDGMENTS

I would like to thank Professor Sarah Nelson and Professor Myriam Rosen-Ayalon for inviting me to participate in this conference. I thank the Rockefeller Foundation for its hospitality at the Villa Serbelloni at Bellagio, Italy, and the Wenner-Gren Foundation for a travel expense. I am especially thankful to Amara Srisuchat for providing information on rock art in Thailand. Thanks are also due to Tristine Smart for commenting on an earlier version of this chapter. Finally, I thank all participants for their support and comments at the conference.

12

Women in the Prehistory of Mainland Southeast Asia

C. F. W. Higham

INTRODUCTION

The principal source material on the status and role of women in prehistoric Southeast Asia comes from cemeteries. This reflects the excellent preservation of bone at some sites, extensive excavations and large samples of skeletons, and the detailed analyses of the human remains and their conjunction with mortuary offerings. A second source is found in the Dian cemeteries of Yunnan, where rich grave offerings contemporaneous with Han-dynasty expansion to the south provide much information on women and their contribution to rituals, subsistence activities, and menial tasks. Despite the rarity of published information, excavations at a number of cemeteries over the past two decades have produced data relevant to women's role in society in terms of production, health, diet, and longevity of men and women and their relative status.

The sequence begins in the late third millennium B.C., when coastal and inland groups of hunter-gatherers came into contact with intrusive rice farmers who ultimately originated in the Yangtze valley. The Neolithic period was of brief duration, and few sites are known. From about 1500 B.C. we find the first evidence for the local casting of bronzes in a distinctive Southeast Asian tradition. Several Bronze Age cemeteries are known. A millennium later, these same groups had mastered the technique of forging iron implements, and major technological, economic, and social changes are evident leading in the early first millennium A.D. to the establishment of a series of states.

COASTAL HUNTER-GATHERERS:
KHOK PHANOM DI

Khok Phanom Di (fig. 12.1) was first occupied about 2000 B.C., when the site was located at the mouth of a major estuary. In terms of bioproductivity, this is one of the richest habitats known. Over the ensuing five centuries, the environmental conditions changed because of fluctuations in the sea level, increasing sedimentation, and probably the relocation of the adjacent river channel (Higham and Thosarat 1994). The mound accumulated rapidly, such that about six meters of cultural material accumulated in four centuries. The dead were interred both alongside their contemporaries, as is often the case, and over the ancestors. We thus have available a "vertical cemetery" comprising clusters of graves in which the skeletal remains are well preserved (figs. 12.2, 12.3). Grave goods varied with the seven successive mortuary phases, the list including pottery vessels of outstanding proficiency; the clay cylinders, anvils, and burnishing stones used in pottery's manufacture; shell, turtle carapace, and fish-bone jewelry; red ochre; wooden biers; shrouds of asbestos or bark cloth; and such rare items as adze heads, a nautilus shell, and the canine teeth of small carnivores.

One way of describing the changes is based on the seven mortuary phases (MP), determined by the sequence and modifications in death rituals. In harmony with the changing environment, subsistence activities were adaptive. During MP1–3, the marine habitat encouraged fishing and the collection of shellfish, although there are some rice remains that could have been obtained through exchange. An increase in freshwater indicators during MP4 permitted the local cultivation of rice: Shell harvesting knives and granite hoes were particularly common at this juncture. A return to marine conditions with MP5–6 probably made local rice cultivation marginal, if not impossible.

To set against this dynamic pattern of change, we have available putative genealogies based on the clustered distribution and sequence of graves (fig. 12.4). The application of a series of statistical tests to the variety and quantity of grave offerings relative to age and sex over time has provided some intriguing patterns. In the first place, during MP1–3, there was very high infant mortality linked, as Tayles (1998) has shown, to an inherited hemoglobinopathy such as thalassemia. While providing some resistance to malaria, people suffered from anemia. Both men and women had physically vigorous lives, with spinal degeneration evident. During MP2, females had a more cariogenic, less abrasive diet than men, but while the same pattern of high infant mortality and physically active lives continued into MP3, the difference in diet ceased. On the basis of the grave offerings, the various statistical manipulations applied to these phases failed to reveal distinctions based on wealth or sex.

However, during MP4, the phase when it is suggested that rice may have been locally cultivated, we find the start of a trend that continued to the end of

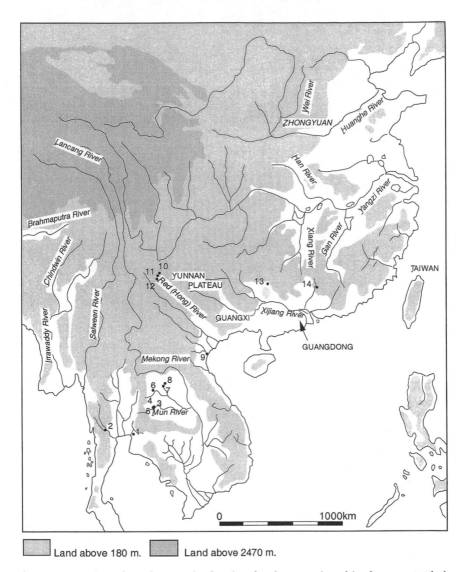

Land above 180 m. Land above 2470 m.

Figure 12.1. Map of Southeast Asia showing the sites mentioned in the text. 1: Khok Phanom Di; 2: Ban Kao; 3: Ban Prasat; 4: Ban Lum Khao; 5: Noen U-Loke; 6: Non Nok Tha; 7: Ban Na Di; 8: Ban Chiang; 9: Dong Son; 10: Tianzimao; 11: Shizhaishan; 12: Lijjiashan; 13: Yinshanling; 14: Shixia.

MP6. Men and women were now distinguished in death. Potters' anvils were found only with some women and young people, and elaborate turtle carapace ornaments were restricted to male graves. These changes occurred at a time when infant mortality fell markedly but deaths among children rose. Women

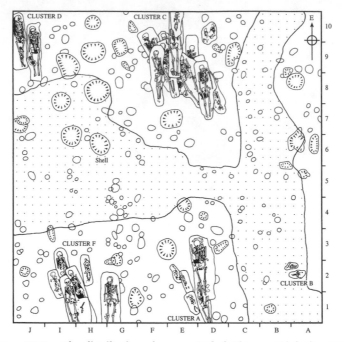

Figure 12.2. The distribution of graves at Khok Phanom Di during MP2.

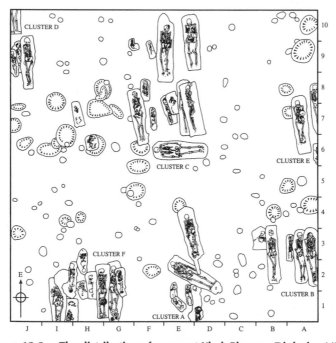

Figure 12.3. The distribution of graves at Khok Phanom Di during MP3.

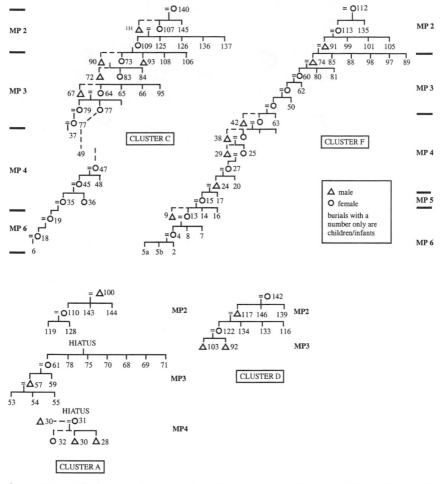

Figure 12.4. The proposed genealogies of four clusters of burials at Khok Phanom Di through five mortuary phases.

were still buried in close proximity to infants (fig. 12.5). Tayles has suggested that the latter would have been a heavy cost to the community as children failed to reach maturity. Life expectancy decreased, and people seem to have led less active lives than hitherto.

A major break with tradition came with MP5. There is evidence for more marine conditions, and the artifacts thought to have been associated with rice cultivation were no longer found. Interment in clusters ceased, and we find only four extremely rich burials in areas not previously used for burial. A woman who died in her mid-30s was particularly rich.

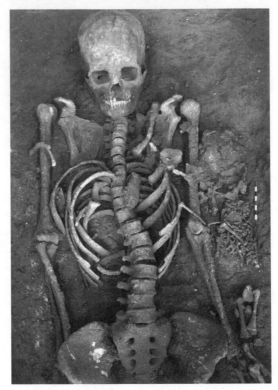

Figure 12.5. Burial 47 at Khok Phanom Di during MP4, a woman buried with an infant on her arm.

Her mortuary ritual incorporated a large and deep grave, and offerings included heaped clay cylinders and pottery vessels over the body, a clay anvil and two burnishing stones contained within a shell, several very finely made pots of novel shape and decoration, and much shell jewelry. The last category included over 120,000 shell-disk beads, almost 1,000 large I-shaped beads, two unique horned shell disks, shell disks near each ear, and a shell bangle (fig. 12.6).

No less intriguing were the burials of two infants on each side of her grave, one of which incorporated a virtually identical set of grave goods, though fewer in number, located in the same relative position. The anvil in this instance was a miniature, as befitted an infant aged about 15 months, and the shell bangle had been placed over rather than on the wrist. We should not overlook a male located some six meters to the east and only partially within the excavated area, for he too was richly endowed with grave goods, including many thousands of shell beads and heavy shell disks.

Figure 12.6.   Burial 15 at Khok Phanom Di during MP5, a woman buried with outstanding wealth.

MP6 saw a further change in mortuary ritual. We found a raised rectangular structure within which a woman had been interred with considerable wealth, though not in the same league as burial 15 from MP5. Her grave goods included a clay potter's anvil, two burnishing stones, several pottery vessels, and over 1,000 shell-disk beads. Adjacent lay two disturbed but also rich burials of another woman and a child. The structure was contemporary with another group of burials to the west, set out in a row, and contained within a set of large postholes that surely represent a wooden collective tomb. Here, we find the remains of two women, two men, and four infants. None could be described as wealthy.

During these two phases, the high sea level remained, and it is unlikely that the environs of the site encouraged the cultivation of rice. There is evidence for poor health, women being affected by anemia. People were shorter in stature and less robust than during earlier phases.

Throughout the prehistoric occupation, Khok Phanom Di was a center for the manufacture of pottery vessels. The inhabitants also had access to coastal resources, although the high-quality conus, trochus, and tridacna shells that dominated from MP5 would necessarily have been obtained from a distant coralline source. The extent of mortuary wealth changed markedly with time, as did the incidence of infant mortality, dental and general health, stature, and life expectancy. The subsistence economy also changed with the environmental modifications, particularly during MP4, when rice cultivation seems to have been undertaken locally. During the first three mortuary phases, it is not possible to pinpoint differences in the treatment of men and women. However, with MP4 there are hints of a change that clarified from MP5: Women and infants were interred with the anvils used to shape pottery vessels, and men were accompanied by large turtle carapace ornaments.

At the same juncture, we note a preponderance of women in the two most enduring putative genealogies: clusters C and F (fig. 12.4). By this period, which belongs in all probability to the period from 1700 to 1500 B.C., many agricultural villages were established in the hinterland. We have suggested that the central role of women in the manufacture of pottery vessels, which Vincent has described as masterpieces, would have enhanced their social status. Again, the retention of girls or young women within the community would have secured the future generation of potters. If, as we have suggested, vessels from Khok Phanom Di were employed in exchange, then we might better understand not only the central economic role of women but also their interment with outstandingly rich and exotic shell ornaments. This emphasizes the importance of women without necessarily ruling out the entrepreneurial role of men. Citing ethnographic parallels in Melanesia, we have found convincing indications that women may not only make ceramic vessels but also take the initiative to exchange their wares by long-distance voyaging (Lepowsky 1983).

In advancing this interpretation, the presence of a miniature anvil with an infant next to burial 15 sharpens our image of a society in which female potters were of central importance and stresses the potential significance of exploring ways of identifying the sex of young people on the basis of their skeletal remains.

THE NEOLITHIC

The Neolithic period in mainland Southeast Asia presents a serious gap in our knowledge. Even the date of the first agricultural communities has not been agreed. I have reviewed the evidence and found no convincing means of identifying the Neolithic prior to about 2300 B.C. in Thailand, Vietnam, or Yunnan and 2800 B.C. at Shixia in Lingnan. White (1997), on the other hand, has suggested, on the basis of pollen cores taken from Lake Kumphawapi in northeastern Thailand that initial settlement could date back to the fifth millennium B.C. The interpretation of evidence for increased charcoal and open land indicators in such cores, however, must take into account the potential impact of either hunter-gatherers or natural conflagrations. If agriculture was involved, then either the impact must have been slight, for no archaeological sites have been found until the initial occupation of Ban Kao and Ban Chiang in the late third millennium B.C., or sites may be so deeply buried below later deposition as to defy archaeological visibility.

Only at Ban Kao has a reasonable part of a Neolithic cemetery been opened (Sorensen and Hatting 1967), but the quality of the human bone is poor, ascription of sex is patchy, and information relevant to the role of women is scarce or absent. Adults were interred in pairs, and there are hints that men and women were oriented in opposite directions. The grave goods comprise mainly pottery vessels and stone adzes, shell-disk beads being present but rare.

THE BRONZE AGE

The Bronze Age in mainland Southeast Asia lasted for about a millennium from 1500 B.C. Large exposures of cemeteries are available from Ban Lum Khao, Nong Nor, and Non Nok Tha. Smaller areas have been opened at Ban Na Di and Ban Chiang (fig. 12.7).

Nong Nor

The Bronze Age cemetery of Nong Nor has been dated between 1100 and 700 B.C., although the presence of a few glass beads from nonmortuary contexts hints at a further few centuries of occupancy (Higham and Thosarat 1998). The distribution of the graves suggests the presence of two groups, one incorporating rows and the other a large cluster within which possible rows may be detected (fig. 12.7). Our analysis suggests that the latter is later. It has been possible to apply a series of statistical analyses, rather than to derive results from visual inspection alone, to identify possible distinctions based on age and sex. Forty-nine graves were sufficiently intact to be incorporated in this sample, and the range of selected grave goods against sex and age is seen in table 12.1.

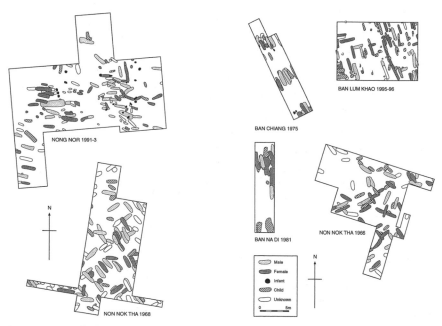

Figure 12.7. The layout of five Bronze Age cemeteries in Thailand, showing the sex and age of each interment.

Table 12.1.   The Relationship between Gender, Age, and the Presence of Selected Grave Offerings from Nong Nor

	Male				Female			
	O (4)	MA (11)	Y(6)	T (21)	O (3)	M (8)	Y (6)	T (17)
Bronze	—	5	2	7	—	9	4	13
Serpentine	3	1	4	8	2	—	2	4
Marble	1	3	—	4	4	2	5	11
Shell bangle	—	2	—	2	1	2	1	4
Shell pendant	—	2	1	3	—	2	1	3
Shell belt	1	—	1	2	1	—	2	3
Shell necklace	1	4	2	7	1	—	2	3
Shell belt	1	—	1	2	2	—	1	3
Dog	1	3	—	4	—	2	2	4
Cattle	2	1	1	4	—	—	—	—
Pig	2	2	2	6	—	1	2	3

Note: O: old, MA: middle-aged, Y: young, T: total.

The application of a principal component analysis to the grave goods themselves suggested that the remains of pigs and dogs and the presence of marble and bronze bangles, shell pendants and necklaces made of disk and barrel beads, shell belts, grinding stones, and certain forms of pottery vessel were prominent in distinguishing between the 49 interments.

The distribution of graves on the basis of the presence or absence of grave goods computed by the principal component analysis shows that there is a group of relatively wealthy graves, a second distinguished by a specific form of pottery vessel, and a third with few or no grave goods (fig. 12.8). The rich graves involve five men and three women. On the basis of the actual number of grave goods, the same statistic separated five graves from the majority. Two were rich males, three were females. One of the males and all the females were grouped together. The separation of a small proportion of the graves on the basis of wealth is also found when applying multidimensional scaling. Again, there are rich men and women.

When seeking evidence for different treatment for men and women on the basis of age, we found no recurrent evidence for older people being more wealthy. Overall, the conclusions are as follows:

1. Some individuals were interred with more grave goods than others. Spatially, a group comprising burials 35, 36, 39, and 105 stands out. It involves a male, burial 105, interred in the largest grave encountered, who wore a bronze bangle unique within the site. His grave was located adjacent to a row of female interments, all of whom were unusually well endowed with grave offerings. It is considered possible that these graves

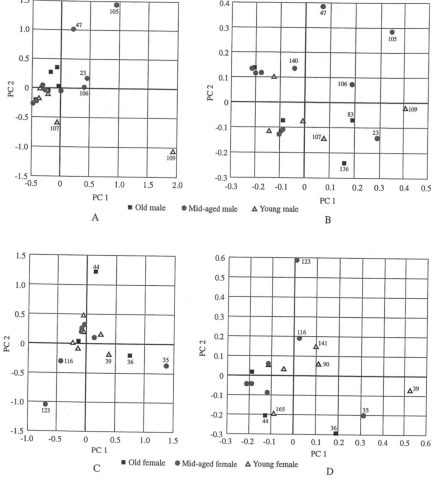

Figure 12.8. The distribution of male and female graves at Nong Nor on the basis of principal component scores. A: males (number of artifacts); B: males (presence or absence of artifacts); C: females (number of artifacts); D: females (presence or absence of artifacts).

are relatively early in the sequence, but there is no conclusive stratigraphic or chronometric evidence for this.

2. There is no evidence for sex or age bias in terms of mortuary wealth.

3. Children were accorded a similar burial rite and range of grave goods as adults.

4. Grinding stones are the only artifact found in the main with one sex (males).

5. There is no sign of a relationship between metal artifacts and wealth.

6. In terms of spatial differences, it is noted that pottery vessel form 10 is restricted to burials in the eastern part of the cemetery.

7. Certain items of jewelry were manufactured from exotic serpentine, jade, talc, and carnelian. They were found so rarely that they have not had a detectable influence on the statistical results. The three burials with carnelian, talc, or jade ornaments are, respectively, a middle-aged male, an adult male, and a middle-aged female. Of the 10 burials with serpentine jewelry, three are old males, one is a middle-aged male, and one is a young male. Three females also had serpentine, all three ages being represented.

With one exception, all the exotic jewelry came from graves in the eastern part of the cemetery.

Ban Na Di, Ban Lum Khao, and Non Nok Tha

The mortuary ritual at Nong Nor is similar to that documented at other Bronze Age sites in Thailand. There is a common theme, with local variations. At the most extensively excavated cemeteries—Non Nok Tha, Ban Chiang, Ban Na Di, Ban Lum Khao, and Ban Prasat (Bayard 1984; Higham and Kijngam 1984; Monkhonkkamnuenket 1992)—males, females, and the young were interred in proximity to each other (fig. 12.8). There is usually a common but not rigidly observed orientation that varies between sites. At Ban Na Di, it was north to south, but at Nong Nor it was east to west. Pottery vessels are the most common grave goods, disposed around the head, over the body, or beyond the feet. There were also items of jewelry, some of exotic origin. Bangles predominate. Bronze specimens are exotic to all the sites mentioned. At Ban Na Di, trochus shell, slate, and marble bangles were also obtained from some distance. Nong Nor is unusual for such cemeteries in the range of exotic stone and metal employed, particularly the serpentine, talc, and the tin examples. Some offerings remain unique to specific sites. Ban Na Di has produced the only large clay animal figurines, whereas Nong Nor is the only site to yield tin jewelry and shell neck pendants.

The bronze artifacts are dominated numerically by bangles. There is no obvious relationship between bronzes and males or females or individuals of greater-than-average wealth or age. Relatively few individuals were associated with bronzes, a situation that is again matched at Non Nok Tha and Ban Na Di. Of all graves at Nong Nor, 12 percent were associated with bronze. The corresponding figure at Ban Na Di is 10 percent. Thirteen percent of the burials from Non Nok Tha listed by Bayard (1984) were associated with bronzes, crucibles, or molds. None of the 110 graves excavated at Ban Lum Khao contained a bronze offering.

At Nong Nor, dog skulls were often interred with the dead. The incorporation of animal remains in graves, presumed to be some form of ritual killing of animals, is again found in other Bronze Age sites. At Non Nok Tha, complete pigs, dogs, and limbs of cattle were encountered. Pigs' jaws were common at Ban Chiang, while the left forelimbs of cattle and pigs were preferred at Ban Na Di. At Ban Lum Khao, pigs' foot bones were often encountered.

The most recent major excavation of a Bronze Age site was undertaken at Ban Lum Khao in Nakhon Ratchasima province, Thailand. The remains of 111 individuals were uncovered, including rows incorporating men, women, infants, and children dating between about 1000 and 500 B.C. It is notable that no individuals stood out in terms of mortuary wealth, nor was it possible to identify a single item that convincingly distinguished between the interment of men and women. Pottery vessels dominated among the grave offerings, and no item of bronze was found in association with any individual, although bronze was locally cast.

As a relatively crude index of mortuary wealth, figure 12.9 shows the number of intact graves at Nong Nor against the actual number of grave offerings. It is seen that a handful are set apart and that the three in question include a man and two women. The complete graves at Ban Na Di also include two rich outliers, one male and the other female. At this site, we also have some evidence for a rich enclave of burials that included most exotic grave goods. The

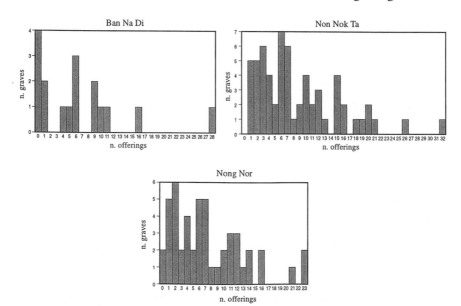

Figure 12.9. The number of grave goods found in intact graves at Ban Na Di, Non Nok Tha, and Nong Nor.

pattern recurs at Non Nok Tha, again with a male and a female being unusually well endowed. If grave goods are a measure of individual attainment, there is a reasonable case for supposing that some men and women achieved high status within their community.

The Bronze Age settlements reflect small, probably autonomous communities with subsistence based on rice cultivation and the maintenance of domestic stock, with considerable hunting, fishing, and collecting. The patterned nature of cemeteries strongly hints at family relationships between those interred in proximity. There is no evidence that men or women achieved significantly higher mortuary wealth, although there does appear to have been a concentration of exotic goods with certain groups defined spatially.

THE IRON AGE

It is most unfortunate that, for this critical period, which lasted for up to 1,000 years from 500 B.C. in parts of Southeast Asia, we have so little information. This is emphasized by the imposition of force by the Han in Lingnan, Yunnan, and Bac Bo and the increased mercantile activity in areas where Indian presence was strongest. Both were instruments for change in Iron Age societies.

In areas ultimately incorporated into the Han Empire, the twilight of prehistory witnessed a swift and marked increase in militarism. Dong Son drums reveal a warrior aristocracy and intensive production of bronze weaponry. In Yunnan, the spectacular mortuary wealth of the Dian, seen in particular at Shizhaishan and Lijiashan, again includes many bronzes and the occasional iron weapon. Both these sites incorporate a royal necropolis. At the latter, Yun Kuen Lee (1996) has applied statistical analyses to the graves and found that the two richest groups are almost certainly distinguished by the sex of the deceased. One contains weaponry, the other superbly crafted implements for weaving.

At Shizhaishan, certain graves contain outstanding wealth, including exotic ornaments, cowry shells, and a mass of weaponry. Cast-bronze scenes on the top of cowry containers reveal warfare, in which the central male figure is gilded and depicted larger than life. However, there are also scenes in which women play a prominent part in ritual and were clearly of exalted status. The woman carried aloft on a sedan chair depicted in a scene found in burial 1, for example, played a central role in a scene celebrating a successful harvest. In another scene, we see women weaving and in another offering bowls of food to a woman whose rank is indicated by gilding. We can also examine scenes of men at war and women bringing in the rice harvest in sacks to be placed in a granary for later distribution. War involved captives, and we can see women being taken, along with cattle, into captivity.

When moving away from royal centers, as, for example, at Tianzimao, the cemetery was dominated by two very large graves containing weaponry and many smaller graves with a minimum of offerings but still including some individuals with weapons and others with ceramic spindle whorls.

Yinshanling

This large cemetery site in Lingnan is dated to the Warring States period, that is, a couple of centuries earlier than Shizhaishan. Again, few human remains survive, but the excavation of 108 graves has provided a large sample of mortuary goods. These have been subjected to the same range of statistical analyses as Nong Nor and Tianzimao, and the results are most intriguing. Fifty-nine categories of grave good were identified, including clay spindle whorls, various types of bronze vessel, swords, arrowheads, halberds, spearheads, bronze tools, bells, belt buckles, whetstones, and jades. Certain of these wield discriminatory power when separating graves on the basis of contents. These are animal-headed staffs, iron scrapers, swords, lances, arrowheads, whetstones, and spindle whorls. In no case, for example, are spindle whorls and swords found in the same grave, and a distinction based on sex is obvious. Of the 18 particularly large and elaborate graves, 11 contained indicators of masculinity, the balance have objects associated with women in the Dian scenes. The presence of such large and rich graves is noted, but they are not, as at Shizhaishan, spatially separated from their contemporaries.

Noen U-Loke

Excavations at this site, located in the upper valley of the Mun River in northeastern Thailand, constitute part of a current project on the origins of the civilization of Angkor directed by the author and Dr. Rachanie Thosarat. Over two seasons, we have uncovered 125 Iron Age graves within a buildup of four meters, dated between about 300 B.C. and A.D. 300. Only preliminary inferences can be drawn from this, the largest sample of such graves with tolerably well preserved human remains in Southeast Asia (fig. 12.10).

There are five phases, the earliest comprising only one grave ascribed at present to the late Bronze Age. Of the remaining four, most graves belong to fourth and fifth phases (MP). Unlike the situation in the Bronze Age, Ban Lum Khao is only a few kilometers from Noen U-Loke, and the MP4 graves were clustered, each containing the remains of men, women, children, and infants. The preferred method of interment was supine with the head pointing to the north. Such clustering ceased with MP5.

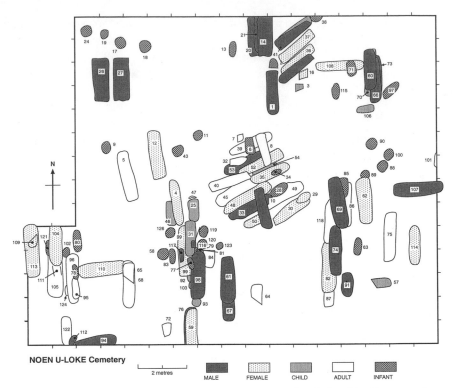

Figure 12.10.   The layout of Iron Age graves at Noen U-Loke, distinguished by sex and age.

Grave goods include many not found in the preceding Bronze Age. Bronzes are abundant, including bangles, earrings, ear spools and coils, finger and toe rings, bells, belts, a headband, and anklets. There are also bronze and iron bimetallic rings. Other ornaments were made from glass, silver, agate, carnelian, and gold. Iron was forged into spearheads, arrowheads, sickles, knives, and spades. Pottery vessels and ceramic spindle whorls were abundant.

During the MP4, we find distinctions based on cluster rather than sex. One cluster had most of the carnelian but few pottery vessels, and another had many pottery vessels but no carnelian. The latter was also distinguished by graves lined and capped with clay, a feature found only rarely in other graves. However, at least three of the clusters contained the grave of a particularly rich individual. Burial 14, for example, included more bronze grave goods by number and weight than could be accumulated from all the Bronze Age cemeteries excavated in Thailand. There were 150 bangles, about 300 finger and toe rings, and three bronze belts. This man also wore silver ear coils sheathed in gold. Burial 69 wore four belts as well as many bangles, finger and toe rings, and weighty ear spools. Burial 113, a woman, had been interred with many bronzes, silver toe and finger rings, pots, and a necklace that incorporated 66 gold beads and beads of agate and glass.

With the final mortuary phase, we find a possibly significant reflection of change. Now women alone were interred with iron sickles, while one man buried prone had a tanged projectile point of iron embedded in his spine. Another adult, of unknown sex, was found with a spearhead as a grave offering. It is suggested that friction was now developing, involving combat, but at the same time iron was being applied to gains in the efficiency of agriculture, which seems to have involved women. Before a final diagnosis of the sex of some skeletons is available, it is noted only that spindle whorls were found with both males and females, though this could change with full laboratory identification.

With the abandonment of Noen U-Loke, we approach the transition into history, when the picture of sex roles may be derived from epigraphic and sculptural sources as well as archaeological evidence. This chapter will not summarize these data, save to note that the achievement and status of women in Southeast Asian society, while lacking in the overt political dominance of the male overlords of the various states, remained a vital element in the maintenance of social cohesion.

SUMMARY

For three millennia, from the coastal hunter-gatherers of Khok Phanom Di to the emergent Iron Age chiefdoms of the Mun valley, we can identify a common element in the place of women in society. Mortuary practices involved the interment of the dead in groups, which probably reflect consanguinal or affinal proximity. Women were often buried near or in the same grave as infants. The diet was at all times good, and the indications of pregnancy even on the bones of young women shows that menarche was probably attained during the mid-teens. When a large sample of remains is available, it is evident that infant mortality was high, but virtually all women had borne children. This relationship would probably have placed a strain on women's health and well-being.

Women tended to live longer than men, with mortality peaking in the late teens and among those over the age of 30 years. Very few women survived 40 years of age. We can trace a relationship between women and key economic or social functions in some of the societies represented: At Khok Phanom Di, they made superb pottery vessels, and at Noen U-Loke some were buried with considerable mortuary wealth and in the latest phase were particularly associated with iron sickles. In Yunnan, they specialized in weaving. Although the advent of the Iron Age and increased militarism clearly favored the rise of men to positions of leadership, a trend continued into the historic period as women continued to achieve high status.

Despite the accumulation of much relevant information, it should be emphasized that much research remains for the future. Foremost is the application of the study of DNA to prehistoric human remains in order to trace relationships between individuals interred in proximity. The second is the identification of some means of sexing immature individuals.

13

Mothers' Workloads and Children's Labor during the Woodland Period

Cheryl Claassen

Several years ago, I proposed that the addition of new activities such as pottery production and horticulture created a time management crisis for women and that our archaeological interpretations consistently produced superwomen, carefree children, and sportsmen (Claassen 1991: 286). I have continued to ponder what time management solutions were employed by prehistoric women and communities of the midwestern United States (Illinois, Indiana, Ohio, and Kentucky) to accommodate new activities. The possibilities for time management solutions are many—specialization (within and across classes, ages, and sexes); the elimination of tasks; increased work from individuals previously working; pulling into the workforce those not previously working; increasing the size of the workforce through birth rate, emigration, and labor tax; and technological changes. Most of the solutions, however, fall into the realm of social changes. In this chapter, I will address the time management problem that arose in or before the Middle Woodland period in the Midwest. Relying on the bioarchaeological literature concerned with adult female workloads and child health, I will propose that a major solution of mothers with increased work demands was to require that older children increase their laboring and also become caretakers for younger children.

The bioarchaeological literature is replete with references to dental caries and abscesses, hypoplasias, musculoskeletal markers, and sexual dimorphism. Dental caries, abscesses, and sexual dimorphism (differences in bone size between females and males) are relatively unproblematic in their causes and securely identified by bioarchaeologists and physical anthropologists. Reliance on musculoskeletal markers—for instance, roughened bony spots for muscle attachment—to indicate habitual activities performed by an individual has been questioned for the possibility that innate biological factors, rather than habitual activity, could be their cause. Recent work by Nagy (1998) leaves little doubt that these markers are determined by behavior. Like musculoskeletal markers, the identification of hypoplasias is not particularly contested, but their cause is, as is their significance. Weaning studies have often examined hypoplasias in infant skeletons, but these hypoplasias may be the result not of weaning but of the factors that caused the child's death.

While it is tempting to talk about gender in this review, the argument presented here is based on sexed skeletons. Gender in these societies was probably based not on soft tissue as it is in our society but on behavior and dress, neither of which is recovered from these burials or typically studied. The terms "male" and "female" are used here to denote the skeletal/biological category but not to imply the genders man and woman or to limit the number of genders to two.

FEMALE WORK IN MIDWESTERN CULTURES

Archaic Period (10,000–3,500 Years Ago)

I hypothesize that the workloads of both females and males in the Midwest increased significantly with the establishment of the Holocene environment by 10,000 years ago. The archaeological evidence indicates that the transition to the Holocene environment of this region is accompanied by increased quantities of artifacts of particular types, increased site numbers, and increased evidence of plant processing. All three observations could be indicating not only an increased number of people in the Early Archaic but also social groupings much smaller than those characteristic on the Pleistocene environment. Where large social groups of Paleo-Indians offered individuals opportunities to borrow equipment and even to specialize in activities, the smaller social groups found in the Archaic must have been fully equipped and members prepared to perform a greater range of activities. The advantage of smaller social groupings was to put less stress on the carrying capacity of the land.

The broader diet of the Early Archaic folks could either increase or decrease search time given a greater geographic diversity of foodstuffs while necessitating frequent harvesting given storage limitations, increased food preparation time due to an increased variety of ways to process the diverse foods, and more time spent in tool manufacture and maintenance.

Group size apparently increased during the Middle Archaic (8,000–6,000 years ago) as many groups in the Midwest adopted a logistical settlement pattern of exploiting resources at least seasonally. Some aggregation loci were at shell mounds in the mid-South, where some of the dead were interred in rituals led by female and male shamans (Claassen 1991). Aggregation points in the lower Illinois valley were the blufftop cemeteries where young and middle-aged adults were buried. The ceremonial life of these aggregate groups surely required significant investments of time by both females and males who prepared foodstuffs and trade/gift items and prepared for and enacted roles in ceremonies.

The bioarchaeological literature contains the best evidence of workloads but is scarce for this region and time period. Noticeable sexual dimorphism in the Archaic Indian Knoll shell mound population indicates that men and women were doing different types of activities (Perzigian, cited in Cook 1984). The higher rates of skeletal stress beginning earlier in life in a subsample of Indian Knoll and Chiggerville male skeletons might mean that males were more physically active than females (Cassidy 1984: 326; Bushée 1995). At Chiggerville, males show more arthritis of the shoulder, while females exhibit more arthritis in the wrist. From the perspective of 793 deciduous teeth of 370 individuals in the Ohio valley of Ohio, diet fostered good dental health, with caries, abscesses, and tooth loss minimal, "reflecting the presumably small amount of simple carbohydrate in the diet" (Sciulli 1998: 190).

How the adults of this era coped with increased work should be the focus of another chapter, but there is in the skeletal data just mentioned evidence from which one could argue that a sexual division of labor, a type of specialization, was in place.

Woodland Period (2,600–1,100 Years Ago)

During the Early Woodland (2,600–1,800 years b.p.) and Middle Woodland (1,800–1,400 years b.p.) periods, females' workloads came to incorporate the new activities of at least clay quarrying and pottery manufacture; new food-getting techniques; storing, preparation, and cooking techniques; and greater effort requirements for burial ceremonialism in mound building, tomb construction, body preparation, grave goods production, and time in ceremony (given the tremendous increase in the number of mounds and the number of burials). As population tripled in south-central Illinois through the Woodland period, birth rates increased so that children were taking more time as well (DeRousseau, quoted in Gardner 1991: 180).

The native cultigens required, by Middle Woodland times, clearance of riverbanks and floodplains, planting, plant breeding, crop tending, harvesting, parching of seeds, preparation of storage containers and pits, selection of seed, travel to rock shelters for storage, and innovations in pottery technology for cooking seeds (Braun 1985). Watson and Kennedy (1991) assert that women were the ones causing the genetic changes in the cultigens and that women were the ones causing the habitat changes.

That these new tasks took greater strength as well as more time for women can be seen in several osteological examinations. From southwestern Ohio sites comes evidence that sexual dimorphism was least among the Late Archaic and most among Middle Woodland peoples (Perzigian, Tench, and Braun 1984: 350). By early Late Woodland (1,400–1,100 years b.p.) times in Illinois skeletal samples (Hamilton, cited in Cook 1984: 243), there is decreased sexual dimorphism from that characteristic of Middle Woodland populations because of increased female size, indicating more strenuous work for women. Greater robustness was particularly evident in the upper arm.

Degenerative pathologies—osteoarthritis, osteophytosis, and degeneration of the vertebral centrum—significantly increase through time in Dickson Mounds of Indiana and are related to work habitually performed (Goodman et al. 1984: 295). Greater stresses were being experienced through health and work, although affecting males more than females.

Lesions on the Elizabeth site Woodland-period skeletons "indicate that Middle Woodland life was more exacting in terms of physical stress than was that of the Late Woodland," conclude Frankenberg, Albertson, and Kohn (1988: 111). Anemia was apparently less common in Late Woodland than in Early Woodland times, while limb-specific periostitis was more common in Late Woodland times.

Dental evidence from Ohio populations indicates continued reliance on native crops and animals. Caries were found in only 2.63 percent of the 34 individuals, and no one had abscesses or tooth loss (Sciulli 1998: 190).

COPING WITH WORK: THE DEVELOPMENT OF THE RESPONSIBLE CHILD

There are several ways mothers and communities can cope with increasing labor demands. They can increase the number of workers, abandon older tasks, or specialize in labor at the level of individuals or communities leading to increased trading for items no longer produced. At this time, I would like to present the evidence for one community-wide solution to the increased work required by the ceremonial life, horticulture, and pottery production that began in the Early Woodland of the Midwest, and that was the deployment of children's labor.

The development of responsible children in native societies appears to have at least one cause in mothers' workloads. Children in hunting-gathering societies may gather food—Hadza children gather up to 50 percent of their food needs—or they may do little to nothing related to the food quest—!Kung children gather none of their food. It has been argued that the !Kung children are not productive because the population density of the Kalahari is so low, the plants and animals are so well known, and water is too heavy for children to carry (Draper 1975). They do not participate in child care because there are enough adults in camp. Although the Hadza camps rarely have adults in them, parents leave children nonetheless but take infants. Children are not used as caregivers in either situation. With the adoption of agriculture or other labor-intensive activities that subtract the mother regularly from camp, however, even infants are left behind. In that situation, infants' diets are supplemented, they are weaned earlier, and they are cared for by children.

Draper (1975) could find no work expectations of !Kung girls or boys, no "cultural pressures," in the bush that determined the sex roles or personality traits so commonly associated with men and women of the world. Yet girls stayed closer to camp or in camp, had more interaction with adults (particularly women), and had less interaction with girl peers than did boys. Play groups were, however, rarely sex segregated, and girls were more often engaged in rough play than were boys before eight years of age. Instead, Draper spoke in terms of proclivities on the part of girls to stay close to adults and that this proclivity came to be exploited by sedentary !Kung. The new types of work for sedentary !Kung women and children are food storage, more involved processing of new foods (corn and sorghum), and keeping domesticated animals out of harm or from harming. Greatly busied mothers in sedentary villages call on girl children to run errands and tend children because, as Draper found, girls are more often at hand.

In a rural Filipino study, girls aged 13 to 15 were observed providing care for older preschool children. In a Peruvian study, daughters were more likely to replace the working mother in non–child care activities, such as cooking and washing. Daughters aged 10 or more had significant roles in meal preparation (cited in Popkin 1980).

When production is centered in the household, when women's work takes them away from home several hours daily, or when women's subsistence work is demanding, children are expected to be responsible and obedient (Draper and Cashden 1988: 341). Responsibility involves child care, field labor, water fetching, food processing, cooking, storage, animal tending, and errand running. Several authors have noted that obedient and responsible children are desired less by adults in foraging and industrialized cultures and most by agriculturists.

The implications for social organization in the history of the Midwest are profound—strong gender role formation would not have been present from the beginning of human occupation in the region but was triggered by workloads so demanding that parents had to call on children for labor and mothers had to leave infants in the care of children. Workloads, while increasing during the Archaic, should not have required women to leave infants behind. I estimate that the need for obedient, responsible children occurred with the move to greater reliance on local domesticates during or prior to the Middle Woodland. It could be that (1) the horticultural intensification (evident in increased seed numbers, decreased natural floodplain woods, and seed-to-nutshell ratios), (2) the production of durables and consumables for gift/trade, and (3) the ceremonial activities of Adena and Hopewell culture combined to produce workloads that took mothers away from home daily, situated some production activities at the home, and taxed mothers' energy. To cope with these demands on their time, they required older children to take on responsibilities—caring for younger children, crop work, food processing, and so on. Child labor would have begun during this period and intensified with the adoption of maize agriculture.

BIOARCHAEOLOGY OF CHILDREN
OF THE MIDWEST

If parents' workloads were such that they called on children to labor and mothers' workloads were such that they left nursing infants behind with older children, then the bioarchaeological data should reveal information on supplementation and possibly evidence of increased work by children.

Weaning

On the surface, there seem to be a number of weaning studies that are relevant to this investigation. Weaning is a change in the water source, from breast water to environmental water; it is the process of stopping breast feeding. Supplementation is less severe than weaning, as nursing often continues even as foreign foodstuffs are given to the child. It involves a change in carbon source. While most bioarchaeologists say that they are studying weaning, they are, in fact, studying supplementation.

Infant dietary supplementation studies have been conducted utilizing dental information (Cook and Buikstra 1979), the ratio of Sr to Ca in juvenile bones (Sillen and Smith 1983), and delta 13C (Katzenberg, Saunders, and Fitzgerald 1993). In the Midwest, supplementation diets have largely been addressed using dental information. Unfortunately, enamel hypoplasias provide much of the information yet are equivocal for determining weaning age. The hypoplasias could be a result of infectious disease rather than weaning/supplementing (Wright and Schwarcz 1998).

Few dental abscesses were observed in subadults of Early Woodland Adena populations (Cassidy 1984: 327). Dental health was quite good in a sample of 14 Early Woodland children from Salts Cave (Cassidy 1984: 329). Cook and Buikstra (1979) argue that increased child dental problems in the Middle Woodland period (after 1,500 years ago) of the eastern United States—including but not limited to the unreliable hypoplasias—are indicative of the use of the native starchy seeds as "weaning" food at this time. Such an observation suggests either that earlier mothers did not supplement children with the native starchy seeds or that their use has been greatly intensified to become more visible archaeologically. Mothers further increased "weaning" efforts in Late Woodland times (Cook and Buikstra 1979).

In children older than six months, cribra orbitalia, an anemia, is associated with other indicators of nutritional stress, supporting "the interpretation of weaning age protein-calorie malnutrition that is most pronounced in the late Late Woodland" (Cook 1984: 258).

Children's Work

There is very little evidence with which to evaluate the activities of children. Unfortunately, stresses on joints from habitual activities and arthritis are age accumulative. Within a subsample of skeletons from Indian Knoll (Archaic), Cassidy (1984: 324–25) found evidence that growth arrests "in utero or in the first few months of life were unusual, growth arrest in the later months and early childhood was frequent but short-lived, and growth arrest in mid-childhood was infrequent and mild." These findings are in keeping with a notion that Archaic subadults were not pressed into much work.

However, there is some evidence that can support the notion that Woodland-period children worked harder. Mild arthritis in Adena subadults has been noted (Cassidy 1984: 327). Bone fractures and juvenile mortality in the Illinois River valley (Buikstra, Konigsberg, and Bullington 1986: 538) were highest in subadults of the Middle Woodland period and decreased through time thereafter. It could be that as these societies came to value children for their labor potential, conditions for children attracted more attention, which enhanced their survivorship.

SUMMARY AND CONCLUSIONS

In this chapter, I have advanced the hypothesis that mothers' workloads increased to the point of needing to employ children as baby-sitters during the Middle Woodland period and thereafter. This use of children for child care and field and home labor gave rise to the strongly gendered work roles recorded in historic documents.

The evidence for Archaic period workloads seems to indicate that all women may have performed more subsistence and food preparation work in the Middle and Late Archaic than had earlier women. Men were under more stress than were women, and women did lighter work than what they performed later in prehistory in the region. Late Archaic women may have performed more production and ritual work than did earlier women.

Both strength and time requirements for work increased with the new Woodland activities. In addition to the increased time and strength requirements for Woodland-period work, mothers bore a greater number of children.

When work demands exceeded time available, it seems that there were several options open to precontact peoples to manage time. Task specialization would exempt most people from doing a particular task. Substituting tasks would keep the number of tasks constant for an individual. Increasing the number of workers would help, perhaps drawing on idle children or elderly individuals.

What indications are there that time management was practiced in this region, and when do these signs appear? The change from shell mounding to dirt mounding at the juncture of Late Archaic and Early Woodland may be such a labor/time-saving decision. The adoption of pottery for direct heat cooking in the late Early Woodland of the Midwest may be another (Sciulli 1998). That both of these changes occur in the Early Woodland period further suggests that time management may be a new concern in the Woodland period. Furthermore, mothers used carbohydrate-rich seeds to wean children earlier in the Middle Woodland and increased these efforts in Late Woodland times (Buikstra et al. 1986). Weaning children earlier would allow infants to be left behind and the mother to work more energetically both because she is unencumbered and undistracted and because the heavy energy demands of lactation and infant carrying (Kramer 1998) will cease sooner.

Buikstra et al. (1986) argue that the population increase of the Midwest during the Woodland period was due to an increase in fertility. They demonstrate that the most likely cause of the increase in fertility was the dietary improvement in supplemental foods that allowed for the absence of mothers and thus shortened periods of postpartum amenorrhea and shortened birth intervals (for an explanation of cause and effect, see Holland 1989). More specifically, "the nutritional mechanism for shortened birth intervals accompanying sedentism lies in access to soft foods appropriate for [supplementation] diets" (Buikstra et al. 1986: 540). They view the crucial step in the supplementation process to be not the wide-scale planting of carbohydrate-rich seeds of goosefoot and knotweed but the innovations in cooking technology (thinner vessel walls) that made it possible to boil these seeds and render both greater carbohydrate returns and a gruel.

Why there would be an interest in better supplemental foods is not explored by Buikstra and her coauthors. One strong possibility for the concern is that mothers' workloads increased after Early Woodland times, necessitating that they expend more energy than previously at work and be absent from home regularly and quite possibly that some production activities be located in the home. Mothers' workloads necessitated the use of baby-sitters who needed a supplemental food while the mother was engaged in work for extended periods of time. (Once children are employed, the later and even more intensive maize agriculture of the Mississippian period would have required a different workload-reduction strategy.)

I propose that the workload level for mothers that necessitated these changes in child labor and infant-feeding practices was present in Middle Woodland societies of the Midwest rather than the Late Woodland, as proposed by Buikstra et al. (1986: 540). The evidence consists of the thinning of vessel walls that occurs in the fifth century A.D., the population increase that begins in the Middle Woodland, the visible use of starchy supplemental food, the energy requirements necessary to establish and maintain the social network of Hopewell societies, and evidence of greater stress in the skeletons of at least some Middle Woodland skeletal populations. The procurement of raw materials and the working of those materials, the construction of mortuary facilities, and the time spent in ceremony and in building extrafamilial social ties were great. Braun (1985) used changes in the diversification of pottery decoration and style to claim greater interaction and cooperation among Middle Woodland groups. At the same time, pottery styles show greater consistency between different localities (Braun 1985). What are the specific types of interactions between women envisioned or implicated by these observations?

It is also during the Middle Woodland that maize first appears in midwestern sites. Bone chemistry studies have failed to find any evidence of Middle Woodland dietary use of maize, but floral analyses contradict this impression. Two explanations for this lag in dietary acceptance—that maize entered eastern U.S. societies first as a ritual plant or that the introduced strains were ill adapted to the eastern environment—have been posited. It may be instead that maize was adopted in the central Mississippi River valley area first as an infant food supplement superior to the local starchy seed gruels but that the practice of excluding infant and children's skeletons from isotopic studies is obscuring this use (e.g., Katzenberg et al. 1993).

Wright and Schwarcz (1998: 2) have addressed the possibility of maize use in infant feeding by pointing out that "if maize gruel was used to feed infants, the practice should be evident as a change in C^{13} of the enamel forming at the age of initial supplementation." Because maize is a plant rich in C^{13} and the mother's diet is low in lipids, the infant supplemented with maize would have enamel enriched in C^{13}. It should further be possible to distinguish between weaning and supplementation of infants by measuring the ^{15}N of bone collagen: The switch from milk proteins to solid food proteins will be apparent in a decrease in the measure (Wright and Schwarcz 1998).

Changing mothers' workloads during the Middle Woodland brought about changes in cooking, vessel technology, juvenile survivorship, fertility, and the social construction of mothering and childhood. The increased number of children resulting from increased fertility would seem to cancel out any energy gained by a society whose mothers weaned children earlier and used child caregivers. Several studies of mother substitutes have shown that mother substitutes, particularly very young ones, do not care for infants as well as do mothers (Popkin 1980). The impact of mother substitutes on infant nutrition in several Filipino communities when very young children are used as caregivers (six to eight years old) is for infant malnutrition to increase to 55 percent, while with older caregivers' (13 and older) malnutrition falls to 21 percent, compared to that of 8.5 percent when mothers themselves are the primary attendants. It could be that the higher subadult mortality during the Middle Woodland period in the Illinois River valley of Illinois was due to the use of mother substitutes to care for infants. Nevertheless, children's labor in the field and at home resulted in a net energy gain for the horticultural societies of the Midwest. The economic cost of children began to decline in the late Middle Woodland, and this may have fueled the increased birth rate in a more meaningful way than did simply a shortened period of amenorrhea, answering Holland's critique of Buikstra et al. (1986) that early weaning was not the only factor affecting fertility and population growth. While mothers' workloads increased significantly with the adoption of cultigens and domesticates, the greatest gain in energy/labor for Woodland groups may well have come from the incorporation of children into the labor pool who are now taught quite early in life the gendered behaviors expected of them.

ACKNOWLEDGMENTS

Thanks to Diane Wilson, Gary Crites, and Jane Buikstra, commentors on a January 1995 version of this chapter.

III

GENDER RELATIONS

SARAH MILLEDGE NELSON

Gender relations have to do with the interactions of various genders, male, female, and any others recognized by a given culture. The focus here is not on men or women or other genders as separate individual categories but on the way the defined genders within a given culture interact. Gender relations may be egalitarian or hierarchical. A particular gender may be disadvantaged economically, politically, and/or psychologically. This can result in other genders having mildly preferential treatment but with no severe consequences to the health and daily activities of others or may result in restrictions for one or more genders on the needs of daily life, such as food and free movement. The chapters in this part focus on gender relations in various ways.

In chapter 14, Bettina Arnold takes up the topic of Iron Age burials in Germany and France. She describes in useful detail the problems of using sex in burials as a proxy for gender and comes to the conclusion that the importance of sex/gender distinction for archaeologists is in perceiving it as a continuum rather than as binary opposites of male/female and man/woman. This makes the interpretation of sex and gender in burials much more difficult but opens up possibilities for better understanding of the culture.

Arnold discusses the possible archaeological ramifications of gender mutability. How could they become visible in archaeological contexts? For example, multiple gender possibilities may be reflected in cross-dressing, which could be visible in grave goods. This is further complicated by the effect that class can have on the appropriateness of cross-dressing. Specifically, Arnold looks at the elite burial at Vix in the Iron Age in France, where the gender ambiguity of the grave goods has been interpreted in various ways. The problem as framed was that the personal adornment and lack of a sword suggest that the burial was that of a female (it was originally called the "Princess of Vix"). However, some scholars felt that elite status is incompatible with femaleness. Tests have shown that the burial very likely is a female, demonstrating that the assumption that women could not be buried with such pomp was the source of the problem, not gender shifting.

In chapter 15, Katheryn Linduff examines women's graves in Anyang, the last capital of Shang China, about 1200 B.C. These burials are among the richest graves from the Shang dynasty that have been professionally excavated and published. This reflects the fact that the king's graves were looted repeatedly over time, but that is not the whole story. Many impressive artifacts presumably came from the kings' graves (indeed, some inscriptions show that they did), but nothing is known of the placement of burial goods or their relationship to each other. The single richest burial ever excavated at Anyang is that of Lady Hao. While this circumstance could be supposed to reflect only the loss of the presumably richer king's graves, it is nevertheless the case that the largest bronze vessel known for the Shang was also from a woman's grave—that of Lady Jing. Both these women were honored with a place in the calendar of ritual worship and became official ancestors after death. The various placement of different classes of women shows that few women were able to exercise power.

The women whose burials are known were queens, consorts, mothers, servants, or sacrificial victims. The use of humans as sacrifices was not confined to women—both women and men are found in the graves of others as sacrifices, and both men and women royalty have sacrificed persons in their graves. Oracle bones reveal some facets of the lives of elite women. They could be military leaders, performers of ritual, and possibly landholders as well as queens or consorts. Linduff suggests that the burials of a few women also reflect political power, with accumulated wealth and status symbols piled into their final resting places.

Linduff connects a two-sided jade figure depicting a male on one side and a female on the other to Daoism, in which a balance between the sexes rather than a dominance of one sex over the other was sought. This jade example is reminiscent of a bronze dagger from the "Northern Zone," north of the line of the Great Wall, at roughly the same time period, with a human figure on the hilt, likewise male on one face and female on the other. However, oracle bone inscription demonstrated that this ideal was not achieved in the Shang dynasty. Kings had multiple wives, and although the wives could be women of power and received honor in their burials and veneration after death, their status still seems to have been dependent on being married to the king, not independently gained recognition. However, Linduff suggests that there may have been "different but parallel" routes to power for women and men.

In chapter 16, Myriam Rosen-Ayalon describes the context of paintings in early Umayyid times and the particular placement of them in buildings dedicated to pleasure and to administration. The buildings are known as "desert palaces," but they seem to have had a variety of functions. In one of these compounds, paintings of women in the bathhouse are nude but not lascivious, showing women (and in one case a child) bathing. In the main hall, women are clothed in a variety of costumes. Another building has sculptures of women in niches and paintings on the floors. Only one of the women is veiled. A third palace complex contains a number of rooms with different functions, including a mosque and a bathhouse. It contains only sculptures and no paintings. The sculptures of women, with bare breasts but with elaborately arranged hair and ornate jewelry, often holding flowers, were placed in niches in the entrance hall and the bathhouse. Rosen-Ayalon suggests that these are ladies to give men pleasure. Handsome young males are also depicted. Seeking antecedents to these representations, Rosen-Ayalon briefly describes Byzantine and Sassanian depictions of the upper classes, where men and women are seen in parallel.

In chapter 17, Elisabeth Bacus provides a new understanding of women in the political economy of the Visaya region of the Philippines in early historic times. Using documents, especially early Spanish accounts, combined with archaeology, she finds that the most significant social categories are elite and nonelite rather than male and female. Chiefs sponsored maritime trade and craft production for elite uses as well as receiving tribute payments, corvée labor, and fees for using their ports. With funds thus acquired, they could expand their power base both laterally and vertically.

It is interesting that early Spanish writers perceived women as equal to men and autonomous in their activities, while Chinese writers appear not to have noticed women at all. These differences surely reflect the cultures of the observers rather than changes in Visayan culture. Women were producers of textiles, a commodity that chiefs controlled. Women of all ranks were weavers, and they learned the skill at an early age. Pottery was also made by women, but less is known about its production. Nonelite women were agriculturalists, especially producers of rice, which was used in elite feasting. Women, from elite to slave women, could be local traders on their own account and even sometimes personally traded with foreigners.

While separation between elite and nonelite appears to have occurred in living arrangements, nonelite men's and women's activities took place in overlapping space. This interestingly echoes the findings discussed in chapter 8 of the Maya region.

Women's production was thus important in both the subsistence and the trade economies. Elite women are noted to have had equal numbers of slaves and dependants as their husbands. Women were important in political alliances and were also ritual specialists, able to heal as well as to mediate with the local gods. Bacus writes of "signs of potency" for women rather than power. Elite women had the trappings of wealth and followers, but they did not control the long-distance trade in wealth items. Earlier in the Visayas, it was possible for women to become chiefs, but as long-distance maritime trade increased and slave capture became important, they were increasingly disadvantaged in the quest for power and potency.

Another kind of images is figurines, which, in chapter 18, Fumiko Ikawa-Smith examines in Jomon, Japan. She focuses on the strange humanoid and female-like figurines that are found unevenly in time and space throughout the Jomon period. The huge numbers of such figurines make them seem unmanageable. Various interpretations of the figurines have been made, but in the end Ikawa-Smith thinks that negotiations of power may provide the best answer.

A. C. Roosevelt takes a different direction in chapter 19. She reviews the sociobiological literature on human evolution and concludes that gender inequality did not exist before the Holocene.

In this final part, we find a variety of kinds of gender relations, ranging from complementarity to inequality. The chapters examine other dimensions of gender relations as well. The topic is complex, as these chapters show, and cannot be reduced to concepts such as "status" or the notion that women can be found in domestic contexts and men in public places. Differences are found in rank and age and perhaps by ethnic groups. Nuances can be found to counter the sweeping generalizations, instead of detailed investigations, that are sometimes offered.

14

"Sein und Werden":
Gender as Process in Mortuary Ritual

Bettina Arnold

Identifying sex and gender in mortuary contexts has always been an important part of archaeological interpretation. There is an ongoing debate over whether to continue to distinguish between the two terms, which have traditionally been defined as biologically (sex) or culturally (gender) determined. Phillip Walker and Della Cook (1998) have argued that conflating the terms "sex" and "gender" in anthropological discourse is a programmatic problem that has negative ramifications for archaeology in particular: "Without the distinction between gender and sex, studying gender roles in ancient societies becomes a virtual impossibility" (256). Others—most recently Kessler (1998) but also Hubbard (1990)—argue that from a contemporary social and political perspective at least, the distinction between the two terms should be eliminated. This chapter attempts to address the challenge to archaeological interpretation of gender configurations presented by the mediation of these two perspectives.

Specifically, I will argue in favor of maintaining the distinction while viewing sex and gender as part of an interconnected continuum rather than as a set of distinctive binary oppositions (two sexes, two genders invariably tied to their "normative" opposite numbers: that is, _ = male/_ = female). In this scenario, there is a complex number of possible biological configurations (morphological as well as chromosomal) arranged along a continuum that occasionally intersect, in certain cultural contexts, with an equally complex set of gender configurations (not necessarily tied to morphological or genetic features) also arranged along a continuum. For example, Herdt has deconstructed the dominant Western dyadic definition of sex very effectively in his introduction to his 1994 volume *Third Sex, Third Gender.* He points out that standard Western clinical practice recognizes four components of the term sex:

chromosomal, gonadal, morphological, and psychosexual or gender identity. He then proceeds to demonstrate that more than two manifestations of each of these components have been documented (1994: 25–33).

Why is the sex/gender distinction important for archaeologists? Ambiguous correlations between (biological/morphological) sex and (extrasomatic) gender in individual burials are more common in the archaeological record than is generally recognized or acknowledged. The complexities of what appear to be mutable gender configurations are often glossed over or ignored in archaeological interpretation, although this situation is improving, as more recent European publications, such as that of Karlisch, Kästner, and Mertens (1997), indicate. Unfortunately, publications in languages other than English tend not to register among American scholars, with the result that excellent work is being done that is not being effectively disseminated.

There are other problems. A consistent bias toward the identification of ambiguous burials as gender-male has tended to skew the interpretation of prehistoric social relationships. In addition, contemporary Western cultures are relatively impoverished with respect to gender categories, with only two genders (corresponding to the two normative biological sexes) being "officially" recognized in most cases. Many archaeologists are unaware of the extensive anthropological literature on the mutability of sex and gender categories (though North American archaeologists working with historical material are an exception; see, e.g., Sandra Hollimon's [1997] chapter in Claassen and Joyce's *Women in Prehistory* [1997]). At the same time, we must beware of chronocentrism as well as ethnocentrism in our discussion of sex and gender in ancient societies. Prehistoric peoples constructed sex and gender on the basis of observed morphological or behavioral features. They could not have distinguished between individuals on the basis of chromosomal features if those features had no phenotypical or behavioral manifestations, for example. At least as importantly, our 20th-century political agendas and concerns were not theirs.

The lack of a systematic approach to this subject constitutes an Achilles' heel in the interpretation of prehistoric gender configurations and their material expression. This chapter presents some suggestions for the construction of such an approach and discusses their potential application to an archaeological context in Iron Age Europe.

"Kleider machen Leute," according to the German adage. This version is more inclusive and gender neutral than the English "Clothes make the man." Clothes make the woman as well as the man, and sometimes they make the man a woman, or the woman a man, or the man/woman something entirely outside the "normative," Western, binary male/female category. The German playwright Carl Zuckmayer made this idea the central point of his 1931 drama *The Hauptmann of Köpenick,* in which a down-at-heel shoemaker appropriates the uniform of a Prussian officer. The inhabitants of his community have been so thoroughly programmed to respond to the trappings of authority that they literally salute the suit and never notice the disjunction between the costume of the pseudo-colonel and his behavior.

People in all societies are, to varying degrees, what they wear and/or wear what they are. Gender is one of the most universal messages communicated by costume and personal ornament. We rarely examine one another's genitals when being introduced for the first time; what we attempt to categorize are the trappings of gender, which may or may not be an accurate reflection of an individual's biological sex. Kessler (1998), for one, would argue that such an examination, even if practiced, would not necessarily lead to an unequivocal sex or gender determination since even the medical profession acknowledges the existence of at least three categories of sex: male, female, and "intersexed" (this last category is itself further subdivided). To further complicate matters, costume may also convey messages regarding social status, ethnicity, age, and other group identity markers. The potential for mystification, misrepresentation, or misidentification of gender, sex, or status on the basis of costume or personal adornment is therefore considerable. Significantly for archaeologists, costume and role-related trappings are frequently included in burial, providing variably complete glimpses of gender configurations in antiquity. Combined with conventional anthropological analysis of preserved skeletal material and, more recently, the analysis of ancient DNA (ADNA), mortuary analysis has the potential to limn gender configurations in the past. This in turn makes possible the recognition of gender categories and configurations, as long as they manifest themselves in some preservable patterned form of material culture in the mortuary context.

The study of sex and gender is extremely complex, not least because notions of femaleness and maleness and what Spector and Whelan (1989) have described as "gender ideology" are simultaneously fundamental to cultural and individual identity as well as highly culturally and individually variable. The individual has recently been getting more attention from archaeologists, who have an historical tendency to focus on "peoples" in the aggregate rather than as unitary actors with their own motivations. This may explain why it is only within the last decade that the mutability of gender categories has been acknowledged in a programmatic way by prehistoric archaeologists. In fact, gender in general, and supernumerary gender categories in particular, have become a serious subject of analysis in archaeology only in the last decade, as a review of the literature clearly shows. Herdt (1994) describes a similar neglect of this subject in cultural anthropology: "But because gendered analyses have typically ignored sexual conduct and practices, they have also tended to marginalize third-sex and/or third-gender categories and representations in culture and society" (44). That the same process of marginalization has been operating in archaeology, particularly in Europe, is demonstrated by the title of a recent publication by Jenny Moore and Eleanor Scott (1997), *Invisible People and Processes: Writing Gender and Childhood into European Archaeology*.

It is also interesting to note that Scandinavian archaeologists seem to have recognized the potential of a gendered approach to the archaeological interpretation of burial practices earlier than most; a representative example of such a gendered mortuary analysis is the recent study by Agneta Strömberg (1993). No corresponding body of literature exists in North American archaeological publications, where gender as a component of mortuary analysis is singularly underrepresented in anthologies and edited volumes. This may be due to the increasing discomfort that many archaeologists feel in their interaction with Native American cultures whose attitude toward the study of skeletal material and burials more generally has been increasingly politicized, most recently in the form of the Native American Graves Protection and Repatriation Act (NAGPRA) of 1990. Even pre-NAGPRA, the close relationship in North America between gender studies in archaeology and feminist thought (itself closely linked to postmodernism and the deconstruction of colonialism) seems to have resulted in the avoidance of potentially culturally sensitive studies such as mortuary analysis in the context of indigenous peoples. As a European archaeologist studying her own ancestors, I have therefore found myself increasingly drawn to European case studies in the formulation of my own research strategies.

One of the key questions in the study of the phenomenon of gender mutability is how to reconstruct motivation. This is highly contested territory in contemporary transgender communities, but it needs to be addressed in any discussion of the archaeological correlates of past gender configurations. For example, there seems to be a correlation between the presence or absence of a gender-transforming category in a society and the way in which the social hierarchy is organized with respect to the relative status of men and women in that society. The tension between gender identity (emic and self-defined) and gender attribution (etic and defined by the social context) exists in all cultures, but to differing degrees. For example, in Western cultures in the late 20th century, it is considered understandable that a woman might want to assume the trappings of the higher-status sex, but it is still relatively rare for a man to voluntarily and publicly "demean" himself by wearing women's clothes in a professional context. (Transvestism in the context of the theater, especially comic theater, is another story, and for reasons that are related.) Upward mobility, in the form of cross-dressing that emulates the higher-status sex, is logically consistent within capitalist societies in many contemporary contexts. Downward mobility, on the other hand, is despised, ridiculed, or pitied. A woman in men's clothes in a late 20th-century American context is considered elegant and dignified (think Julie Andrews in *Victor, Victoria*), whereas a man in women's clothing is seen as a spoof or is an object of amusement (think Harvard's Hasty Pudding Club).

A complicating factor in the interpretation of past gender configurations as manifested in dress is that in Western society today, women's clothing is much more highly sexualized than men's clothing.[1] The sweat sock is not the equivalent of the stocking. The literature on Western transvestism, which is typically presented as primarily male to female, often includes some discussion of fetishism or sadomasochism (King 1981). This underscores the sexual component of contemporary transvestism in Western culture. Such behavior is erotic primarily because it is illicit and taboo, which means that this form of transvestism is probably not a good analogue for societies in which gender transforming is institutionalized. Cross-dressing is not deviant in and of itself but only if the reason for its occurrence is not considered legitimate, that is, when time, place, and audience are inappropriate (Woodhouse 1989: 15). It is the social context (and complexity) of gender transforming generally, and transvestism in particular, that archaeologists need to consider in their interpretations.

Another key point is that there *are* individuals who voluntarily cross-dress in this as well as other societies despite the social costs of such behavior. This means that archaeologists have to assume that gender transformers[2] existed in prehistoric contexts, whether or not they are always archaeologically recoverable. Gender transformers, or two-spirit people, are documented in over 150 North American tribes, for example, in every region of the continent, among every type of native culture, from small bands of hunters in Alaska to the populous, hierarchical city-states of Florida (Roscoe 1994: 330). They are found in Africa among various peoples, in the Near East, in South and East Asia, and in Europe. In short, there are virtually no ethnographically recorded cultures that do not exhibit some type of gender mutability. The issue is not whether gender transformers were present in prehistoric societies but rather how to define the social conditions under which male or female gender transformers will be reflected in the archaeological record. The mortuary record is the most fruitful context for such evidence, and it is here that we need to focus our attention.

Archaeologists have an advantage over ethnographers in that they are able to determine the biological sex of an individual on the basis of skeletal remains as well as ADNA. However, in blind studies of skeletal samples, the bias consistently favors the identification of borderline individuals as male, following the Western cultural tendency to accord males higher status than females. In

addition, archaeologists tend to oversimplify the relationship between gender and culture by reducing their interpretations to the sex-gender binary formula. Cross-dressing is a symbolic incursion into territory that borders gender categories—a liminal zone that manifests itself as sex-gender disjunction (not necessarily merely inversion) in the burial record. Too often sex and gender configurations in prehistoric burials are forced into categories that are considered normative in Western European society.

The first task of the archaeologist should be to identify patterned correlations between morphologically identifiable sex and the material culture expression of gender within a specific prehistoric mortuary context before attempting to define the range of possible social categories. This requires cemeteries of sufficient size to provide a significant sample and burials that are well preserved and that have been systematically excavated. Needless to say, this happy conjunction of circumstances is comparatively rare, at least in Iron Age European contexts, my own field of study.

The hypothetical cemetery should be analyzed according to the following criteria:

1. How many different categories of grave-good assemblages or burial treatments are identifiable?
2. Which ones appear to be age specific, that is, correlate primarily with the age of the individual?
3. Are the patterns bipolar or multipolar with respect to some variables?
4. How do these correlate with biological sex as determined morphologically and (where possible) genetically? Is there genetic evidence for chromosomally "intersexed" (Kessler 1998) individuals?
5. Where are the areas of overlap between the identifiable patterned categories? That is, are there any individuals who exhibit a sex-gender disjunction with respect to anatomical or chromosomal features and grave-good assemblage or burial treatment? In the best of all possible worlds, different researchers would be responsible for the gender analysis on the basis of grave goods and the sexing of the skeletal material and DNA. The results of the various analyses would then be compared in an attempt to identify and interpret possible disjunctions.
6. Are these disjunctions found in association with males, females, and possible intersexed individuals, or are they restricted to a single sex? What are their relative proportions?

We also need to consider what Woodhouse (1989: xii) calls the "sociology of appearance," the "apparent divorced from the real." The "apparent" for archaeologists corresponds to personal ornament and other grave goods, whereas the "real" in burial is represented by the morphologically observable biological sex of the individual.[3] The assumption made by most mortuary analysis, that the external appearance of an individual indicates not only biological sex but also a person's gender, is upset by transvestism, whether female to male, male to female, or intersex to male, female, or some other mutable gender category.

The emphasis in this discussion is on transvestism or, perhaps less exclusively, multivestism, not because it is the only way in which gender identity is expressed but because it is the principal way in which gender identity is likely to manifest itself archaeologically as compared to biological sex. Transvestism is motivated by a number of different factors in contemporary societies, including but not limited to sexual orientation and enhanced economic opportunities. The ethnographic evidence for transvestites suggests that they may be a-, bi-, hetero-, or homosexual. The extent to which a society emphasizes the sexual orientation of an individual when defining gender role is highly variable. A number of researchers have emphasized the secondary significance of sexual orientation in the definition of the Native American gender transformers sometimes referred to as "berdache," or more recently "two-spirit beings" (Angelino and Shedd 1955; Whitehead 1981; Whitam and Mathy1986; Roscoe 1988, 1994; Jacobs, Thomas, and Lang 1997). The sexual orientation of such individuals was not the primary reason for their inclusion in a gender-transforming category. Scholars such as Havelock Ellis and Magnus Hirschfeld, writing in the 1920s and 1930s, also made a point of distinguishing transvestism from homosexuality (King 1981: 163).

Contemporary American society has a tendency to define transvestism primarily in terms of sexual orientation, which has affected the archaeological interpretation of this category of person in prehistoric contexts. Ultimately, the sexual orientation of a gender transformer who shows up in the archaeological record is of secondary importance unless all members of an institutionalized gender-transforming category shared the same sexual orientation as a condition of membership. Even then, there would be no way to distinguish archaeologically (assuming the absence of written records) between such groups and those in which sexual orientation has no or little bearing on membership. It is the material culture correlates of gender transformation that we have to consider and the fact that in order for gender transformers to form an archaeological pattern, they must constitute a normative category within their society. The ethnographic evidence suggests that institutionalized gender-transforming groups include all possible permutations of sexual orientation. The common thread is not sexual orientation but the appropriation of the costume and trappings of a gender incongruent with morphologically observable biological sex.

Native American gender transformers (most recently baptized "two-spirit people" [Jacobs et al. 1997], although each tribe or tribal group may have their own specific terms for such individuals) offer an alternative model to the traditional Western bimodal pattern for interpreting sex/gender disjunction within mortuary contexts. One of the most famous and well-documented cases is the Zuni gender transformer Whe'wa. In traditional Native American societies, gender transformers were not anomalous but rather were integral, productive, and valued members of their communities (Roscoe 1991: 5). By virtue of their liminal status—half within the sphere of one gender, half within the sphere of the gender consistent with their biological sex—they were in a particularly favored position, and their relatively high status in most ethnographically documented Native American societies reflects this.

Native American societies also provide a good demonstration of the extent to which the presence of a female gender-transforming category varies from one group to the next and how it correlates with gender ideology. Blackwood (1984: 29) argues that evidence from 33 Native American tribes indicates that the cross-gender role was as viable an option for women as it was for men. She also believes the nature of the kinship system played a role in whether cross-gender roles were available to women as well as men (1984: 33). The status of women relative to men in a given society seems to play a role in the presence and frequency of female gender transformers.

There has been a lot of debate surrounding the question of whether male dominance is universal. It is certainly true that the extent to which women are subordinate to men is highly variable cross-culturally. That is why the presence or absence of female gender transformers and their relative frequency compared to male gender transformers might be useful as an indicator of the relative status of males as compared to females in a prehistoric society. For example, if men and women were of comparable status and there were no specific injunctions against gender transforming, one would expect to see a similar male-to-female gender transformer ratio. Deviation from this pattern in either direction implies corresponding gender ideologies.

Western history, for example, records more women who not only cross-dressed but who also lived and worked as men than vice versa (Bullough and Bullough 1993: ix). This is because, on the one hand, women are subordinate to men in Western cultures but, on the other hand, individuals have considerably more leeway with respect to personal expression in this society than in many others, past or present. In other words, gender transforming is not institutionalized, but the punishment for transgressing gender lines is not so severe that individual women have been unwilling to take the risk. It is significant that, in fact, the risk in contemporary Western society is considerably higher for men than for women.

The ethnographic record also provides us with examples of how gender transformers may be recognizable in the archaeological record under certain conditions. Harriet Whitehead (1981), for example, has emphasized that the definition of an individual as a gender transformer in Native American societies was dependent on participation in work inconsistent with the biological sex of the individual. This presupposes two things: (1) that gender is defined primarily in terms of the work performed, and the tools, costume, and behavior of the performer determine how an individual's gender is classified, and (2) that the choice of occupation and associated paraphernalia is both individual and communal, that is, that the "two-spirit person" represents an institutionalized supernumerary gender category.

As Halberstam (1992) points out, "Gender is always posthuman, always a sewing job which stitches identity into a body bag" (51). This view represents gender as a process rather than a product (Plummer, in Ekins and King 1996: xiv) and is supported by ethnographic evidence. The Zuni lhamana Whe'wa illustrates the mutable quality of the Native American gender transformer especially well. He participated in activities associated with both women and men in Zuni society. He wore women's clothing, although some features of his costume were specific to his status as a gender transformer, that is, were not typical of either male or female costume.

At Whe'wa's death, his grieving relatives put a pair of pants on under his skirt to represent the rejoining of his biological sex to his cultural identity as a gender transformer in the female sphere at the moment of death. For the Zuni, biological sex represents the "raw" identity of the individual at birth. It is superseded by the "cooked" gender identity that the individual chooses for him- or herself as part of the social induction process; this adult gender identity may or may not correspond to the individual's biological sex at birth. At death, an individual's "raw" identity resurfaces and is represented together with the acquired, "cooked" cultural identity in the mortuary ritual (Roscoe 1988: 145). Or, as Ru Paul recently put it, "You're born naked and the rest is drag" (quoted in Denny 1994: 217).

Male Zuni lhamanas underwent one of two male initiation rites and participated in the all-male kachina societies responsible for sacred masked dances. They were referred to by male kinship terms, and, especially significant, they were buried on the male side of the cemetery. In other words, even though in Zuni gender ideology lhamanas occupy a third gender status in life, one that combines men's and women's traits, in death they are treated as biologically male (Roscoe 1988: 129). Archaeologically, there would be a conjunction between the evidence for anatomical sex and the placement in the cemetery with other anatomically male individuals and a disjunction with the imperishable parts of the personal costume typically found associated only with biologically female individuals and some found with neither biological males nor females.

What would archaeologists make of a male-female gender transformer such as Whe'wa? He was above average height—contemporary observers referred to him as "the tallest person in Zuni" (Roscoe 1998a: 128), and his robust physique was the subject of much commentary. Despite his morphologically male exterior, when Whe'wa visited Washington and spent several weeks on the social circuit, he was thought by Washington "society" to be female and was allowed access to the dressing rooms of "society" ladies. Washington society saw a Pueblo "princess" because that was what they had been told to expect and because Whe'wa's costume was consistent with the label. *The Hauptman of Köpenick* discovered the uses of this phenomenon in 1931 Prussia, as did Whe'wa in 1882, when he watched Washington's crème de la crème put on their hairpieces and adjust their corsets in their boudoirs.

In the same way, European observers seem to have been unable to recognize the transgendered individuals they encountered in native societies in the course of the 19th century, even though later ethnographers, such as Elsie Parsons in 1916, found ample evidence for the existence of such a category (Blackwood 1984: 38). The Zuni seem to have linked both male and female gender transformers to the same supernatural archetype. In Zuni ideology, there were three genders: male, female, and liminal. As Roscoe points out, the answer to the question "Was Whe'wa a man or a woman?" is "Neither" (1991: 145; 1994). He argues eloquently for a new form of discourse that can handle the complexity of gender transformation. What is needed is a "multidimensional model, one that recognizes not only the sexual and gender features of these alternative roles, but their economic, religious, social, and kinship facets as well" (Roscoe 1988: 213).

As early as 1955, Angelino and Shedd asked the question whether there are certain types of social organization that are correlated with the presence or absence of gender transformers (1955: 121). They argued that one of the principal problems with the analysis of the gender-transforming phenomenon is that there is no agreement on what the term means. I would suggest that there are at least seven possible categories of gender/sex configurations in mortuary contexts, including gender transformers. The list in table 14.1 is not intended to be exhaustive, but it attempts to provide a starting point for a more concrete discussion of gender mutability in the context of archaeological praxis.

It is worth mentioning here that pseudohermaphrodites are relatively common (Kessler 1998: 135), but the range of variation with respect to genital configurations is quite extensive and in most cases probably would not lead to the "recategorization" (by self or by others) of the individual with respect to sex or gender. True hermaphrodites, on the other hand, are extremely rare,

Table 14.1. Possible Categories of Gender/Sex Configurations in Archaeological Mortuary Contexts

1. Biologically male/gender male	Sexual orientation[a]
Identifiable[b c]	Not archaeologically identifiable
Archaeological correlate:	Gender/sex conjunction
2. Biologically male/gender female	Sexual orientation
Identifiable[b c]	Not archaeologically identifiable
Archaeological correlate:	Gender/sex disjunction possible
3. Biologically female/gender female	Sexual orientation
Identifiable[b c]	Not archaeologically identifiable
Archaeological correlate:	Gender/sex conjunction
4. Biologically female/gender male	Sexual orientation
Identifiable[b c]	Not archaeologically identifiable
Archaeological correlate:	Gender/sex disjunction possible
5. Biologically male or female/neither man nor woman ("living outside gender" or "gender outlaws") Identifiable[b c]	Sexual orientation
[Whittle 1996])	Not archaelogically identifiable
Archaeological correlate:	Gender/sex disjunction possible
6. Pseudohermaphrodite[d]	Sexual orientation
Identifiable[c]	Not archaeologically identifiable
Archaeological correlate:	Gender/sex disjunction possible
7. True hermaphrodites[d]	Sexual orientation
Identifiable[c]	Not archaeologically identifiable
Archaeological correlate:	Gender/sex disjunction possible

[a]Sexual orientation categories: asexual, bisexual, homosexual, heterosexual.
[b]Morphologically.
[c]Genetically.
[d]Gender categories: male, female, intersex.

and any archaeologically identifiable (i.e., socially acceptable or institutionalized) gender-transforming category is unlikely to include many or any individuals with this trait.

Since gender is attributed to social actors by self as well as by others (Kessler and McKenna 1978; Kessler 1998), how these categories are represented archaeologically is dependent on the gender ideology of the society in question (Spector and Whelan 1989). This involves not only the way in which the genders are ranked relative to one another but also the way in which the gender cosmology of the society operates and to what extent gender identity intersects with gender role and attribution as well as rank and status. The gender ideology of a society usually extends beyond people to other living things as well as the inorganic world of material culture and indeed the world itself in the form of gendered space. Although we are unlikely to be able to recover or correctly identify all the gendered messages embedded in the archaeological record of prehistoric cultures, we can establish guidelines for recognizing patterns that may relate to gender ideology. The identification and interpretation of gender transformers constitutes one of these patterns.

Throughout much of history, trans- or multivestism was not viewed as an aspect of sexual conduct at all but often played a major role in religious cults. This is true for some, but not all, ethnographic examples of gender transformers. Cross-dressing is considered to be a sign of spirituality among many groups. Yakutian shamans in Siberia wore women's clothing, while among the Chuckchee in the same part of the world, shamans exchanged rifle, lasso, and harpoon for a woman's needle and skin scraper (Bullough and Bullough 1993: 17). Among the Winnebago, male gender transformers performed women's tasks and were thought to be able to tell the future. On the other hand, as Lurie (1953: 708) points out, not all Winnebago seers were gender transformers.

Nor is the phenomenon of the spiritually favored gender transformer restricted to so-called less complex societies (Harlow 1997). In early medieval Europe, a number of transvestite saints are known, all female-to-male gender transformers who entered male monastic communities in masculine dress: Hugolina, Agnes of Monçada, Angela of Bohemia, Apollonaris, Euphrosyne, Eusebia, Margareta, Anastasia, Callisthene, Glaphyra, and Wilgefortis are just some examples (Hotchkiss 1996: 22–23). Hotchkiss asks the provocative question, If disruptions of gender hierarchy were not encouraged, why were there so many sympathetic and popular female saints? In part, she argues, because "radical transformation—water to wine, death to life, male to female—informs Christian doctrine on many levels" (19). In addition, the act of inverting sex, which rejects sexual relations, "reflects the growing emphasis in the early centuries of Christianity on celibacy and sexual renunciation" (19). Monks as well as priests, with their long robes, represent another version of this costume-based de-sexing through transvestism. By wearing what is in effect a form of dress, a costume ordinarily associated with women, they enter a zone between the sexes in which, as an institutionalized third gender, they are protected from sexual interaction with women.

Bullough and Bullough (1993: 24) argue that biologically male and biologically female individuals, when viewed from a historical perspective, cross-dressed for different reasons. They argue that women cross-dressed and impersonated men to gain what they could achieve only as men, while men were more likely to cross-dress for erotic or religious reasons. While this is a generalization, it should be considered a possible model for interpreting prehistoric gender transforming in societies where women are accorded lower status than men. On the other hand, Hotchkiss's work makes clear that the relationship between social-political organization as expressed in gender ideology and the presence, absence, and nature of female-to-male, male-to-female, or inter-sex-to-supernumerary gender is complex and requires more in-depth cross-cultural analysis.

We must also consider the way gender and social status or class intersect. Cross-dressing by women rulers such as the Egyptian pharaoh Hatshepsut, who was represented in numerous statues wearing male clothing and a beard, occasionally even with a penis, is only indirectly useful in understanding the relative status of women in general in Egyptian society. We cannot conclude on the basis of the existence of morphologically female rulers that women were considered on a par with men. In fact, the opposite seems indicated: that in Egyptian gender ideology, men were ranked higher than women. Inscriptions on some of Hatshepsut's monuments use feminine pronouns when referring to her, even though she is represented in male regalia. This suggests that male clothing and appearance were seen as the prerequisite to rule — an Egyptian version of *The Hauptmann of Köpenick* (Bullough and Bullough 1993: 24). This category of gender transformer is a manifestation of what Antonia Fraser (1988) has called the "honorary male" syndrome. This phenomenon may be restricted to elites in societies with inherited status that are also patriarchal, as in the case of ancient Egypt. The biologically female elite individual in such cases takes on a position of political and economic power by being expediently gendered male (Arnold 1996). This allows the gender ideology of male supremacy to remain unchallenged while fulfilling the requirement of hereditary succession in the absence of a male heir. However, examples of nonelites "standing in" for deceased or never-born siblings of the opposite sex are also documented (Whitehead 1981), so the honorary male/female category is not necessarily restricted to elites.

Julie Wheelwright's (1989) study of cross-dressing women in Western military history emphasizes the fact that they did so as much for economic as for sexual orientation reasons. The handful of women who have historically cross-dressed have had little impact on the relative status of women in Western societies over time. She concludes, "It would appear that women have simply borrowed male dress as an avenue to gain power denied them elsewhere in their lives" (15). The comparative freedom for women to engage in such "liberating" behavior in Western cultural contexts is a relatively recent phenomenon, however.

For example, the fact that Elizabeth I (referred to by contemporary chroniclers as the "singular exception"; Fraser 1988) reviewed her troops in full male regalia, avoided marriage and childbearing, and ruled England more successfully than any previous monarch did nothing to improve the lot of women as a group in Elizabethan England (any more than Margaret Thatcher and her all-male cabinet did). An understanding of the different forms of mortuary ritual in a society and the ability to identify status differences as well as gender distinctions are critical to understanding gender ideology. Whether sex organizes culture or vice versa (Herdt 1994: 37), the two are inextricably linked.

Here again, only gender transforming that is institutionalized rather than occasional will have archaeological correlates. The Greeks and Romans, for example, practiced religious rites that included cross-dressing, but they did not have cross-dressing shamans who took on the attributes of the other or both sexes throughout their adult lives. Periodic or temporary gender transmutation is unlikely to leave archaeological traces. This also means that the absence of evidence for gender transforming in burial ritual may mask occasional cross-dressing behavior practiced by certain individuals at specifically regulated times. The whole point of cross-dressing at certain European festivals (the German Fasching or Mardi Gras are good examples) is that it represents a temporary suspension of restraint as well as a controlled inversion of normative behavior. Whether or not this is true in all cultural contexts, in cases where cultural continuity can be demonstrated with preliterate societies in the same geographic area, such observations may have significance for the interpretation of archaeological evidence. What is required at this point is a cross-cultural study of mutable gender categorization in order to determine whether and in what ways they might be archaeologically visible.

Gender transformers currently represent a "hidden" archaeological population because of the dependence of most European archaeologists on the normative two-sexes/two-genders model. When gender transformers *are* invoked by archaeologists, it is often to avoid attributing social power to biologically female individuals. We need to distinguish between patterned sex/gender disjunction in burial and the reluctance of a largely male archaeological establishment to accept the possibility that particular women as women may have achieved considerable social power under certain circumstances.

I have written elsewhere about one of the best documented of these cases, the early Iron Age burial of Vix in Burgundy, one of the richest, best-preserved Iron Age graves ever discovered (Arnold 1990). Apart from the spectacular bronze, gold, and silver drinking equipment, a four-wheeled wagon, a unique gold *torc* (neck ring), and other grave goods, the personal ornament included symmetrically placed bead bracelets, anklets, and a multiple-bead necklace. The latter three categories of personal adornment, especially the anklets, are found in morphologically female burials of the time in cemetery contexts where a larger sample is available. Also significant, there were no weapons in the grave, which is atypical for contemporary burials of high-status morphologically male individuals. The most recent analysis conducted on the skeletal material from the grave identified it as biologically female on the basis of 7 out of 10 diagnostic tests (Langlois 1987: 214). Currently pending ADNA analysis of the remains should confirm the biological sex of this individual.

In other words, this burial is *not* an example of sex/gender disjunction. Rather, it is an example of the *Hauptmann von Köpenick* phenomenon again: Archaeologists such as Konrad Spindler (1983), who interpret this grave as that of a transvestite male priest, in fact are reacting to a perceived gender/ *status* disjunction viewed through a contemporary androcentric filter. Is there any concrete evidence for the existence of a mutable, nonbinary system of gender categorization in Iron Age Germany, or are we dealing with the *Hauptmann von Köpenick* syndrome in the few documented cases of possible sex/gender disjunction that have been identified?

Several problems plague the investigation of this question. Most significant is the ancient looting of many of the high-status central burials that were the focus of most of the variably systematic 19th- and early 20th-century excavations. Another problem is the possibility that the high-status graves are more standardized than nonelite burials of the same period, forming an elite sodality, possibly linked by marriage, across regions. Our understanding of late Hallstatt and early La Tène social organization is too sketchy at present to allow us to say much about gender configurations. There is a binary pattern in the burial goods that seems to relate to gender, but how this relates to biological sex in a larger sample than a handful of high-status graves is unclear.

Kinship, sex, and gender are the primary structural elements on which ancient social organization was based. These parameters determined inter- and intracommunity relationships, status and position within the sociopolitical hierarchy, and inheritance of social prerogatives. Traditionally, sex and to some extent kinship have been assessed through archaeological context and conventional physical anthropological analysis. This analysis, however, has been limited by factors such as the degree of preservation of the remains, ambiguities in physical markers, and researcher bias. Recent advances in the study of ADNA (Hummel and Herrmann 1994) provide a means to mitigate some of these limitations by enabling genetic discrimination between closely related individuals and precise determination of sex for burials in which only a small quantity of hard tissue, ideally teeth, has been preserved.

The analysis of mtDNA (mitochondrial DNA) in particular has the potential to revolutionize our understanding of early Iron Age social organization since it provides the opportunity to ask precisely the kinds of questions that conventional analysis cannot answer.

Mitochondrial DNA, which is maternally inherited and nonrecombining, is particularly useful for relationship analysis because the effectively haploid genome accumulates mutations faster than nuclear DNA, allowing for the differentiation of individuals along maternal lines. As a method, this approach differs from allele frequency–based surveys of nuclear-encoded variants in several respects: (1) The variation is very extensive and is not scrambled by recombination; (2) the effective population size is roughly one-quarter of that for nuclear variants, which enhances the effect of genetic drift; (3) because mtDNA is maternally inherited, only female lineages are relevant; and (4) deducing the phylogenetic relationships within and between haplotype clusters is relatively straightforward and allows divergence and expansion times to be estimated (Richards et al. 1996).

Comparing the populations in early Iron Age tumuli, for example, could make it possible to determine what motivated the construction of a new mound as well as how individuals were related to one another within and between mounds. The analysis of multiple burials, which often contain both a male and a female individual, has an obvious gender component. Interpretations of this type of burial tend to assume that the male individual represents the primary interment, whereas the female burial is merely another category of grave good. And what of female burials that are in a grave of their own? DNA analysis makes it possible to rigorously test many of the assumptions that have hitherto dominated our interpretations of early Iron Age social organization in west-central Europe.

For example, matrilineal succession is documented in a number of Celtic cultures in the British Isles and is also hinted at in the Classical texts. Mitochondrial DNA analysis would enable the identification of a system of matrilineal succession if it existed in the early Iron Age of southwestern Germany. This in turn will allow the formulation of hypotheses regarding the presence and nature of gender transformers in Celtic societies on the Continent as well as the British Isles.

The handful of "ambiguous" gender cases known to date from Iron Age Germany, for example (Arnold 1990), could be analyzed from a genetic perspective to determine whether a mutable gender category in fact existed in the cultures of early Iron Age Europe. The evidence at the moment based on conventional morphological analysis is equivocal. The Vix burial is less an ambiguous gender burial than an example of the reluctance of the male-dominated academic community to recognize the major roles played by women in the pre-Roman Iron Age, both on a political and a socioeconomic level. The Stuttgart-Bad Cannstatt "transvestite warriors" (Arnold 1991: 96), on the other hand, are a good example of the kind of confusion that arises when the grave-good inventory contains objects with conflicting gender associations. The most common pattern of conflicting grave-good inventories seems to be spear points, either singly or in sets, in association with symmetrically arranged bracelets, earrings, and other "normatively" female personal ornament. The "conflict" is at least as likely to be an artifact of the 20th-century analytical approach as an example of a transgendered category in the sixth century B.C. Occasionally, burials are found that do not contain any "gender diagnostics" in the form of weapons or personal ornament. Both of these burial categories are in the realm of the "ambiguous," but neither necessarily supports the idea that Hallstatt society included a transgender category.

That gender configurations were mutable, at least as reflected in mortuary ritual, seems certain. This is reflected not only in the degree of regional variation found in burial ritual but also in terms of chronological shifts within specific cemeteries. The cemetery of Jogasses à Chouilly (Aisne-Marne), which spans the Hallstatt D/La Tène A (LT A) transition, is a good example (Demoule 1989: 157–58). During the first phase of use, male and female burials were physically separated. The only wagon burial attributable to this phase was found directly on the boundary between the two "gender zones." By the second phase of use, this distinction between male and female burials became blurred, and "family" tumuli containing individuals of both sexes and presumably at least two genders appear on the periphery of the phase I cemetery. During the third phase of use (LT A), the cemetery experienced an explosive growth, initially indiscriminate with respect to age and sex, but gradually, in the course of the fourth phase of use, beginning to differentiate on the basis of social status. The cemetery was abandoned before La Tène B2. This example demonstrates (1) the complexity of early Iron Age European gender configurations both spatially and temporally, (2) the need for extensive excavation of cemeteries (rather than recovery of selected burials), and (3) the fact that gender segregation and differentiation have to be viewed from a diachronic perspective, as an ongoing performance of negotiation and expression rather than a synchronic representation that is then made to "stand for" the society as a whole as well as through time.

A triunal approach involving ADNA analysis, conventional physical anthropological analysis, and archaeological context should contribute significantly to our information on the chronology and social organization of the early Iron Age and its gender configurations. If there are gender transformers out there in the archaeological record of the pre-Roman Iron Age, we will find them only if we apply a systematic approach to their identification and interpretation. The ethnographic record suggests a number of approaches that can be incorporated into research strategies, as I have tried to demonstrate here. We have to salute both the suit and the person wearing it in order to move beyond *The Hauptmann von Köpenick* in our reconstructions of prehistoric gender configurations.

NOTES

1. This continues to be true despite semifacetious attempts to resexualize men's clothing, such as a recent Web site with the motto "Bring Back the Codpiece!"

2. The terminology available to researchers engaged in the study of the mutability of gender categories is highly problematic, and there is no consensus as to what constitutes the most neutral term for individuals whose gender identity does not conform to their biological sex (however that is defined). Native Americans, members of the gay and lesbian com-

munity, transsexuals, transvestites, and others all have their own views on how such individuals should be defined and labeled. Terms such as "berdache," "man/woman," and "two-spirit person" are generally rejected by one group or another as pejorative, limiting, or too culturally specific. It is unlikely, given the complexity of this topic, that any single term will encompass all possible permutations of this phenomenon. Under the circumstances, it seems perhaps most useful to identify the terminology used on a case-by-case basis, within the specific cultural context of the research. Since this chapter discusses archaeological evidence from Western Europe, specifically from Iron Age Germany, France, and Switzerland, I have chosen to use the term "gender transformer" to describe the mutable gender categories represented in that specific context. This refers to the archaeologically recoverable evidence for individuals where the correlation between biological sex and gender as represented in mortuary remains is ambiguous. It is conceded that we cannot know whether the individuals in question viewed themselves as "transformed." The term is therefore acknowledged as representing an entirely etic construction.

3. In the context of archaeological analysis, biological sex must be limited to what is phenotypically observable or, in the rare cases where funding for ADNA analysis is available and preservation allows, genotypically identifiable. The key question is, If genetic anomalies are present, would they have been identifiable in the prehistoric context in terms of morphology and/or behavior? Prehistoric peoples could not have distinguished between individuals or created their own identities on the basis of chromosomal anomalies that do not have a phenotypic or behavioral expression. In addition, even though there are demonstrably more than two biological sexes when the number and morphology of sex chromosomes are considered the defining characteristic, such anomalies are too rare to constitute the basis of an institutionalized gender-transforming category, even if they occasionally are expressed phenotypically (enlarged clitoris, late descending male genitalia, and so on) (Kessler 1998: 135).

15

Women's Lives Memorialized in Burial in Ancient China at Anyang

Katheryn M. Linduff

INTRODUCTION

The jade figurine in figure 15.1 represents a female on one side and a male on the other. It is a unique piece from ancient China, excavated at Anyang (Henan province) in 1980 in the intact tomb of Lady Hao (Tomb 5), dating from about 1200 B.C. Its balanced view of the female and male brings to mind early Chinese Daoist thinking about the structure of the universe. The indigenous Chinese philosophical system called Daoism was a school of thought associated with several texts dating from the late Zhou dynasty, or from about 500 B.C. to about 200 B.C., but surely representing thinking from a much earlier period. The main source of information about the principles of this early movement is a book titled the *Taiping jing* (Classic of the Way of Great Equilibrium). The earliest surviving version of this book refers to the *taiping* ("great equilibrium" or "great peace"), a state sought by many to actualize.

The society of the great equilibrium was a utopian, "golden age" concept shared among several late Zhou schools of thought. A sage ruler presided effortlessly over a perfectly harmonious society that was itself perfectly attuned to a harmonious cosmic order. A perfect system of justice was provided where, if everyone occupied his or her proper place, he or she would be justly rewarded, with no one in want.

At the level of the community, failure to attain the great equilibrium was thought to be caused by the imposition of obstacles to the circulation of the "essences" (*qi*). For example, in relations between the sexes, sexual abstinence was condemned because it upset the interaction of the yin (female) and yang (male) essences, and killing of infant girls was severely condemned because

Figure 15.1.   Jade figurine excavated from Tomb 5 of Lady Hao, Anyang. From *Yinxu Fuhaomu* (1980: plate XXV).

the practice caused an imbalance in the strength of yin and yang. This must reflect a censuring of the practice of female infanticide in the everyday world of Chinese society in which the philosophic system provided checks and balances as well as explanations for this and other ills of the world.

This figure immortalized in jade a balanced picture of the male and female, perhaps reflecting the principles embodied in the beliefs just described. If that is the case, this figure confirms the beginnings of Daoist thought several hundred years earlier than extant texts will allow. The prospect that this sort of thinking existed so early in Chinese history is exciting to contemplate, but like most living in early dynastic times, the life of the deceased woman in Tomb 5, a consort of the third king, Wu Ding (c. 1200 B.C.), of the Shang dynasty (c. 1550–1050 B.C.) was not nearly so ideal.

Chinese society at least as early as the Shang was hierarchically ordered rather than egalitarian, and Lady Hao lived in a community that placed only men on the throne and lavished them with high rank while expecting women to bear male heirs and sometimes to provide spiritual and military guidance. This figurine must have represented an idealized, philosophic position (certainly conceived of by male philosophers) against which the everyday world could be measured and explained. To learn about the atmosphere in which the daily lives of Lady Hao and her female contemporaries took place, one may begin with evidence associated with the excavations at the royal ceremonial center at Anyang.

THIS STUDY

Naturally, the degree to which these research questions can be addressed must be seen within the context of the past 50 years of archaeological recovery in China during which archaeologists hoped to retrieve and reconstruct the heritage and lineage of male rulers. As a subdiscipline of history in China, archaeological analysis has respected official, historical writings as accurate and inclusive and sees social, cultural, technological, and other changes as advances provoked in the political capitals and because of the wisdom of their leaders. Recorded history defined what and who were culturally Chinese and civilized and what and who were not. This official model was extended to analysis of all in the realm and beyond, leaving little room to explore the roles of living men and women or of "others" either inside or outside of the world of the Chinese, except within the vagaries of later political Confucianism and philosophical Daoism.

Official written histories of the Shang in China list the names of kings who ruled in the last capital and were thought of as the supreme rulers of a large state. Initial excavations at Anyang in the late 1920s located and unearthed what has been identified as the royal cemetery and ritual center of the late period of the dynasty. It is not certain that this is other than a ceremonial center, as the lack of a wall and commercial district typical of later Chinese cities has disqualified it as a large urban community (Li Chi 1977; Wheatley 1972; Chang 1980). The 12 largest tombs there, all looted before scientific excavation, are thought to be those of the political rulers who reigned between c. 1350 B.C. and 1050 B.C., or until the end of the dynasty. The measure of women's lives in this research atmosphere is dependent on what has been sought in relation to their male counterparts. Archaeological data on women at Anyang is limited because research and excavation plans have simply not included questions about them.

Nevertheless, in the past three decades, many additional tombs have been excavated, especially in locations outside the burial ground of the kings. Several of the most lavish are the unlooted burial remains of females (e.g., M5 and HPKM1550:49) (fig. 15.5). In a polygamous elite society where position and status of official women might have been flexible and/or unstable, accounting for the elaboration of certain tombs of females in death introduces a particular dilemma requiring caution in interpretation.

This study begins inquiry into how members of the social and political elite at Anyang buried their female dead and how they expressed sex and gender in that context. Because the evidence is exclusively from burials, we must consider whose perception was being commemorated—was it the memory of the family of the deceased, the king who must have had to play out an official view, the deceased themselves, or some or all of the above? With the analysis of the published archaeological data from the burials as well as related contemporary written materials, I will attempt a reconstruction of the status, roles, and cultural heritage of the women celebrated in this royal burial site at Anyang (figs. 15.2, 15.3, 15.4).

THE EVIDENCE

Analysis of all known burials of females throughout the site (nine single burials, sacrificial pits) (tables 15.1, 15.2; fig. 15.3) and of contemporary written

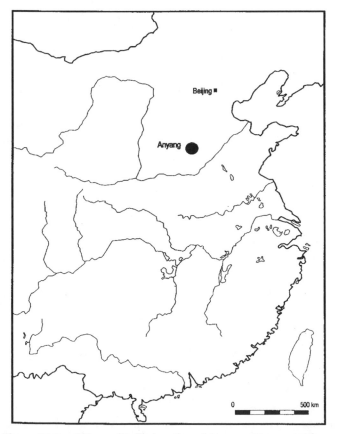

Figure 15.2.   China, with the location of Anyang, Henan province.

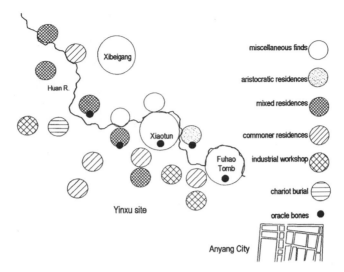

Figure 15.3.   The Yinxu urban area. The late-Dhang capital stretches over 5.8 kilometers along the Huan River northwest of modern Anyang, Henan province. From Barnes (1993: 128, Figure 57).

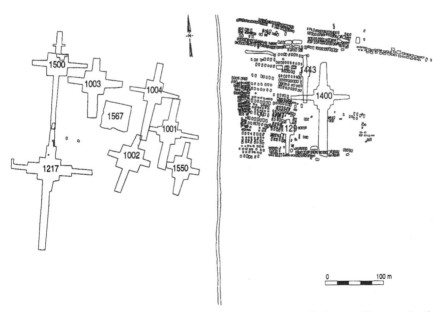

Figure 15.4.   The royal cemetery site of Houjiazhuang, including small graves in the eastern sections of Xibeigang excavated in 1969 and 1976 and royal burials in western and eastern sections of Xibeigang. From Li Chi (1977: 83, Figure 9) and Chang Kwang-chih (1980: 122, Figure 36).

262   *Katheryn M. Linduff*

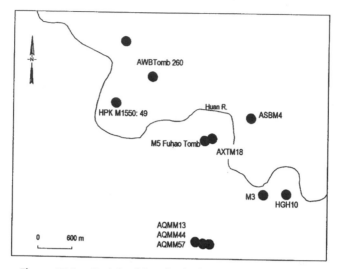

Figure 15.5.   Burials of females in the Yinxu site at Anyang.

documentation from inscriptions on ritual bronze vessels and oracle bones suggests that the status and roles of women buried at Anyang were varied. Women were queens, military leaders, consorts, wives, probably slaves, and artisans whose status was determined according to lineage, cultural heritage, marriage alliance, and/or job specialization. In addition, for a few women, such as those buried in M5 and HPKM1550:49, status appears to be tied to political power, whether accrued from their affiliation with royalty or inherited, as perceived at the time of death. Their power and position were notable, as they commanded significant accumulation of wealth and status symbols at death, even though their authority may have been gained and limited in relation to their kingly counterparts.

However, interestingly, as women's status and influence in society was expressed in burials, it suggests that a different but parallel route to power existed for women and for men. That is, women were ranked among women, as well as by comparison to men, sketching out an expanded set of hierarchical relations based on gender. Whereas the official view located political, economic, and social power with males, it did not record the types of power experienced by women and implied in the archaeological record as seen below. Women lower in the hierarchy, perhaps because of their less prestigious positions in marriage, cultural backgrounds, and/or roles in society, were not mentioned in the written documents at all, so their burials yield the only available data on their lives.

EVIDENCE OF WOMEN IN
BURIALS AT ANYANG

Excavation of Anyang has been ongoing since the late 1920s (Li Chi 1977). From what has been reported thus far, there are three circumstances in which females can be identified in tombs: (1) in large and small tombs of single individuals; (2) in tombs containing kings, either in their own coffins or in unadorned spaces inside the king's burial chamber; and (3) in graves or pits, both singly and as part of group burials (figs. 15.4, 15.5; table 15.1). In addition, burial patterns can be observed. First, the overwhelming number of burials contain the bodies of males—royalty, nobility, and commoners or anonymous individuals in mass graves. Second, the females were all buried for special purposes at this site—as queens, consorts, servants, or mothers. Third, all burials at Anyang, whether male or female, were associated somehow with glorification of the kings. The site was, evidently, the official cemetery and ritual center for royalty and their entourages; the site did not accommodate burial of the rest of the Shang population.

Observations about status and role are possible as well. Royal wives and other high-level women were buried in their own tombs (AWBM260 and M5) or near the king's burial chamber (M1550:49). Commoner women were interred in single, casketed tombs (AQMM13, 44, and 57), and those sacrificed (voluntarily or otherwise) were placed either inside or outside of royal burials or burial grounds (M4, 5, 6, 7, 12, 13, and 17 and HGH10; see fig. 15.3).

Burials of Royal Women

Not surprisingly, among all female burials, those of royal women are clearly the richest in content and can be discussed using contemporary written materials. Two tombs of this sort are preserved and published: the tombs of Lady Jing (AWDM260; Anyang Work Team 1987)[1] and Lady Hao (M5; *Yinxu Fuhaomu* 1980). Both were wives of the third Shang ruler named Wu Ding (c. 1250 B.C.–c.1200 B.C.)[2] (see table 15.1). The tombs are distinguished by number and elaborateness of their grave goods that identify them as prestigious women. For instance, the single, largest bronze ritual vessel ever excavated at Anyang comes from the tomb of Lady Jing—the Simuwu *fangding* (fig. 15.6). She was the first wife of Wu Ding, and her tomb is found in the same precinct as the kings' tombs (fig. 15.7). On the other hand, the richest, intact tomb yet excavated at Anyang is that of Lady Hao, the third wife of Wu Ding. Her tomb is located across the river from the king, outside the royal cemetery (fig. 15.3).

The shapes and sizes of these tombs are significant. The tomb of Lady Jing has one ramp (fig. 15.7), and that of Lady Hao has none but is large (5.6 by 4 meters)

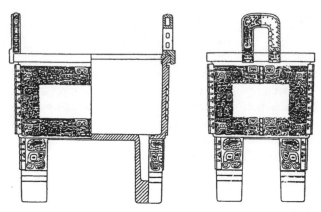

Figure 15.6. Simuwu *fangding* excavated from AWBM260 at Xibeigang, Wuguancun, Anyang. From Feng (1981: 180, Figure 7).

(fig. 15.8). All the supposed royal tombs of the kings at the site, including the one usually assigned to King Wu Ding (HPKM1001), are shaft tombs, are rectangular in shape, have a stepped profile, and have multiple ramps. The only exception is one known as the Wuguan tomb (*Yinxu de faxian yu yanjiu* 1994), which has only two, but like the other tombs of males it is much larger than those of Ladies

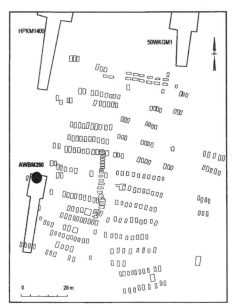

Figure 15.7. Plan of the tomb of Lady Jing (AWBM260) at Anyang. From Anyang Work Team (1987: 100, Figure 3).

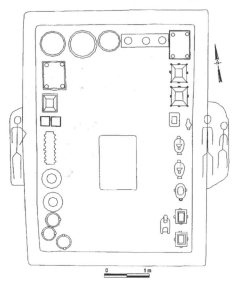

Figure 15.8.   Plan of the tomb of Lady Hao (M5) at Anyang. Based on *Yinxu Fuhaomu*
(1980: Figure 7).

Jing and Hao (fig. 15.4). Both of the tombs of females are outfitted with royal
style ritual bronzes, jades, and auxiliary materials, such a pottery vessels and
stone, bone, ivory, shell, and wooden items, and each tomb held sacrificial victims in the royal fashion (table 15.2). All together, there are 38 victims in Lady
Jing's tomb: four on the upper level and one male with a dog on the lower level
in a special pit beneath the coffin called a "waist pit." In addition, there are 11
more skulls in the grave and 22 on the ramp leading into the tomb. In Lady Hao's
tomb, the sacrificed victims are found in equal numbers and in equivalent positions (fig. 15.8).

According to inscriptions on oracle bones found at Anyang, King Wu Ding
reigned for 59 years and had many, many consorts (50–60). Three of his wives
were given the name *mu* (translated as "mother," or as the name of a place or
a person) and were recorded in the ritual worship calendar. Both Lady Jing and
Hao were given this status. The *Shiji,* an official history written in the Han
dynasty during the second century B.C. but thought to reflect earlier customs,
claimed that Shang kings were polygamous. Even so, only one to three of their
female associates were eligible to be ritually recognized as "*mu,*" according to
the *Shiji* (Hu 1970; Huang 1995). The burial and inscriptional evidence on
Lady Jing and Lady Hao bear out this record, and, although the kings might
have had only one official wife (queen), they may have kept others as consorts
and ranked them in order of their accession, ability to bear male descendants,
and/or their favor with the king (Liu 1982).

This is differentiated in burial as well as through designation in inscription. Elaborateness of burial and use of the title "*mu*" is afforded at least two of Wu Ding's wives: the Lady Jing and Lady Hao. The graves do not differ in number or opulence of goods, but they do differ in type of goods: Lady Jing's tomb held the Simuwu *fangding,* cast in the hallmark style and decoration of royal Chinese patronage, and Lady Hao's included many such items, if not so large, as well as frontier materials and a collection of new and old jades (table 15.1; *Yinxu Fuhaomu* 1980). Lady Jing was buried in the precinct of the kings themselves and was afforded a tomb with a ramp. These features set her apart from the "consort" wife, Lady Hao, who was buried, albeit elaborately, in a position outside the official cemetery. The location and type of Lady Jing's tomb as well as her title as first wife imply a rank higher than that of Lady Hao.

Shang-date inscriptions document that both past kings and certain consorts or queens were paid respect by their descendants in special state-level ceremonies. For instance, the appellation "*mu*" was attached to some personal female names, including Jing and Hao. Why they in particular were designated with this title is not clear, especially since Hao did not have male children, but the title apparently was respected. Women at court could be recognized in other ways as well. All consorts of direct kings (*zhixi*) could receive special ceremonies (*teji*), and, during the Wu Ding period (c. 1250 B.C.–1200 B.C.), the king's pseudonym was always placed in front of the names of his consorts. The pseudonym was associated with lineage because on the day the king was given this name, rituals for the ancestral female (*xianbi,* or past mother) were held (Huang 1995), forming a bond not only between Wu Ding and his women but also with the distaff side of his heritage.

Questions about health, weather, harvest, and military success in the future were frequently asked by Chinese kings, and the responses of the higher powers were recorded on oracle bones and tortoise shells in ceremonies at the Shang court. From inscriptions dating from Wu Ding's reign, we know that three of his consorts, Jing, Hao, and Zi, performed rituals that requested information on the growth of grain and/or on harvest. Were these women actually enfeoffed and officially in charge of royal lands and crops (Hu 1970)? This cannot be determined with the evidence currently available, but the inscriptions do tell us that women were active in the royal rituals of oracle taking and that they held and gained power through the activity. It also shows that the role of women in agricultural production, either symbolically or actually, included ritual performance by them.

In addition, a military role was played by Lady Hao and perhaps by others. She is recorded in oracle bone inscriptions as a famous military leader. The inscriptions say that she was frequently sent out by Wu Ding to conquer peoples hostile to the Shang, including the *bafang,* the *tufang,* and the *yifang*

(Yang 1983), all non-Shang groups living on the borders of the Shang domain and ones with whom the Shang vied for control of land and people. Her special role in battle is underscored by the abundance of weapons, including many *ge* halberds, in her tomb (fig. 15.9) (*Yinxu Fuhaomu* 1980; Linduff 1996). Military equipment was also found in the tomb of Lady Jing—a bronze general's helmet and several *ge*—and she too might have had a military role or been from a military family.

It is clear from all the evidence from Anyang that within the royal circle, highly ranked women were given special status. On what grounds they gained these favors is not completely clear. Biographical information given about Lady Hao, the structure of her tomb, and some special tomb contents suggest that she was married in and perhaps from one of the peoples whom she was "commanded" by Wu Ding to conquer (Linduff 1996). She was described as a military leader and was outfitted with weapons in her tomb, but other items, included with her personal property, were quite distinctive non-Shang objects: bronze mirrors, bow-shaped objects, check pieces, bits and bronze ornaments for horse gear associated with chariots and horse management, and curved knives of the frontier type.

These items might very well identify her with peoples who lived outside of the Shang political realm but inside the sphere of contact. These groups raised horses, probably controlled routes of trade for strategic metal ores and other goods, were aligned frequently with other powerful clans in northern Asia, and were therefore quite important for the stability of the Shang kingdom (Linduff 1996). They posed a particular threat during the reign of Wu Ding, a situation that could have readily provoked a marriage alliance (Linduff 1996). Marriage of elite women was recorded between the Shang and the Zhou, for instance, strategically aligning the two contending groups with the hope of formalizing relations between equally capable and powerful groups (Hu 1970). In the case of Lady Hao, she probably was not a Shang elite but one who was afforded all the luxury of a royal Shang burial as the wife of the king while still maintaining her identity as an outsider as marked by artifacts of frontier manufacture and style in her tomb.

These women, Lady Jing and Lady Hao, were special cases but must be assumed to stand for others whose graves have not yet been discovered. They were buried with all the trappings of Shang royalty, although the amount of grave goods and the size of their tombs are smaller than those of their husbands. They were official wives of the king and were held in high esteem because of it, but probably because of their own identity and skills as well. In the case of Lady Hao, it was her marriage, the intergroup relationship, and probably her talent that afforded her special status even though she was not thought of as the number one wife and had not borne male children.

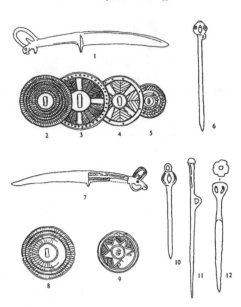

Figure 15.9. Bronzes of the northern zone type unearthed from the FuHao tomb and their northern counterparts. 1–6: from FuHao tomb; 7–12: from various sites in the northern zone. From Lin Yun (1986: 252, Figure 51).

Burial of Another Elite Woman

Another very special burial, HPKM1550:49, is not precisely dated to a subperiod at Anyang but is clearly associated with a large burial (M1550) thought to be a king's tomb (fig. 15.4). Included in this tomb was the body of a noble female with her head pointed south and her body covered with red pigment (Li Chi 1977). The most distinguishing feature of this burial is the group of about 130 hairpins that adorned her hair (fig. 15.10). We do not know who she was, but from the elaborate display of hairpins, known to designate rank (Li Chi 1959), and her position in relation to the king's burial, we can assume that she is of noble position. Although grave goods included three bronze vessels, several jades, a circular turquoise disk, and four shells found in her right hand, these artifacts are of modest scale and design, and it is the hair ornaments that mark this grave in a significant way. She may have been a lower-ranked wife of noble birth or a favored consort of the king buried in the outer chamber at the time of his death.

From analysis of the distribution of carved bone items in tombs at Anyang, a proposal about status within gender can be made. For instance, the number and type of carved bone spatulas found in tombs indicate male rank, while among females rank was indicated by the number of bone hairpins (Wang

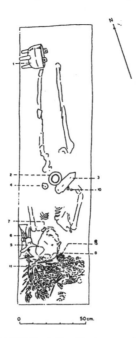

Figure 15.10.   Plan of HPKM1550:9 at Houjiazhuang, Anyang. From Liang (1976: 14, Figure 5).

1999). The royal consort Lady Hao, buried in Tomb 5, had 449 bone hairpins placed with her, while the female in Tomb 1550:49, clearly of lower rank, had 130 hairpins arranged in her hair (fig. 15.11). The arrangement of pins in an even smaller Tomb ATXM18 (see the next section; fig. 15.5) is similar to that in Tomb 1550:49 but includes only 25 pieces. The number is smaller, as is the tomb's scale, underscoring the lower social position of this woman. As adornments for women, these bone hairpins signified not only social position but also a gender role and in ways not assigned to the ritual bronzes and jades that appear in both male and female tombs.

Single Graves of Other High-Ranking Women

Another single burial, AXTM18, is shaped like and has the trappings of elite burials at Anyang already discussed—secondary ledges for placement of burial goods, sacrifice, a waist pit, and bronze, jade, shell, and bone grave goods (90 pieces), including sacral bronze ritual vessels and weapons (figs. 15.10, 15.11). This tomb has been dated from the same period as the tombs of Lady Jing and Lady Hao, as the bronzes are of the same style (Anyang Work Team

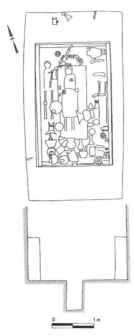

0   1 m

**Figure 15.11.   Plan of AXTM18 north of Xiaotun village, Anyang. From Anyang Work
Team (1981: 492, Figure 1).**

1987: 99–118). The coffin was painted red in the fashion of the elite and held
within it the body of the deceased as well as jades commonly found in upper-
class burials. The deceased was 35 to 40 years of age, but the inscriptions do
not precisely identify her. The inclusion of bone hairpins does, however, identify the interred as female, but her age alone must have afforded her special
status.

Although the life span of Shang people has not been well studied, an analysis of bones from the small tombs of "commoners" (tombs other than royal
tombs or sacrificial pits) buried far from the royal tombs at Anyang has yielded
the following statistics. Men's life span averaged 33.29 years and women's
29.41 years; 83 percent of them died between 14 and 55 years of age, of which
22 percent died in youth; 13 percent died under 14 years of age, and only 4.2
percent lived into old age (Han and Pan 1985). Although the authors themselves question the reliability of the data, the age estimates are considerably
lower than the deceased in AXTM18 and suggest that she was an elite who
probably lived longer than average. According to the *Shiji,* for instance, King
Wu Ding lived a long time and ruled 59 years (Dong Zoubin 1945). The length
of reigns of three other kings was recorded as more than 30 years.[3] One could

expect that the life span of the elites buried at Anyang reflected this same variation and that they lived longer than commoners.

Another very interesting tomb varies in treatment and type from those already mentioned. This tomb, AQMM13, is dated from the same period (c. 1250 B.C.–1200 B.C.) and contains two bodies: an older female and a younger male (*Zhongyuan Wenwu* 1986; fig. 15.12). The bodies are contained in one large outer coffin inside of which are two smaller coffins, one for each body. The body of the female is oriented to the east and is held in a wooden coffin painted red; the male, laid on his side, is contained in a wooden coffin painted black and oriented to the west. Under the female grave is a waist pit containing a sacrificed dog, a custom found only in elite tombs. Four clay objects are placed on a secondary terrace, and the rest of the grave furniture is inside the coffin of the female. These include two bronze ritual vessels, an unidentified object in her hand, and three jade objects. Modest by comparison to the other tombs discussed here, this must be a mother and young son of a lower-ranked family. The male must not yet have come of age, for he was not afforded a tomb of his own. It is not clear whether they died at the same time or by what means.

Two other female tombs have been excavated in the same region, and they too are modest in size and content (fig. 15.4). Both tombs (AQMM44 and AQMM57; *Zhongyuan Wenwu* 1986) date from the third and fourth phases of occupation at Anyang (c. 1200 B.C.–1050 B.C., respectively) and contain wooden coffins painted red. Grave goods in these tombs are limited to pottery jars and jade items. Although AQMM57 was looted at the time of excavation

Figure 15.12.   Plan of AQMM13 southeast of Xuejiazhuang, Anyang. From *Zhongyuan Wenwu* (1986: 16, Figure 4).

and only fragments of bronze were found there, its size precludes large numbers of goods even in its original state. This is a cemetery in which there are numerous simple graves, probably of commoners. The deceased mother and son in AQMM13 must have been of higher status within the group, as their tomb is the most elaborate in that cemetery.

Women as Sacrificial Victims

In general, women were not favored for sacrifice at Anyang but must have been put to death under very special circumstances. For instance, in 1976, 19 sacrificial pits were excavated (*Yinxu de faxian yu yanjiu* 1994) (see Appendix 2; fig. 15.13), and only seven held the bodies of females. The largest pit contained

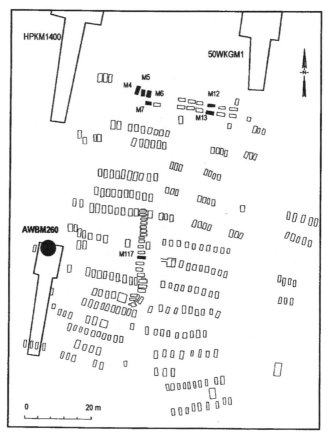

Figure 15.13.   Plan of sacrifice pits (AWBM4, M5, M6, M7, M12, M13, and M117 are female burials) north of Wuguan village, Anyang. From Anyang Work Team (1977: 21, Figure 2).

339 persons executed at one time, and the others included fewer than 100 (fig. 15.13). The practice of sacrificing can be illustrated by looking at the latest of these pits, HGH 10 (fig. 15.14). In the vertical pit, there were three distinct layers in which 73 human victims were placed. In the most recent layer near the top, there were 25 persons: 16 intact, 2 beheaded, and 7 severed heads. Some were buried alive with mouths still open in burial; others killed before being interred. Among the deceased were found a bronze *ding* (a type usually found in elite graves), pottery, pilled silk, linen fabric, and millet. In the middle layer, there were 29 victims: 19 intact, 1 beheaded, and 9 skulls only. They were placed with faces up or on their sides, and some were kneeling. Both hairpins and jades were found in the layer, suggesting that they were female, slaughtered, and then placed carefully in position in the pit. In the lowest level, there

0   1 m

Figure 15.14. Plan of sacrificial pits north of Wuguan village, Anyang. AWBM6, shown here, is a female burial. From Anyang Work Team (1977: 23, Figure 3).

are 19 victims: 17 intact bodies, 1 skull, and 2 undetermined human bones. Three females, as well as infants and children, were identified in the remains of the lowest level, and all other victims were male. Hairpins, shells, and carved bones were also found in this layer, the usual trappings of the elite and females. These sacrificial offerings must have been made as part of the funerary ritual associated with royal kings' burials since the pits are close to and aligned with the large shaft tombs in the royal cemetery in Huojiazhuang (fig. 15.3).

In the 19 pits excavated in this area, two pits contain exclusively females, one (HGH17) contains one male and one female, and all others are male (Anyang Work Team 1977:1). The pits containing females are located in one corner of the site and suggest that there was some reason, historical or religious, for their sacrifice and placement. Although it is generally assumed that many of these victims are war captives and that women were not captured, there were special circumstances for which women were offered. There is inscriptional evidence that female servants, or slaves, bore children of the master or even the king and that women were sacrificed in rituals to bring about peace (Sun 1987). These oracle bone inscriptions frequently recorded questions asked (by the king) of his female ancestors about fertility—whether he would have another son, whether a certain female was pregnant, or about rituals arranged for the day of delivery. The birth of a female child was thought to bring bad fortune and sickness caused by concubines. In the mind of the king, misfortune of this sort could, presumably, have been reason to "sacrifice" the woman who brought the bad luck.

FURTHER OBSERVATIONS

As has been described, there are three types of burials at Anyang that include females: those of royal wives or other elite women buried in their own tombs (AWBM260 and M5) or near the king's burial chamber (M1550:49); those of lesser elites in single, casketed tombs (AQMM13, 44, and 57); and those of sacrificial victims buried either inside or outside royal burials or burial grounds (M4, 5, 6, 7, 12, 13, and 17 and HGH10). The overwhelming number of burials contain the bodies of men, whether those of nobility, commoners, or sacrificial victims, and we know that these women were buried in this location for reasons associated somehow with glorification of the kings. They were queens, consorts, servants, mothers, and military leaders. In this royal context, it is clear that women received burial treatment according to a system of ranking: queens and noble women at the top, lesser elites below the former, and servants or slaves who went to their deaths at Anyang for some special ritual purpose.

At least two customs identified women and distinguished them from each other and from males. The cultural identity of Lady Hao was probably maintained through special burial items associated with the frontier and the great flurry of hairpins as worn by the woman in Tomb 1550:49 designating her and the others as women of rank. The display of frontier items identifies Lady Hao's birth families, while the luxury accumulated in the burials as well as the style and layout of the tombs of Lady Jing and Lady Hao are marked by their marriage to royalty. The lower-ranked, elite tombs are comparable to those of males of the same social rank and position, except that some have hairpins or are buried with another person, such as the young man buried in Tomb AQMM13. These include limited grave goods but are individual, single burials. The sacrificed females would seem to have been chosen for some very particular purpose and took place on a limited scale, unlike males.

These observations have revealed that upper-class Shang women did have power and individual identity and that these were recognized in burial. We know that Fu Hao, for instance, played a significant political as well as military role during the reign of Wu Ding; others must have done the same. In addition, she retained her cultural identity and amassed great wealth while living amidst the powerful Shang. In the context of this royal center, the memory of these women's family backgrounds and positions in society was marked in their graves. The jade figurine visualized an idealized physical comparability between the sexes, perhaps as a reminder, for it was finally placed in a chthonic world where sexual differences and gender roles were both confirmed and ranked.

APPENDIX

Table 15.1. Burials of Women at Anyang

Tomb	Period	Location	Tomb	Tomb Master	Sacrifices	Burial Objects
AXT* M18	II. Second phase of Yinxu	South of Tomb 5 (about 22 m east of Tomb 5), north of Xiaotun village	South-north oriented. It is a rectangular earthen pit furnished with secondary terrace and waist pit (L 4.6 m, W 2.2–2.3 m, 5.6 m below the ground). The remains of wood and paint were found, which suggest that painted wooden coffin was used.	35–40-year-old female (? The excavator is not quite sure about the gender.)	5 humans and 2 dogs (location as shown in the map).	Total 90 objects including bronzes 43, pottery 4, jade 11, bone 28, shells 4. Pottery: Bronze: ritual bronzes: 24, *ding* 3, *yan* 2, *gui* 1, *zun* 2, *lei* 1, *you* 1, *jia* 2, *jue* 5, *gu* 5, *pan* 1, and *qi*-shaped object 1 weapons: *ge* 9 and 10 arrowheads. Jade: *ge* (inscribed), *qi*, knife, ear spoon, awl-shaped object, hairpin, handle-shaped ornament, cylinder-shaped object, fish and

AQM* II. Second phase of Yinxu					rectangular-shaped object. Others: bone 28, shells 4.
M13	Liujiazhuang, Tiexi, 2 km south of Xiaotun village, Anyang	2.8 cm long, 1.4 cm wide, and 2.7 cm below the ground. Furnished with secondary terrace. One outer coffin and 2 inner coffins (Plate 4).	2 deceased with their heads oriented in opposite directions. To the east, the deceased is an old female with stretched burial in a red wooden coffin (2.04 cm long, and 0.54 cm wide). To the west is a young male with extended burial and laid on side in a black wooden coffin (2 cm long and 0.32 cm wide).	A waist pit under the deceased woman is dug below the coffin with a dog inside.	Except the 4 objects put at secondary terrace, all the burial goods are inside the coffin. Pottery: *gui* 1, *guan* 1, *lei* 1, and bowl 1. Bronze: *gu* 1, *jue* 1 (Plate 6), unidentified object (in the hands of the deceased) 1 Jade: *bi* 1 and *huan* 1, . *qi* (ax).

continued

Table 15.1. Burials of Women at Anyang (Continued)

Tomb	Period	Location	Tomb	Tomb Master	Sacrifices	Burial Objects
M3	II. Early second phase of Yinxu	Southeast of Xuejiazhuang, Anyang	8°, north-south oriented. The pit is 2.4 m below the ground, 2.8 m long, 1.6 m wide; bottom 5.2 m below the ground. Secondary terrace Waist pit	Stretched burial with the head to the north.	The tomb is furnished with waist pit with a dog inside. Two dogs are buried. Secondary terrace: on the east is a *female sacrifice* with her head to the north; the remains of the wood are found below her body (1.5 m long, and 0.4 m wide); on the south are 2 dogs with the heads to the east; on the west is a dog with the head to the south. All the sacrifices are covered with the painted fabric (? not quite sure).	Pottery 3. *li* 1, *gu* 1, *jue* 1. Bronze 19. *ding* 1, *jue* 1, *gu* 1, *ge* 13, bell 3. Jade 3. *ge* 1, pendant 1, handle-shaped object 1. Stone 3. bird-shaped object 2, *ge* 1. Shellfish 30. Spiral shells 4.
AWB* M260	II. Early second phase of Yinxu	North of Wuguan village	50°, north-south oriented, rectangular "*jia*"-shaped pit with a ramp on the south.	Lady Jing, *muwu* or *piwu*, the legal wife or consort of king *wuding* or *zujia*.	1. In the chamber, 22 skulls distributed in different directions.	Jade *ge* and 3 shells from the waist pit, undisturbed. Other objects all disturbed.

The roof of the tomb is 9.6 m long and 8.1 m wide, and the bottom is 6.35 m long, 5 m wide, and 8.1 m below the ground. The roof of the ramp is 24 m long, and the south part of it is 4.1 m wide. The south part of the ramp is a slope, 20 m long. Below it, a square sacrificial pit, 3.9 m long, 3.3 m wide, and 0.6 m deep. Three sacrifice pits: M133, M179, M256. M133, east of the burial pit, 8 skeletons without heads. M179, top of the tomb 2.2 m long, 0.9 m wide, and 1.5 m below the ground, 7 du. 8 torsoes with4 pointing

2. Among the earth of the pit 7 m below the ground, 6 skeletons with-out heads.
3. The square pit at the bottom of the chamber, 4 skele-tons, disturbed.
4. Around the outer coffin, 5 skeletons, disturbed.
5. At the bottom of the pit and in the earth, the bones of horses, cattle, sheep, pigs, and dogs, seriously disturbed.
6. Among the earth of the pit, 5.9 m below the ground, a skeleton of an animal.

Pottery: gray and white pottery in sandy and earthen clay, cord and rope pattern. *zu, basin, li, gui,* and general helmet (no statistical of the number of the objects). White pottery, 90 shards, rope, and negative line pattern, *gui* and *zu*. White pottery *gui,* 01.

Bronzes: Dome-shaped objects 65. Cattle-shaped objects 8, 6 intact. Profile of the cattle with an arched latch on the back. Arrowheads 36, broken *nei* of *ge* 13, *silengqi* 2, awl-shaped object 1, fragments of bronzes 8.

continued

Table 15.1. Burials of Women at Anyang (Continued)

Tomb	Period	Location	Tomb	Tomb Master	Sacrifices	Burial Objects
			north and 4 south. M256, west of the burial pit, unexcavated.			Gold: 15 fragments of thin gold from the outer coffin. Stone: grid stone 1 (037), broken, *chu* 2, *qing* musical instrument 1, stone 1, other broken parts of the stone objects. Jade: *ge* 1, arrowhead 1, ornament 1, animal-shaped decoration 1, *sun tou* (joinery-shaped object) 1, tube-shaped object 1, handle-shaped object 1, small stripe-shaped object 2, square-shaped object 5, small rectangular jade 1, turquoise animal head 3, turquoise ornaments 33. Bone and antlers: arrowheads 251, awl-shaped object 1,

| M5 | II. Early second phase of Yinxu | About 100 m northwest of Xiaotun village, Anyang | Rectangular pit. The roof of the tomb is 5.6 m long, 4 m wide, 8 m below the ground. The coffin (lacquered) is 5 m long, 3.4–3.6 m wide, 1.3 m high. A ramped foundation above the pit is possibly used as a ritual shrine. | Lady Hao, the legal wife or consort of king *wuding* | 16 sacrificial humans (4 on the top of the outer chamber, 2 in the eastern niche, 1 in western niche, 1 in the outer chamber ouside the coffin). 6 sacrificial dogs (1 in the waist pit, 5 on the top of the outer chamber). | 1,928 objects and 6,800 shells. 460 bronze objects and 210 ritual vessels. 750 jade and stone objects. 560 bone objects. | hairpin 1, handle-shaped fragments 4, teeth-shaped fragments 3, inscribed dagger 3, dagger 2, tube 2, unknown objects 2, awl-shaped object with a hole near the tip, antler 1, antler with a hole 2. Shell and ivory: fragments of clam shells bubble-shaped clam 1, stripe-shaped ivory 21, shells 21. Wooden object: shovel 8. |

continued

Table 15.1. Burials of Women at Anyang (*Continued*)

Tomb	Period	Location	Tomb	Tomb Master	Sacrifices	Burial Objects
AQM* M44	III. Third phase of Yinxu	Liujiazhuang, Tiexi, 2 km south of Xiaotun village, Anyang	2.5 m long, 1.05 m wide, and 2 m deep. 2.95 m below the ground. Furnish with secondary terrace. Red wood coffin.	Adult female, stretched burial.		Pottery: *lei* 1, *hu* 4 Jade: *Zhang* 1.
ASB* M4	IV. The fourth phase of Yinxu	North of Dasikong village	190°, north-south oriented. The pit is 2.3 m long, 1 m wide, and 1.15 m below the ground. Wooden inner coffin.	Stretch burial.		Pottery: *li* (Plate 8–8) shells (from the mouth of the deceased).
AQM* M57 (looted)	IV. Late fourth phase of Yinxu	Liujiazhuang, Tiexi, 2 km south of Xiaotun village, Anyang	East-west oriented furnished with secondary terrace and waist pit. It is 3.1 m long, 1.55 m wide, and 4.15 m deep. Secondary terrace.	Unknown.	One young female is buried at the western part of the secondary terrace.	Pottery: *gu* 1, *ban* 1, *lei* 1. Shells: 3. Mother-of-pearl inlay: 110. Bronze: fragment 1 with the remains of fabric. Jade: *Zhang* 24, among which 20 have red inscriptions.

HPK* M1550: 49	?	Northeastern part of tomb 1550	The burial pit is in the stamped earth located at the north-eastern part of tomb 1550, north-south, 2.2 m, east-west 0.55 m, 0.11 m below the ground.	A noble female, extended burial, head oriented south, red pigments all over the body, about 60–70 bone hairpins decorated the hair.	Bronze: *di* 1, *jue* 1, *gu* 1. Jade: *bi* 1, *ge* 1, green jade frog 1, carved rabbit 1, hairpin 1, *jue* 1, *qinbo* (the object used to play musical instrument) 1. Bone: hairpins 60–70. Turquoise: circular form. Shells: 4 found in the right hand of the deceased.

*AXT = Xiaotun village at Anyang; AWB = north of the Wuguan village at Anyang; ASB = north of Dasikong village at Anyang; AQM = Liujiazhuang, Tiexi, 2 km south of Xiaotun village at Anyang; HPK = Houjiazhuang at Anyang; HG = Hougang at Anyang.

Table 15.2. Sacrificial Pits of Females at Anyang

Tomb	Period	Location	Tomb	Sacrifices	Burial Objects
AWB* M4	?	North of Wuguan village (the former west of Xiaoying and the royal burial area)	2.10 × 1.00–2.30, north-south oriented.	2 skeletons, 25–28 years old. Laid on one side. M117: 2.05 × 0.90–1.60, north-east oriented.	Stone frog 1, jade ornament 1, jade hairpin 1 (looted).
AWB* M5	?	As above	2.20 × 1.10–2.30, north-south oriented 9	9 female (?), 1 unidentified, 30–35 (8), adult (2), 2 extended burial, 7 prone burial (not sure is the burial practice of nine female).	
AWB* M6	?	As above	2.05 × 1.25–3.35, north-south oriented	7 skeletons, 6 female, 30–30 (4), 35 (1), adult (1) (can not tell which is for women). There are evidence of their hands and legs bound.	
AWB* M7	?	As above	1.88 × 1.00–3.1, east-west oriented	9 skeletons, 4 female, adult (3), children (6), prone burial.	

continued

Tomb	Period	Location	Dimensions/Structure	Burial	Finds
AWB* M12	?	As above	2.25 × 1.15–3.00, east-west oriented	4 female, 25–30 (2), adult (2), 2 prone burial and 2 extended burial.	Pottery *lei* 2, lids of the pottery, bone hairpin 1.
AWB* M13	?	As above	2.3 × 1.45–1.84, east-west oriented	7 adult women, 22–28 (5), adult (2). One of them was headed, the other 6 were all skulls. 4 prone burial, 3 laid on one side.	
AWB* M117	?	As above	2.05 × 0.90–1.60, north-east oriented	20+years old female, only skull, extended burial.	
HG* H10	IV, the fourth phase of Yinxu, *yi* or *xin* period	The south slope of Hougang, 105 m north of Gaolouzhuang village, northwest of Anyang	Vertical pit, 0.8 m below the ground, the roof of the pit is 2.2 m diameter, the bottom is 3.6 m below the ground, 2.3 m diameter. The bottom was pounded and covered with small stones and sand.	There are totally 73 human sacrifices and buried in three layers. From top to bottom, women were found only in the bottom layer, the third layer. It is 2.2–2.3 m below the ground. The 19 skeletons were distributed southeast of the pit. Three women were identified.	Shells, bone hairpin, and carved bones 2.

continued

Table 15.2. Sacrificial Pits of Females at Anyang (Continued)

Tomb	Period	Location	Tomb	Sacrifices	Burial Objects
				Skeleton no. 3: southern wall of the pit, facing northeast, about 25 years old, laid on one side with contracted burial, the skull broken, backbone rotten, the right leg over the left one, phalanxes (feet bones). Skeleton no. 4: eastern part of the pit, facing east, about 35 years old, prone burial, skull broken, no tibia and phalanxes. Skeleton no. 9: below the left part of skeleton no. 3, about 30 years old, the upper palatine bone and teeth (not quite sure if female).	

*AXT = Xiaotun village at Anyang; AWB = north of the Wuguan village at Anyang; ASB = north of Dasikong village at Anyang; AQM = Liujiazhuang, Tiexi, 2 km south of Xiaotun village at Anyang; HPK = Houjiazhuang at Anyang; HG = Hougang at Anyang.

ACKNOWLEDGMENTS

My thanks to Profs. Sarah Milledge Nelson and Myriam Rosen-Ayalon for leading the way to Bellagio and for making me stretch beyond the limits of common knowledge in early Chinese studies. I am grateful to Sun Yan for her assistance and interest in this research and to Hsu Miao-lin for helping with the tables, figures, and bibliography. Both asked pointed questions that sharpened my observations and strengthened my discussion. Wang Ying's research on the carved bones in tombs at Anyang has also informed me about the status of women there.

NOTES

1. The identity of the deceased is not absolutely certain. She is thought to be either the legal wife or the consort of King Wu Ding or King Zuni, a later king at Anyang. For the purpose of this discussion, I will discuss her as a partner of Wu Ding and assume that chronology is debatable. See Anyang Work Team (1987).

2. The identity of Lady Hao is also debated. Most, however, argue that she is the third wife of King Wu Ding. See Cheng-lang (1986: 103–19).

3. From Dong Zoubin (1945): Wu Ding 59 reigned years, Zugeng 7 years, Zujia 33 years, Lin Xin 6 years, Kangding 8 years, Wuyi 4 years, Wenwuding 13 years, Diyi 35 years, and Dixin 52 years.

16

The Female Figure in Umayyad Art

Myriam Rosen-Ayalon

In view of the commonly held misconception of Islam as an iconoclastic religion, our topic calls for a few preliminary words. To persons outside the field of Islamic studies, it often comes as a surprise to discover that Islamic art is populated with paintings and sculptures of animals and human beings. Throughout its 1,400-year duration, Islamic art is hardly devoid of human representations, for the Koran—the basic guide for Muslim daily life and religious attitudes—contains no interdiction whatsoever against producing two- or even three-dimensional representations of either animals or humans. Indeed, there is a considerable literature on the subject, generally referred to under the label of "on the lawfulness of painting in Islam"(Ettinghausen 1962: chap. 1; Creswell 1969: 409–14; Allen 1988: 19–37).

In all Muslim lands and in a variety of media, an impressive number of such representations are found (fig. 16.1). There have, of course, been ups and downs in such creativity: periods in which the *Ulema,* the theologians, had the upper hand in their opposition to such depictions, which they considered abhorrent and diametrically opposed to orthodox doctrine, and more lenient periods, as well as particular regions, where graphic creativity was more popular (e.g., Iran as against North Africa, where such depictions were generally avoided). On the whole, however, human and animal depictions can be found in most facets of Islamic art. Islamic archaeology has been blessed with an abundance of discoveries demonstrating such a presence, and certain of these animated figures provide the basis of this chapter.

The Umayyad period (661–749/50) is undoubtedly one of the most intriguing periods of Islamic history. It is the very beginning of the meaningful political might of Islam, and in many respects this period reflects the true impetus

289

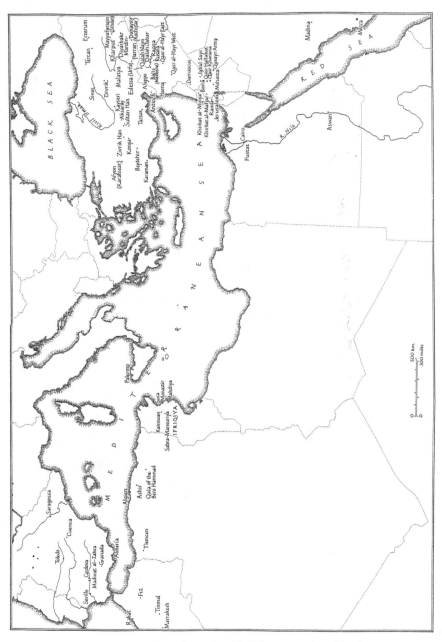

Figure 16.1. Locations of Umayyad buildings mentioned in the text.

of Islamic civilization. As to Islamic art, it would be difficult to say whether its Islamic character had already become defined by then, given the complex nature of the Umayyad period. However, Umayyad art was undoubtedly the cornerstone for much of what was later to emerge in the Islamic arts. Scholars have been attracted to this significant period, but the contemporary historical sources in Arabic are scarce (Elad 1994: 1–3). Needless to say, interpretation and speculation have, thus, been all the more common, often based on later writings and possibly reflecting later developments of society. Some of these later writings were also tainted by a biased view of their predecessors, the Umayyads (Humphreys 1991: 69–89).

Contrary to the paucity of written sources concerning this period, the artistic, visual arts provide us with considerable information, though this evidence is uneven in various respects. As important as this dynasty was, the main artistic production can be traced over some six decades, with the pace increasing from the beginning of the eighth century on. Geographically, too, artistic production under the Umayyads is unevenly distributed. Some areas were more favored than others, as the examples discussed here amply illustrate. Of the various sources of information that are available for the study of this period, archaeology is probably the most fertile.

One of the most striking subjects, relevant to our examination of Umayyad art, is the group of Umayyad "desert palaces." With their discovery and identification, it has become obvious that they represent a widespread phenomenon throughout the Syrian Desert and its immediate surroundings—Jordan, Israel, and Lebanon. It has been pointed out by several authors that many of these "palaces" share a number of characteristics, furthering their investigation and understanding. It is now clear that no two of these monuments are alike; each one differs in specific elements, and this could be said also for their decoration.

The principal media used in decorating the palaces were painting (walls and floors), sculpture (in stone or stucco), and mosaics (floors), only the first two of which are relevant to our topic. The fresco paintings form an overwhelming majority of the wall decoration, spreading not only over the walls but also on vaults, arches, domes, and—as we will see at one site, Qasr al-Hair al-Gharbi—even over the floors. In several cases, as in Jerusalem (Mazar and Ben-Dov, n.d.: 32–33), only a few fragments have survived; in other cases, surviving compositions are elaborately rendered. The richest concentration of such wall paintings is to be found at Qusayr 'Amra (Musil 1907).

Having laid the ground for our investigation, it should be emphasized that, of the many palaces (Creswell 1989) and their respective ornamentation, only three are truly relevant to our context. Only in these three do we find artistic depictions of women—at Qusayr 'Amra in Jordan, Qasr al-Hair al-Gharbi in Syria, and Khirbat al-Mafjar in Palestine (listed chronologically). Whether

painted or in the round, the presence of depictions of women at these three sites
is overwhelming, although their occurrence at each palace is very different. It
should be emphasized that, insofar as Islamic art is concerned, the study of
female depictions has not even reached infancy but is still "in utero" (Hambly
1998). These are certainly not the only source for depictions of women in
Islamic art. Over the ages, the depiction of women had its ups and downs
throughout the Islamic world, but the focus here is on this well-defined chapter of art history. However, for the presence of women as subjects in the art of
Islam during its first century, particularly during the first half of the eighth century, it is precisely these palaces that are so important.

Let us then begin with the earliest of these monuments, that at Qusayr 'Amra
(fig. 6.2). This building had long been associated with the person of Walid I
(705–715) (Creswell 1989: 112–13), until in recent years its date was pushed
forward to the days of Walid II (743–744) (Hillenbrand 1982). It is a rather
small structure, comprising one main hall with two small side rooms and an
attached bathhouse. The interior is entirely covered with a very diverse group
of wall paintings, among which are numerous depictions of women. No satisfactory interpretation has been offered for the painted scenes, and they do not
appear to have any coherent system to them. In other words, we are still at a
preliminary stage of identification and interpretation, and the key to decoding
the overall composition is so far elusive.

Disregarding those scenes where no female depictions are present, there
seems to be a very distinct difference between the scenes located in the bathhouse and those in the main hall. No two scenes are alike, but in the bathhouse

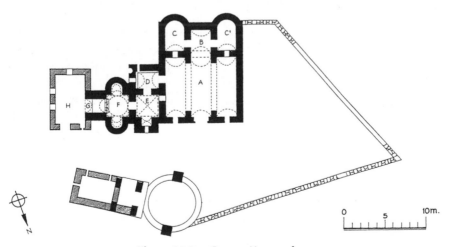

Figure 16.2.   Qusayr 'Amra: plan.

there seems to be a preponderance of nude women, there being no porno-graphic sexual intent evident in them, not even a wink to the observer. Such depictions, of course, are most natural in the context of a bathhouse. They are very naturalistically rendered, shown in profile, *en face,* or from the back. Pro-portions are good, and the depictions are well defined by contour lines. In one case, the woman holds a small child in her arms, and the scene possesses an air of intimacy and reality. This "true life" atmosphere is accentuated in one depiction where a large vessel for washing (fig. 16.3) is shown next to the woman in a rather informal manner. Next to her is another woman holding a bucket and quite naturally proceeding with her bath. These depictions are directly related to the activity carried on in this part of the structure. The depic-tions do not seem to reflect any established trend in pre-Islamic art, and they can probably be regarded as a "modern" artistic trend, a phenomenon of the new civilization that produced them. This naturalistic style in the nude, in all probability with roots in the Classical tradition, reflects a well-defined taste for plump women, as are admired in Jahiliyyah poetry (Ettinghausen 1962: 32).

On the other hand, the complexity of the role of the female depictions in the main hall is striking. Here the surface of the wall paintings is much greater, and walls, ceilings, vaults, and arches are all covered with frescoes containing

Figure 16.3.   Qusayr 'Amra. Fresco of a woman in her bath (after Ettinghausen 1962).

floral, animal, and human depictions. Though still incompletely interpreted, there seems to be no clear system to the female depictions. The various scenes differ greatly from one another, as do the roles of the respective figures. The scenes seem to be disconnected, and even the women's costumes appear to be diverse. Further, the women here seem to be depicted in passive roles, relegated to mere "wallflowers" rather than participants in a live scene (as in the baths).

It should be emphasized again that no two female depictions here are alike. Such a great diversity, with an emphasis on the naturalistic painting, does convey a message of realism, and in one way or another, most of the scenes at Qusayr 'Amra carry the flavor of authenticity, making them all the more significant as a source for understanding their context. These figures are depicted with great care, and all the details are diligently painted and include numerous traditional features, such as a dancer in the Classical tradition (fig. 16.4).

At Qasr al-Hair al-Gharbi, the problem is somewhat different, for the placement of the female depictions is rather odd (fig. 16.5). Here there are both paintings and stucco sculptures, some of which are almost completely in the round. The sculptures have been identified as belonging to the decoration of the facade of the main entrance to the palace and had been positioned at various heights there. Such prominent positioning surely reflects a pre-Islamic tradition, but the figural repertoire clearly indicates a new and quite different interpretation (fig. 16.6) with, inter alia, the female figure depicted in a fuller, "fleshier" manner.

Another entirely different feature is the occurrence here, on the floors, of painted depictions of women. These "floor paintings" draw on both the Classical

Figure 16.4. Qusayr 'Amra. Fresco depicting a woman (after Creswell 1969).

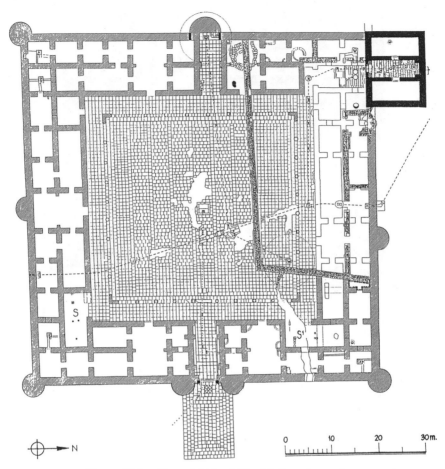

Figure 16.5.   Qasr al-Hair al-Gharbi: the palace, plan.

and the Sasanian traditions. On the one hand, we see a medallion enclosing the head of a woman accompanied by agricultural crops—to be identified with the goddess Gea (Schlumberger 1946–48); on the other hand, there are such elements as beaded decoration, which distinctly indicate oriental sources of inspiration (fig. 16.7).

In a second "floor painting," the composition itself is based on "strips," as in ancient reliefs—an Eastern concept. These figures too are clearly of Sasanian inspiration, as are numerous details over which we may skip here in our brief discussion. The costumes are clearly Near Eastern, in the best Sasanian tradition, and this is especially striking among the musicians depicted on the upper register of the "floor paintings" (fig. 16.8). Not only are they clad in Iranian

Figure 16.6. Qasr al-Hair al-Gharbi. Stucco sculpture (after Schlumberger 1946–48).

garb, but they appear to have been taken over directly from Iranian iconography. However, they have undergone "acclimatization," for nothing precisely parallel exists in Sasanian art. Truly, they are Umayyad, for the entire concept of "floor paintings" is otherwise unknown. Could they merely have been preliminary sketches for a mosaic never executed?

One figure of a woman at this site, on a fragment of a wall painting, clearly depicts a "Muslim" woman. Though a mere fragment, it shows her realistically and modestly, with a traditional veil covering her head (fig. 16.9).

The most interesting female depictions, however, would seem to be those found in the Umayyad Palace at Khirbat al-Mafjar, near Jericho in Palestine. Although fragments of wall paintings were also excavated here, not even a hint of a painted depiction of a woman was found. On the other hand, the quantity of sculpture here is astounding, by any criterion. All the sculptures are of stucco, originally covered with polychrome painting. They are in the round or almost so and are more or less of natural size (fig. 16.10).

The palace complex at Khirbat al-Mafjar includes various architectural units, including a mosque and a bathhouse (fig. 16.11). The several elements were constructed at slightly different times (Hamilton 1949), though this is of little consequence to our discussion. The fact that the bathhouse seems to have been completed first and the palace proper only later may indicate a later style

Figure 16.7. Qasr al-Hair al-Gharbi. "Floor painting" of "Gea" in medallion (after Schlumberger 1946–48).

in the palace depictions (fig. 16.12). Female figures are found, however, in both units: The entrance hall of the palace had such figures placed in niches in the upper part of the main gateway, and another series of female figures was located inside the porch of the entrance to the bathhouse (fig. 16.13).

Even so, and leaving aside stylistic differences, the female figures from the two architectural units do differ in dress, facial features, and even facial expressions. Yet they all share a similar concept: They are decorative elements on the upper portions of the walls. Further, they are all what we would call today "topless" and have elaborate coiffures (which differ in the two units) and are prominently adorned with jewelry, whether earrings or necklaces. Their most impressive feature, worn by all the female figures, is the long skirt, pleated and with a wavy hem all around. Besides their not-so-modest dress, they were notably holding either a "bouquet" or a basket of flowers.

Figure 16.8.   Qasr al-Hair al-Gharbi. "Floor painting" of two female musicians in upper register (after Schlumberger 1946–48).

Figure 16.9. Qasr al-Hair al-Gharbi. Fresco fragment depicting a modest woman (after Schlumberger 1946–48).

Figure 16.10. Khirbat al-Mafjar. Female figure in stucco in the entrance hall of the palace (courtesy Israel Antiquities Authority).

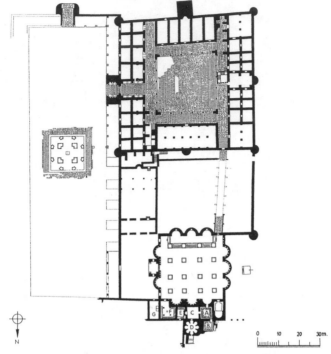

Figure 16.11.   Khirbat al-Mafjar: plan (from Hamilton 1949).

Such an iconography directly reflects Sasanian prototypes (1993: 234–39), most of which are found on silver objects. This general comparison has led to the suggestion that the Khirbat al-Mafjar ladies originally held a cup of wine in their second hand (for various arms are missing from the Mafjar sculptures), as did their Sasanian counterparts (Hillenbrand 1982). However, the Sasanian figures all have a mythological association, their role being interpreted either as the goddess Anahita herself or as that of a religious consort, a priestess. Such roles, however, are entirely out of place under Islam, and here their role was clearly to extend a pleasing welcome to those entering the palace or bath-house. Whether courtesans, concubines, "filles de joie," or otherwise, they are surely to be associated with the pleasures of the Umayyad court—a life indeed essentially one of amusement and leisure (Hamilton 1988).

The Sasanian association acknowledged, along with the essential differences in meaning, another dimension remains to confront us. This is the new trend of Umayyad esthetics—and the Mafjar finds represent significant new data for this facet. Here, as we have noted also at Qusayr 'Amra, a taste for a new sort of female figure can clearly be distinguished, in comparison with that

Figure 16.12.   Cross section of the porch of the bathhouse at Khirbat al-Mafjar.

found in Sasanian art. The stucco figures here are somewhat plump, with full bosoms, whereas Sasanian depictions are of delicate, lithe women, often sinuously dancing.

The one exception to the fullness of the Mafjar women is to be found in the decoration of the dome of the *diwan,* or private audience room in the palace. The large rosette, carved in stucco, is made up of several concentric rows of leaves, with "buds" in the form of human heads, alternating male and female. Patches of color emphasizing the hair and eyes (and in the case of the men, beards) are still preserved. Here, indeed, the women are rather more delicately rendered. At the same time, it should be pointed out that their depiction is only partial, and the lower parts of the body do not appear at all (fig. 16.14). The ornamentation of the dome here is rather enigmatic, not only in its composition but in the very presence of female heads above a *diwan* (unless the function of this room was something entirely different from that assumed previously). As noted, the locations of the other female depictions in the palace can be explained as a sort of welcoming feature, to create a favorable ambiance. However, the female depictions in the dome, though very much in the general

Figure 16.13. Khirbat al-Mafjar. Female figure in stucco in the hall of the bathhouse (courtesy Israel Antiquities Authority).

style of the entire group of sculptures at Mafjar, call for some other explanation, one that so far eludes us.

The male figures here, who appear young and handsome, may be a reference to the various games played under the Umayyads, favoring "ephebes" as amusement partners. Together with the young ladies, they might be an indication of the animated life of the palace (Hamilton 1988).

This brief survey of the female depictions at three Umayyad desert palaces clearly reveals that the individual groups are quite different from one another. There are no overall stereotypes here, and though they share common stylistic denominators, each group conveys a message of its own and seems to be inspired by different motives. In general, however, all these female depictions seem directed toward the pleasure of the male-oriented Umayyad court. There is no evidence to assume any "divine" interpretation of the figures, and even

Figure 16.14.   Khirbat al-Mafjar. Alternating female and male heads in the dome of the *diwan* **(courtesy Israel Antiquities Authority).**

in the one case of a "floor painting" at Qasr al-Hair al-Gharbi, which has roots in Classical mythology, such symbolism had surely lost all meaning within the Islamic context.

At this point, another significant question arises, for no similar examples are provided by pre-Islamic art. Thus, where does this iconography originate? As is well known, two prominent factors contributed to early Islamic culture: Byzantine civilization, the legacy of Western culture up to that time, and Sasanian civilization, the custodian of the legacy of Mesopotamian-Iranian culture in the period of the rise of Islam. While not seeking to compare these two sources of inspiration, several basic trends should be noted.

In Byzantium, the pinnacle of any female cult was obviously Mary. As Christianity was the official state religion, depictions of biblical scenes and personages (both Old and New Testaments) abounded. In this context, Mary occupied the prime position. Another very significant female depiction is the unique portrait of the empress Theodora in the mural mosaics of the Church of San Vitale in Ravenna, shown along with her retinue. As impressive as the scene is, it is enhanced and emphasized by the fact that on the opposite wall, across the nave, is a parallel scene with the emperor Justinian accompanied by members of his court. This constellation of emperor and empress facing each other outwardly emphasizes an equality of roles, expressing Justinian's official policy. However, this is a representation of the highest social rank within Christian Byzantium.

Beyond the imperial level, Byzantine secular art is not widely preserved. It would be difficult to envisage sources of inspiration within the Byzantine realm for the female depictions in Umayyad art despite the unequivocal Western-Classical trend so clearly evident in the paintings, particularly at Qusayr 'Amra and Qasr al-Hair al-Gharbi.

Turning to the Sasanian world, the evidence is of a somewhat different nature, spread over a broader social panorama. On the one hand, we see the goddess Anahita and her priestesses (referred to earlier) among the quite common representations, for example, on Sasanian silver. However, in two other contexts, depictions of woman also find a role. In the one, the investiture of the king as the divine king-of-kings shows him receiving an insignia from the Persian deity Ahura Mazda as well as from a goddess. Here, too, her role is supreme, delegating both earthly and divine authority to the king, and here again, the female role is parallel to that of the god in the hierarchy of the Sasanian context.

On a more down-to-earth, Sasanian level, male nobility and other high-ranking figures (not necessarily of royal descent) are shown together with their female counterparts. They are often depicted facing or seated next to one another in more or less equality, though there are often slight differences in scale (in favor, of course, of the male depictions). Here, too, as in the Byzantine world, a queen could be seen depicted on coins, alongside the king—a possibility completely ruled out under Islam (Evans and Wixom 1997: 214–15; Ghirshman 1962: 246).

A third component contributing to the formation of Islamic art—somewhat overlooked—is undoubtedly Coptic art. Here, a real close relationship between Islamic and Coptic art undoubtedly existed, bearing direct influences, for example, on some of the sculptures of Khirbat al-Mafjar (Rosen-Ayalon 1975: plates 39, 40). As much as the similarities appear convincing, and as much as Coptic art is interrelated with Islamic art, the implications are particularly valid for the specific discussion of the Khirbat al-Mafjar sculptures.

None, however, of the types of depictions in either of these two pre-Islamic cultures is to be found in the early Islamic context. It is paradoxical—despite the abundant evidence that Islamic art was a true heir to both those civilizations in the visual realm—that Islam adopted the outer shell but discarded the inner content. In this context, it is of particular interest to observe the symbiosis occurring in the early Islamic period: The Umayyad depictions of women remain close to their artistic sources, but they appear in entirely different contexts. This is all the more striking when it is realized that many specific elements of both the two pre-Islamic traditions were adopted into the Islamic world. These influences have often been noted in reference to objects, motifs, and stylistic particulars in the major arts, such as architecture, and in the more prosaic world of metalwork, pottery, and the like. However, here the context is rather one of mentality, of the attitude toward gender relationships. It is in this realm that the comparison must be made between Islam and the patterns established within the Byzantine and Sasanian cultures, respectively.

However, in overall analysis it becomes evident that none of these main sources of inspiration for the Umayyad art provides either precise parallels or patterns for the panorama of the female figure and her role in the respective monuments. It would be significant to further examine the physical context of these representations. One hint in this direction may be cited: a curious report by Ibn Batutta, in the later part of the Middle Ages. Having been admitted to visit the palace of an Ottoman prince, he was greeted in the entrance hall by 20 servants in the hall. (On leaving the palace, he was presented with one of the slave women as a gift [Pierce 1993: 35].) One cannot avoid at least associating this with the display of stucco sculptures in the entrance hall at Khirbat al-Mafjar (fig. 16.15).

Women, of course, played a significant role throughout Islamic history and Islamic society, though they were not often in the limelight (Yamani 1996). Despite this, depictions of females in Islamic art have been neglected almost entirely. Though the evidence is not evenly distributed either chronologically

Figure 16.15. Khirbat al-Mafjar. Reconstructed view of the entrance hall (after Hamilton 1949).

or geographically, a fuller picture of the role of woman in the world of Islam can surely be obtained. The material presented here represents the earliest phase and still calls for a much more thorough study. This evidence is unique, for there is nothing even remotely comparable in later Islamic society. Thus, these rich Umayyad female depictions cannot be extended as a valid sample for the lengthy history of Islam, nor can they be taken in any way to represent the entire realm of Islam, which stretched from Spain in the west to Southeast Asia.

An accessory question is, Who could have served as the models for these female depictions in the Umayyad period? There is not even a clue. Though this trend depicting the female figure had no immediate predecessors, there must have been some means for fulfilling this need.

Unfortunately, our information on daily life in the Umayyad realm is scant, hardly enabling an interpretation of the activities that took place in the desert palaces. Much more detailed research into the decoration of these palaces is essential, and it is hoped that it will lead to a closer identification of the roles of the respective female depictions. Still enigmatic are such questions as, Were there women present in these compounds? Did they have any special quarters? Were the bathhouses used by both males and females? Was such use simultaneous, or was it segregated?

Though our discussion has focused on female depictions, a complementary examination of the parallel imagery of male depictions in Umayyad art should also be initiated to determine how the subject is treated and how it compares with our present topic, but this must await some later study.

Although Umayyad secular art has been regarded as less innovative than religious art (Grabar 1993: 98 [where he even suggests "gender" studies to contribute to our understanding of this art]), what we are actually seeing here is an entirely new crystallization of artistic components. These animated depictions of the "bucolic" world of the Umayyad palaces seem a major novelty of Umayyad art, even more striking when set against the blank backdrop of antecedents.

17

Accessing Prestige and Power: Women in the Political Economy of Protohistoric and Early Historic Visayan Polities

Elisabeth A. Bacus

Western observers of many of the societies in both mainland Southeast Asia (Burma, Thailand, Cambodia, Laos and Vietnam) and Island Southeast Asia (. . . Malaysia, Indonesia, and the Philippines, plus Brunei and Singapore) have been struck by the complementarity of men's and women's work and the relative lack of ritual or economic differentiation between men and women there.

In Island Southeast Asia, differences between people, including men and women, are often attributed to the activities the people in question engage in or the spiritual power they exhibit or fail to exhibit. If we want to understand gender there, we . . . must understand local ideas of power and prestige; the next step is to ask how people defined as male, female, or something else are mapped onto . . . the prestige and power systems.

— Shelly Errington,
  in *Power and Difference: Gender in Island Southeast Asia* (1990)

INTRODUCTION

A Philippine perspective on the archaeology of women and gender is difficult to provide; currently, there are no archaeological studies of past gender systems in the archipelago. In this chapter, I consider gender in the political economy of early historic (1521 to early 1600s, the early period of Spanish contact) and protohistoric (ca. 10th to early 16th centuries A.D.) Visayan polities. The reasons for doing so are twofold. First, the nature and dynamics of protohistoric Philippine political economies have received considerable archaeological attention in recent years. Within the Visayas (the islands between Luzon and Mindanao; see fig. 17.1), projects in the Dumaguete-Bacong region (e.g., Bacus 1995, in press), Tanjay region (e.g., Junker 1990), and Cebu City

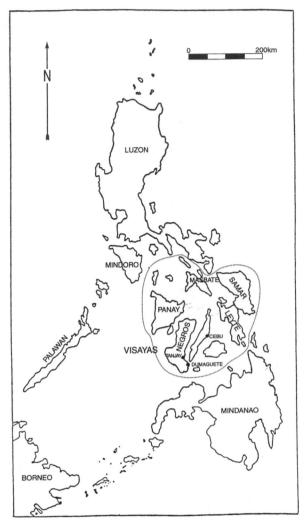

Figure 17.1. **Philippine Islands showing the area of the Visayas and the location of the protohistoric centers of the Dumaguete, Tanjay, and Cebu polities.**

(Nishimura 1992) have examined the organization of craft production, chiefly control over the wealth sector of the economy, political uses of local craft goods, and their various transformations during the protohistoric period, a period marked by intensive and competitive participation by Philippine polities in trade with China and mainland Southeast Asia states. The only social categories considered thus far as relevant to understanding Visayan political economies have been those of the elite and nonelite. However, economic systems are gendered systems (see, e.g., Brumfiel 1991, 1992; Costin 1996;

Wright 1996), and in complex polities, women and men cannot be assumed to participate in or be affected by political-economic processes in the same way. Furthermore, the approach I have taken in my own studies of protohistoric Visayan polities, one based on anthropological political economy, emphasizes agency and structure in analyzing social relations based on unequal access to wealth and power; however, the only actors I have considered thus far have been the ruling elite.

The second reason relates in part to the chapter-opening quote from Shelly Errington. Since our archaeological research on protohistoric Visayan polities has focused on systems of prestige and power (as political authority), it may provide a basis for beginning to understand past gender systems. Recent anthropological research on contemporary centrist archipelago societies (i.e., the Malay peninsula, the Philippines, and most of Indonesia except for Sumatra, the Lesser Sundas, and Moluku) has been interested in why, in a region where men and women are viewed as complementary, women tend to be systematically disadvantaged in the effort to achieve prestige and power. Studies (see papers in Atkinson and Errington 1990) suggest that this results from "practice rather than stated rules" (Errington 1990: 54). Thus, by identifying the activities (economic and otherwise) of women (vis-à-vis men) in contact and early historic Visayan society, we may begin to understand why, despite fairly egalitarian gender relations, elite women did not hold positions of political authority.

This chapter begins with an overview of the sociopolitical and economic organization of early historic (i.e., 16th-century) Visayan polities, specifically the reconstructions used to inform current archaeological interpretations of the protohistoric period. I then present Spanish observations of women based on my study of accounts from 1521 to the early 1600s, particularly in regard to ascertaining their economic activities. As I discuss next, many of the types of archaeological data used to study gender in complex polities elsewhere in the world are currently lacking for the Philippines; nonetheless, I consider some of the implications that a gendered view has for our understanding of protohistoric Visayan political economies. Finally, I consider possible relations between Visayan women's activities and their access to prestige and power, as political authority, and some resulting implications for changes in protohistoric gendered prestige systems that should be manifested in the material record.

EARLY HISTORIC
VISAYAN POLITICAL ECONOMIES:
WITHOUT AND WITH WOMEN

Much of our current understanding of protohistoric Visayan sociopolitical and economic organization derives in large part from early Spanish accounts (and to a lesser extent from the few but informative Chinese records of the 10th to 16th centuries). Though Tagalogs of the Manila Bay region were literate in an indigenous script called *baybayin* when Spaniards first arrived there in the mid-1560s (Scott 1984: 52–53), only one apparently authentic pre-Hispanic document has been found thus far (a 10th-century copper plate inscription of an acquittal of debt that mentions a noblewoman; Postma 1991). Archaeologists (as well as cultural anthropologists and historians) thus rely on analyses of European accounts to construct early contact "ethnographies" for insights into interpreting the material record of the immediate protohistoric period.

Beginning with the first Spanish expedition to the archipelago in 1521, and especially after 1565, the beginning of Spanish colonial rule, accounts of various kinds (e.g., church records, missionary accounts, colonial reports, administrative records, travelers accounts, and accounts of military expeditions) were written about the archipelago and its inhabitants. Among the most important of the primary sources for the contact and early historic period in the Visayas are Pigafetta's *Primo viaggio intorno al mondo* (1524), the main account of Magellan's 1521 expedition and the earliest of the European eyewitness descriptions of the archipelago, and the following first-generation colonial descriptions, many written in response to a royal order to report on native conditions and customs: Miguel de Loarca's *Relación de las Yslas Filipinas* (1582), the anonymously authored Boxer MS (ca. 1590), Antonio de Morga's *Sucesos de las Islas Filipinas* (1609b), and Pedro Chirino's *Relación de las Islas Filipinas* (1604b). The somewhat later *History of the Bisayan Islands* (1668) by Ignacio Alcina, who lived in the Visayas for 35 years, is considered by scholars to be the most extensive work on the Visayas (and Philippines generally) until the ethnographies of the 20th century. I, as well as other archaeologists, have analyzed these accounts, along with the large corpus of other types of Spanish accounts translated by Blair and Robertson (1903–6), to construct an historic baseline for comparison with aspects of protohistoric sociopolitical organization and political economy (for discussion of some of the problematic uses of these accounts, see, e.g., Fernandez 1996; Bacus, in press).

These early accounts describe, in varying degrees of detail, aspects of various lowland polities throughout the archipelago. Some polities, such as Manila and Cebu, appear to have exhibited greater sociopolitical stratification and were more regionally extensive than the other numerous smaller-scale lowland polities described. Early commentators on 16th-century Visayan society noted three classes of people (largely hereditary but with some possibility of mobility). *Datu* referred to the hereditary elite and was a political title of both local and regional chiefs; the former were chiefs of a *barangay*—a settlement of 30 to 100 households—and the latter of a *bayan,* comprising a number of *barangay*. *Tumao*, a lesser lineage of nobility, were "descendants of other or former *datus*, or of an immigrating *datu*'s original comrades, or the kin of a prominent local ruler" (Scott 1982: 113–14). A ruling *datu*'s counselors were chosen from this group. *Timawa*, often the relatives or illegitimate sons of the *datu*, were the personal vassals of the *datu*. They served as warriors and participants in trading and raiding expeditions and neither paid tribute nor performed agricultural labor (de Loarca 1582; Chirino 1604b; Scott 1982, 1994). *Oripun* included commoners and "slaves" (i.e., the lowest subclass of commoners who had become domestics or field chattel through debt bondage, capture in raiding, or voluntarily because of dire economic circumstances or who were second-generation slaves; it also included those killed for ritual purposes) who provided the obligatory agricultural and other labor and/or tribute for the support of the elite (Scott 1982: 112–13). Finer subdivisions existed within *timawa* and *oripun;* for the latter, these were reflected in the amount of and types of services owed the *datu*.

While Spanish accounts do not provide a detailed description of the political economy of any one polity, they do provide a broad outline. Accounts indicate that chiefs derived support from agricultural and other tribute, various labor services, payments for services they performed, and fees for use of their ports and through their sponsorship/leadership of maritime expeditions for the purposes of exchange within the archipelago, long-distance trade, warfare, and raids (e.g., de Loarca 1582; Scott 1982, 1994). These provided the financing for various political activities important to the maintenance and expansion of a chief's power base, which consisted of various horizontal and vertical alliances. Chiefs appear to have sponsored some craft specialists (primarily part time), with some specialists located at political centers. Most of the craft goods described were produced for elite consumption, including use as export items in intra-archipelago exchange and foreign trade. Craft specialists mentioned in accounts include goldsmiths who produced gold ornaments that were items of wealth worn in most abundance by chiefly elite (Boxer MS 1590), iron and other unspecified smiths (Boxer MS 1590; Alcina 1668), skilled carpenters who constructed chiefs' and other elites' houses (Boxer MS 1590; Alcina 1668), shipwrights (with full-time specialists mentioned within only the context of a Spanish shipyard; de Loarca 1582; de Morga 1609b; cf. Bacus 1995), and textile producers. Chiefs controlled the distribution and exchange of other goods as well, such as fine earthenwares, though possibly not their production. Likewise, chiefs had varying degrees of control over certain resources and foods valuable as trade exports. These included gold ore, iron, raw cotton, rice, and beeswax, which either were acquired by their own slaves or received as tribute (de Morga 1609a; Alcina 1668). For most items (gold and other jewelry, iron objects, and boats), there is little information on the organization of production, whether or not it occurred under elite sponsorship, and on the location of the various production activities. Similarly, little information exists on the production and distribution of utilitarian and nonelite goods.

As this summary of current reconstructions of early historic Visayan political economies shows, consideration of these various producers and laborers as gendered individuals is lacking. Though partially due to the information contained in accounts, it also reflects the use of general models (e.g., see Junker 1990; Bacus 1995), such as Frankenstein and Rowlands's (1978) prestige goods model, D'Altroy and Earle's (1985) wealth finance model, and Wright's (1984) tributary model to investigate aspects of political economy. Consequently, we have a rather genderless view of protohistoric Visayan polities and have yet to investigate the nature of and changes in Visayan women's activities during this period and the impacts of various forms of political economies on women and of women on these structures.

SEEING WOMEN

Cristina Blanc-Szanton (1990) has noted that Spanish and other foreign writers describing Philippine cultures made many insightful observations through their fundamentally comparative and contrastive approach. Early Spanish observers "were struck by the generally autonomous behavior and customs and by the egalitarian views of Visayans concerning the sexes, which were in implicit contrast with their own traditions" (Blanc-Szanton 1990: 356). They also noted marked differences between Visayan customary law and Spanish laws regarding women. For example, "Illongo women inherited equally, had equal rights to their children after a divorce, and could independently decide whether they wanted to stay married or not" (Blanc-Szanton 1990: 357). In addition, women also could own property and, in the company of other women, travel some distance from home. Such early Spanish observations suggest that in Visayan culture of the immediate pre-Hispanic period, gender relations and images of gender were reasonably egalitarian (Blanc-Szanton 1990: 379; cf. Eviota 1992). Such images may also be seen in Visayan creation myths (some versions recorded in the early historic period; see, e.g., Scott 1994) in which the first woman and man spring simultaneously from two sections of the same piece of bamboo (Locsin-Nava 1996: 61).

Any attempt to understand women within early historic Visayan political economies from written accounts, though, is hampered by the relatively few references to them overall and to the activities they engaged in (with the exception of their sexual practices and acts of Christian devotion). The only illustrations of 16th-century Visayan women and men comes from the Boxer MS

(1590), with changes in attire due to the Spanish presence already evident. What can be discerned about their activities from early Spanish accounts is discussed here. In the case of Chinese writers (of the 10th to 16th centuries), the few references to women are not surprising given their particular interest in trade and the archipelago's products and natural resources. Nonetheless, women are not completely invisible; one can see the products of their labor, specifically textiles (see the following discussion), among the Chinese descriptions of goods exported from the archipelago (e.g, Chao Ju-Kua 1225).

Among the various craft-related activities noted earlier, textile production (of cotton and abaca cloth) was clearly a female activity. Male transvestites were also weavers during the 16th century (Scott 1994: 69), though accounts do not provide any detailed information on this gender. Textile making is certainly the most explicitly discussed women's economic activity, and it is mentioned more often than any other craft. Spanish observations also provide some insight into the organization of its production (especially of cotton cloth). As previously discussed, chiefs controlled the distribution of some textiles (i.e., their use in foreign trade; Echevarria 1974: 1, 4–6) and, as shown in the following, also some of its production. The considerable Spanish interest in Philippine textiles may reflect the importance of textiles in Spanish New World colonial economies as tribute and trade items (e.g., in 1572, one year after Legazpi's conquest of Manila, galleons sailed for Acapulco with 22,600 pesos worth of cloth; Scott 1994: 70).

From a young age women, regardless of their status, spun and wove (on backstrap looms) cotton cloth and abaca cloth (known as *habul* or *medriñaque,* which was made from the fibers of a species of the banana plant family) for their own household's needs, for use in their own local exchange activities, and for payment of tribute (e.g., Scott 1994). Visayan women wove not only items of clothing and blankets but also the important male status-marking *pinaiosan,* a distinguishing red-dyed abaca cloth worn only by men who had personally killed an enemy (Alcina 1668). Abaca cloth was also an exported foreign-trade good by the early 13th century (Chao Ju-kua 1225).

Female slaves also spun and/or wove for their masters (de Loarca 1582; Dasmarinas 1591; de Morga 1609a; Alcina 1668; Blanc-Szanton 1990: 356). As previously noted, there were different grades of slavery; for female slaves, this meant differences in the location of and time spent in cloth-making activities. Alcina (1668) noted that female household slaves wove in Visayan chiefs' residences. According to de Loarca (1582), slaves who had their own residences varied in the amount of their spinning and weaving obligations:

The *tumaranpoque* women [who worked one day out of four for their master], if they have children, serve half of the month in spinning and weaving cotton, which their masters supply. . . . The *tumatalan* women [those who worked in their master's house

only when there was a banquet or celebration] spin only one hank of cotton each
month for their masters, who furnish to them the cotton in the boll. (145)

Not all islands or regions within islands were suitable for growing cotton
(e.g., Cuyo Island, near Panay, which nonetheless produced large quantities of
cotton textiles; de Loarca 1582). In such cases, the chiefly elite would have
acquired raw cotton through intra-archipelago exchange. Given women's primary role in agriculture (see the following discussion), they presumably grew
the cotton, which chiefs then received as tribute and subsequently used, in part,
in such trade activities.

Pottery appears to have been the only other craft material produced by
women in the early historic period (Scott 1994); unfortunately, Spanish
accounts do not provide descriptions of women's specific activities in pottery
production. Besides domestic uses, earthenware vessels were used in mortuary and other ritual contexts (e.g., Pigafetta 1524; de Loarca 1582; Boxer MS
1590; Chirino 1604a). Again, accounts lack details of the organization or specialization in production of these different types of vessels.

The significance of local pottery in early historic political economies is difficult to ascertain from written records, in contrast to that of foreign porcelains
and stonewares. There is some evidence that chiefs distributed earthenwares,
though the context (i.e., to slaves on the arrangement of marriage; de Loarca
1582) indicates that it was not for political purposes. More relevant to the latter is the use of earthenware pottery as an item of exchange between coastal
polities and interior upland groups (de Loarca 1582: 121–22). Such exchange
was important to a coastal chief's ability to participate in foreign trade since
the items highly sought by Chinese and other traders were interior forest products (e.g., resins, aromatic woods, and beeswax). Women's ceramic and textile production in the protohistoric period and implications of these craft activities for women's prestige are explored in the next section.

Another women's activity that yielded goods essential to the maintenance
of contact period Visayan political economies was farming, especially of rice
(de Loarca 1582; Boxer MS 1590; Scott 1994). Nonelite women engaged in
planting, weeding, and harvesting of rice and other crops such as millet, taro,
yams, and bananas. These were cultivated primarily in swidden fields, though
rice was sometimes grown in irrigated pond fields (Scott 1994: 36). Rice,
which accounts suggest could not be grown in sufficient quantity in most areas
to support populations year-round (Pigafetta 1524; Alcina 1668), was an item
of tribute. Chiefs used rice in feasts and rituals, as an export in archipelago-
wide exchange (since not all areas cultivated rice), and in foreign trade (including with those traders who resided for months at their ports) (e.g., Lavezaris
et al. 1567: 216).

Visayan women (including slaves) also engaged in trading activities within their own and neighboring settlements. Interestingly, women could also trade with foreigners (much to Legazpi's, the governor of the first Spanish settlement, disapproval; Anonymous 1565–67: 138). Unfortunately, the types of goods they used in exchange are not specified in early historic accounts (though textiles are mentioned by Scott 1994), and thus the implications for political and economic control of women's production are difficult to ascertain.

Though 16th-century Spanish accounts provide few detailed descriptions of women's economic activities, this is not significantly different from their recorded observations of men's economic activities (cf. Eviota 1992), with the exception of trade. Even in the case of the latter, Spanish interest focused on the items of trade rather than on their production. For several crafts, such as iron smithing, shipbuilding, woodcarving, and jewelry making, it is not clear whether these were domains exclusive to men. It may be reasonable to assume that the absence of Spanish commentary on the gender of these craft specialists indicates consistency with their own notions of gendered activities.

WOMEN IN PROTOHISTORIC VISAYAN POLITICAL ECONOMIES

As noted in the beginning of this chapter, gender has not been an area of research in Philippine archaeology. In the following discussion, I point out some of the current problems but also, more important, the potentials for engendering Visayan protohistory.

Comparisons of the relative status of, as well as within, genders during this or any other period are currently difficult to make, as we lack the mortuary data necessary to examine differential treatment of males and females. Large cemeteries do exist for this period (e.g., Kay Thomas with 297 burials and Pulung Bakaw with 208 burials [Fox 1959], Pingabayan with 238 burials [Tenazas 1968], and Santa Ana with 299 [Peralta and Salazar 1974]); however, problems of preservation, mortuary treatment (i.e., cremation and secondary burial), and/or the absence of the necessary specialists on site precluded sex determination of the skeletal remains. Of the several sites where skeletal remains have been sexed, the samples are too small for meaningful analysis (e.g, Cebu has two burials [Miracle et al. 1991]; Tanjay has 36 burials, of which 14 could not be sexed [Junker 1993a]) or have not been fully published (e.g., Panhutongan with 53 burials [de la Torre 1996]). Burials, though, are not the only source for constructing gender images. Clay figurines/sculptures clearly portraying females and males (and possibly specific individuals) have also been recovered from archaeological sites (e.g., Tabon cave [Fox 1970] and Ayub cave [Dizon 1996]). Until their dating is clear, though, it is difficult to interpret them within any larger cultural context.

A few other problems exist in archaeologically investigating gender and, of particular concern here, women in the protohistoric period. For example, houses were built primarily on poles, and thus we lack architectural evidence related to women's (and others') domestic activities and use of space. It should be possible, though, to compare household and intrasettlement midden deposits to investigate differences in activities within and between social classes since, for example, the elite and nonelite do appear to be residentially segregated within the political centers (see, e.g., Junker 1990; Nishimura 1992). Interestingly, there is evidence from the protohistoric Dumaguete polity (e.g., Bacus 1995, in press) and Tanjay polity (e.g., Junker 1990) for the association of pottery making and iron-smithing locales at the centers. This suggests spatial overlap in these possibly exclusively gendered activities (based on the historic and ethnographic evidence) and/or nonexclusive gender participation in these crafts. Such evidence suggests greater flexibility in gendered activities in the protohistoric period, at least in comparison to reconstructions based on historic and later ethnographic accounts, and highlights future research that can contribute to our comparative understanding of gender and craft production in complex polities.

Of a more temporary problem is the current lack of published archaeological data related to textile production. Spindle whorls for producing cotton cloth have been recovered from archaeological contexts, including from burials. Of the 238 burials from around the 12th to 14th centuries at the Pingabayan site, only two had spindle whorls among their respective mortuary goods. This suggests that it was not significant to mark an individual's role in textile production at death. In comparison, the late 14th- to late 15th-century burials at the Pulung Bakaw (208 burials) and Kay Thomas (297 burials) sites had 30 and 31 graves, respectively, with spindle whorls (found primarily with adult individuals, though Fox [1959] does not provide the number of each age class of individuals or describe any other mortuary goods with these burials). Whether this higher percentage of burials containing textile-making equipment relates to regional differences in raw materials, changes in the significance attached to cloth production (e.g., increased importance in exchange during a period in which polities' participation in international trade was increasing), or other factors remains to be investigated. Clearly, analyses of spindle whorls within their domestic and mortuary contexts should provide insights into activities conducted by women and transvestites as well as into issues concerning relations of status (i.e., slave, commoner, and elite), gendered craft activities, and exchange. Evidence pertaining to abaca cloth production may be more difficult to obtain since this fiber did not require spinning; instead, the fibers were tied together with fine knots prior to weaving.

Despite some of the current limitations we face in engendering Visayan protohistory and prehistory, we can at least recognize that women's production
would have been central to the political economy of these polities and would
have been impacted by these polities' increasing participation (as documented
in the archaeological record) in trade with China and Southeast Asia. Both textile and nondomestic pottery production would have become more important
to the political economy after involvement in foreign trade, consequently
entailing changes in women's productive work and/or in the nature of gendered craft production. For example, there is evidence for a standardized earthenware type in the 15th to 16th centuries suggestive of full-time pottery specialists at or near the center of the Tanjay polity that may have been used in
exchange with upland populations for forest products (Junker 1993b). By recognizing women, we can begin to investigate the possible implications of specialization for changes in gendered pottery production.

Chinese silks and porcelains, mainland Southeast Asian porcelains, and textiles from these and other regions replaced some native textiles and, in some
contexts, local earthenwares. As suggested in the following discussion, some
of the local goods may have marked prestige, whereas others were central to
ritual practices (e.g., earthenware burial jars). Consequently, some of
women's ceramic and textile production may have been reduced with the
beginnings of intensive foreign trade. At the same time, some of it would have
increased with the use of earthenware vessels in local exchange and of textiles
in foreign trade. The details of such foreign-trade impacts on the activities and
statuses of women in Visayan polities will require further archaeological
investigation.

TOWARD AN UNDERSTANDING OF
GENDERED PRESTIGE AND POWER IN
VISAYAN POLITIES

Early Spanish accounts suggest that the immediate pre-Hispanic period gender relations in the Visayas were reasonably egalitarian. De Loarca (1582:
119) describes elite Visayan women as highly praised and powerful (though
in what ways is unspecified), with possibly as many dependents and slaves as
their husbands. Daughters of powerful *datu* were sought for marriage by lesser
and potential *datu* who consistently tried to marry upward. The latter often
traveled great distances to find daughters of more powerful *datu*. In addition
to women's economic and political alliance roles, they were most commonly
the ritual specialists (*baylane*) who were healers and mediators between the
community and the local animistic spirits and gods (Pigafetta 1524; Anonymous 1565–67; Blanc-Szanton 1990: 357; Geremia-Lachica 1996; Salazar

1996). A position held in great respect in Visayan society, *baylanes* appear to have been close advisers of the *datu* in such matters as religion, medicine, and natural phenomena (as observed in the early to mid-17th century; Alcina 1668, cited in Geremia-Lachica 1996: 53), a role with potential political influence (Geremia-Lachica 1996; cf. Salazar 1996). (This may relate to *baylanes*'s ability to lead uprisings against missionaries and Muslims, in some areas of the Visayas, beginning in the late 16th century; Geremia-Lachica 1996). Though Visayan women had autonomy, equality, and power in several spheres, they nonetheless do not appear to have held positions of political authority as ruling *datu* during the early years of Spanish contact.

As mentioned in the beginning of this chapter, anthropologists studying contemporary gender systems in island Southeast Asia have been investigating why women in centrist Archipelago societies tend to be systematically disadvantaged in the effort to achieve prestige. In centrist societies, "male and female are viewed as basically the same sort of beings. . . . Gender differences tend to be downplayed in ritual, economics, and dress; kinship terminology and practice tend to be bilateral; and male and female are viewed as complementary or even identical beings in many respects" (Errington 1990: 39). Studies of women and prestige in these societies suggests that this results from "practice rather than stated rules; women are not prohibited from becoming shamans, meditating, or being highly respected, but their life circumstances and everyday tasks are such that they are disadvantaged" (Errington 1990: 55).

Anthropologists argue that the Western notion of political "power" is better understood as "potency" or "spiritual potency" in island Southeast Asia—an "intangible, mysterious and divine energy which animates the universe" (Anderson 1972: 7). Potency is something leaders seek to accumulate, and since it is invisible, it can be known only by its signs. Signs of a person's potency include large amounts of wealth and substantial numbers of followers. Prestige derives from having potency. Within hierarchical polities, power/potency can be used to support those activities (such as ceremonies; see, e.g., Geertz 1980) that themselves are indicators of a person's or center's potency (a "circular reciprocal relationship"; Errington 1990: 44).

These anthropological insights identify two important questions for investigating relationships between Visayan women and prestige/power systems: What were the signs of prestige and potency in early historic Visayan polities? What activities provided access to or accumulation of such signs? Although the information contained in early accounts does not allow these questions to be fully answered, it does allow for some potentially interesting connections to be made. These questions may even be possible to partially answer for the protohistoric period using current archaeological evidence.

In the early historic Philippines, as in other historic and some contemporary island Southeast Asian polities, prestige was marked by items of wealth that

Spanish described as including local and foreign goods—gold jewelry, porcelain, silk, some iron objects, bronze gongs, and slaves (e.g., Pigafetta 1524; de
Artiedo 1573; Chirino 1604b; Scott 1994). Wealth items were generally, but
not exclusively, restricted to members of the *datu* nobility, and in cases where
they were not (e.g., because *datu* distributed them, for various reasons/pur-
poses, to their followers), *datu* held them in greater quantity.

Elite women certainly owned items of wealth. However, their direct access
to these goods, and hence their ability to accumulate greater quantities of
wealth, were limited. The two primary means of wealth acquisition were
through marriage, when grooms paid "bride-price," some (possibly all) of
which went to the woman (de Loarca 1582; Boxer MS 1590), and through
inheritance. Elite women, as described in Spanish accounts, limited the number of children that they had to ensure that their children inherited well. *Baylanes* appear to have been the only group of women who received wealth items
as a result of their religious activities and specifically when performing ceremonies sponsored by prominent *datu* (Scott 1994). *Baylanes* thus could potentially accumulate further signs of potency. However, *baylanes,* by definition,
must have exhibited spiritual potency. An important question that arises
(which is not yet possible to answer) is, Why, if this "is culturally the sine qua
non for political power and authority in the archipelago" (Atkinson and
Errington 1990: 60), was this not the case for these women? Potency's relation to political power and authority seems to be mediated by gender.

The direct acquisition of slaves and foreign items of wealth was key to accumulating signs of potency and prestige. Although women produced goods (i.e.,
textiles, rice, and the pottery that was used in exchange with interior groups
for valuable export resources) that were important to the foreign trade that ultimately provided the exotica that signified potency, they did not control, sponsor, or engage directly in this trade (though some accompanied their husbands
on "tributary missions" of trade to the Chinese court). Nor were women active
in slave raiding. In this context, it is interesting that in a courtship passage from
a Visayan folk epic, it is said to the heroine, "You raid with your eyes and capture many, and with only a glance you take more prisoners than raiders do with
their *pangayaw* [slave raids]" (Alcina 1668). Marriage, like slave raiding, provided wealth. Slaves provided much of the labor, of which there appear to have
been shortages, for the extractive and productive activities (e.g., pearl diving,
coral and tortoise-shell collecting, hunting of civet cats and deer for skins, and
collecting of various forest products; Morga 1609a; Alcina 1668; Scott 1994)
that produced the surplus required by elites for participating in foreign trade.

Long-distance trade and slave raiding, along with warfare, were male activities; *datu* sponsored and participated in long-distance maritime trade expeditions and were the leaders in warfare and of slave raids. More important, the
men who participated in these activities, regardless of whether they were lesser

nobles, commoners, or slaves, received some of the acquired wealth (de Loarca 1582; Scott 1982). Amounts varied according to status. Men, of all statuses, thus had greater opportunities for acquiring and accumulating potent objects than women (especially nonnoble women). For those men (again, regardless of class) who distinguished themselves in such activities, it was possible to become *datu* since membership in this class was not strictly hereditary in the Visayas.

Interestingly, Reid (1988: 170) has noted that between the 15th and 17th centuries, in areas of Southeast Asia not strongly Hindu, Buddhist, or Islamic, "there was a remarkable tendency for those states that participated most fully in the expanding commerce of the region to be governed by women." Whether this would have been the case in the Visayas (or other areas of the archipelago) had not the Spanish colonial government usurped control over trade with China is, of course, unknown. Nonetheless, it suggests that when foreign trade became a commercial enterprise, presumably entailing alienated goods less tied to prestige systems, women could hold positions of political authority.

Archaeological evidence suggests that some of the items of potency in the historic period (particularly porcelain) were status and prestige goods during the 12th to early 16th centuries (e.g., Junker 1990; Nishimura 1992; Bacus 1995, in press). Differences in men's and women's access to, and accumulation of, such items, though, is currently difficult to ascertain, particularly given the available mortuary data. For the two to three centuries prior to more regular trade with China and Southeast Asian polities (i.e., pre-12th century), it is unclear what preceded foreign exotica as signs of potency in these polities. Some archaeologists (e.g., Dalupan 1985) have suggested that the elaborately decorated earthenwares found throughout the islands were items of prestige in this earlier period, and there are some foreign items (though in significantly smaller quantities than is found in the protohistoric record). Unfortunately, the dating of many of these decorated wares is unclear. If indeed porcelain vessels replaced local ceramic vessels as markers of potency, there may well have been changes in women's status corresponding to the devaluation of their ceramic goods, particularly if they had previously been producers of such signs. The relations between gender on the one hand and potency/power and prestige on the other during the protohistoric period represents an important topic for future research on complex polities in the Visayas.

CONCLUSIONS

Though this chapter has not presented analysis of archaeological data with regard to specific questions of gender, it has sought to highlight some areas within recent research on protohistoric Visayan polities that require gendered rethinking. An anthropological political economy approach dictates that we focus on the activity of human actors—within the circumstances associated with getting a living, within the structures of power that shape and constrain activity, and at the intersection of local and global histories (Roseberry 1988)—who, as we well recognize (at least now), are all gendered. Thus, it is no longer possible to employ general models of economic organization or dynamics without also considering, or at least bearing in mind, the implications for gendered actors (not to mention ethnic- and class-bound actors; see, e.g., Brumfiel 1992). Our aim should be to provide a more nuanced and "peopled" understanding of political economy in the Visayas (along the lines of, e.g., Brumfiel 1991; see also Conkey and Gero 1997).

I have also attempted to contextualize the limited political authority of Visayan women during the early historic period, which, I would suggest, probably extends back into the early second millennium A.D. (i.e., the period of increased and intensified participation in foreign trade). That it was not impossible for women to achieve such positions is suggested by later historic accounts of women chiefs (e.g., Blanc-Szanton [1990], though some references appear to be of legendary figures [Quindoza-Santiago 1996]), and, of course, it is highly likely that early European explorers and colonizers did not recognize politically potent women. However, what I have tried to explore is how women, despite economic autonomy and the similar notions of male- and femaleness that characterize centrist Archipelago societies both historically and in the present, tend to be systematically disadvantaged in their achievement of prestige and power, specifically of political authority. As Errington (1990) points out for contemporary centrist societies, it is not the stated rules but rather women's life circumstances and their everyday tasks that disadvantage them. Visayan women during the early years of Spanish contact owned wealth (in the form of slaves, gold, and porcelain), created wealth (i.e., certain textiles and rice), and produced goods exchangeable for wealth (i.e., earthenware pottery and other textiles). However, they did not control the political uses of such goods (e.g., in intra-archipelago exchange, formation of alliances, and foreign trade), nor could they directly acquire them via foreign trade and slave raiding, which would have enabled them to increase their holdings of essential markers of potency and prestige (e.g., slaves, followers, and porcelain). If slave raiding and foreign trade were activities essential to establishing political authority, as suggested by some (see, e.g., Wolters 1982; Rafael 1988), and at least the latter was not regularly engaged in until the protohistoric period, then this suggests transformations in the systems of prestige and power that should be manifest in the material record. Furthermore, research focused on elucidating specific gendered activities in the pre- and protohistoric periods will thus be essential to understanding such systems within this region (for further discussion of the importance of gender attribution in studies of craft specialization, see Costin 1996). By engendering Visayan political economies, the archaeology of this region can contribute to understanding the interrelations of women's practices and their access to prestige and political power in complex polities.

ACKNOWLEDGMENTS

An earlier version of this chapter was presented at the conference titled "Worldwide Archaeological Perspectives on Women and Gender" held amidst the beautiful surroundings of Bellagio, Italy. My thanks to the organizers of this conference, Sarah Nelson and Myriam Rosen-Ayalon, for inviting me to participate. I am grateful to them and the other participants for the stimulating discussions on gender and archaeology and their helpful and insightful comments on my chapter. My thanks also to the Institute of Archaeology for funding additional research at the Newberry Library on women in the early historic Philippines.

18

Gender in Japanese Prehistory

Fumiko Ikawa-Smith

INTRODUCTION

As in many parts of the world, gender studies in Japanese archaeology is in a very early stage of development. In our first exploration into the studies regarding gender and women in Japanese prehistory (Ikawa-Smith and Habu 1998), we have shown that women are grossly underrepresented among those archaeologists who plan and execute archaeological investigations and who interpret and disseminate the results to students and the public. We then suggested that this underrepresentation may, in part at least, be responsible for the stereotypical manner in which women's activities are presented in publications and museum displays directed to the general public. In this second exploration, I continue in this vein, starting with a historical review of Japanese scholarship on women in ancient Japan, followed by an update on the data about women in the archaeological profession. I will then examine the effects of the demographic structure of the archaeological profession and the methodological orientations of Japanese archaeology on the studies of baked clay figurines from the Jomon period. I concur with Nelson (1997: 13) when she comments that "gendered power imbalances in the present among living archaeologists still contribute to obscuring parts of the archaeological records" because there is a clear need to break out of the one-sided constructions of these representational images.

The prehistoric period of Japan comprises the time span from the initial peopling of the Japanese archipelago to about A.D. 600, when events recorded in *Kojiki* (A.D. 712) and *Nihongi* (A.D. 720), with the inevitable distortions to suit the political agendas of those who are doing the recording, are generally considered to reflect what actually happened. This block of time is usually divided into four segments: Paleolithic, Jomon, Yayoi, and Kofun periods. For the purpose of this chapter, I define these periods as follows. The Paleolithic covers the immense time span from the first arrival of humans, which could have taken place over half a million years ago, to the appearance of pottery, which now seems to date about 13,000 radiocarbon years ago, or about 14,550 calibrated years B.C. (Nakamura and Tsuji 1999). The Jomon period, often divided into five or six subperiods (Incipient/Initial, Early, Middle, Late, and Final), lasts for some 14,000 years until the establishment of a social system based on effective rice agriculture in paddy fields about 300 B.C. The protohistoric Yayoi and Kofun periods, by contrast, are shorter, being assigned about 600 and 300 years, respectively, with the dividing line marked by the appearance of the keyhole-shaped mounded tombs, or *kofun,* about A.D. 300.

STUDIES OF WOMEN IN ANCIENT JAPAN

It should be noted at the beginning that archaeology in Japan, as in other East Asian countries, is considered a branch of history (Ikawa-Smith 1999). I have noted elsewhere the historical circumstances in which the subfields of the North American anthropology (archaeology, biological anthropology, sociocultural anthropology, and anthropological linguistics) became established as, or associated with, separate academic disciplines in Japan (Ikawa-Smith 1982) and commented on how the archaeology of Japan, as an aspect of national history, is influenced by, and in turn promotes, the ideology of ethnic and cultural homogeneity (Ikawa-Smith 1990).

Studies regarding women's roles and positions in ancient Japan was initiated by historians. Although archaeologists have began showing interests in this area of inquiry, the majority of contributions continue to be the result of the work conducted within the framework of study groups of feminist historians (e.g., Joseishi Sogo Kenkyukai 1989, 1990; Sogo Joseishi Kenkyukai 1993).

Historical Research before 1945

Scholarly inquiry into women in ancient Japan began as part of the reorientation of the discipline of history that occurred in the second decade of the 20th century, when historians' perspectives broadened to include social, economic, and cultural histories of "common people," which comprised women. Nishino (1990) places this shift in the global context of the social and intellectual climate of the time and suggests that the reaction to the situation in Japan included the uneasy realization that the common people's ways of life are rapidly disappearing forever in the process of modernization. This led to the development of folklore as a scholarly discipline, and information gathered by this new methodology contributed significantly in historical reconstruction of gender roles, having lasting influence on the scholarship on women in ancient Japan. For example, Yoshie Akiko goes out of her way to refute the view about spiritual superiority of women in ancient times, espoused by Kunio Yanagida (1875–1962), a prominent early leader of folklore.

The second significant development was the introduction of the Marxist perspective on the development of human society, which held that matriarchy preceded patriarchy. An additional factor at this time was the growth of women's liberation movement, symbolized by the launching in 1911 of a literary journal for women named *Seito* (literally "blue steps" but usually translated back into English as "Bluestocking," which *Seito* was originally meant to represent). The first issue of this journal contained an essay by Hiratsuka Raicho (1886–1971) titled *"Genshi, josei wa taiyo de atta"* (In the beginning, woman was the Sun). "It became the early manifesto for *Seito* women and the battle cry for newly emerging feminists" (Copeland 1994: 140). As Copeland points out (141), the reference here is to the sun goddess Amaterasu, described in ancient mythology as the supreme deity and the ancestor of the Imperial Household.

It is interesting to note at this juncture that the romanticized image of the past, when women were thought to have enjoyed higher status and greater prestige than in recent years, was sustained by two sets of ideological systems that are, in a sense, contradictory. On the one hand was the Marxist doctrine, which ran counter to the imperial ideology of the early 20th-century Japanese state. On the other was the mythological accounts of ancient Japan as recorded in *Kojiki* and *Nihongi,* which, Marxists would have said, provided the ideological basis for the very system that enslaved women.

Be that as it may, critical reexamination of extant historical records, along with the folklorists' field research in rural areas, produced during the 1920s and 1930s a number of important works on women's contribution to agricultural production, their position in the official status system, marriage, and household composition in ancient Japan. It should be noted (1) that "ancient Japan" usually meant the 7th to 12th centuries, for which reliable documents existed; (2) that for earlier times, reconstruction was based on interpretation of "survivals" in the historical records and oral traditions, not on archaeological data; and (3) that authors were all men, with one significant exception. This was Takamure Itsu (1894–1964), a poet, social activist, and feminist scholar who, in her 686-page volume based on meticulous analysis of the 9th-century genealogical records, argued that matrilineal descent system existed in ancient Japan (Takamure 1938). Takamure chose this deliberately academic style of presentation because, as she notes in her autobiography (1965: 246–47), the very use of the word "matrilineal" was likely to invite an unwelcome attention of the Special Security Police: the police did come knocking on her door in any case (1965: 274–75). She continued her work to prove the prior existence in Japan of a woman-centered society under the extremely difficult conditions of wartime Japan. Her next major opus, the 1,208-page *Study of Matrilocal Marriage,* was published in two volumes after the war (Takamure 1953).

Studies of Ancient Women in the Postwar Years, 1945–70

During the first decade after World War II, reinterpretations of Japanese history from the Marxist perspective enjoyed a great popularity among Japanese historians. The removal of restrictions on academic inquiry and expression, however, did not result in noticeable advance as far as the history of women was concerned because, as Nishino (1990: 6–10) explains, the interests of progressive historians of the time were focused on the transformational processes of ancient society, such as the formation of the Asiatic mode of production and the state in Japan, and women were treated simply as part of the subjugated masses.

Two developments that occurred in the early postwar years seem to have lasting effects on the direction of studies about women in ancient Japan. One of these is the keen interest, on the part of the historians of the time, in the Marxist constructions of the "ancient family" and the "primitive community" as they applied to Japanese material. These topics continue to serve as the points of reference in the more recent attempts at reconstruction of gender roles. It is in part because archaeology, as noted previously, has been closely linked with history in Japan, and prominent archaeologists who form today's archaeological establishment spent their formative years in history departments of early postwar Japan. It is also because the interest in the "ancient family" and the "primitive community" gave rise to the pioneer work by Wajima (1948), who applied these concepts to actual archaeological data on prehistoric settlements. For the Jomon period, he remarked that the small house pits in clusters, female figurines, and burials without rich funeral goods suggested an egalitarian, matrilocal, and matrilineal clan community.

The second development that helped shape today's gender studies in prehistoric Japan is the rise of ethnology/cultural anthropology as an academic discipline. One of the leading figures in this development was Oka Masao, who, in his 1934 doctoral dissertation presented to the University of Vienna, *Kulturschichten in Alt-Japan,* argued that the Japanese culture was made of a series of cultural complexes that arrived from various sources over the years. His views, along with Egami Namio's now famous horse-rider theory of Japanese state origins, were first brought to public attention at a symposium held in 1948, where they were compared and correlated with archaeological information then available (published as Ishida et al. 1949, 1958; Egami 1995). The prehistory volume of the first of the many illustrated series on Japanese history and archaeology contains a chapter by Oka (1956), in which he suggests the arrivals during Jomon of two cultural complexes in which women made important contributions as plant cultivators and the societies were organized along matrilineal, matrilocal, and matriarchal principles: one during Middle Jomon without rice and another during the Final Jomon with rice. These were followed by male-oriented cultural complexes during the Yayoi and Kofun periods. It is noteworthy that this illustrated history for students and educated laypeople, published in the mid-1950s, contained a chapter in which gender roles were suggested for specific subperiods in Japanese prehistory. Even though this approach, inspired by the *Kulturkreise* methodology, will not find sympathetic ears in North America today, it continues to thrive in Japan, as seen in the works by such ethnologists as Obayashi Taryo (1991) and Sasaki Komei (1997). Its influence is also evident in archaeologists' preoccupation with rules of descent and postmarital residence patterns when they venture into reconstruction of cultural practices, including gender roles, in prehistoric Japan (e.g., Komoto 1975; Hayashi 1977; Harunari 1979, 1986; Tsude 1982).

It should be noted here as well that during this time there was no significant contribution, as yet, by female historians or archaeologists, with a single exception. This was a paper by Yoshiko Makabe (1962), in which she compiled osteological data, comparing biological sex identification of personages buried in two kinds of mortuary sites of the Kofun period: mounded tombs and simpler cist graves. As she told me during a conversation in July 1998, she had wanted to find out whether the central personages buried in those impressive mounded tombs really were all men, as they were often implicitly assumed, and, if women were present, whether they were underrepresented in comparison with the sex distribution in graves of lesser grandeur. She also said that no one paid any attention to her 1962 paper. Indeed, I was not aware of this paper, published in a local university bulletin, until Makabe herself brought it to my attention. Even though her sample was small (21 mounded tombs and 60 cist graves where the condition of skeletal remains made sex identification possible) and the conclusion somewhat ambiguous, the paper, in retrospect, is significant in the history of studies on women and gender in prehistoric Japan.

Gender Studies since 1970

It was during the 1970s, particularly after the 1975 International Year of Women, that *joseishi,* or "the history of women," became established as a field of specialization within the discipline of history. Various associations and study groups, with considerable overlaps in membership, were formed during the "boom" years in the 1970s. *Zen-Kindai Joseishi Kenkyukai* (Association for the Study of Premodern History of Women), which was formed in 1977, was one of these groups. Another was *Joseishi Sogo Kenkyukai* (Association for the Integrated Study of the History of Women), which covered the entire span of time from the prehistoric to contemporary periods. The results of the inquiry of this latter group were published as two sets of multivolume collections of essays and a three-volume bibliography on the history of women by the University of Tokyo Press. The first volume of both sets contained chapters on gender roles in prehistoric periods, particularly about division of labor in subsistence activities. These were written by archaeologists (Tsude 1982; Ogasawara 1990), but not by women archaeologists.

About the time the historical study of women was becoming established and gaining popularity, profound changes were taking place in the practice of archaeology. The changes actually began in the mid-1960s with the rapid industrial expansion in Japan. With that came the need for emergency investigations of archaeological sites, and the number and scale of archaeological activities changed dramatically (fig. 18.1). Data increased both in volume and in quality as new methods and techniques for data recovery and analysis were employed. The increased activity for the salvage archaeology, as well as the expansion of the postsecondary educational system, meant new job opportunities for archaeologists, both as cultural resource management administrators and as teachers/researchers at colleges and universities.

In our earlier work referred to at the beginning of this chapter (Ikawa-Smith and Habu 1998), we sought to confirm our suspicion that women were not benefiting from these expanded job opportunities, apart from temporary employment as laborers at excavation sites and cleaners/catalogers in laboratories. Female students are numerous in undergraduate programs in archaeology, sometimes forming the majority, and they continue to be well represented in graduate programs. Somewhere along the line, however, they disappear from the scene. During the 1960s and 1970s, I could think of only two women who were employed as archaeologists in Japan. One was Okada Atsuko, who held a series of academic positions and is currently serving as the dean of humanities at Hokkaido Takai University. The other is Makabe Yoshiko, referred to in the previous section, who has long been affiliated with the Kurashiki Museum of Archaeology and is now professor at Kobe Women's University.

We were surprised to find that, as late as 1995, women accounted for only 2.77 percent of those who were admitted to the Japanese Archaeological Association (table 18.1). As it is necessary to meet a series of criteria and be approved by the Membership Committee and the General Assembly, the association's membership is an affirmation of one's status as a "professional

NOTICES OF EXCAVATIONS OF BURIED CULTURAL PROPERTIES, 1950/56 - 1998/99

Sources: Agency of Cultural Affairs, Center for Archaeological Operations of the Nara National Institute for Cultural Properties (various publications)

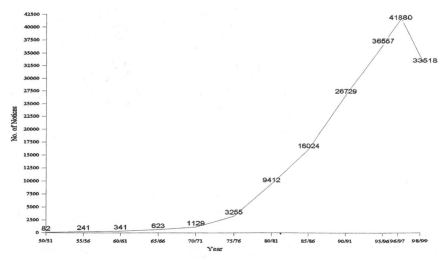

Figure 18.1.   Notices of excavations of buried cultural properties, 1950–95/96. (From Agency of Cultural Affairs, Center for Archaeological Operations of the Nara National Institute for Cultural Properties, various publications).

archaeologist." In order to show the historical trend of women's participation, we wished to examine the membership list at the 10-year interval, but the lists for 1987 and 1964 had to be substituted for the ones for 1985 and 1965, respectively. The earlier lists, for 1955 and 1945, are unavailable at this time.

Table 18.1.   Membership in the Japanese Archaeological Association[a]

Year	Total Membership	No. of Women (%)
1964	397	4 (1.01%)
1975	818	17 (1.34%)
1987	2,005	42 (2.09%)
1995	2,851	79 (2.77%)

[a]Criteria for membership:
1. Be engaged in archaeological research at present and in the future.
2. Be 25 years of age or older.
3. Have publication records to satisfy one of the following:
    a. At least one scholarly paper based on archaeological methodology or on integration of interdisciplinary approaches.
    b. At least one excavation report, which must be written and/or edited entirely or substantially by the applicant.
    c. At least three book reviews, brief communications, and/or co-authored excavation reports.

Most professional archaeologists do one of the two things to earn the living:
(1) hold an academic position and do research and disseminate information
through teaching and publication, or (2) engage in cultural resource management and be involved more directly in producing archaeological information.
With the tremendous increase in emergency archaeological projects (fig.
18.1), these two roles are increasingly bifurcated in Japan (Kobayashi 1986;
Fawcett 1995). For academic appointments, *Archaeologia Japonica* (Annual
Reports of the Japanese Archaeological Association) provides very useful
information. Each issue lists all the names of universities and colleges that
offer archaeology programs and the course titles and full names of the instructors who give these courses. It is usually possible from the given names to
know, within a small margin of error, whether the instructor is male or female.
Table 18.2 is the result of our attempt to go over the lists for every five years,
beginning with 1950. All the courses listed as part of archaeology programs in
all the universities and colleges are given in column 3. Not all the courses are
about archaeology: It would be easy to exclude a course called "Physical
Anthropology," but the contents of some of the others are not so easy to guess
from the titles. Therefore, none was excluded so as to not distort the data. The
number in column 4 is the number of courses given by women, not the number of women giving the courses. For example, for 1985, four of the ten
courses given by women are by the same person, and two of the remaining six
are by another, reducing the total number of women instructors to six. Furthermore, I happen to know that the woman whose name appears with four of
the courses is an ethnologist by training, and the courses are likely to be more

Table 18.2. Courses in Archaeological Programs Offered by Women, 1950–95

Year	No. of Institutions Offering Archaeology Courses	Total No. of Courses in Programs (Not All Are on Archaeology)	Courses Offered by Women Instructors (% of Total Courses)
1950	28	61	0
1955	26	73	0
1960[a]			
1965	73	254	2 (0.79%)
1970	39	235	0
1975	63	381	1 (0.26%)
1980	97	499	3 (0.60%)
1985	103	609	10 (1.64%)
1990	153	765	11 (1.44%)
1995	147	1,168	25 (2.14%)

[a]Data for 1960 are not available.
Sources: *Archaeologia Japonica* (*Annual Reports of the Japanese Archaeological Studies and Excavations*),
Japanese Archaeological Association, Vol. 3 for 1950 (published in 1955), Vol. 8 for 1955 (1959), Vol. 18
for 1965 (1970), Vols. 21, 22, and 23 for 1968, 1969, and 1970 (1981), Vol. 28 for 1975 (1977), Vol. 33
for 1980 (1983), Vol. 38 for 1985 (1987), Vol. 43 for 1990 (1992), Vol. 48 for 1995 (1997).

ethnological than archaeological in content. In any event, it is abundantly clear that the proportion of academic positions held by women remains amazingly small.

Figure 18.2 is a graphic presentation of historical trends, comparing the proportion of women in the association's membership (table 18.1) with that of women holding academic positions (table 18.2).

As to employment as cultural resources management (CRM) professionals, very precise data are published periodically by the Center for Archaeological Operations of the Nara National Institute for Buried Cultural Properties Research, but gender breakdowns of these employees are seldom indicated. A rare exception was for fiscal 1981, when a total of 2,145 persons were employed by various municipal and prefectural governments and affiliated foundations, of which 2,077 (99.7 percent) were male and only 68 (0.3 percent) were female (Center for Archaeological Operations 1981: 1). The proportion has increased to 6.5 percent for 1992, when there were 4,846 CRM archaeologists, of which 314 were women (personal communication, Kobayashi Masaru, Agency for Cultural Affairs, July 22, 1998). In 1998, the total for CRM archaeologists is 6,872 (Center for Archaeological Operations 1999: 7), but the proportion of women in this enlarged group is unknown. It is my impression that women are gaining some ground in this area, and this is confirmed by the figure that Fujimura Junko has kindly assembled for Hyogo prefecture in western Honshu, where she herself works (personal communication, August 26, 1998). In this prefecture, just west of Osaka, there were

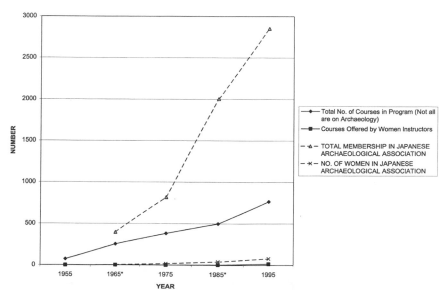

Figure 18.2. Comparison of association membership with number of courses given by women instructors.

202 cultural properties professionals working in May 1998, either with permanent (187) or part-time (15) terms of employment. Of the total, 22 (10.4 percent) were women, although eight of the 15 nonpermanent members were women: thus, of the permanent staff, only 14 (7.5 percent) are women. Even that number is impressive, as Fujimura recalls that, when she joined the service in 1985, the total of CRM professionals in Hyogo prefecture had just reached 100, of whom three were women.

As noted before, Okada Atsuko and Makabe Yoshiko are two pioneer women who have been practicing archaeology over the past few decades. While Okada has not written extensively on gender issues, Makabe continued to present painstaking analysis of mortuary data (Makabe 1990, 1992b). As chapters on women, women's work, and social position has become regular features in those numerous semipopular series on Japanese history and archaeology, Makabe is in high demand as one of the few potential suppliers of such chapters (1985, 1987, 1992a, 1996). Makabe, fortunately, is being joined by several younger women who write about recent development in gender archaeology in the English-speaking world (e.g., Fujimura 1996, 1998), and present useful review articles on such topics as division of labor (Fujimura 2000) and power and prestige (Terasawa 2000). I am also encouraged by the editorial leadership of Tsude Hiroshi and Sahara Makoto, who presented, as part of the six-volume series Issues in Ancient History (Tsude and Sahara 2000), a volume focusing on gender, household, and community, with half the chapters written by women historians and archaeologists.

CLAY FIGURINES OF THE JOMON PERIOD

I now turn to the studies of Jomon clay figurines, most of which are thought to depict women. I begin with a general outline of the number and time-space distribution and depositional contexts of these figurines. I will then review some examples of the interpretations that have been offered regarding the function and meaning of these figurines. I will conclude with observations about what appears to be the major themes that dominated figurine research so far and about the prospects for future research.

The Jomon period as a chronological unit is unmanageably long and getting longer with new finds and calibration, as noted previously. For points of reference, we will use the most frequently used version of sixfold division of the Jomon period: Incipient, Initial, Early, Middle, Late, and Final. Although some of the numerous radiocarbon dates for Jomon sites have been calibrated, most have not been. For the sake of consistency, we will use uncalibrated radiocarbon years throughout this discussion. The subdivisions of the Jomon period, with approximate time ranges, are as follows (Taniguchi 1999: 27):

Incipient Jomon: 13,000–10,000 years b.p.
Initial Jomon: 10,000–6,000 years b.p.
Early Jomon: 6,000–5,000 years b.p.
Middle Jomon: 5,000–4,000 years b.p.
Late Jomon: 4,000–3,000 years b.p.
Final Jomon: 3,000–2,300 years b.p.

Number and Time-Space Distribution of Jomon Clay Figurines

The total number of Jomon figurines is estimated to be about 15,000 (Harada 1999). The estimate starts with the total number (10,683) of figurines documented as of 1991 in the database compiled by the study group organized by Yaegashi Junki at the National Museum of Japanese History (National Museum of Japanese History 1992) and adds estimated finds of about 400 per year in the last eight years since that tabulation. Harada cites Kobayashi Tatsuo as saying that, given that 15,000 have been recovered, as many as 300,000 may have been produced. Divided by the whole length of the Jomon period, however, the rate of production is not exactly staggering (only about 30 figurines per year) had they been evenly distributed in time and space.

Figurines are not evenly distributed both in time and space. Figure 18.3, slightly modified from a computer-generated map in the National Museum of Japanese History (1992: 490) study, shows the figurine frequency by prefectures, and table 18.3, also taken from the same study (1992: 484), gives the actual numbers of specimens reported, by prefectures and by Jomon subperiod. No figurine has been recovered from three of the 47 prefectures, including Okinawa at the southern end of the island chain. In fact, figurines are very sparsely distributed in the southwestern half of the archipelago, with the exception of Nara and Kumamoto prefectures, where 195 and 108 specimens are reported, respectively, toward the end of the Jomon period. We will refer to these occurrences later. In general, the heaviest figurine concentrations are found in the northern end of Honshu and the mountainous area of central Honshu.

Table 18.3 shows that baked clay figurines are not numerous in the first three of the six subperiods of Jomon, which in fact represent 8,000 radiocarbon years, or 75 percent of the Jomon period. According to this table, based on the 1991 database project (National Museum of Japanese History 1992), not a single clay figurine is attributed to the Incipient Jomon. As the result of recent recovery of one complete and one fragmentary pieces from the Kayumi Ijiri site, however, this should now be amended to show "2" for the Incipient Jomon of Mie prefecture (No. 24). Harada (1999: 133) finds stylistic affinity of these specimens with the famous "Venuses of Kamikuroiwa," in that ample breasts are realistically represented in both cases and at least one of the

334 Fumiko Ikawa-Smith

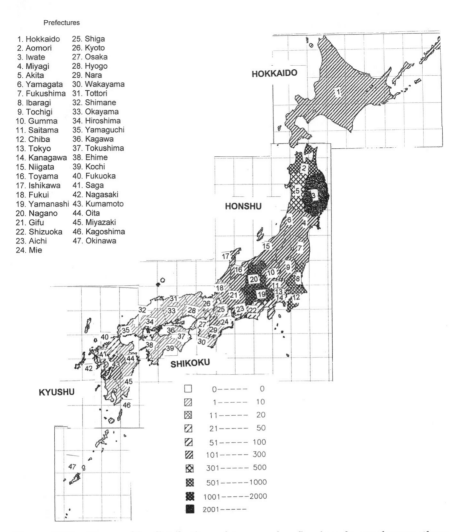

Prefectures

1. Hokkaido	25. Shiga
2. Aomori	26. Kyoto
3. Iwate	27. Osaka
4. Miyagi	28. Hyogo
5. Akita	29. Nara
6. Yamagata	30. Wakayama
7. Fukushima	31. Tottori
8. Ibaragi	32. Shimane
9. Tochigi	33. Okayama
10. Gumma	34. Hiroshima
11. Saitama	35. Yamaguchi
12. Chiba	36. Kagawa
13. Tokyo	37. Tokushima
14. Kanagawa	38. Ehime
15. Niigata	39. Kochi
16. Toyama	40. Fukuoka
17. Ishikawa	41. Saga
18. Fukui	42. Nagasaki
19. Yamanashi	43. Kumamoto
20. Nagano	44. Oita
21. Gifu	45. Miyazaki
22. Shizuoka	46. Kagoshima
23. Aichi	47. Okinawa
24. Mie	

0----- 0
1----- 10
11----- 20
21----- 50
51----- 100
101----- 300
301----- 500
501-----1000
1001-----2000
2001-----

Figure 18.3. Geographic distribution of Jomon clay figurines by prefecture (from National Museum of Japanese History 1992: 490).

Kayumi Ijiri specimens, unlike most Jomon clay figurines, were found intact, as were the Kamikuroiwa pebbles (figs. 18.4, 18.5), recovered during the excavations in 1962 from the level dated to 12,165 ± 600 years b.p. (Esaka and Nishida 1967). At Kamikuroiwa, there were seven flat pebbles, about five centimeters in the longest diameter, with incised lines suggesting anthropomorphic features. The lines on two of the seven are thought to represent breasts and skirts made of grass fiber, while the remaining five were variously interpreted as representations of adult males or adolescent females (Ono

Table 18.3.   Time-Space Distribution of Jomon Figurines[a]

Prefectures[b]	Incipient Jomon	Initial Jomon	Early Jomon	Middle Jomon	Late Jomon	Final Jomon	Unknown/ Unentered	No. of specimens[c]
1. Hokkaido	0	0	2	39	48	193	11	285
2. Aomori	0	1	2	105	207	306	12	629
3. Iwate	0	0	89	166	739	1,261	25	2,182
4. Miyagi	0	0	4	113	49	35	1	188
5. Akita	0	0	1	50	157	227	1	446
6. Yamagata	0	0	1	59	67	69	4	179
7. Fukushima	0	0	0	40	169	36	3	241
8. Ibaragi	0	12	1	10	636	160	16	803
9. Tochigi	0	0	0	0	99	11	0	106
10. Gumma	0	0	7	4	100	59	15	152
11. Saitama	0	1	1	15	81	120	6	217
12. Chiba	0	24	2	15	393	359	7	788
13. Tokyo	0	0	2	246	60	71	2	373
14. Kanagawa	0	0	0	58	38	11	2	108
15. Niigata	0	0	0	127	53	4	1	183
16. Toyama	0	4	5	112	50	37	0	180
17. Ishikawa	0	0	0	33	117	113	3	168
18. Fukui	0	0	0	2	4	0	0	6
19. Yamanashi	0	0	12	1,319	76	22	39	1,469
20. Nagano	0	1	1	812	256	96	1	1,169
21. Gifu	0	0	0	59	22	35	4	105
22. Shizuoka	0	0	0	18	16	10	9	53
23. Aichi	0	4	3	2	63	147	2	218
24. Mie	0	1	0	0	1	2	0	3
25. Shiga	0	0	0	0	2	5	0	6
26. Kyoto	0	0	0	1	4	2	0	5
27. Osaka	0	2	0	0	8	44	0	46
28. Hyogo	0	0	1	0	1	0	0	2
29. Nara	0	0	0	0	2	193	1	195
30. Wakayama	0	0	0	0	1	1	0	2
31. Tottori	0	0	0	0	1	0	0	1
32. Shimane	0	0	0	0	0	0	0	0
	0	0	0					
33. Okayama	0	0	0	0	6	3	0	6
34. Hiroshima	0	0	0	0	2	0	0	2
35. Yamaguchi	0	0	0	0	3	2	0	3
36. Kagawa	0	0	0	0	1	0	6	7
37. Tokushima	0	0	0	0	0	0	0	0
	0	0						
38. Ehime	0	0	0	0	3	0	0	3
39. Kochi	0	0	0	0	1	0	0	1
40. Fukuoka	0	0	0	0	17	13	7	24
41. Saga	0	0	0	0	0	3	0	3
42. Nagasaki	0	0	0	0	7	8	0	8
43. Kumamoto	0	0	0	0	108	108	0	108

continued

Table 18.3.   Time-Space Distribution of Jomon Figurines[a] (*Continued*)

Prefectures[b]	Incipient Jomon	Initial Jomon	Early Jomon	Middle Jomon	Late Jomon	Final Jomon	Unknown/ Unentered	No. of specimens[c]
44. Oita	0	0	0	0	7	0	0	7
45. Miyazaki	0	0	0	0	2	2	0	2
46. Kagoshima	0	0	0	0	1	3	0	3
47. Okinawa	0	0	0	0	0	0	0	0
	0							
Totals	0	50	134	3,405	3,675	3,774	178	10,683

[a]Modified after table 6 in National Museum of Japanese History (1992: 484).
[b]The numbers given to prefectures correspond to the numbers shown on the map of figure 18.3.
[c]Total specimen number is sometimes less than the sum total of the subperiod specimen numbers because, when a specimen is assigned to Late or Final Jomon, for example, it is entered under both Late and Final subperiods.

1984: 8). Many scholars, however, found it difficult to link these pebbles with the baked clay representations of women that were then thought to occur for the first time in the Initial Jomon (e.g., Mizuno 1974: 307; Yoneda 1984: 64–65). They not only are stylistically different but also are found intact, while clay figurines are almost always recovered as broken fragments. Even with this addition, the number in the Incipient Jomon is very small, and it continues to be low through the Initial and Early Jomon, with less than 2 percent of the grand total recovered (by the National Museum database of 1992) for 75 percent of the time span. The number suddenly increases during the Middle Jomon, particularly in central Honshu, and then the center shifts to northern Honshu in the Final Jomon. Two centers of concentration are evident in the map (fig. 18.3): the Pacific side of northern Honshu, particularly Iwate prefecture, and the central mountainous region of Honshu, covering Nagano and Yamanashi prefectures.

Even within the area and period of concentration, the figurine occurrence is uneven. There are a handful of Middle Jomon sites in central Honshu where hundreds of figurines were recovered, while only a few or none at all occur at other sites in the same general area. Some of the prolific sites are large habitation sites, while others are thought to represent special activity locations, possibly devoted to ritual performance.

Depositional Contexts of Jomon Figurines

As noted previously, Jomon figurines are recovered, almost always, as broken fragments scattered throughout the site, along with pottery sherds and broken stone tools. Some authors argue that there is nothing unusual about this since ceramic vessels, stone tools, and other artifacts are usually found as broken fragments as well (e.g., Fujinuma 1979: 182–83; Noto 1983: 80–82). Most other

Figure 18.4.   Map showing the locations of the sites mentioned in text.

researchers believe, however, that the figurines are not only broken intentionally and deliberately but also manufactured to be fragmented in a prescribed
way. Ono (1984: 110–12), for example, notes that at the Tateishi site in Iwate
prefecture, none of the 212 figurines dating to the Late Jomon was found intact
and that conjoining parts were recovered from the site for only 8 percent of the
figurines. In other words, most of the missing parts are completely absent from
the site. Ono therefore suggests that the fragments were deposited at different
parts of the site as well as at other settlements and ceremonial locations. Harada

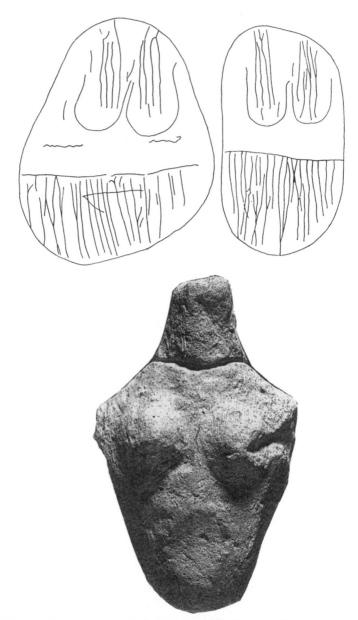

Figure 18.5.   Anthropomorphic figures from Incipient Jomon. Above: Incised pebbles, Kamikuroiwa rock shelter, Ehime prefecture, about 5 cm high (after Esaka and Nishida 1967: 233). Below: The earliest clay figurine, Kayumi Ijiri site, Mie prefecture, 6.8 cm high (after Bunkacho 1997: 15, with the courtesy of the Mie Prefectural Center for Buried Cultural Properties, where the specimen resides.)

(1995: 68) also observes that, at the Shakodo site in Yamanashi prefecture, where 1,116 figurine fragments were recovered mostly from the perimeter of the large settlement consisting of over 200 pit houses, only one was in a relatively intact state, missing the right arm only. In the case of 22 of the 1,116 fragments that could be conjoined, the pieces were recovered from different parts of the site, sometimes as much as 230 meters apart: Harada therefore believes that they do not represent the remnants of figurines that were accidentally broken; the broken pieces were deliberately placed as far away from one another as possible so as to prevent a possibility of ever "coming together" again.

Kobayashi (1977) summarized the breakage patterns of the Middle, Late, and Final Jomon figurines as shown schematically in figure 18.6. The patterns suggest to him that the anthropomorphic forms were "divided into" several pieces, or certain body parts were "torn away" along the lines of cleavage that had been intentionally worked into figurines when they were made. In his words, the figurines were made to be broken in a prescribed manner, just as chocolate bars are manufactured today to be broken off at predetermined lines. Noto (1983: 79–81), on the basis of his analysis of the 188 figurine fragments from Tateishi, is inclined to believe, however, that the figurines broke along the lines of structural weakness inherent in the way that they were made by joining molded pieces together.

In a very small number of cases, Jomon figurines are recovered from contexts where their deliberate and intentional placement is evident. Ono (1984: 116–29) notes that 26 such sites, involving 28 specimens, were known at the time of her writing. They include the Tochikura site in Niigata prefecture (fig. 18.7A), where a figurine fragment, missing the head and arms, was found upside-down in a pit, dug about 50 centimeters deep into the pit house floor, dating to the Middle Jomon. Pottery fragments were placed along the pit walls in the upper part of the pit, and another sherd was placed near the figurine as if for support. Another example is the Gohara site in Gumma prefecture (fig. 18.7B), where the famous figurine with a "heart-shaped" face (fig. 18.8A), dating to the Late Jomon, was found in three conjoinable pieces, inside a stone enclosure measuring about 150 by 50 by 40 centimeters deep. At the Sugisawa site in Yamagata prefecture (fig. 18.7C), a Final Jomon figurine, in an almost intact condition, was found buried in a supine position, inside an enclosure made of large cobbles, covered by another flat stone. If there was a human burial at these sites as well, the skeletal remains did not survive. A clear use of clay figurines as burial goods occurs only at some Hokkaido sites toward the end of the Jomon period, when the nature of the figurines seems to change significantly, just before their final disappearance from prehistoric Japan (Harada 1999: 140–43).

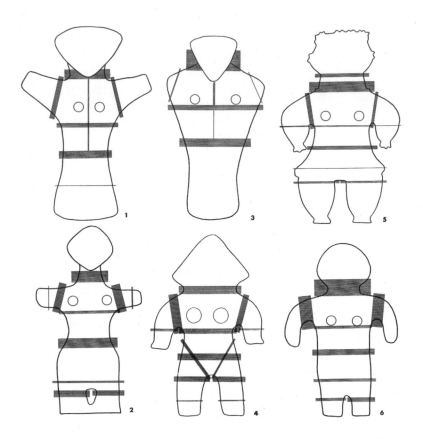

Figure 18.6. Breakage patterns of Jomon figurines (after Kobayashi 1977: 53). Middle Jomon: Tochikura site, Niigata prefecture (1), Mashino Shinkiri site, Nagana prefecture (2); Late Jomon: Chikano site, Aomori prefecture (3), Saihiro shell mound, Chiba prefecture, and Tatsuki shell mound, Ibaraki prefecture (4); Final Jomon: Korekawa site, Aomori prefecture (5), Kashihara site, Nara prefecture (6).

Interpretations of Jomon Figurines

Early Interpretations

Artifacts that appear to be Jomon figurines were occasionally mentioned in chronicles and travelogues since the early 17th century, but the first "anthropological" discussion is attributed to Shirai Mitsutaro (1863–1932), one of the cofounders of the Anthropological Society of Tokyo (the current Anthropological Society of Nippon). Soon after its founding in 1884, Shirai (1886) addressed the question of their possible functions, suggesting three possible uses: children's toys, representations of a deity, or ornaments. Referring to ethnographic examples from New Zealand, he concluded that it was probably personal ornaments,

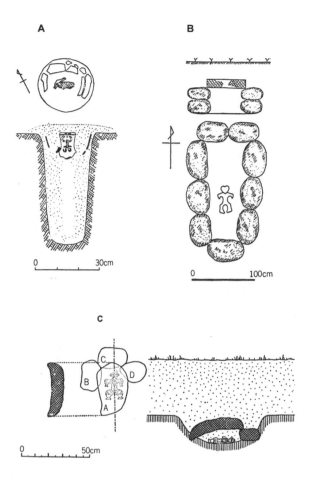

Figure 18.7.   Figurines in special features (modified after Ono 1984: 119). (A) Pit dug into the pit-house floor, Tochikura, Niigata prefecture (Middle Jomon). (B) Enclosure made of cobbles, Gohara, Gumma prefecture (Late Jomon). (C) Cobble-outlined pit, Sugisawa site, Yamagata prefecture (Late Jomon).

worn by the prehistoric people, which may also have served as amulets (as summarized in Yoneda 1984: 10; Watanabe 1997: 833).[1] It was the use/function of these objects that was first addressed by the early practitioners of the nascent discipline. Over the years, the majority opinion leans toward the view that they represent some sort of deity, with a smaller proportion of professionals suggesting the use as protective amulets or a combination of the two (i.e., a deity who provides risk protection). As Watanabe (1997: 833–84) remarks, what is meant by "deity" or "protection" (against what?) is not always clear.

The question of the gender representation was also considered early. Tsuboi Shogoro (1863–1913), another cofounder of the Anthropological Society, classified in his 1898 paper figurines into males and females on the basis of the

Figure 18.8.   Examples of Middle Jomon figurines. (A) Slab-form figurine (15.1 cm high), Ishigami site, Aomori prefecture. (After Nagamine 1986: 257.) (B) Figurine with a baby (7.1 cm high), Miyata site, Tokyo. (After Kobayashi 1977, Plate 18.) (C) Standing figurine (16 cm high), Sakai site, Yamanashi prefecture. (After Harada 1995, Plate 16, with the courtesy of Sakai Archaeological Museum.) (D) Figurine with "wildcat face" (25,7 cm high), Kurokoma site, Yamanashi prefecture. (After Nagamine 1986: 258.)

Figure 18.9.   Examples of Late Jomon figurines. (After Nagamine 1986: 259–260.) (A) Figurine with "heart-shaped" head (30.5 cm high), Gohara site, Gumma prefecture. (B) Figurine with "heart-shaped" head and "arched eyebrows" (20cm high), Sensui site, Nagano prefecture. (C) Figurine with "pointed head" (12.1 cm high), Shiizuka shell mound, Ibaraki prefecture. (D) Figurine of "horned owl" type (16.4 cm high), Chojayama shell mound, Chiba prefecture.

size and shape of the breasts and abdomen, hairdo, and clothing (Yoneda 1984: 14–16). Ohno Nobutaro (1863–1938), applying a similar set of criteria to a larger sample of specimens (287 figurines then known), classified them into 213 females, 47 males, and 27 ambiguous (Ohno 1910, as summarized by Noguchi 1974: 93–94; Yoneda 1984: 16–22). On the basis that 213 out of 287 figurines (73 percent) show secondary sexual characteristics of a female (or disregarding the 27 percent where such characteristics are absent), Ohno concluded that Jomon figurines represented a deity for women, one that protected women from the risks of childbirth. This view received further support from

Torii Ryuzo (1870–1953), who, citing examples from Paleolithic Europe to the Bronze Age Middle East, suggested that the occurrences of these figurines indicated "the cult of goddess" in Stone Age Japan, as they did elsewhere in the Old World (Torii 1922). Characterization of the Jomon figurine as female representation continues to be the dominant view. Ono (1984: 16), for example, notes that all the figurines could be considered female representations since the example from the Sakai site in Yamanashi prefecture, which was once thought to represent a man with a penis, is now reinterpreted as a representation of a birthing mother with an emerging fetus. Nagamine (1986: 255) therefore "would argue that there are no figurines that manifest concrete male characteristics." The characterization of Jomon figurines as female representations forms the basis of several interpretative attempts, such as by Mizuno (1974) and Watanabe (1997, 1998, 1999), as will be discussed later.

When Tsuboi classified the figurines into males and females, he was working with the assumption that the figurines were the Jomon people's self-images, represented as realistically as the techniques and the nature of the medium allowed. Thus, the clothing, hairstyles, and personal ornamentation, including possible tattoos, were carefully observed, and ethnographic analogues were sought. Distinctive features of male versus female attire were important in this comparative exercise. He found that Jomon figurines shared many items of clothing and decoration with peoples of northern Eurasia, but they did not resemble the historic Ainu of northern Japan. Assuming again that such customs remained unchanged for thousands of years, Tsuboi concluded that the Jomon people, who made these figurines, were unrelated to the Ainu. Figurines were used by Tsuboi in support of his argument that the Jomon pottery was made not by the ancestral Ainu but by the pre-Ainu inhabitants of the Japanese archipelago, in the "Who were the Jomon people" debate that preoccupied the anthropologists of the time. This particular brand of "Who were the Jomon People" debate, often referred to as the "Korobokkuru Controversy," ended with Tsuboi's death in 1913 (cf. Ikawa-Smith 1990: 58; 1995: 46–48), as did the use of the figurines as an indicator of Jomon ethnicity.

Shattered Goddesses in the Classificatory-Typological Framework

The breakage pattern, which as we have seen previously makes one of the important elements in the interpretations today, was noted relatively early as well. According to Kobayashi (1977: 49), it was Oba Toshio (1899–1975) who first remarked on the possible significance of the fact that figurines were often found in fragmented state and suggested that they probably were used in magicoreligious rituals and discarded when they were broken and lost their potency (Oba 1926). In the same paper, Oba also divided Jomon figurines into three categories and related them to pottery styles. Thus, the twin themes in figurine research, the classificatory-typological studies and interpretation of Jomon figurines as sacred images loaded with mythical potency, were established in the mid-1920s and continue to this day.

The shift in figurine studies, from the concern with the makers' ethnicity to emphasis on typology, echoes the similar shift of direction of the Jomon research in general toward a greater precision in time-space systematics based on stratigraphy and typology. Going beyond discussion of chronology and typological classification was generally frowned on among the mainstream archaeologists as mere "speculation." Consideration of function and meaning of clay figurines fell into this category of speculative and unprofessional endeavor. The great volume of literature on Jomon figurines that has accumulated since the mid-1920s, therefore, consists mainly of detailed description and typological classification. They attempt to determine temporal and geographic distribution of figurine types and to establish their affiliation with ceramic types and other artifacts and features. Esaka Teruya's (1919–) monograph (Esaka 1960) is generally regarded as the culmination of this trend of inquiry, but the work continues along this line as the increasing number of archaeological investigations, mostly of salvage nature, brings out hundreds of specimens with intriguing features each year. The 22 articles that accompany the computerized database are good examples of detailed descriptive accounts on the regional scale (National Museum of Japanese History 1992). As will be mentioned later, the continuing work in this format is adding to the rich and valuable database, which is yet to be explored to its full potential. In the meantime, very little "interpretative" work has been done, even though Japanese archaeologists are less reticent in recent years to discuss issues other than time-space systematics and culture-historical affiliation.

Among the few exceptions in this vast body of descriptive-classificatory literature on Jomon figurines is the contribution by Mizuno Masayoshi (1934–). His interpretation of clay figurines formed an important element in his very influential series of publications regarding symbolic structure of the Jomon settlement system. The first of those focusing on the meaning of the figurines and their disposal patterns (Mizuno 1974) appeared in a special issue of a local journal, *Shinao,* dedicated to the memory of Fujimori Eiichi (1911–74), an eminent avocational archaeologist. Fujimori (1963) had used the occurrence of numerous figurines in the Middle Jomon in the central mountainous area of central Honshu as one of the 12 reasons why plant cultivation may have been practiced by Middle Jomon people of the area, the view not supported by the majority of professional archaeologists at the time. He argued that the Middle Jomon figurines of central Honshu, unlike the Late and Final Jomon figurines elsewhere, clearly represented women and were intended to express the desire for life and fertility of humankind and the earth. While Fujimori explicitly stated that his remarks are limited to the Middle Jomon in central Honshu because figurines in other areas and other periods even included those showing males, Mizuno (1974) begins with the assertion that all the Jomon figurines are representational images of women and, more specifically, adult women in their reproductive prime. This is because there is no figurine that shows an adolescent or elderly woman, while there are those that clearly depict women with enlarged abdomens (fig. 18.10A) or a woman holding an infant (fig. 18.8B). Thus, to Mizuno, even those figurines that do not show any sign of pregnancy are the images of "women who are meant to become mothers" (1974: 299–300). Mizuno suggested that the figurines were made by women and were used in a three-stage ritual celebrating conception, pregnancy, and delivery: They were "killed " (broken) at this simulated childbirth at the peak of their reproductive potency. The fragments, charged with mythical powers of regeneration, were then scattered throughout the site to the benefit of the entire community. The broken pieces that are found away from habitation sites are likely to be those placed in fields and under fruit trees to ensure their productivity. Even though there are differences in the form of the figurines themselves, as well as in the disposal pattern through the various phases of the Jomon period, Mizuno (1974: 311) emphasizes unity and continuity of the idea system behind figurine production and disposal. The differences are merely variations in emphasis of the "leitmotiv" of Jomon culture as it underwent its own developmental cycle.

Watanabe Hitoshi (1919–98), best known in the West for his work on the Ainu ecosystem (e.g., 1968, 1972), has presented, as what turned out to be his last major contribution to the discipline, a very ambitious set of papers (1997, 1998, 1999 [the latter two published posthumously]) with a view to developing "a scientific interpretation of the function of those figurines" (1997: 829), which, as he rightly points out, has not seen much progress. He expresses dissatisfaction both with studies of temporal-spatial distribution of figurine types as exemplified by the National Museum of Japanese History database (1992) and with the more recent emphasis on the intrasite distribution and conjoining of fragments. The notion that the figurines were ritually broken and scattered over the site, he observes, is not supported by firm evidence and ignores the effects of weathering and taphonomic processes (1999: 359–62). He is highly critical of Mizuno's work as an example of the recent trend in which something akin to detective fictions passes as archaeological discourse (1999: 360, 395).

He believes that the question of the function of figurines themselves can be answered only through an ethnoarchaeological study. He then develops a wide-ranging discussion of ethnographic examples of anthropomorphic artifacts and the myths and rituals associated with such artifacts. Archaeological examples from the European Paleolithic through the Neolithic of the lower Amur region are also reviewed and incorporated into the discussion. He concludes, on the basis of comparison of the overall outline (cylindrical, waisted, bulging shouldered, and so on) and eyebrow shapes, that the origin of the

Figure 18.10.   Examples of Final Jomon figurines. (After Kobayashi 1977.) (A) "Pregnant" woman (19.5 cm high), Kamegaoka site, Aomori prefecture. (B) Sitting figurine (10.5 cm high), Gohonmatsu, Aomori prefecture. (C) "Goggle-type" figurine (20 cm high), Yoka-machi, Aomori prefecture.

Jomon figurines is to be found in the Paleolithic of the Lake Baikal area. Jomon figurines, according to Watanabe, are images of a "mother goddess as protector of their fertility or reproduction" (1997: 830) who also had "a wider function as tutelary goddess of family welfare" (1998: 130, 205). Watanabe devotes considerable space to discussion of folkloristic practices of Japanese mountain villagers, who until recently depended on hunting and logging rather than on agriculture. The wooden images of a mountain goddess kept in their households, he believes, represent the survival of the Jomon goddess belief after the end of the Jomon period over 2,000 years ago.

Even though Watanabe is critical of Mizuno's approach and conclusions, he, like Mizuno (1974), seeks to find a single "function" that applies to all the Jomon figurines, and, like Mizuno again, he characterizes all the Jomon figurines as representing females. On the latter point, he does look for empirical evidence for his characterization by examining and tabulating the illustrations contained in the National Museum database (National Museum of Japanese History 1992). He finds that 655 of the illustrated pieces showed the chest portions, of which 451 (69 percent) showed breasts (1997: 885, table 2). He notes that his enumeration confirmed the intuitive observations made years ago by Ohno (1910) and Torii (1922). Apparently 69 percent is enough to make an assertion that all the Jomon figurines are meant to represent biological females: There is no explanation for the 104 cases (31 percent) that do not clearly show female sexual characteristics. This last opus by Watanabe (1997, 1998, 1999), with an impressive literature survey of both ethnographic and archaeological sources, certainly is a credit to his long and distinguished career of scholarship, but as an interpretation of archaeological phenomena, in methodology, and in conclusion, it curiously takes the figurine research all the way back to the 1920s, when sweeping generalizations about Jomon figurines, based on archaeological and ethnographic analogues, prevailed. That could very well have been his intention, as he concludes the long treatise by stating (1999: 391–95) that, because of the sterility of the typological-chronological approach of the Japanese archaeology in recent decades, no significant progress has been made in the study of Jomon figurines since the days of Tsuboi, Ohno, and Torii, whose contributions we have noted in the previous section.

In contrast to the single-function view of Jomon figurines presented by Mizuno and Watanabe, a number of archaeologists have noted that the figurines would have served in a variety to ways to meet the needs of Jomon people. Noguchi (1974: 98), for example, remarks that figurines would have been used in some cases in magical practices, in other cases in religious ceremonies, and in still others in funeral contexts. He admits that this sounds vague, but he believes that this is the best one could do at this time and that it describes the situation better than to assume a single function for all the figurines. Nagamine (1986: 263) concludes his survey article on Jomon figurines by citing Noguchi (1974) and stating that "the use of the figurines was diverse, depending on the area and time period, and we should always be aware of that diversity for figurines in Jomon society." Similarly, Yoneda (1984: 92) observes that figurines are morphologically diverse and that depositional patterns are also varied. It is therefore to be expected that they would have been used in a variety of ways. To suggest probable diversity in the use and function, in fact, is the corollary of the classificatory-typological framework that emphasizes detailed description of form and precise time-space assignments of typological units. The authors did not venture beyond listing several possibilities. Suggestions for diverse uses and function, therefore, are tantamount to saying that the meaning/function/use of the figurines is too complex and hence unknowable. In this sense, Watanabe is quite right when he pointed the finger at the prevailing methodological framework of Japanese archaeology as the cause of the stagnant state of Jomon figurine research.

Prospects for Future Research

The baked clay figurines from the Jomon period (ca. 14,500–300 B.C.), represented by over 15,000 specimens, collectively form a very rich corpus of data yet to be fully explored by gender-informed archaeologists. Part of this body of data comes from early excavations and surface collections, but hundreds of pieces being unearthed annually in recent decades are recovered during well-documented excavations under CRM operations. It is the standard practice of CRM archaeologists in Japan to record the provenience of each fragment in three dimensions. Conjoining of fragments is also part of the routine practice, as is placement of their occurrence in a culture-historical context with respect to associated ceramic types, settlement forms, and other noteworthy artifacts and features. Reporting of all the finds within a very short time frame is mandatory under the cultural properties preservation laws and regulations. These reports are highly descriptive but detailed, and almost all the significant pieces are illustrated.

Very little of these data is known outside Japan. Only cursory references are made to Jomon figurines in general introductory books on Japanese prehistory (e.g., Kidder 1966; Aikens and Higuchi 1982; Imamura 1996). Maringer's (1974) brief piece is now over a quarter of a century old, and it was in any event based largely on even older Western-language sources, such as Kidder's (1957) book on Jomon pottery and a general survey of Japanese archaeology by the same author (1959). Of the leading scholars in this field, English translation is available only of Mitsukazu Nagamine's (1986) summary article.

The reverse is also true. Very little, if any, of the Western-language literature on the use of baked clay figurines in archaeological constructions of past societies seems to be read by the active practitioners of figurine research in Japan. Of all the authors I consulted, only Watanabe (1997, 1998, 1999) cites Marja Gimbutas, for example, but one of her earlier publications only (Gimbutas 1982)—with approval, I might add. None of her later works is mentioned, nor is any reference made to the ongoing debate on the "mother goddess" in particular and to the use of anthropomorphic imagery in general (e.g., Joyce 1993; McCafferty and McCafferty 1994; Conkey and Tringham 1995; Haaland and Haaland 1995; Meskell 1995, 1998; Bolgar 1996; Brumfiel 1996; Hamilton et al. 1996; Frankel 1997; Hamann 1997; Hutton 1997; Goodison and Morris 1998). It is hoped that the critical insights being gained through the discourse would be profitably applied to Jomon figurines.

As seen in the previous section, much of the work presented by professional archaeologists in the last few decades is descriptive and culture-historical. As noted previously as well, the major strands that make up the "interpretative" attempts date back from the early years of anthropology in the late 19th century. The dominant themes are (1) that the figurines are representational images of women; (2) that the single most important attribute of a female is her ability to give birth, though the process is fraught with risks to the woman,

the child, and the demographic future of the group; (3) that the Jomon figurines
are a reification of this procreative power and metaphorically symbolize productivity of the earth and nature in general; and (4) that the figurines served
some important role in the Jomon society that was thought to have been ruled
by magic. I quite agree with Watanabe (1999: 391) when he said that the
Jomon figurine research is in urgent need of a new paradigm.

Before turning our attention to possible ways to break out of the narrow con-
fines of this interpretative framework, I want to note that all the sources cited
in the section "Interpretations of Jomon Figurines," with the single exception
of Ono (1984), are by men. This is not surprising, in view of the pronounced
gender imbalance among professional archaeologists, of whom only 1.34 percent and 2.77 percent, respectively, were women in 1975 and 1995 (table
18.1). It is not surprising as well, therefore, that Jomon figurines are "mind-
lessly gendered" (Nelson 1997: 84). It strikes me as the ultimate in "essential-
izing" prehistoric women to the extent of reducing them to baby-making
machines when Mizuno (1964) views all the Jomon figurines, including those
who do not show any explicit attributes of pregnant women, as mothers or
"women who are meant to become mothers." In Mizuno's scenario, these clay
women are supposed to possess mythical power of procreation and creation,
but they themselves are expendable, as they are to be destroyed in order to
release the power for the good of the entire community. Watanabe Makato
(1996: 121–34), on the other hand, after enumerating various views about the
apparently deliberate breaking of figurines, states that they are most likely to
represent the goddess of rebirth and regeneration, but he does not necessarily
exclude the idea that the breaking was done in a ritual of sympathetic magic
because the kind mother goddesses would not have been averse to serving as
proxies for the sick and injured as well. He concludes his book by saying that
the figurines represented the benevolent mother goddess to whom one could
make all sorts of requests and appeals, "just as we do with our own mothers
today" (Watanabe 1996: 134). Here we see a male child's idealized image of
a mother of 20th-century Japan. It is interesting as well to note that it is
Fujimura Junko , a young woman archaeologist, who questions whether the
Jomon hunter-gatherers really wanted so many children: She wonders whether
they could possibly be concerned about keeping a reasonable space between
births in order not to strain the resource base (2000: 87). She also notes, citing
Makabe Yoshiko (another woman archaeologist), that if the figurines were
indeed amulets for safe delivery, the major purpose could have been to ensure
the safety of the mother, whose productive, rather than reproductive, capabil-
ity was important for the economic well-being of the community.

Returning now to the major strands of interpretations, there has always been
a minority of scholars who objected to the blanket generalization of Jomon fig-

urines as representational images of women who were reduced to the basic
biological function of procreation. We have already seen that Fujimori (1963)
felt that some of the figurines represented males. Harada (1999: 139–43), on
the other hand, states that sexual characteristics are not clearly discernible in
figurines of the Late and Final Jomon. These figurines are not meant to represent actual human beings but rather to reify the concept of supernatural being
that transcends sex and gender (1999: 140).[2] Kobayashi Tasuo (1937–), a leading scholar in Jomon studies, goes even further and maintains that all the
Jomon figurines are not representational images at all but rather objectifica-
tions of abstract concepts. The figurines, along with such artifacts as masks,
ear spools, mace heads, and engraved stone tablets, formed "the second category of tools," to be contrasted with "the primary category of tools" that were
used directly in subsistence activities (e.g., Kobayashi 1977: 45; 2000:
136–39). Kobayashi's "second category of tools" appears to be rather similar
to Binford's (1962) "ideotechnic" and/or "sociotechnic" items. While
Kobayashi believes that the content of the idea system represented by the figurines is unknowable and, on that ground, strongly disagrees with the mother
goddess interpretation of Jomon figurines (2000: 149–50), he makes an interesting comment regarding the sudden appearance of figurines in the southern
part of Japan during the Late Jomon. As seen in the map and the table showing figurine distribution (fig. 18.3, table 18.3), figurines are virtually absent in
the southwestern part of the archipelago until Late Jomon times, when as many
as 108 occur in Kumamoto prefecture in west-central Kyushu. This is when
the domesticated rice (*Oryza sativa*), which was to become the major crop in
the Yayoi period (300 B.C.–A.D. 300), first appeared in Kyushu. Since the rice
is not native to Japan, it must have been brought in from abroad, most likely
via Korea. Kobayashi (1993: 92) interprets the sudden appearance of the figurines in Kyushu at this time as an indication of "a strengthening of Jomon tradition" in reaction to the encroachment of a new culture. The "resistance
movement" did not succeed, however, and the new culture moved farther to
the east. The cluster of figurines from the Final Jomon Kashihara site in Nara
prefecture signifies the last stronghold of the Jomon tradition in western Japan.
The figurines are seen here as the unifying symbol of Jomon ideology.

It seems to me that Jomon figurines, some of which have very unusual facial
expressions (figs. 18.8D, 18.9, 18.10), could be interpreted to indicate tension
and negotiation of power. Kobayashi posited the increased production of figurines during the Late and Final Jomon in western Japan as an indication of
assertion of Jomon ideology at the time of intergroup tension between the
indigenous Jomon and encroaching Yayoi groups. Many years ago, Fujimori
(1963: 26) remarked that, in contrast to the Middle Jomon figurines of central
Honshu, which appear to him to be expressing a naive hope and prayer for life

and abundance (fig. 18.8C), some of the Late and Final Jomon figurines had stern expressions "as if they were insisting on some prerogative." Fujimori did not elaborate which ones he was speaking of. Therefore, it is possible that he was referring to the same ones as Kobayashi's "resistant" fighters. Alternatively, Fujimori may have had in mind other examples that could be better understood in terms of intragroup conflicts of power and prestige. The intragroup frictions may have to do with gender roles and hierarchies arising from relative economic contributions to the subsistence system. Finally, the "magic," which is thought by many authors to be so important in Jomon society, may not always have to be benevolent in nature. If the figurines were indeed deliberately "torn apart" and scattered over and around the settlement or buried in special features, that could have been an act of malevolent witchcraft. There are a number of possibilities once we get out of the preoccupations with the mother goddess, fertility cult, and sympathetic magic.

All these ideas are yet to be fully developed and tested against an independent set of data. It seems to me to be particularly worthwhile to explore the possibility of the link between the probable contribution of women in economic activities on the one hand and the causes for inter- and intragroup tensions on the other. To this end, we need to be especially conscious of the diversity of the cultural systems grouped under the rubric of "Jomon culture."[3] It is now increasingly clear that not all the Jomon groups were hunter-gatherer-fishers. For example, if the chestnuts were semicultivated at the Sakuramachi and Sannai Maruyama sites in central and northern Honshu during Middle Jomon times (Takahashi et al. 1998), who did the cultivating, and why? Is there any contextual evidence to infer the identity of the cultivators? Is there any environmental or demographic data to suggest the desirability of such an endeavor? Salmon was caught and processed for later use as early as the Incipient Jomon at the Maeda Kochi site near Tokyo (Matsui 1996), and meat and fish were smoked in a special oven and acorns gathered and stored in large quantities at such Incipient and Initial Jomon settlements as Kakoinohara, Sojiyama, Okunonita, and Uenohara in southern Kyushu (Shinto 1999, summarized in Ikawa-Smith 2000). Was the fish, meat, and acorn processing done by women, and, if so, is it a coincidence that figurines, clearly depicting female sexual characteristics (fig. 18.5), appear with the establishment of this Jomon subsistence pattern? Most of the large shell middens are thought to be the places where mass processing of shellfish took place for later use or for trade, and salt making is inferred for some of the coastal sites on the Pacific side of north and central Honshu during the Late and Final Jomon. It is particularly intriguing to find that a quantity of coarse pottery, which is thought to have been used in boiling down seawater to obtain salt, has been excavated at the Tatsuki site (Sugihara and Tozawa 1965), where over 1,000 figurine pieces, mostly of the "pointed head" type, with some "horned owl" ones (fig. 18.9C, D), have also been recovered over the years (Ono 1984: 44; Kawarabuki 1992: 183). As boiling seawater in pots seems like an extension of boiling food in pots, it may have been women who produced salt through the labor-intensive efforts. Salt would have been useful as preservative anytime, but it is considered to have become increasingly important in the Jomon diet as the proportion of carbohydrate from plant sources increased at the expense of meat and fish. The control of production and distribution of the highly valued commodity, representing high labor cost, could have been a source of much tension. Other commodities that are known to have circulated widely are lacquer, jade, and adhesive bitumen. It would be interesting to see how the frequencies of figurines covary with the evidence for procurement and circulation of these probable "valuables."

I am certain that answers to these questions are already there in the mass of data that have been accumulated over the decades through the careful excavations and recording by Japanese colleagues. Their concern with time-space systematics has placed the data in neat classificatory slots, and their passion for conjoining has brought out many linkages that are otherwise invisible. Jomon figurines have a great potential for informing us not only about myths and rituals surrounding women but also about their economic roles and the sociopolitical organization of Jomon societies in general.

ACKNOWLEDGMENTS

I would like to thank Professor Sarah Nelson for inviting me to participate in the conference and giving me the opportunity to explore the topic that I had always intended to do "some day." I am grateful to Dr. Junko Habu of the University of California, Berkeley, for permission to use portions of the paper that we jointly prepared (Ikawa-Smith and Habu 1998) as well as for her kind assistance in obtaining information; Ms. Hishida (Fujimori) Junko of the Office of Buried Cultural Properties Research of the Hyogo Prefectural Board of Education; Professor Makabe Yoshiko of Kobe Women's University and Professor Okada Atsuko for their time in discussing issues with me; and Mr. Kawai Nobukazu of the Asahi Shimbun Newspapers, Professor Kishigami Nobuhiro of the National Museum of Ethnology, Mr. Kobayashi Masaru and Mr. Okamura Michio of the Agency for Cultural Affairs, Professor Sahara Makoto of the National Museum of Japanese History, and Professor Tsude Hiroshi of Osaka University for their assistance in obtaining publications and other data used in this paper. Finally, Nana Kodama and Rosanna Chan, as students at McGill University, helped me prepare figures and tables.

NOTES

1. Probably because of an error in converting the publication date given as "the 19th year of Meiji" into the Christian calendar, Watanabe refers to this paper, both in his text and his bibliography, as "Shirai 1896."

2. One wonders with these "a-sexual" figurines whether we are dealing with a case of the "two-spirits," third-gender category (Hollimon 1997; Munson 2000), but this possibility is not considered.

3. I have commented on a number of occasions (e.g., Ikawa-Smith 1980: 139) that the practice of referring to all the cultural manifestations of the very long Jomon period collectively as "Jomon culture" in the uppercase singular is misleading when it should actually be "Jomon cultures" in English, even though the concept is hard to convey in the Japanese language, which lacks the obligatory plural. I was therefore pleased to see Taniguchi (1999: 21) go out of the way to use the phrase "Jomon cultures" in transliterated English, as he emphasized the high degree of temporal and spatial variability among the cultural systems assigned to this long block of time.

19

Gender in Human Evolution: Sociobiology Revisited and Revised

A. C. Roosevelt

INTRODUCTION

Early sociobiological theory sought to characterize gender patterns among the hominids, our earliest ancestors. Gender roles of modern humans were attributed to genetic hard-wiring developed for a lifestyle of big-game hunting in savanna environments. Males were characterized as violent hunters and innovative toolmakers. They were the breadwinners, jealously dominated families, and defended against predators. Females were submissive and dependent and cared for the young at the home base. This division of labor and functions created the pair bond.

Since the early days of the theory, quite a different picture of early hominid lifeways has emerged from primatology, prehistory, and ethnology. The early picture turns out to be closer to ideal gender roles in Western society than to current data from anthropoid apes, hominid sites and skeletons, and living tropical foragers. Although the early scenarios generally have not been upheld, their assumptions about human nature and human evolution are widely held among scientists and broadly disseminated in the media as explanations for racism, sexism, inequality, and violence. Given the salience of these ideas in both scholarly and popular thinking, it is important to challenge the incorrect tenets with basic empirical evidence and explore its theoretical implications. The poor fit between data and theory encourage a paradigm shift in the science of human nature.

On rereading Darwin (1979), more than a century after he proposed the theory of evolution, one is struck by the similarity of his ideas and those of late 20th-century scientific evolutionary consensus. Views on this important subject jelled long before relevant data became available. Darwinians believed that the locus of human origins was the temperate savanna or steppe and assumed that the change to bipedal locomotion was an adaptation to such habitats. The early industrial revolution saw rapid temperate-zone deforestation and colonial expansion into the humid tropics. Naturally, to late Victorians their natal habitat was natural and salubrious, and hot, forested habitats conquered were unhealthy, evolutionary backwaters. Although England was led by a powerful woman and endowed with a history of appreciable gender balance (e.g., Shteir 1996), an assumption of natural gender inequality became enshrined in ideologies of the rising middle class and overseas expansion of Christian missions (Snyder and Tadesse 1995). White Christian European males exemplified the advanced human heritage, and their civilization was to be conferred on natives in the tropics. The image of person, subject, or doer was generally male. Men were strong intellectually and physically and should work, lead, and support their families; women were weak physically and mentally and should be obedient, raise their children, and keep the domestic sphere. Other family patterns were unnatural or bestial. A man's jealous defense and control of his family were protected both by legal practice and widespread sentiment. In Darwin's time, mainly white men were recognized openly and formally accredited as professors, scientists, engineers, and artists, so it is not surprising that they imagined that ancient males developed the first tools for their pursuits, invented agriculture, created the fine art, and were the sages of society (Conkey and Spector 1984; Hager 1997). In this time of economic stratification and agribusiness, the presumed ancient subsistence, hunting, was a prized masculine activity (Cartmill 1993), and its products were luxuries. Upper-class or financially independent Victorian women could contribute in the public sphere, and some were active in arts and other intellectual pursuits, but increasingly most had to do so privately, as associates of men or as outsiders (Shteir 1996).

Darwinism flourished in early 20th-century biology and anthropology (Haraway 1989; Gould 1996). Scientists assumed that European white men in charge of society were the most genetically fit and that women and lower classes, immigrants, and indigenous people were insufficiently evolved. A less overt version survives in today's behavioral ecology (Tiger and Fox 1971; Barash 1977; Wilson 1978). Although Darwin's theories have survived the last 100 years surprisingly intact, neo-Darwinism has inscribed on them some additions. One of the most important is the idea of the selfish gene and sexual selection (Hamilton 1964; Dawkins 1989). Darwin had seen natural selection as what we now call a stochastic process. He did not accept that it was directed to a goal by a providential hand. He cautioned that creatures did not necessarily compete violently or purposefully, as some held at the time, but that individuals prospering under current conditions would become more common. Those less suited eventually would diminish. However, after Mendel, the overarching teleology of the selfish gene replaced Darwin's more restrained view. The engine of evolution became the goal-seeking gene; the individual became almost irrelevant. In this extreme view, a creature's behavior and morphology became directed for the sole purpose of proliferation of the genes in future generations. This is the theoretical foundation for interpreting action and form as primarily self-serving and for the assumption that what exists is necessarily functional and adaptive. Related to this concept were the different sexual adaptations of males and females. Males spread their seed far and wide, but females invested in one male and in long-term care for the helpless offspring.

In a recent popularization by primatologists Richard Wrangham and Dale Petersen, *Demonic Males* (Wrangham and Petersen 1996), the men who are dominant in modern society are destined genetically to be natural leaders, achievers, and killers, and women to be submissive, nurturing, and attracted to such men. This genome developed through cooperative male big-game hunting in savannas and female specialization on domestic and reproductive functions. However, the evidence that the authors offer for genetic patterns and their prehistory is entirely anecdotal. Despite the lack of empirical data, such ideas are the foundation for both paleoanthropological and archaeological scenarios not explicitly referenced to the paradigm (Conkey and Spector 1984; Hager 1997; Kent 1998; Watson and Kennedy 1991).

The premise of this chapter is that human evolutionary theory and its implications are too important to be allowed to skirt the data. The emerging data on environment, food getting, social behavior, and genetic variation in apes, hominids, and living humans requires revisions in our understanding of the behavioral ecology of human evolution. They indicate the following: (1) The habitat for human emergence was tropical rain forest, not steppe. (2) Big-game hunting has never been a significant food source for apes or small-scale human societies in the tropics; broad-spectrum gathering of plants, supplemented with small game and invertebrates, furnished most food until the terminal Pleistocene and Holocene, when fishing and shellfishing were intensified and in some places plant domestication began. (3) Males were not the breadwinners; where provisioning was done, females did most of it. (4) Females make and use tools more frequently than males among apes and hunting-and-gathering societies, and food tools have been mainly for gathering, not for big-game hunting. (5) The enduring anthropoid and human social group and locus of socialization has been the mother and her young; she often bonds with male and female associates, not necessarily only with her relatives or her mate, who may have peripheral or no ongoing social interaction with her and their young. (6) In primate and tropical hunter-gatherer societies, either males or females can be dominant, but dominant individuals are not genetically more fit; their sociopolitical roles may to lead to lowered fitness, in the Darwinian sense. (7)

Dominance in social apes and nomadic hunter-gatherers is more about avoiding violence than doing it, and beatings and killings, especially of females and infants by males, have not been frequent, except during episodes of unusual stress or contact with humans from complex, sedentary societies.

The chronological data suggest that the traits that Darwinists and sociobiologists thought innate and primeval in humans have appeared mainly since the end of the Pleistocene, amid growing populations, settlements, complex social organization, and warfare. As such, they appear to be recent human behavioral and cultural responses to more sedentary lifestyles and consequent ecological stress and social crowding. Just as many social animals become more hierarchical, aggressive, and murderous in conditions of crowding and resource scarcity, so, apparently, do humans. If this is the explanation for current human social ills, it is important to recognize its timing and causal nexus. Misinterpreting such behaviors as embedded in our early hominid genetic heritage would take us down a wrong path for explanation and distract from practical solutions. The balance of this chapter will summarize current evidence on relevant aspects of human ecology, human behavior, human evolution, and their implications for understanding human nature. It is important to define the environment adequately since archaeologists and sociobiologists tend to assume that habitat sets the pattern of evolution. Subsistence also is the major link between populations and their environment and a possible causal factor in day-to-day behavioral and biological adaptation.

THE ENVIRONMENT OF EARLY HUMANS: SAVANNA OR TROPICAL FOREST?

The savanna as the primary habitat of human evolution is central to the original sociobiological vision (Wilson 1978) and to mainstream paleoanthropology and African archaeology (Washburn and DeVore 1961; Howell and Bourliere 1963; Clark 1971; Isaac 1977; Lovejoy 1981; Tooby and DeVore 1987; Phillipson 1994; Boaz 1997), but there is no conclusive paleoecological evidence to support this idea. Geomorphological evidence, pollen profiles, macroplants, isotopic chemistry, and bioarchaeological evidence all indicate tropical forest habitats, not savannas, during the emergence of hominids and earliest lithic cultures (Plummer and Bishop 1994; WoldeGabriel et al. 1994; Bonnefille 1995; Hill 1995; Reed 1997; Spencer 1997). For more than three decades, natural scientists have insisted on the prehistoric savanna habitat (Tricart 1973; Flenley 1979; Hamilton 1982; Prance 1982; de Menocal 1995; Maley 1995; Vrba 1995). At the time, there was little direct evidence in the form of dated, quantified samples of biota and biochemical results, so researchers interpreted inadequately understood indirect evidence in favor of theory. Little was known then about present-day humid tropical environments, so interpretations were uninformed about plants, fauna, ecology, sediments, rocks, climate, and carbon cycles in the equatorial zone.

The "evidence" claimed for arid prehistoric climates was geomorphological, palynological, paleontological, and biogeographic. Proponents felt that sand, pebbles, carbonate, and silicified rocks developed under sparse, open arid-adapted vegetation. However, sand and gravel are produced by abundant, moving water, not aridity (Thomas 1975; Hauer and Lamberti 1996); the supposed aeolian sands were shown to be particles created by river action (de Ploey et al. 1968); and the relevant sands, clays, and silica deposits are types produced through chemical weathering by rain under dense forest vegetation (Moss 1968; Buol et al. 1989), not open vegetation. The lime was from earlier marine deposits, from calcareous tuffs in East Africa and dolomitic limestone in South Africa (Furon 1963). The early prehistoric grass pollen levels—from less than 10 percent up to about 60 percent (Lanfranchi and Schwartz 1990; Lanfranchi and Clist 1991; Elenga et al. 1994; Bonnefille 1995)—are ranges normally found in tropical lowland rain forests and their wetlands (Absy 1979), not in savannas, where grass is over 99 percent of ground cover. The assemblages of animal bones in hominid sites have been reinterpreted as indicating wooded landscapes with water bodies, not savannas (Plummer and Bishop 1994; Kappelman et al. 1997; Spencer 1997; Fernandez-Jalvo et al. 1998), and the isotopes of prehistoric fauna and hominid bone (Ambrose and DeNiro 1989; Kingston et al. 1994; Lee-Thorp et al. 1994; Hill 1995; Sikes and Potts 1999; Sponheimer and Lee-Thorp 1999) are more negative than expected for savanna, if about 10 percent diagenesis from geological marine carbonate is taken into consideration. Bipedal hominids appear first in wooded, not open habitats (e.g., WoldeGabriel et al. 1994), and joint and limb forms indicate continued travel in trees (Zihlman 1996). The diversity of modern species had been assumed to reflect the effects of Pleistocene savannas. For biogeographers now, however, current diversity patterns in central Africa suggest persistence of rain forest until deforestation for ironworking, cattle, agriculture, timber, range management, and urbanization (e.g., White 1983; Colyn et al. 1991; Lovett and Wasser 1993; Scholes and Walker 1993).

Thus, the paleoecological evidence indicates heavily wooded, humid environments, not desert or savanna, in East and South Africa in but a few areas of very high elevation or distance from the equator until about 2 million years ago, when there were some changes but vegetation remained more wooded and humid than today. The Central African rain forest itself was a closed, canopied formation until the development in the later Holocene of more sedentary, populous, and complex human societies. Human ancestors did not leave humid warm wooded environments for open cool regions until well after the initial appearance of *Homo* and the first tool cultures. So, if the environment had any effect on early hominid behavior and genetics, it was the tropical rain forest and its water bodies that were involved, not temperate, arid savanna or desert.

The specific nature of habitat is significant in evolutionary adaptation. In tropical rain forests, plants dominate ecosystems. Large game animals are minuscule in the biomass and carnivores even less. Dense vegetation cover reduces predation pressure. Animals evolved in rain forests, such as great apes, have greater encephalization and dexterity for harvesting fruits, nuts, pith, and insects with hands or tools; they have less seasonal behavior, more neoteny, less territoriality, slower reproduction, greater parental investment, less aggressiveness, and more sociality and intraspecific tolerance than savanna animals (Kingdon 1997). Physiologically, tropical forest animals are adapted for moderately warm and stable temperature. All these traits are precisely those that distinguish humans, their primate relatives, and their ancestors from savanna animals. In contrast, animals that evolved in savannas or steppes, such as the bovids, show less encephalization, less foot dexterity, more rapid reproduction, more precocial young, less parental care, less sociality, more aggressiveness, more territoriality, more male dominance and sexual competition, and less egalitarian organization. Physiologically, they show adaptations to open, seasonally hot and dry habitats: urine concentration, estivation, seasonal migration, seasonal mating, and so on. Contrary to the idea that bipedal locomotion was an adaptation to the high heat or open vistas of savannas, savanna-adapted animals more often are obligate quadrupeds than are tropical rain forest animals. In accordance with a rain forest habitat, human evolution can be seen as exemplifying further development of the changes that the forest great apes underwent in their earlier evolution. Neither in behavior nor in physiology does the human phenotype manifest any evolutionary shift in the direction of a genetic adaptation to savanna.

SUBSISTENCE: CARNIVORY OR BROAD-SPECTRUM FORAGING?

Big-game hunting by males as the subsistence of early human ancestors is not supported by accumulated evidence for ape, hominid, and human subsistence. The staple carnivory of the early hominids in this scenario would be a contrast to modern anthropoid ape practice. In most ape diets, meat is rare or absent (McGrew et al. 1996). Bonobos, chimps, and gorillas are considered our closest living relatives and the closest to hominid ancestors (Marks 1992; Zihlman 1996). Of these, lowland gorillas never eat meat and eat invertebrates mainly during short dry seasons (Carroll 1997). Apes rarely scavenge for meat. Some chimps and bonobos catch animals and sometimes eat them (Boesch 1994; Wrangham and Petersen 1996). Nonetheless, when strictly measured, meat is an extremely small part of their food, usually less than 1 percent, and most individuals never hunt and never eat meat. Also contrary to evolutionary theory, when apes hunt, both males and females do it. Male hunting may be more common, but hunting is not a uniquely male adaptation (Goodall 1986; de Waal and Lanting 1997; Morbeck et al. 1997). The sharing of meat observed is not unique, either. Large fruits also are shared on demand.

Early paleoanthropologists initially supported big-game hunting because early hominid bones sometimes occurred with bones of large game. On this basis, Raymond Dart (1953) claimed that our ancestors were bloodthirsty, ruthless, "killer" apes, a idea that was the basis for key evolutionary popularizations (Ardrey 1961, 1970) that influenced generations of Americans. However, systematic taphonomy studies show the early hominids and the game were not predators but prey of carnivores (Brain 1981; Klein 1999). Their bones shows carnivore teeth marks, not marks of stone tools or human teeth.

Similarly, both morphology and wear patterns on *Australopithecine* and early *Homo* teeth are consistent with plant processing, not with gnawing meat or bone (Klein 1999). In addition, the stable carbon isotopes of *Australopithecine* bones do not necessarily indicate reliance on meat, although some have claimed so (Sponheimer and Lee-Thorp 1999). If a 10 percent diagenesis of bone mineral from geological marine carbonates is factored in, the chemistry indicates a C-3 plant-based diet. No direct faunal or artifactual evidence for hunting is found before the later Paleolithic, the time of early modern human emergence (Klein 1999). Even then, archaeological associations do not prove that big-game was the staple. Rather, the preponderance of large bones in some sites reflects collecting procedures. Large-mesh screening or no screening makes big game the main food; fine screening, flotation, and archaeobotany make plants and small fauna the main foods. Where proper collection and recording methods are employed in well-preserved Late Pleistocene tropical sites, the main food is largely plants and small aquatic fauna, not big game (e.g., Roosevelt et al. 1996; Roosevelt 1998).

Ethnographic evidence similarly shows that plant gathering, not big-game hunting, is the main subsistence of tropical-subtropical foragers, supplemented with small amounts of invertebrates and small game and only occasional large game (Hames and Vickers 1983; Beckerman 1994; Roosevelt 1998). Meat from large game is a minor calorie source in a year's diet, less than 1 percent. Pygmy people of the African rain forests eat mainly plant foods, whether in forests or in horticultural villages (Bailey and Peacock 1988; Hewlett 1991; Sarno 1993). Periods of intensified meat eating is associated with researcher-elicited hunting (Hladik et al. 1993) and colonial trading in ivory and bush meat (Turnbull 1983). The savanna woodland Hadza in East Africa eat mainly plants: starchy roots, berries, and nuts (Hawkes et al. 1995; Hawkes 1997). !Kung Bushmen in steppes rely on a tree nut, mongongo (Lee

1968). Amazonian Indian part-time foragers also mainly eat plants (over 90 percent), with small amounts of fish and insects and game (Beckerman 1994; Dufour 1994). The subtropical forest Ache "foragers" eat crops and collected plants, supplemented with invertebrates, small game, and domestic animals. The 90 percent meat consumption often cited (Hill and Hawkes 1983) happened only during hunting trips commissioned by the anthropologists. The plant-based tropical forest diet is not protein or fat deficient, for the frequently eaten leaves, shoots, stems, roots, nuts, and fruits of palms and trees are rich in high-quality protein and/or fat (Mitani et al. 1994; McGrew et al. 1996).

Carnivory is not a viable scenario for hominids and early humans. Patterns of human anatomy, physiology, metabolism, and pathology do not indicate that carnivory is a strategy appropriate for our species (Milton 1987). Hominids are supposed to have become carnivores to support their large, calorically "expensive" brain with high-nutrient food (Aiello and Wheeler 1995), but genetically determined human physiology and metabolism resemble those of omnivorous primates whose staples are high-nutrient plant foods, not those of carnivores. Modern humans are ill suited physiologically for high-meat diets, which predispose them to early degenerative disease. At any rate, the nutrients in short supply for hunter-gatherers are calories, not protein. Analyses of actual ethnographic food consumption indicate that when food is scarce, calories and, to a lesser degree, vitamins, such as A and C, are lacking, not protein, which usually is eaten in adequate levels per capita (Beckerman 1994; Dufour 1994). Large carnivores are rare in rain forests because prey is dispersed and cryptic. Carnivory is thus an expensive adaptation, requiring large expenditures in calories for those gained because of long searches and energetic pursuits, and it is dangerous since large ungulates are aggressive (Kingdon 1997). Lean, wild animals are a poor and costly calorie source compared to oily or starch-rich seeds (Beckerman 1994). Plants are the majority of available biomass, while vertebrates are a tiny minority (Fittkau 1973). According to existing evidence, big game has been an insignificant food among great apes, early hominids, and humans in the lowland tropics. It would have been too rare to be an important selective factor in human evolution. If subsistence were an evolutionary factor, then the activity of interest would have been intensive plant harvesting, supplemented by small fauna.

GENDER BEHAVIOR FROM APES TO TODAY

Divison of Labor in Subsistence

One of the most striking differences between evolutionary theory and data lies in provisioning. Theoreticians assumed that hunting by males provided the food in the first families. However, the evidence does not indicate significant male provisioning. Where provisioning is done, it is primarily by females, and, in some groups, the young contribute significantly to their own support and to that of others.

Most adult apes get their own food (McGrew et al. 1996). When there is provisioning, mostly females do it, not males, and only females functionally nurse young. When animals share food, the food tends to transfer from females (de Waal and Lanting 1997; Zihlman 1996). Females spend significantly more time than males foraging and making and using tools for subsistence. Male apes contribute little food to others. They make food-getting tools less frequently and spend much less time using tools for food-getting. For hominids, no researcher has detected physiological evidence for a sexual division of labor. Among prehistoric human foragers, females were physically active in subsistence. For example, the large early skeletal population from Paloma, Peru (c. 9,000 to 5,000 b.p.) showed heavy participation by both men and women (Benfer 1990). During periods when fish and shellfish were staples, both men and women were muscular and arthritic from lifting nets and carrying loads. Early cross-cultural surveys (Murdock and Provost 1973) suggested that men produced the most food or contributed equally with women, but they lacked actual measurements of time spent and food acquired and equal observation of mens', womens', and children's activities (Spector 1983; Wadley 1998). In addition, as mentioned above, researchers exaggerated the contribution of male big-game hunting in food economics (Roosevelt 1998; Hill and Hawkes 1983; Hladick et al. 1993).

In present-day tropical and subtropical hunter-gatherer and horticulural societies, quantified studies show that most food is produced by women and children, who spend the most time foraging (Hawkes 1997; Hawkes et al. 1995; Lee and Daly 1999; Martin and Voorhies 1975; Roosevelt 1998). Among Amazonian foragers, women and children contribute most food as gathered plants, fish, and shellfish (Beckerman 1994; Hames and Vickers 1983; Roosevelt 1998; Wust 1994). Among nineteenth-century Fuegians, women and children collected most of the food, and women owned and maintained the fishing boats, and built the hearths and houses (Steward 1946). Even where aquatic fauna supplemented crops, women and children were important in fishing. In rural Japan (Kawanabe et al. 1999), their fishing provided most of the protein in the cereal diet. After industrialization, they lost that role.

Woman's lack of hunting has also exaggerated (for example, Kelly 1995; as Wadley 1998 points out). Their lack of active participation in large-game hunting has obscured the quantitative importance of their hunting. In tropical and subtropical foraging, women may be as active or more active than men in hunting, whether in time spent or in productivity (Lee and Daly 1999). Women and men usually are equally involved in Pygmy net-hunting (Hewlett 1991; Sarno 1993; Turnbull 1981, 1983). In some groups, women act as beaters and men kill the netted animals; in others, the women and men regularly trade off these roles. Sarno judges women more effective; they run faster, more nimbly set nets, and kill more animals (personal communication, 1999). Even when hunting is not considered a typical female activity, women regularly hunt (Lee and Daly 1999; Spector 1983). And when women hunt, they often produce the majority of the meat because the small game they catch are the majority of faunal biomass (Martin and Voorhies 1975). In Amazonian and Mayan societies, the raising of young captured animals also tends to be women's work. (By analogy, animal domestication would be expected to have been by women.)

Women tend to be the main horticultural food producers in tropical South America and Africa (Hames and Vickers 1983; Martin and Voorhies 1975). Some researchers note cooperation between men and women, implying parity. But men assist women in clearing and weeding for a few weeks, and women spend nearly 365 days a year weeding, harvesting, and planting, and they process, cook, and distribute most produce, as well. For example, among the Yanomamo, an Amazon society considered to represent primeval savanna lifeways, over 90% of the calories are provided by women (Smole 1976). Worldwide, also, females have been the main transporters of food, and they carry children and tools simultaneously. Even prehistoric populations show an association of tump-line cranial indentations with female, not male, crania (e.g., Geller 1998). In this context, the idea that hominid females required the help of men to carry food because they were weak and had to carry young is ludicrous.

The large subsistence contribution of women, among other things, gives them substantial economic power, because in small-scale societies, one usually owns the product of one's work and has the right to allocate it. Women often distribute others' products, too, because of their roles in food processing and food service. Such roles gives them broad power in decision-making.

Tool Use

One assumption of evolutionary theory was that tools were invented by males for hunting or warfare, but data from primatology, paleoanthropology, and ethnology do not fit that scenario.

In apes and monkeys, most tools and tool use are for gathering and processing food, not for hunting or conflict. They use tools for nut cracking, chopping and pounding of starchy pith, digging holes, insect dipping, leaf sponging, etc. (Goodall 1986; Joulian 1986). The tools intensify extraction of keystone resources, such as nut and legume oilseeds, root and pith starch, and invertebrates, resources exploited when fruit and herb staples decrease seasonally. Females use tools more often and for longer than males, as mentioned above, and the difference is substantial: fifteen times more in some cases. Observers report that the innovators in food and tools are females and children; teaching is mainly done by females, by example and by helping the young. Tools are rarely used threateningly within groups, although they are used in many social interactions. For example broken-off branches are waved or dragged for attention, angrily or in a friendly manner. Both apes and monkeys throw stones or branches or drop feces on intruders. Tools are not, however, usually used in combat; teeth and hands are.

The fact that females are the main users and the probability that plants have been the main foods for all tropical primates suggest that early hominid tools should reflect female activities in plant harvesting and processing. We have no way, at present, to determine the truth of this. Individual hominid osteology might be expected to reflect tool use as human's does, in arthritis from digging, etc., but studies have not been conducted. The shapes and wear patterns of early tools suggest cutting, chopping, prying, and scraping (flakes, hand-axes, cleavers, choppers, denticulates, chisels, and discoid cores), digging (handaxes, picks, cleavers), pounding, and mashing (battered rocks, spheroids, polyhedrons). For late Pleistocene human cultures, the usewear on stone tools from Brazil, Argentina, and France indicates that tropical belt cultures' tools were used more on plants than on animal products, in contrast to high-latitude cultures, where tools show more contact with animal products (Mansur 1986). This pattern fits the expectation that plants will be more important where biomass is high than where it is low. Thus, high-latitude tool use for big-game hunting should probably not be projected back earlier than the upper Paleolithic, when *Homo sapiens sapiens* appears.

Among ethnographic foragers, most material is made and used by women, and most food getting and processing is by women, as mentioned (Martin and Voorhies 1975; Spector 1997; Wadley 1997). In tropical foragers, the morphological descendants of early tools are axes, machetes, mashers, pounders, scrapers, knives, and awls, primarily used for plant processing, not for processing animal carcasses. The hand-axe's descendants, the hafted stone axe or the steel-head hatchet or machete, are owned and used by women as well as men as everyday tools for cutting wood, digging, and dispatching animals. In such societies, except for steel tools, women tend to make the tools they use. An Australian woman makes the stone flakes and points that she uses, for example, and Amazonian women make the chips for their manioc graters, by bipolar method.

In sum, the assumption that early hominid males were responsible for inventing and using tools for hunting and group aggression does not have support in the primate, prehistoric, or ethnographic record. Given existing information, it is more probable that tools were invented by adult females and children primarily for plant food getting and processing.

The Pair Bond in Reproduction and Social Organization

Key in early scenarios was the formation of the pair bond, considered a basic hominid grouping. Even this part of the scenario does not survive close scrutiny.

In Neo-Darwinian views of sexual selection, hominid males should try to control the females that they mate with to ensure a conduit for their genes, rather than those of others. This was one of the reasons for the pair-bond and nuclear family. Such concepts survived a long time because researchers did not collect the genetic data to test them. As pointed out by feminist scholars (e.g., Hager 1997), early primate researchers tended to study the mating behavior of males, not females. The dominant male was classified as the mate of the females and father of the young because this seemed self-evident. But the genetics of individuals was not known until recent DNA studies.

Among tropical forest primates most closely related to humans, there is no evidence for a "nuclear" family and pair-bond for breeding purposes (Manson 1997; McGrew et al. 1996; Reynolds and Harvey 1994). Instead, the common pattern is that the cohabiting, genetic family is the mother and her young. This pattern is even found in savanna baboons. Researchers had identified marriage-like pairings, called "consortships," but these were usually temporary, lasting a week or at most a month. The DNA studies, further, do not show that the "husbands" are necessarily the fathers, for the females do not mate exclusively with "consorts." The social "fathers" and "husbands" are giving help to individuals who are unrelated to them as often as not. (Even monkey mothers readily adopt unrelated young.) Long-term mutual male-female social relationships can be important in adaptation and survival, but this often is independent of the breeding contribution by the male to that female. The general mating pattern in great apes is promiscuity, not exclusive pair-bonds (Fuentes 1999; Small 1993). Contrary to selfish gene theory, males tend not to act to achieve exclusive mating. Certainly they try hard to mate, but in general they do not try to prevent others from mating and do not necessarily determine others' mating patterns. In both chimps and Bonobos, females commonly take the initiative by "presenting." In Bonobos, females frequently initiated sex in tense situations.

To understand these cases, "selfish gene" and kin selection theory are inadequate. They make the scenario of sedentary, domestic mothers-with-children paired with mobile, breadwinning fathers an unlikely pattern for hominids, who morphologically closely resemble anthropoid apes in most traits except for bipedality and small canines. The early hominid remains themselves give little support for the nuclear family idea. Earlier, hominid activity areas were interpreted as family home bases, on analogy with African hunter-gatherers

(Isaac 1977; Turnbull 1983). But a wide range of taphonomic studies do not support this interpretation (summarized in Klein 1999). They indicate natural causes for assemblages as carnivore dens or alluvial deposits, as mentioned above. No early sites record structures that might have housed male-female mating pairs and their young, and the famous Laetoli footprints claimed to represent a male and female pair could equally well represent an older and younger animal. On analogy with ape behavior, it is more likely that the prints were made by a mother and child.

In the ethnographic record, generally, co-resident pairs of men and women are only assumed, not proven to be the mating pair that produced co-resident children. The genetic tie between mother and a particular child is usually recognizable, through parturition, but the husband's genetic tie with the young is not easily verifiable. Researchers have not tested the relatedness of the males and young but simply assumed spouses are genetic parents. But if people are sexually unfaithful, the husband might not be the father. Few small-scale societies espouse the idea, valued in the West, that families should be couples and that paternity should be exclusive (Fuentes 1999). In fact, men other than the husband who have sex with a woman during her pregnancy are considered to contribute to the child's substance and spirit and are obligated to give food to the mother and child in Amazonia (Beckerman et al. 1998). Furthermore, the importance of geneaological paternity in the Western sense does not figure in most ethnographic accounts, especially when residence is matrilocal and/or relatedness is counted through the female line, a common pattern in lowland South American forager groups (Roosevelt 1998; Steward 1946; Wust 1994). For example, among the Cuiva, Yaruro, Maku, Bororo, Ache, Siriono, and Yuqui, the most common long-term residence of a woman is in her parents' house. They marry males from other villages. Thus young males, not females, are exchanged. The role of husband is impermanent and insecure and involves long and heavy labor for the woman's family. Regardless of residence, women are not assumed to be chaste or faithful to spouses, and informants characterize female promiscuity as frequent.

In tropical foragers, then, like among the great apes, resident groups often are not coterminous with the mating pair and their young. "Marriage" is a social entity that may or may not involve the husband as progenitor. Sexual promiscuity is common, and there are no data that suggest that males are more likely than females to mix sexually. Thus, the term "polygyny," favored by sociobiologists, is not as appropriate as "polygamy." Marriage, per se, through a ceremony and/or contract between individuals or families is rare in such societies. A couple becomes a pair by living together and cooperating in food-getting, domestic activities, and child-rearing. Formal marriage is more common to sedentary and/or complex societies and has an important function in management of property. Sex, marriage, and child-rearing do not fit sociobiological theory even in modern societies. Large numbers of people do not reproduce, and many families raise adoptees who appear to be not less cared for than biological children. Furthermore, the educated, privileged, powerful, and economically well-off have the smallest number of living offspring.

Ape, hominid, and modern human mating and family life do not fit sociobiological theory.

Parenting

A key assumption was that the care of helpless (altricial) young would remove females from full-time foraging, so males would become the provisioners. This assumption is not borne out by studies of parenting in apes or humans, and the small amount of hominid data tends to accord with the other data.

Most primate infant and weanling care is given by mothers, who are serious, vigilant, assertive, and affectionate caregivers (first-time mothers are less so) (McGrew et al 1996; Morbeck et al. 1997; Kano 1992; Small 1993). Mothers carry out care at the same time that they forage. They either carry the infant or put it down nearby. Males also have the capacity to be caregivers, given experience, but the fact that infants are born to females gives them much more experience. Males, other females, and adolescents all spend time with others' young (Hrdy 1999). Adolescent males actively interact with young, and when young are orphaned, adolescent males have been observed to take over their care successfully (Goodall 1986). The young are a magnet for social activity, and there is competition to be in the central group of females and young. One social cue in begging for food is to briefly "baby-sit" an infant by holding or playing with it, to get food from the mother.

We do not have much information about hominid care of the young. As altriciality, tool use, and food-sharing increased during evolution, females would have had to carry young more, and that would have encouraged more bipedal locomotion, as many have pointed out. Paleoanthropological research needs to collect evidence for such changes. Theoretically, genetic changes in morphology should be preceded by physiological effects of changed behavior (Slobodkin 1968). Bones can be screened for arthritis from changes in locomotion, and research can define weaning age and other physiological stresses in young by study of tooth enamel. Current studies reveal stress lines at approximately the time for weaning, but no researcher has synthesized the data. Osteological research suggests that hominid young were active physically, presumably in foraging, a pattern that continues with Neandertals, whose young and adults have similar ontogenetic bone changes (Klein 1999; 367–393).

Among ethnographic foragers, females care for young while foraging, aided by carrying aids. Women do not opt out of foraging because of child care, although one may "rest" doing lighter foraging immediately after parturition (e.g., Hawkes 1997). Men in Pygmy societies do substantial amounts of child-care compared to 20th century U.S. men (Hewlett 1991). Others also share child care: older children, other women, and especially adolescents and older men. Even small children get substantial food for themselves and for others. They make up much labor in fruit collection (Hawkes et al. 1995) and mass fishing and shellfishing (Steward 1946).

Existing knowledge about both apes and human foragers suggests that females rear the young and still do the majority of subsistence. The two activities are not incompatible. On the other hand, both apes and humans rely to some degree on caregiving by others. It is interesting that humans show the greatest within-species extremes in contributions by social fathers. In U.S. societies at certain periods, the men gave negligible direct care, but among certain tropical forest foragers they give almost the same amount as mothers (Hewlett 1991). The potential for childcare seems to exist in most ape and human individuals, whether it comes from a genetically determined capacity for affect to young or from learned inclination. However, such traits do not seem to function primarily to ensure the survival of relatives but seem a more general trait that underlies affective social behaviors in both human and non-human primates.

Dominance, Aggression, and Violence

When Neo-Darwinians assumed that primate males were universally aggressive, dominant, and violent this was an interpretation more theoretically than empirically derived.

In primates, patterns of gender dominance vary, and male dominance is not necessarily the most common (de Waal and Lanting 1997; Fedigan 1986; Goodall 1986; Kinsey 1997; McGrew et al. 1996; Morbeck et al. 1997). Among apes, only some common chimp groups exhibit male dominance. In these populations, especially those provisioned at Gombe, males are rough with females, push by them to feed, hit them, bite them, and force them to mate. The females do not seem to resist but do try to escape. The males also push forward aggressively in contacts with outsiders and are thought to aggressively "patrol" borders against outsiders (based on ancedotal evidence). But among other common chimp groups, there is balance between male and female dominance or even a tendency to female dominance.

In Bonobo populations, females are considered the dominants, judged by the standards for assessing male dominance (de Waal and Lanting 1997; Kano

1992). Females threaten, hit, and bite males, and males retreat. The reverse is not often seen. Females dominate access to food. They push males out of the way and take what they want. Males must make do with what is left. They do not resist but rely on subterfuges to feed. Bonobo females also dominate in relations with outside groups. They go together in vanguard; the males hold back. Recent studies of the correlates of primate gender dominance cite the influence of socialization patterns related to demography, life history, and "settlement patterns" (Morbeck et al. 1997). In Bonobos, for example, males stay with their mothers their whole lives. Their mothers dominate them, due to seniority and female coalitions, and males develop submissive behaviors. In common chimps, in contrast, males may grow up mainly interacting with each other, a very different context.

Discussions of the evolutionary role of violence and aggression tend to gloss over the fact that primates are rarely violent to conspecifics. The terminology of behavioral ecology can be misleading. Most of the time when writers use the word aggression, they are referring to activities that would in common parlance not be "aggressive." Examples include staring to make another individual look down or step aside. Social primates use chivvying for place to avoid true aggression and physical violence (de Waal 1996). Dominance interaction thus deters animals from physical conflict most of the time.

In primates and other mammals, bloody fighting, murder, and infanticide, ordinarily absent, arise in conditions of spatial crowding and food scarcity (Dagg 1999). This is shown in numerous laboratory studies of manipulated conditions and in studies of free-ranging populations under ecological or population pressure. The famous killings at Gombe took place in explosive situations due to intensive provisioning and disruption by humans. Only a few individuals were murderous, and they did not have significantly more young than others. Some lived longer but this correlated with selective care of these individuals by humans (Goodall 1986). Males were not the only killers; a substantial proportion were females. But conspecific murder is not observed in populations such as Bonobos, who inhabit large, undisturbed rainforests, so the expectation for early human evolution is that such violence would not be a selective factor, since forests were more extensive than today.

For hominid populations, there is no direct evidence for dominance or violence of males against females. The degree of sexual dimorphism is disputed because of taxonomic problems (a large male may be a different species than a small female; a small individual may be a male of a small species or a female of a large species.) In any case, dimorphism is considered more an element in male-male competition than male-female interaction, and humans and apes tend to be less dimorphic than other animals. In terms of violence, Wragham only cites Dart as his source for violence and killing in hominids, and Dart's interpretation of sites as loci of hominid violence was later overturned, as explained above.

In prehistoric small scale societies, social dominance seems to have been more balanced than predicted by sociobiological theory. Ideotechnic and sociotechnic materials do not suggest male dominance in ritual and politics. In fact, female images are more common and prominent than those of males in early art, compared to more recent art. The large, central, frontal figure in art is often female, not male; males and female "ancestors" are equally often depicted; and males become more prominent later rather than earlier, in evolutionary terms. The more statelike the society, the more males dominate politically, ideologically, ritually, and economically (Nelson 1993). However, even for complex non-state societies, like the Maya, the decipherment shows women were much more common as rulers, ritual specialists, and architecture patrons than archaeologists assumed (Schele and Freidel 1990).

In terms of physical dominance or abuse, as determined by pathology patterns, there is no osteological evidence for frequent beating of women (or men) until late prehistory in a context of socioeconomic and political differentiation (Cohen and Bennett 1993). In most sites, there are abundant materials traditionally produced by women: remains of weaving, and pottery and food and food-processing tools. These products presumably were the maker's to dispose of, since they were dispersed in domestic contexts, rather than at centrally controlled loci. Only in states, which take control of most peoples' labor, does women's labor and its product seem to be expropriated by others, and only in such societies do traditional women's industries get relegated to economic unimportance or be taken over by men.

In ethnographic hunter-gatherer and many simple horticultural populations, political, social, ritual, and economic interaction is usually described as egalitarian, not male-dominated, and in many non-state complex societies, gender roles are considered "balanced" and complementary (Kaplan 1997; Martin and Voorhees 1975; Lee and Daly 1999; Sanday 1981; Wust 1994). Societies vary in how similar or different men's and women's activities are, but women's activities are not considered less important. Men and women tend to have more similar activities than in states. Social dominance and political leadership are not primarily male, and it has not been the case that women were rarely leaders. According to ethnographic accounts, females were often leaders of corporate groups. For example, women frequently negotiated and signed treaties for tribes in the eastern U.S., political assemblies included both men and women; and, where men are chiefs, women's groups had the right to elect them (Etienne and Leacock 1980: 44–87).

There is little mention of husbands striking wives more than wives strike husbands in hunting-and gathering societies, even larger and more muscled men who could presumably overpower women (Burbank 1994; Lee and Daly 1999). The pattern of male physical dominance or abuse of women and children assumed by neo-Darwinians to be a primeval, selective, and genetically embedded human trait of hominid origin is rare in descriptions of these societies. Since documents do record men's violence against the women in their families in more sedentary tribal (such as the Yanomamo) and state societies (Justice Department 1998; Davies 1994; Downs 1996; Dutton 1995; Gordon 1998; Monahan 1998), this seems another gender trait appearing during later human cultural evolution rather than in earlier periods. Although treated by sociobiologists as an adaptive trait conducive to the abuser's fitness, a propensity to violence is correlated with poverty, substance abuse, and lack of social skills. Domestic violence is favorable neither to the proliferation of violators' genes nor to the subtraction of competitors' genes. Most of the killed are related to or affiliated with the killer. In addition, contrary to the theory, males are not more violent than females in domestic contexts. According to statistics women strike the first blow more often, and violence initiated by them is more likely to end in a man's death (Archer 1998; Heidensohn 1995). But contrary to the idea that violent males are more attractive and more successful propagators, violent male offenders tend to be avoided by females, according to rehabilitation studies.

In terms of gender dominance in apes, factors of ontogeny and demography seem important, as mentioned above. In humans, there are several possible factors. There is a strong scular trend from patterns of gender equality in hunting-gathering societies to relative inequality in state societies. Gender equality is associated with strong economic and social power for women and gender-balanced ideologies; inequality is associated with organized physical coercion and centralized political and economic control in stratified communities oriented to value males more than females (Sanday 1981). A genetic basis for the different patterns of gender-dominance is not, therefore, indicated. Rather, patterns created by governmental, religious, and community organizations in sedentary and crowded contexts are the correlates.

In regard to genetic bases of violence, it is significant that apes are less violent and murderous than humans. We share the great majority of our genetic heritage with them, so a solely genetic explanation for the contrast seems unlikely. Rather, modern studies of both humans and animals suggest a correlation between violence and conditions of crowding, resource scarcity, and social inequality, all characteristic of later prehistory, not human origins.

Infanticide

According to selfish gene corollaries evolutionary theory, males kill the young of other males to bring females into oestrus so they can father their own.

This kind of behavior is so rare in great apes that it is unlikely to be a selective factor as hypothesized. Most cases of infanticide discussed in the literature were not observed (e.g., Goodall 1986). An infant disappeared, and the researchers assumed it was killed by a conspecific male. Since death of infants by accidents, such as falling, is relatively common, this is not a safe assumption. Furthermore, the observed incidents involved female killers as well as males, so the pattern of gender participation does not fit the theory. Among hominid skeletons, infants are rare, but the most famous one was dispatched by leopards, not by hominids (Brain 1981). As mentioned above, osteological evidence of violence to women tends to be confined to sedentary, stratified societies; it does not seem prominent in prehistoric small-scale societies (Cohen and Bennett 1998). In ethnographic foraging societies, nonrelatives commonly share child-care, as mentioned, and children are said to be valued. When infanticide occurs within groups, it is more likely done by women (Kelly 1995: 233–244). The hypothetical pattern of baby-killing by men desirous of taking over another's mate is not often recorded. In modern societies, both women and men are involved in infanticide. As mentioned above, its main U.S. correlates are poverty, lack of education, and substance abuse. The idea that most infanticide would be by stepfathers interested in fathering their own children with mates is not upheld by research, which indicates that genetic relatives predominate among those violent to the young (see violence references, above.) Whether people kill their young because they are incapacitated by substance abuse, unable to support them, or unwilling to sacrifice to do so, their behavior is not that predicted by natural selection, sexual selection, or selfish gene theory.

CONCLUSIONS

When one looks closely at the data of paleoecology, paleoanthropology, primatology, prehistory, and ethnology and compares it to the evolutionary theoretical foundation that underlies the gender interpretations of materialist archaeology, the results are surprising. Time-honored assumptions enshrined in the working hypotheses and conclusions of many studies are not upheld. The ensuing patterns are very different from what was expected.

The data suggests that the environment of early human evolution was tropical forest not savanna. Forest fruits, nuts, and herbs were the staple foods of ancestral hominids, supplemented by small amounts of invertebrates and small game. To judge from primate and ethnographic studies in the tropical and subtropical zones, females, not males, would have been the main provisioners, tool makers, and users. With their young and their male and female associates, they constituted the only enduring social group. Mating was promiscuous, so the only strong genetic tie in social dominance was between mother and young. Males did not dominate females, and their social ranking was based on the influence of their mothers, to whom they deferred. Males were part of family groups primarily as sons and friends, not as progenitors. Since females tended to change troups in adolescence, they bonded with unrelated females and mated with the descendants of their associates.

The hominid record is still too poorly known to offer much evidence to test this scenario but one can say that the existing evidence does not contradict this scenario. Prehistory and paleoanthropology suggest that the earliest hominids and earliest tool makers did occupy the tropical rainforest and rely primarily on plant foods. The revised evolutionary theory can be used to design research to investigate specific, relevant features of the paleoanthropological record.

Comparable female provisioning and gender balance are characteristic of recent tropical and subtropical foragers. Only the most recently evolved human patterns resemble the patterns assumed to be innate and primeval by evolutionists. It is in some sedentary segmentary or ranked societies and in many state societies that one finds strong patterns of gender inequality, male dominance, provisioning, and violence toward women and children. What are the causal factors creating these distinct patterns through time? In primates, females are more parental than males because they have the most intimate experience with bearing and raising young. When males are faced with young to care for, they can do it, showing many of the same responses as females. In primates, females dominate sons due to seniority and sons' long conditioning as juniors leads to more submissive adult behavior. It is by grouping together and bonding with their sons and affiliates that females establish strong social positions and prevent harassment by males, who may be larger and stronger. Because mothers and their allies help each other and the young, when threatened, children's rank is influenced by mothers' rank. The females are more innovative and active with tools because they have the most experience using them. Because of the comparative abundance of food dispersed in the forests, food is either eaten individually or shared, not fought over violently. For the same reasons, relations with outsiders are not usually violent, and, because of the vegetation cover and ecology, predation is not a constant threat.

In hominids, many of these patterns would have continued, since we still see them at work among modern human foragers, but we know that systematic changes were taking place. Females would have had to increase the intensity of their gathering to support increasingly altricial young. Since presumably consumption of perennial staples could not be greatly increased, the increase would have to come from keystone foods, such as hard nuts, stem starch, or termites, which require tool-aided exploitation or preparation. Increasingly helpless young and having tools and food to carry would have encouraged bipedal locomotion. Those more successful at caring for altricial young, forming coalitions, intensifying food-getting, using tools, and walking upright would have had more young survive, and, slowly, infant helplessness, affect, intelligence, and social capacity would increase in successive generations and eventually reach the stage of fully human growth patterns, capacities, and skills. Males who could get along with the females and their young, rather than attacking and disrupting them or living alone or only with other males, would benefit from more access to food and mating opportunities, as well as group protection from predators. Their improved survival over the males who dispersed or were prone to conflict would increase sociality, affect, and non-aggressiveness in successive populations.

Among human foragers, females and their young are the core social group, because they are the main subsistence producers and socializers. Males depend on them for most of their food and social contact. In these groups, the product of one's labor tends to belong to oneself, so, since food is shared, women would have the most influence and independence. Because of the visibility of genetic relatedness of individuals to their mother, the matrilineal line tends to be an important tie, whereas, because of sexual promiscuity, the position of father as genitor may be weak. Because of the importance of female reproduction, female characteristics, such as menstruation, are considered ritually important and dangerously powerful. The craft products of females have ritual importance, and all who wish to participate in ceremonies need women to exchange ritual materials with. Residential associations are built on such webs of benefits and obligations. Even if a man has the physical strength to overpower a woman, the group usually does not permit this, and, if it happened, the man would lose social and economic support he required for survival and risk ritual defamation and death.

When societies became sedentary and produced their food, this allowed more permanent relation of individuals or corporate groups to resources, and differential capacity of land to produce led to differential wealth. Ape and hominid evolution had enhanced sociality and tolerance among individuals, so cultural conditioning for fierceness and fighting skill was necessary to prepare individuals to defend themselves violently and attack others. Crowding and fighting over resources eventually led to conquest of some groups over others, and socio-economic hierarchies of conquerors and conquered appeared. The development of military forces and strategic facilities to defend resources and structures allowed policing and further conquest. Some groups then had the force and economic power to compel rather than negotiate cooperation of others. Ownership of resources by some prevented economic independence and self-sufficiency of others. State structures tended to expropriate individual or corporate ownership of space, resources, facilities, and tools and conferred formal economic status on men through gender biased taxation. Women's ownership of goods and facilities were for the most part not formally recognized in these systems, which thus took away womens' power from their labor, know-how, and the products of their work. Men gained power through the establishment of formal military and political roles, tipping power relationships in favor of males over females. With time, these changes were written into laws and policies. Ruling groups worked to immobilize all local groups competing for power, including women's groups. Residential and social groupings that favored women's power and influence were outlawed, and nuclear households headed by males often became required by law. Women's and local corporate groups lost status and power in this process. Women's roles were also inhibited by gender biased regulations and laws about employment, craft production, and religious participation.

Although in small-scale societies women's reproductive functions do not prevent them from being the main food producers, complex societies sometimes force women to withdraw from work during menstruation and pregnancy. The political and ritual power that women have held through their reproductive and genealogical roles become limited through imposition of patriarchal genealogy incorporated in property and inheritance laws. In addition, some state religions have eliminated administrative positions for women and pushed them out of the religious hierarchy. This happened both in Islam and the Christian church. Anglo-Saxon women clergy not only ran nunneries and parish churches but also monasteries, but no Catholic women head parishes or monasteries today. In nineteenth- and early 20th-century Euroamerican nations, the law as well as customs of middle-class propriety often prevented women from attending universities, medical schools, and law schools. Limited in this way from professional education and credentials, women were kept out of the most lucrative and influential professions. International aid organizations to postcolonial countries introduced forms of economic and educational gender bias by giving agricultural extension and fellowship only to men, even where women continued to be the main food-producers. Thus, the patriarchal societies of the temperate regions were imposed upon the tropics.

In this sequence, the social conditions for systematic gender inequality did not exist until the Holocene in most regions and thus would not have been present during the evolution of most of our genome. The ideologies and social systems of patriarchal states have all appeared on a time-scale too short to allow for significant genetic embedding. On both counts gender inequality cannot therefore be attributed to ineluctable genetic patterns. Rather, the conditions for their appearance are historically situated and explained. Encouraged or enforced by enculturation, education, law, administration, and religion, they obviously can be undone.

Bibliography

Absy, M. L. 1979. "A Palynological Study of Holocene Sediments in the Amazon Basin." Ph.D. diss., University of Amsterdam.

Ahlstrom, Richard V. N., Mark L. Chenault, M. Zyniecki, and David H. Greenwald. 1995. "Chronology, Compound Growth, and Demography." In David H. Greenwald, Mark L. Chenault, and Dawn M. Greenwald, eds. and comps., *The Sky Harbor Project: Early Desert Farming and Irrigation Settlements: Archaeological Investigations in the Phoenix Sky Harbor Center, Volume 3: Pueblo Salado* (379–92). SWCA Anthropological Research Paper No. 4, Flagstaff, Arizona.

Aiello, L., and P. Wheeler. 1995. "The Expensive-Tissue Hypothesis: The Brain and Digestive System in Human and Primate Evolution. *Current Anthropology* 36: 199–221.

Aikens, C. M., and T. Higuchi. 1982. *Prehistory of Japan.* New York: Academic Press.

Albeck, María Ester. In press. *Areas de Actividad Doméstica en Pueblo Viejo de Tucute.* Estudios Atacameños, Universidad Católica del Norte, Jujuy, Chile.

Alcina, Francisco I. 1668. *History of the Bisayan Islands,* pt. 1, bk. 4. Translated by P. S. Lietz. Chicago: University of Chicago, Philippine Studies Program.

Allan, Sarah 1991. *The Shape of the Turtle: Myth, Art, and Cosmos in Early China.* Albany: State University of New York Press.

———. 1997. *The Way of Water and Sprouts of Virtue.* Albany: State University of New York Press.

Allen, Terry. 1988. *Five Essays on Islamic Art.* Sebastopol, Calif.: Solipsist Press.

Alt, K., Munz, M., and W. Vach. 1995. "Hallstattzeitliche Grabhügel im Spiegel ihrer biologischen und sozialen Strukturen am Beispiel des Hügelgräberfeldes von Dattingen, Kr. Breisgau-Hochschwarzwald." *Germania* 73(2): 281–316.

Ambrose, S. H., and M. DeNiro. 1989. "Climate and Habitat Reconstruction Using Stable Carbon and Nitrogen Isotope Ratios of Collagen in Prehistoric Herbivore Teeth from Kenya." *Quaternary Research* 31: 407–22.

Anderson, Benedict. 1972. "The Idea of Power in Javanese Culture." In C. Holt, ed., *Culture and Politics in Indonesia* (1–69). Ithaca, N.Y.: Cornell University Press.

Anderson, Wendy R. M. 1989. "Badarian Burials: Possible Indicators of Social Inequality in Middle Egypt during the Fifth Millennium B.C." M.A. thesis, McGill University.

———. 1992. "Badarian Burials: Evidence of Social Inequalities in Middle Egypt during the Early Predynastic Era." *Journal of Archaeological Research Center in Cairo* 29: 51–66.

Angelino, Henry, and Charles L. Shedd. 1955. "A Note on Berdache." *American Anthropologist* 57(1): 121–26.

Anonymous. 1565–67. "Relation of Occurrences in the Philippines after the Departure of 'San Pedro' to New Spain." In E. Blair and J. Robertson, eds., *The Philippine Islands,* vol. 2 (1903) (77–160). Cleveland: Arthur H. Clark Company.

Anthony, David. 1986. "'The Kurgan Culture,' Indo-European Origins, and the Domestication of the Horse: A Reconsideration." *Current Anthropology* 27(4): 291–313.

Anyang Work Team, Institute of Archaeology. 1977. "Anyang Yinku nuli jisikeng de fajue" [Excavation of the sacrificial pits of slaves at Yin ruins in Anyang]. *Kaogu* 1: 20–36.

———. 1981. "Anyang Xiatun cunbei de liangzuo yindaimu" [The two tombs of the Yin Dynasty excavated in the north of Xiaoton village, Anyang County]. *Kaogu Xuebao* 4: 491–518.

———. 1987. *Kaogu Xuebao* 1: 99–118.

Anyang Fajuedui, the Institute of Archaeology, CASS. 1976. "1975 nian Anyang Yinxu de xinfaxian" [New Discoveries at Yinxu, Anyang]. *Kaogu* 1: 264.

Aranyanak, Chiraporn. 1985. "Ancient Fabric Fragments from the Ban Chiang Culture Site." *Muang Boran* 11(1): 47–54.

Archer, J. 1998. *Report to the Meeting of the International Society for Aggression.* Ramapo, N.J.

Ardener, Shirley, ed. 1981. *Women and Space.* London: Croom Helm.

Ardrey, R. 1961. *African Genesis.* New York: Atheneum.

———. 1970. *The Social Contract: A Personal Inquiry into the Evolutionary Sources of Order and Disorder.* New York: Delta.

———. 1976. *The Hunting Hypothesis.* New York: Atheneum.

Arnold, Bettina. 1990. "The Deposed Princess of Vix: The Need for an Engendered European Prehistory." In Dale Walde and Noreen D. Willows, eds., *The Archaeology of Gender: Proceedings of the Twenty-Second Annual Conference of the Archaeological Association of the University of Calgary* (366–74). Calgary: University of Calgary.

———. 1991. "The Material Culture of Social Structure: Rank and Status in Early Iron Age Europe." Ph.D. diss., Harvard University.

———. 1996. "'Honorary Males' or Women of Substance? Gender, Status and Power in Iron Age Europe." *Journal of European Prehistory* 3(2): 153–68.

Arnold, Dean E. 1985. *Ceramic Theory and Cultural Process.* Cambridge: Cambridge University Press.

Arnold, Jeanne E. 1997. "Revisiting Power, Labor, and Kinship: Thoughts for the Development of Social Theory." Paper presented at the Social Theory in Archaeology: Setting the Agenda meeting, Snowbird, Utah.

Arnold, Philip J. III, and Robert Santley. 1993. "Household Ceramics Production at Middle Period Matacapan." In Robert S. Stanley and Kenneth G. Hirth, eds., *Prehispanic Domestic Units in Western Mesoamerica: Studies of the Household, Compound, and Residence* (227–48). Boca Raton, Fla.: CRC Press.

Arvey, Margaret. 1988. "Women of Ill-Repute in the Florentine Codex." In Virginia E. Miller, ed., *The Role of Gender in Precolumbian Art and Architecture* (179–204). Lanham, Md.: University Press of America.

Atkinson, Jane M., and Shelly Errington. 1990. *Power and Difference: Gender in Island Southeast Asia.* Palo Alto, Calif.: Stanford University Press.

Aziz, S. Atiya, ed. "Islamic Influences on Coptic Art." In *The Coptic Encyclopedia* (1310–12). New York: Macmillan.

Bacus, Elisabeth A. 1995. *Political Economy and Interaction: Late Prehistoric Polities in the Central Philippine Islands.* Ann Arbor, Mich.: University Microfilms, Inc.

———. In press. "Prestige and Potency: Political Economy of Protohistoric Visayan Polities." In E. A. Bacus and L. J. Lucero, eds., *Complex Polities in the Ancient Tropical*

World. Archaeological Papers of the American Anthropological Association No. 9. Washington, D.C.: American Anthropological Association.

Bacus, Elisabeth, et. al. 1993. *A Gendered Past: A Critical Bibliography of Gender in Archaeology.* University of Michigan Museum of Anthropology Technical Report 25. Ann Arbor, Mich.: Museum of Anthropology Publications.

Bailey, R., and N. Peacock. 1988. "Efe Pygmies of Northeastern Zaire: Subsistence Strategies in the Ituri Forest." In I. De Garine and G. Harrison, eds., *Coping with Uncertainty in Food Supply* (88–117). Oxford: Clarendon.

Baldwin, Robert. 1985. "Plutarch's Wife as Mirror in a German Renaissance Marriage Portrait." *Source: Notes in the History of Art* 4 (2/3): 68–71.

Barash, D. 1977. *Sociobiology and Behavior.* New York: Elsevier.

Bard, Kathryn A. 1987. "An Analysis of the Predynastic Cemeteries of Nagada and Armant in Terms of Social Differentiation, the Origin of State in Predynastic Egypt." Ph.D. diss., University of Toronto.

———. 1988. "A Quantitative Analysis of the Predynastic Burials in Armant Cemetery 1400–1500." *Journal of Egyptian Archaeology* 74: 39–55.

———. 1989. "The Evolution of Social Complexity in Predynastic Egypt: An Analysis of the Nagada Cemeteries." *Journal of Mediterranean Archaeology* 2(2): 223–48.

Barnard, Alan. 1992. *Hunters and Herders of Southern Africa: A Comparative Ethnography of the Khoisan Peoples.* Cambridge: Cambridge University Press.

Barnard, A., and T. Widlock. 1996. "Nharo and Hai//om Settlement Patterns in Comparative Perspective." In *Cultural Diversity among Twentieth-Century Foragers: An African Perspective,* ed. S. Kent, pp. 87–107. Cambridge: Cambridge University Press.

Barnes, Gina. 1993. *The Rise of Civilization in East Asia.* London: Thames and Hudson.

Barrett, J. 1994. *Fragments from Antiquity.* Oxford: Blackwell.

Bashilov, Vladimir A., and Leonid T. Yablonsky. 1995. "Introduction." in Davis-Kimball et al., eds., *Nomads of the Early Iron Age* (xi–xv). Berkeley, Calif.: Zinat Press.

Basilov, V. N. 1984. "The Study of Shamanism in Soviet Ethnography." in M. Hoppal, ed., *Shamanism in Eurasia* (46–63). Gottingen: Herodot.

———, ed. 1989a. *Nomads of Eurasia.* Seattle: Natural History Museum of Los Angeles County.

———, ed. 1989b. "Introduction." in *Nomads of Eurasia* (1–8). Seattle: Natural History Museum of Los Angeles County.

Basilov, V. N., and Natal'ya L. Zhukovskaya. 1989. "Religious Beliefs." In V. N. Basilov, ed., *Nomads of Eurasia* (161–81). Seattle: Natural History Museum of Los Angeles County.

Baumgartel, Elise J. 1947. *The Cultures of Prehistoric Egypt.* London: Oxford University Press.

———. 1970. *Petrie's Nagada Excavation: A Supplement.* London: Bernard Quaritch.

Bawden, Garth. 1982. "Community Organization Reflected by the Household: A Study of Pre-Columbian Social Dynamics." *Journal of Field Archaeology* 9(2): 165–81.

Bayard, D. T. 1984. "Rank and Wealth at Nom Nok Tha: The Mortuary Evidence." In *Southeast Asian Archaeology at the XV Pacific Science Congress* (82–128). Dunedins: Otago University Studies in Prehistoric Anthropology.

Beckerman, S. 1994. "Hunting and Fishing in Amazonia: Hold the Answers, What Are the Questions?" In A. C. Roosevelt, ed., *Amazonian Indians from Prehistory to the Present* (177–202). Tucson: University of Arizona Press.

Beckerman, S., R.Lizarralde, C. Ballew, S. Schroeder, C. Fingelton, A. Garrison, and H. Smith. 1998. "The Bari Partible Paternity Project: Preliminary Results." *Current Anthropology* 39(1): 164–647.

Benfer, R. A. 1990. "The Preceramic Site of Paloma, Peru: Bioindications of Improving Adaptation to Sedentism." *Latin American Antiquity* 1: 284–318.

Berberian, Eduardo, et al. 1989. *Sistemas de Asentamiento Prehispanicos en el Valle de Tafí.* Cordoba, Argentina: Comechingonia, Revista de Antropología e Historia.

Biesele, Megan. 1993. *Women Like Meat: The Folklore and Foraging Ideology of the Kala-hari Ju/'hoan*. Johannesburg: Witwatersrand University Press; Bloomington: Indiana University Press.

Binford, Lewis R. 1962. "Archaeology as Anthropology." *American Antiquity* 28(2): 217–25.

Blackwood, Evelyn. 1984. "Sexuality and Gender in Certain Native American Tribes: The Case of Cross-Gender Females." *Signs: Journal of Women in Culture and Society* 10(1): 27–42.

Blair, Emma, and James Robertson. 1903–6. *The Philippine Islands*. 55 vols. (1493–1898). Cleveland: Arthur H. Clark Company.

Blake, T. Michael, and John Clark. 1989. "The Emergence of Hereditary Inequality: The Case of Pacific Coastal Chiapas, Mexico." Paper presented at the Circum-Pacific Pre-history Conference, Seattle.

Blanc-Szanton, Cristina. 1990. "Collision of Cultures: Historical Reformulations of Gen-der in the Lowland Visayas, Philippines." In J. M. Atkinson and S. Errington, eds., *Power and Difference: Gender in Island Southeast Asia* (345–83). Palo Alto, Calif.: Stanford University Press.

Blanton, Richard E. 1994. *Houses and Households: A Comparative Study*. New York: Plenum Press.

Bleek, D. F. 1928. *The Naron, a Bushman Tribe of the Central Kalahari*. Cambridge: Cam-bridge University Press.

Bleek, W. H. I. 1924. *The Mantis and His Friends; Bushman Folklore Collected by the Late Dr. W. H. I. Bleek and the Late Dr. Lucy C. Lloyd*, ed. D. F. Bleek. Cape Town: T.M. Miller; London and Oxford: B. Blackwell.

Boaz, N. T. 1997. *How the Human Being Emerged from the Cataclysmic History of the Earth*. New York: Basic Books.

Bodenhorn, Barbara. 1990. "I'm Not the Great Hunter, My Wife Is." *Études/Inuit/Studies* 14(1–2): 55–74.

Boesch, C. 1994. "Is Nutcracking in Wild Chimpanzees a Cultural Behavior?" *Journal of Human Evolution* 26(4): 325–38.

Bolgar, Diane. 1996. "Figurines, Fertility and the Emergence of Complex Society in Pre-historic Cyprus." *Current Anthropology* 37(2): 365–72.

Bonnefille, R. 1995. "A Reassessment of the Plio-Pleistocene Pollen Record of East Africa." In E. S. Vrba, G. H. Denton, T. C. Partridge, and L. H. Buckle, eds., *Paleocli-mate and Evolution with Emphasis on Human Origins* (299–310). New Haven, Conn.: Yale University Press.

Borkovenko, N. A. 1994. "Tomb of Saka Princes Discovered in the Sayans, Siberia." In A.G. Kosintsev, ed., *New Archaeological Discoveries in Asiatic Russia and Central Asia* (48–53). St. Petersburg: Institute of History of Material Culture.

Bourdieu, Pierre 1973. "The Berber House." In Mary Douglas, ed., *Rules and Meaning* (98–110). London: Penguin Books.

Boxer MS. 1590. "Boxer's Codex." In F. L. Jocano, ed., *The Philippines at the Spanish Contact* (1975) (188–235). Manila: MCS Enterprises.

Brain, C. K. 1981. *The Hunters and the Hunted? An Introduction to African Cave Taphon-omy*. Chicago: University of Chicago Press.

Brandt, Elizabeth, and Katherine A. Spielmann. 1998. "Sociopolitical Organization in the Pueblo IV Period." Prepared for *Migration and Reorganization: The Pueblo IV Period in the American Southwest*. Manuscript in possession of the author, Department of Anthropology, Arizona State University, Tempe.

Braun, David. 1985. "Ceramic Decorative Diversity and Illinois Woodland Regional Inte-gration." In Ben Nelson, ed., *Decoding Prehistoric Ceramics* (128–53). Carbondale: Southern Illinois University Press.

Brown, Betty Ann. 1983. "Seen but Not Heard: Women in Aztec Ritual—The Sahagun Texts." In Janet C. Berlo, ed., *Text and Image in Pre-Columbian Art* (119–54). British Archaeological Reports International Series 180. Oxford: Oxford University Press.

Browner, C. H. 1991. "Women and Economic Change in Rural Mexico." *Peasant Studies* 19(1, fall): 5–20.

Brumbach, Hetty Jo, and Robert Jarvenpa. 1990. "Archeologist-Ethnographer-Informant Relations: The Dynamics of Ethnoarchaeology in the Field." In Sarah M. Nelson and Alice B. Kehoe, eds., *Powers of Observation: Alternative Views in Archeology* (39–46). Archeological Papers of the American Anthropological Association No. 2. Washington, D.C.: American Anthropological Association.

Brumfiel, Elizabeth M. 1991. "Weaving and Cooking: Women's Production in Aztec Mexico." In J. Gero and M. Conkey, eds., *Engendering Archaeology: Women and Prehistory* (224–51). Cambridge: Basil Blackwell.

———. 1992. "Distinguished Lecture in Archaeology: Breaking and Entering the Ecosystem—Gender, Class, and Faction Steal the Show." *American Anthropologist* 94: 551–67.

———. 1996. "Figurines and Ideological Domination." In R. P. Wright, ed., *Gender in Archaeology: Research in Gender and Practice* (143–66). Philadelphia: University of Pennsylvania Press.

Brunton, G. 1937. *Mostagedda and the Tasian Culture*. London: Quartich.

———. 1948. *Matmar*. London: Quartich.

Brunton, G., and G. Caton-Thomspon. 1928. *The Badarian Civilization and Prehistoric Remains near Badari*. London: Quartich.

Buikstra, Jane, Lyle Konigsberg, and Jill Bullington. 1986. "Fertility and the Development of Agriculture in the Prehistoric Midwest." *American Antiquity* 51: 528–46.

Bullough, Vern L., and Bonnie Bullough. 1993. *Cross-Dressing, Sex and Gender*. Philadelphia: University of Pennsylvania Press.

Bunkacho (Agency for Cultural Affairs), ed. 1997. *Hakkutsu sereta Nippon Reto '97* [Excavations in the Japanese archipelago '97]. Tokyo: Asahi Shimbunsha.

Bunker, Emma. 1970. "The Animal Style." In Emma Bunker, Bruce Chatwin, and Ann Farkas, eds., *"Animal Style" Art from East to West* (12–15). New York: Asia Society.

Buol, S. W., F. D. Hole, R. J. McCracken. 1989. *Soil Genesis and Classification*. Ames: Iowa State University Press.

Burbank, V. C. 1994. *Fighting Women: Anger and Aggression in Aboriginal Australia*. Berkeley and Los Angeles: University of California Press.

Bushée, Eric. 1995. "Degenerative Joint Disease of the Chiggerville Site (15)h1) as an Indicator of Biomechanical Stress." Paper presented at the annual meeting of the Kentucky Heritage Council Archaeological Conference, Richmond.

Butler, Judith. 1990. *Gender Trouble: Feminism and the Subversion of Identity*. New York: Routledge.

———. 1993. *Bodies That Matter: On the Discursive Limits of "Sex."* New York: Routledge.

Carr, C. 1995. "Mortuary Practices: Their Social, Philosophical-Religious, Circumstantial, and Physical Determinants." *Journal of Archaeological Method and Theory* 2(2): 105–200.

Carroll, R. W. 1997. "Feeding Ecology of the Western Lowland Gorilla (*Gorilla gorilla gorilla*) in the Central African Republic." Ph.D. diss., Yale University.

Cartmill, M. 1993. *A View to Death in the Morning: Hunting and Nature through History*. Cambridge, Mass.: Harvard University Press.

Cassano, S., and A. Manfredini, eds. 1983. *Studi sul Neolitico del Tavoliere della Puglia*. British Archaeological Reports International Series 160. Oxford: Oxford University Press.

Cassano, S. M., A. Cazzella, A. Manfredini, and M. Moscoloni. 1987. *Coppa Nevigata e il suo territorio: Testimonianze archeologiche dal VII al II millennio a.C.* Rome: Quasar.

Cassidy, Claire. 1984. "Skeletal Evidence for Prehistoric Subsistence Adaptation in the Central Ohio River Valley." In Mark Cohen and George Armelagos, eds., *Paleopathology at the Origins of Agriculture* (307–45). Orlando: Academic Press.

Castillos, Juan José. 1979. "An Analysis of the Tombs in the Predynastic Cemetery N 7000 at Naga-ed-Der." *Journal of the Society for the Study of Egyptian Antiquities* 10(1): 21–38.

———. 1982. "Analyses of Egyptian Predynastic and Early Dynastic Cemeteries: Final Conclusions." *Journal of the Society for the Study of Egyptian Antiquities,* no. 12: 29–53.

Center for Archaeological Operations. 1981. *Maizo Bunkazai Nyusu* [Buried Cultural Properties News], No. 34. Nara, Japan: Nara National Institute for Cultural Properties Research.

———. 1999. *Maizo Bunkazai Nyusu* [Buried Cultural Properties News], No. 89. Nara, Japan: Nara National Institute for Cultural Properties Research.

Chang, Kwang-chih. 1980. *Shang Civilization.* New Haven, Conn.: Yale University Press.

———. 1983. *Art, Myth and Ritual: The Path to Political Authority in China.* Cambridge, Mass.: Harvard University Press.

Chao Ju-Kua. 1225. *Chu Fan Chih* [An account of the various barbarians]. Translated in W. H. Scott, *Prehispanic Source Materials for the Study of Philippine History* (68–70). Quezon City: New Day Publishers.

Cheal, David. 1989. "Strategies of Resource Management in Household Economies: Moral Economy or Political Economy?" In Richard R. Wilk, ed., *The Household Economy: Reconsidering the Domestic Mode of Production* (11–22). Boulder, Colo.: Westview Press.

Cheng-lang, Chang. 1986. "A Brief Discussion of Fu Tzu." In K. C. Chang, ed., *Studies of Shang Archaeology* (103–19). New Haven, Conn.: Yale University Press.

Childs-Johnson, Elizabeth. 1991. "Jades of the Hongshan Culture: The Dragon and Fertility Cult Worship." *Arts Asiatiques* 46: 82–95.

Chirino, Pedro. 1604a. "Of Marriages, Dowries, and Divorces among the Filipinos." In F. L. Jocano, ed., *The Philippines at the Spanish Contact* (125–46). Manila: MCS Enterprises.

———. 1604b. *Relacion de las Islas Filipinas.* Translated by R. Echevarria. Historical Conservation Society 15. Manila: Bookmark, 1969.

Chlenova, Natal'ya L. 1994. "On the Degree of Similarity between Material Culture Components within the 'Scythian World.' " In Bruno Genito, ed., *The Archaeology of the Steppes: Methods and Strategies* (499–540). Naples: Instituto Universitario Orientale.

Cipolloni Sampò. 1983. "Scavi nel villaggio neolitico di Rendina." *Origini* 11: 183–323.

Cipriani, L. 1953. "Report on a Survey of the Little Andaman during 1951–53." *Bulletin of the Anthropological Survey of India* 2(1): 61–82.

———. 1966. *The Andaman Islanders.* London: Weidenfeld and Nicolson.

Claassen, Cheryl. 1991. "Gender, Shellfishing, and the Shell Mound Archaic." In Joan Gero and Margaret Conkey, eds., *Engendering Archaeology: Women and Prehistory* (276–300). New York: Blackwell.

Claassen, Cheryl, and Rosemary A. Joyce, eds. 1997. *Women in Prehistory, North America and Mesoamerica.* Philadelphia: University of Pennsylvania Press.

Claessen, Henry J., and Jarich G. Oosten, eds. 1996. *Ideology and the Early State.* Leiden: E. J. Brill.

Clark, J. D. 1971. *The Prehistory of Africa.* New York: Praeger.

Clark, John E. 1983. "A Preclassic Mesoamerican Society: Analysis of Francesca-Phase Burials from Chiapa de Corzo, Mexico." Unpublished paper.

Clark, John E., and William J. Parry. 1990. "Craft Specialization and Cultural Complexity." *Research in Economic Anthropology* 12: 289–346.

Clark, R. T. 1959. *Myth and Symbol in Ancient Egypt.* London: Thames and Hudson.

Cohen, M. N., and S. Bennett. 1993. "Skeletal Evidence for Sex Roles and Gender Hierarchies in Prehistory." In Barbara D. Miller, ed., *Sex Roles and Gender Hierarchies* (273–96). Cambridge: Cambridge University Press.

———. 1998. "Skeletal Evidence for Gender Hierarchies." In K. Hays-Gilpin and D. Whitley, eds., *Reader in Gender Archaeology* (297–317). New York: Routledge.

Collier, J., and R. Rosaldo. 1981. "Politics and Gender in Simple Societies." In S. Ortner and H. Whitehead, eds., *Sexual Meanings: The Cultural Construction of Gender and Sexuality* (275–329). Cambridge: Cambridge University Press.

Collins, Jane L. 1986. "The Household and Relations of Production in Southern Peru." *Comparative Studies in Society and History* 28: 651–71.

Colyn, M., A. Gautier-Hion, and W. Verheyen. 1991. A Re-Appraisal of Palaeoenvironmental History in Central Africa: Evidence for a Major Fluvial Refuge in the Zaire Basin." *Journal of Biogeography* 18: 403–7.

Condominas, George. 1977. *We Have Eaten the Forest*. New York: Hill and Wang.

Conkey, Margaret, and Joan Gero. 1991. "Tensions, Pluralities, and Engendering Archaeology: An Introduction to Women and Prehistory." In J. Gero and M. Conkey, eds., *Engendering Archaeology: Women and Prehistory* (3–30). Oxford: Basil Blackwell.

———. 1997. "Programme to Practice: Gender and Feminism in Archaeology." *Annual Review of Anthropology* 26: 411–37.

Conkey, Margaret W., and Janet Spector. 1984. "Archaeology and the Study of Gender." *Archaeological Method and Theory* 7: 1–38.

Conkey, Margaret W., and Ruth E. Tringham. 1995. "Archaeology and the Goddess: Exploring the Contours of Feminist Archaeology." In D. C. Stanton and A. J. Stewart, eds., *Feminism in the Academy* (199–247). Ann Arbor: University of Michigan Press.

Cook, Della. 1984. "Subsistence and Health in the Lower Illinois Valley: Osteological Evidence. In Mark Cohen and George Armelagos, eds., *Paleopathology at the Origins of Agriculture* (235–69). Orlando: Academic Press.

Cook, Della, and Jane Buikstra. 1979. "Health and Differential Survival in Prehistoric Populations: Prenatal Dental Defects." *American Journal of Physical Anthropology* 51: 649–64.

Cooper, Zarine. 1985. "Archaeological Explorations in the Andaman Islands." *Bulletin of the Indo-Pacific Prehistory Association* 6: 27–39.

———. 1987. "A Report on Archaeological Investigations in the Andaman Islands from 1984 to 1986." Unpublished manuscript.

———. 1988. "Shell Artifacts from the Andaman Islands." *Australian Archaeology* 26: 24–41.

———. 1989. "Analysis of the Nature of Contacts with the Andaman Islands during the Last Two Millennia." *South Asian Studies* 5: 133–47.

———. 1990. "Archaeological Evidence for Resource Exploitation in the Andaman Islands." *Man and Environment* 15(1) : 73–81.

———. 1993a. "The Origins of the Andaman Islanders: Local Myth and Archaeological Evidence." *Antiquity* 67: 394–99.

———. 1993b. "Perceptions of Time in the Andaman Islands." *World Archaeology* 25(2): 261–67.

———. 1994. "The Relevance of the Study of Abandoned Onge Encampments in Understanding the Archaeological Record in the Andaman Islands." In B. Allchin, ed., *Living Traditions: Studies in the Ethnoarchaeology of South Asia* (235–63). New Delhi: Oxford University Press and IBH Publishing.

———. 1997a. "The Salient Features of Site Location in the Andaman Islands, Indian Ocean." *Asian Perspectives* 36(2): 220–31.

———. 1997b. *Prehistory of the Chitrakot Falls*. Pune: Ravish Publishers.

Cooper, Zarine, and Sandra Bowdler. 1998. "Flaked Glass Tools from the Andaman Islands and Australia." *Asian Perspectives* 37(1): 74–83.

Cooper, Z., and H. Raghavan. 1988. "Analyses of Sediments from a Cave in the Andaman Islands." *Man and Environment* 12: 67–74.

————. 1989. "Petrographic Features of Andamanese Pottery." *Indo-Pacific Prehistory Association Bulletin* 9: 22–32.

Copeland, Rebbeca L. 1994. "Hiratsuka Raicho." In Chieko I. Mulhem, ed., *Japanese Women Writers: Bio-Critical Sourcebook* (132–43). Westport, Conn.: Greenwood Press.

Costin, Cathy L. 1991. "Craft Specialization: Issues in Defining, Documenting and Explaining the Organization of Production." *Archaeological Method and Theory* 3: 1–56.

————. 1996. "Exploring the Relationship between Gender and Craft in Complex Societies: Methodological and Theoretical Issues of Gender Attribution." In R. Wright, ed., *Gender and Archaeology* (111–40). Philadelphia: University of Pennsylvania Press.

Creswell, K. A. C. 1969. *Early Muslim Architecture*. Oxford: Clarendon Press.

————. 1989. *A Short Account of Early Muslim Architecture*. Revised and supplemented by James W. Allen. Cairo: The American University in Cairo Press.

Crown, Patricia, and W. H. Wills. N.d. *The Origins of Southwestern Ceramic Containers: Women's Time Allocation and Economic Intensification*. Albuquerque: University of New Mexico Press.

Csordas, Thomas, J., ed. 1994. *Embodiment and Experience: The Existential Ground of Culture and Self*. Cambridge: Cambridge University Press.

Cyphers Guillén, Ann. 1993. "Women, Rituals, and Social Dynamics at Ancient Chalcatzingo." *Latin American Antiquity* 4: 209–24.

Dagg, A. I. 1999. "Infanticide by Male Lions Hypothesis: A Fallacy Influencing Research into Human Behavior. *American Anthropologist* 100(4): 940–50.

Dahlberg, Frances, ed. 1981. *Woman the Gatherer*. New Haven, Conn.: Yale University Press.

D'Altroy, Terrance, and Timothy K. Earle. 1985. "Staple Finance, Wealth Finance, and Storage in the Inka Political Economy." *Current Anthropology* 26: 187–206.

Dalupan, Maria. 1985. "Long-Distance Trade and Pre-Hispanic Social Differentiation in the Lowland Philippines: A View from the Grave." Paper presented at the 12th Congress of the Indo-Pacific Prehistory Association. Penablanca, Philippines.

Dart, R. A. 1953. "The Predatory Transition from Ape to Man." *International Anthropological and Linguistic Review* 1: 201–18.

Darwin, C. 1979. *The Descent of Man and Selection in Relation to Sex*. Norwalk, Conn.: Easton Press. Original edition, New York: George Macy Companies, 1871.

Dasmarinas, G. P. 1591. "Letter to Felipe II." In E. Blair and J. Robertson, eds., *The Philippine Islands,* vol. 8 (1903) (142–68). Cleveland: Arthur H. Clark Company.

Davies, M., ed. 1994. *Women and Violence: Realities and Responses Worldwide*. London: Zed Books.

Davis-Kimball, Jeannine. 1995. "Excavations at Pokrovka, Russia 1990–1994." *Old World Archaeology Newsletter* 18(2): 12–17.

————. 1997/98. "Amazons, Priestesses and Other Women of Status." *Silk Route Art and Archaeology* 5: 1–45.

————. 1998. "Statuses of Eastern Early Iron Age Nomads." In Mark Pearce and Maurizio Tosi, eds., *Papers from the EAA Third Annual Meeting at Ravenna 1997,* vol. 1 (142–52). British Archaeological Reports International Series 717. Oxford: Oxford University Press.

Dawkins, Richard. 1989. *The Selfish Gene*. Oxford: Oxford University Press.

De Artiedo, Diego. 1573. "Relation of the Western Islands Called Filipinos." In E. Blair and J. Robertson, eds., *The Philippine Islands,* vol. 3 (1903) (190–208). Cleveland: Arthur H. Clark Company.

De la Torre, Amalia. 1996. "The Surigao del Norte Archaeological Project." *Indo-Pacific Prehistory: The Chiang Mai Papers. Bulletin of the Indo-Pacific Prehistory Association* 14: 177–85.

De Lavezaris, Guido, et al. 1567. "Letter to Felipe II from the Royal Officials." In E. Blair and J. Robertson, eds., *The Philippine Islands,* vol. 34 (1906) (204–12). Cleveland: Arthur H. Clark Company.

De Loarca, Miguel. 1582. "Relacion de las Yslas Filipinas." In E. Blair and J. Robertson, eds., *The Philippine Islands,* vol. 5 (1903) (34–187). Cleveland: Arthur H. Clark Company.

De Menocal, P. B. 1995. "Plio-Pleistocene African Climate." *Science* 270: 53–58.

De Morga, Antonio. 1609a. "Relation of the Philippine Islands and of Their Natives, Antiquity, Customs, and Government." In M. Garcia, ed., *Readings in Philippine Prehistory* (1979) (266–306). Manila: Filipiniana Book Guild.

———. 1609b. "Sucesos de las Islas Filipinas." In E. Blair and J. Robertson, eds., *The Philippine Islands,* vol. 16 (1904) (25–209). Cleveland: Arthur H. Clark Company.

Demoule, Jean-Pierre. 1989. "D'un âge a l'autre: Temps, style et société dans la transition Hallstatt/La Tène." In M. Ulrix-Closset and M. Otte, eds., *Hallstatt: La Civilisation de Hallstatt* (141–71). Etudes et Recherches Archéologique de l'Université de Liège No. 36. Liège: Université de Liège.

Denny, Dallas. 1994. *Gender Dysphoria: A Guide to Research.* New York: Garland.

De Ploey, J., J. Lepersonne, and G. Stoops. 1968. *Sedimentologie et Origine des Sables de la Series des Sables Ocre et de la Serie des "Gres Polymorphes" (Systeme du Kalahari) au Congo Occidentale.* Serie Sciences Geologiques No. 61. Tervuren, Belgium: Musee Royal de l'Afrique Centrale.

DeRaedt, Jeles. 1991. "Similarities and Differences in Lifestyles in the Central Cordillera of Northern Luzon, Philippines." In A. Terry Rambo and Kathleen Gillogly, eds., *Profiles in Cultural Evolution.* Museum of Anthropology Papers No. 85. Ann Arbor: University of Michigan.

Derrida, J. 1967. *Writing and Difference.* Translated by Alan Bass. Chicago: University of Chicago Press.

De Waal, F. 1996. *Good Natured: The Origins of Right and Wrong in Humans and Other Animals.* Cambridge: Harvard.

De Waal, F., and F. Lanting. 1997. *Bonobo: The Forgotten Ape.* Berkeley and Los Angeles: University of California Press.

Dizon, Eusebio. 1996. "The Anthropomorphic Pottery from Ayub Cave, Pinol, Maitum, South Cotabato, Mindanao, Philippines." *Indo-Pacific Prehistory: The Chiang Mai Papers. Bulletin of the Indo-Pacific Prehistory Association* 14: 186–96.

Dobres, Marcia-Anne. 1995. "Gender and prehistoric technology: on the social agency of technical strategies." *World Archaeology* 27 (1) : 25–49.

Dong Zoubin. 1945. *Yin Lipu.* Li-chuang: Institute of History and Philology, Academia Sinica.

Dornan, S. 1975. *Pygmies and Bushmen of the Kalahari.* Cape Town: C. Struik.

Downs, D. 1996. *More Than Victims: Battered Women, the Syndrome, Society, and the Law.* Chicago: University of Chicago Press.

Dowson, T. A. 1992. *Rock Engravings of Southern Africa.* Johannesburg: Witwatersrand University Press.

Dowson, T. A., and D. Lewis-Williams, eds. 1994. *Contested Images: Diversity in Southern African Rock Art Research.* Johannesburg: Witwatersrand University Press.

Draper, Patricia. 1975. "Cultural Pressure on Sex Differences." *American Ethnologist* 2: 602–16.

Draper, Patricia, and Elizabeth Cashden. 1988. "Technological Change and Child Behavior among the !Kung." *Ethnology* 27: 339–65.

Dufour, D. 1994. "Diet and Nutritional Status of Amazonian Peoples." In A. C. Roosevelt, ed., *Amazonian Indians from Prehistory to the Present* (123–59). Tucson: University of Arizona Press.

DuQuesne, T. 1995. " 'Semen of the Bull': Reflections on the Symbolism of Maat with Reference to Recent Studies." *Discussions in Egyptology* 32: 107–16.

Dutton, D. G. 1995. *The Domestic Assault of Women.* Vancouver: University of British Columbia Press.

Echevarria, Ramon. 1974. *Rediscovery in Southern Cebu.* Cebu City: Historical Conservation Society.

Eder, James F. 1984. "The Impact of Subsistence Change on Mobility and Settlement Pattern in a Tropical Foraging Economy: Some Implications for Archaeology." *American Anthropologist* 86: 837–53.

Egami Namio, ed. 1995. *Nippon Minzoku no Genryu* [Origins of the Japanese people]. Tokyo: Kodansha.

Ehlers, Tracy Bachrach. 1990. *Silent Looms: Women and Production in a Guatemalan Town.* Boulder, Colo.: Westview Press.

Ehrenreich, Robert M., Carole L. Crumley, and Janet E. Levy, eds. 1995. *Heterarchy and the Analysis of Complex Societies.* Archeological Papers of the American Anthropological Association No. 6. Washington, D.C.: American Anthropological Association.

Ekins, Richard, and Dave King. 1996. *Blending Genders: Social Aspects of Cross-Dressing and Sex Changing.* New York: Routledge.

Elad, A. 1994. *Medieval Jerusalem and Islamic Worship: Holy Places, Ceremonies, Pilgrimage.* Leiden: Brill.

Elenga, H., D. Schwartz, and A.Vincens. 1994. "Pollen Evidence of Late Quaternary Vegetation and Inferred Climate Changes in Congo." *Palaeogeography, Palaeoclimatology, Palaeoecology* 109: 345–56.

Eliade, Mircea. 1972. *Shamanism: Archaic Techniques of Ecstasy.* Princeton, N.J.: Princeton University Press.

Ellis, Chris. 1992. "A Statistical Analysis of the Protodynastic Burials in the 'Valley' Cemetery of Kafr Tarkhan." In Edwin C. M. van den Brink, ed., *The Nile Delta in Transition: 4th–3rd Millennium B.C.* (241–58). Distributed by Israel Exploration Society, Jerusalem.

Errington, Shelly. 1990. "Recasting Sex, Gender and Power: A Theoretical and Regional Overview." In J. M. Atkinson and S. Errington, eds., *Power and Difference: Gender in Island Southeast Asia* (1–58). Palo Alto, Calif.: Stanford University Press.

Esaka Teruya. 1960. *Dogu* [Clay figurines]. Tokyo: Azekura shobo.

Esaka Teruya, and Sakae Nishida. 1967. "Ehime-ken Kamikuroiwa ganin" [The rich shelter of Kamikuroiwa, Ehime prefecture]. In Special Committee to Investigate Cave Site, the Japanese Archaeological Association, ed., *Nippon no Dokutsu Iseki* [Cave sites of Japan] (224–36). Tokyo: Heibonsha.

Estioko-Griffin, A., and P. B. Griffin. 1981. "Woman the Hunter: The Agta." In F. Dahlberg, ed., *Woman the Gatherer* (121–51). New Haven, Conn.: Yale University Press.

Etienne, M., and E. Leacock. 1980. *Women and Colonization.* New York: Praeger.

Ettinghausen, Richard. 1962. *Arab Painting.* London: Skira.

Evans, Helen C., and William D. Wixom, eds. 1997. *The Glory of Byzantium: Art and Culture of the Middle Byzantine Era A.D. 843–1261.* New York: Metropolitan Museum of Art.

Eviota, Elizabeth Uy. 1992. *The Political Economy of Gender: Women and the Sexual Division of Labour in the Philippines.* London: Zed Books.

Fang Dianchun and Liu Baohua. 1984. "Discovery of the Hongshan Culture Jade Tombs at Hutougou of the Buxing County in Liaoning." *Wenwu* 6: 1–5.

Fang Dianchun and Wei Fan 1986a. "Excavating a Lost Culture." *China Reconstructs* (December): 33–39.

———. 1986b. "Brief Report on the Excavation of Goddess Temple and Stone Graves of the Hongshan Culture at Niuheliang in Liaoning Province." *Linohai Wenwu Xuegan* 8: 1–17.

Fawcett, C. D., and A. Lee. 1902. "A Second Study of the Variation and Correlation of the Human Skull, with Special Reference to the Nagada Crancia." *Biometrika* 1: 408–67.

Fawcett, Clare L. 1995. "Nationalism and Postwar Japanese Archaeology." In P. L. Kohl and C. Fawcett, eds., *Nationalism, Politics, and the Practice of Archaeology* (232–46). Cambridge: Cambridge University Press.

Fedigan, L. M. 1986. "The Changing Role of Women in Models of Hominid Evolution." *Annual Review of Anthropology* 15: 25–66.

Feng Fugen. 1981. "Simuwu ding zhuzao gongyi de zai yanjiu" [A reexamination of the casting technology of the Simuake tripod]. *Kaogu* 2: 177–82.

Fernandez, Albina P. 1996. "If Women Are the Best Men in the Philippines, Why Are They Invisible in History?" *Review of Women's Studies* 5–6: 123–40.

Fernandez-Jalvo, Y., C. Denys, P. Andrews, T. Williams, Y. Dauphin, and L. Humphreys. 1998. "Taphonomy and Palaeoecology of Olduvai Bed-I (Pleistocene, Tanzania)." *Journal of Human Evolution* 34: 137–72.

Fiddes, Nick. 1991. *Meat: A Natural Symbol*. London, New York: Routledge.

Fine Arts Department. 1986. *Archaeology of Four Region*. Bangkok: Hattasilpa. (in Thai)

———. 1988a. *Adit Isan*. Bangkok: Rongpim Kan Satsana. (in Thai)

———. 1988b. *Kanchanaburi: Background Information*. Bangkok: Department of Archaeology.

Fittkau, E. J., ed. 1968. *Biogeography and Ecology in South America*. The Hague: W. Junk.

Flenley, J. R. 1979. *The Equatorial Rain Forest: A Geological History*. Boston: Butterworth.

Fourie, L. 1928. "The Bushmen of South West Africa." *The Native Tribes of South West Africa*. Cape Town: Cape Times Limited.

Fox, Robert B. 1959. "The Calatagan Excavations: Two 15th Century Burial Sites in Batangas, Philippines." *Philippine Studies* 7(3) (entire issue).

———. 1970. *The Tabon Caves: Archaeological Explorations and Excavations on Palawan Island, Philippines*. Monograph of the National Museum No. 1. Manila: National Museum.

Frankel, David. 1997. "On Cypriot Figurines and the Origins of Patriarchy." *Current Anthropology* 38(1): 84–88.

Frankenberg, Susan, Donald Albertson, and Luci Kohn. 1988. "The Elizabeth Skeletal Remains: Demography and Disease." In Douglas Charles, Steven Leigh, and Jane Buikstra, eds., *The Archaic and Woodland Cemeteries at the Elizabeth Site in the Lower Illinois Valley* (103–19). Kampsville Archeological Center Research Series Vol. 7. Kampsville, Ill.: Center for American Archeology.

Frankenstein, Susan, and Michael Rowlands. 1978. "The Internal Structure and Regional Context of Early Iron Age Society in Southwestern Germany." *University of London Bulletin of the Institute of Archaeology* 15: 73–112.

Fraser, Antonia. 1988. *The Warrior Queens: The Legends and the Lives of the Women Who Have Led Their Nations in War*. New York: Random House.

Fuentes, A. 1999. "Re-Evaluating Primate Monogamy." *American Anthropologist* 100(4): 890–907.

Fujimori Eiichi. 1963. "Jomon chuki bunka no kosei" [The structure of the Middle Jomon culture]. *Kokogaku* 9(4): 18–29.

Fujimura (Hishida) Junko 1996. "Nippon kokogaku to genda" [Gender and Japanese archaeology]. *Joseishigaku* 6: 83–89.

———. 1998. "Genda kokogaku" [Archaeology of gender]. *Daikokai* [Voyages into History, Literature, and Thought] 22: 70–74.

———. 2000. "Danjo no bungyo no kigen" [The origins of the male/female division of labor]. In H. Tsude and M. Sahara, eds., *Kodaishi no Ronten 2: Onna to Otoko, Ie to Mura*

[Issues in ancient history 2: women and men, household and village] (77–98). Tokyo: Shogakkan.

Fujinuma Kunihiko. 1979. "Dogu" [Clay figurines]. In *Sekai Toji Zenshu. Vol. 1: Nippon Genshi* [Earthenware and porcelains of the world. Vol. 1: Ancient Japan] (177–84). Tokyo: Shogukkan.

Furon, R. 1963. *The Geology of Africa.* Translated by A. Hallam and L. Stevens. Edinburgh: Oliver and Boyd.

Garcia Moll, Roberto, Daniel Juarez Cossio, Carmen Pijoan Aguade, Maria Elena Salas Cuesta, and Marcela Salas Cuesta. 1991. *Catálogo de entierros de San Luis Tlatilco, México, Temporada IV.* Mexico, D.F.: Instituto Nacional de Antropología e Historia.

Gardner, Peter G. 1991. "Forager's Pursuit of Individual Autonomy." *Current Anthropology* 32, no. 5 (December 1991): 543–72.

Garlake, Peter S. 1995. *The Hunter's Vision: The Prehistoric Art of Zimbabwe.* Seattle: University of Washington Press.

Geertz, Clifford. 1980. *Negara: The Theatre State in Nineteenth Century Bali.* Princeton, N.J.: Princeton University Press.

Geller, P. 1998. "Analysis of Sex and Gender in a Maya Mortuary Context at Preclassic Cuello." M.A. thesis, University of Chicago.

Geniola, A, and A. M. Tunzi. 1980. "Espressioni cultuali e d'arte nella Grotta di Cala Scizzo presso Torre a Mare (Bari)." *Rivista di Scienze Preistoriche* 35: 125–46.

Geremia-Lachica, Maria M. 1996. "Panay's Babaylan: The Male Takeover." *Review of Women's Studies* 5–6: 52–60.

Gero, Joan. 2001. "Field Knots and Ceramic Beaus: Interpreting Gender in the Peruvian Early Intermediate Period." In C. Klein, ed., *Gender in Pre-Columbian America* (15–55). Washington, D.C.: Dumbarton Oaks Pre-Columbian Library.

Gero, Joan, and M. Cristina Scattolin. In press. "Hacia la Comprensión de la Jerarquización: Un Estudio desde Yutopian, Valle de Cajón." *Actas y Memorias del XI Congreso Nacional de Arqueología, Mendoza, Argentina.*

Ghirshman, R. 1962. *Parthes et Sassanides.* Paris.

Gilchrist, Roberta. 1999. *Gender and Archaeology: Contesting the Past.* London: Routledge.

Gilman, Patricia A. 1987. "Architecture as Artifact: Pit Structures and Pueblos in the American Southwest." *American Antiquity* 52(3): 538–64.

Gimbutas, Marja. 1982. *The Goddesses and Gods of Old Europe, 6500–3500 B.C.: Myths and Cult Images.* 2nd ed. London: Thames and Hudson.

Ginter, B., and J. K. Kozlowski. 1994. *Predynastic Settlement Near Armant: Studien zur Archaologie und Geschichte Altägyptens.* Band 6. Heidelberg: Heidelberger Orientverlag.

Goffman, Erving. 1979. *Gender Advertisements.* London: Macmillan.

González, Luis. 1994. "Producción Metalúrgica y la Emergencia de Jefaturas en el Noroeste Argentino." *Actas y Memorias del XI Congreso Nacional de Arqueología, Mendoza, Argentina* 1: 137–41.

Goodall, J. 1986. *The Chimpanzees of Gombe: Patterns of Behavior.* Cambridge: Belknap Press.

Goodison, Lucy, and Christine Morris, eds. 1998. *Ancient Goddesses: The Myths and the Evidence.* London: British Museum Press.

Goodman, Alan, John Lallo, George Armelagos, and Jerome Rose. 1984. "Health Changes at Dickson Mounds, Illinois (A.D. 950–1300)." In Mark Cohen and George Armelagos, eds., *Paleopathology at the Origins of Agriculture* (271–305). Orlando: Academic Press.

Gordon, L. 1998. *Heroes of Their Own Lives: The Politics and History of Family Violence.* New York: Penguin Books.

Gould, S. J. 1996. *The Mismeasure of Man.* New York: W. W. Norton.

Grabar, O. 1993. "Umayyad Palaces Reconsidered." *Ars Orientalis* 23: 98.

Grach, A. D. 1980. *Drevniye kochevniki v tsentre Asii.* Moscow: Nauka.

Graziosi, P. 1980. *Le pitture preistoriche della Grotta di Porto Badisco*. Firenze: Istituto Italiano di Preistoria e Protostoria.

Gregg, S. A. 1979–80. "A Material Perspective of Tropical Rainforest Hunter-Gatherers: The Semang of Malaysia." *Michigan Discussions in Anthropology* 5 (1–2): 117–35.

Griffin, P. Bion, and Agnes Estioko-Griffin, eds. 1985. *The Agta of Northeastern Luzon: Recent Studies*. Cebu City: San Carlos Publications.

Griswald, William A. 1992. "Measuring Social Inequality at Armant." In R. Friedman and B. Adams, eds., *The Followers of Horus: Studies Dedicated to Michael Allen Hoffman* (193–98). Oxford: Oxbow Books.

Guenther, Mathias Georg. 1989. *Bushman Folktales: Oral Traditions of the Nharo of Botswana and the /Xam of the Cape*. Weisbaden: F. Steiner Verlag.

Guo Dashun. 1995. "Hongshan and Related Cultures." In S. M. Nelson, ed., *The Archaeology of Northeast China: Beyond the Great Wall* (21–64). London: Routledge.

———. 1997. "Understanding the Burial Rituals of the Hongshan Culture through Jade." In Rosemary E. Scott, ed., *Chinese Jades* (27–36). Colloquies on Art and Archaeology in Asia No. 18. London: Percival David Foundation of Chinese Art.

Guo Dashun and Zhang Keju. 1984. "Brief Report on the Excavation of Construction Sites of Hongshan Culture at Dongshanzui in Kezuo County, Liaoning Province." *Wenwu* 11: 1–11.

Guthrie, T. D. no date. *Breaking the Code of Palaeolithic Art*. Unpublished manuscript.

Haaland, Gunnar, and Randi Haaland. 1995. "Who Speaks the Goddess's Language? Imagination and Method in Archaeological Research." *Norwegian Archaeological Review* 28: 105–121.

Hager, L. D., ed. 1997. *Women in Human Evolution*. London: Routledge.

Halberstam, Judith. 1992. "'Skinflick': Posthuman Gender in Jonathan Demme's 'The Silence of the Lambs'." *Camera Obscura* 27 (September 9): 35–52.

Hamada Kosaku and Mizuno Seiichi. 1938. *Hung-shan-hou, Chihieng, Prehistoric Sites at Hung-shan, Chihieng, in the Province of Jehol, ManchuEuo*. Ser. A, Vol. 6. Tokyo: Archaeologia Orientalis.

Hamann, Bryon. 1997. "Weaving and the Iconography of Prestige: The Royal Gender Symbolism of Lord 5 Flower's /Lady 4 Rabbit's Family." In C. Claassen and R. A. Joyce, eds., *Women in Prehistory: North America and Mesoamerica* (153–72). Philadelphia: University of Pennsylvania Press.

Hambly, Gavin R. G. 1998. *Women in the Medieval Islamic World*. New York: St. Martin's Press.

Hames, R. B., and W. T. Vickers. 1983. *Adaptive Responses of Native Amazonians*. New York: Academic Press.

Hamilton, A. D. 1982. *Environmental History of East Africa: A Study of the Quaternary*. London: Academic Press.

Hamilton, Naomi, et al. 1996. "Can We Interpret Figurines?" *Cambridge Archaeological Journal* 6(2): 281–307.

Hamilton, R. 1949. "Who Built Khirbat al-Mafjar?" *Levant* 1: 61–67.

———. 1988. *Walid and His Friends: An Umayyad Tragedy*. Oxford: Oxford Studies in Islamic Art.

Hamilton, W. D. 1964. "The Genetical Evolution of Social Behavior." *Journal of Theoretical Biology* 7: 1–52.

Hammel, Eugene A. 1984. "On the *** of Studying Household Form and Function." In Robert M. Netting, Richard R. Wilk, and E. J. Arnould, eds., *Households: Comparative and Historical Studies of the Domestic Group* (29–43). Berkeley and Los Angeles: University of California Press.

Hammond, Dorothy, and Alta Jablow. 1973. "Women: Their Economic Role in Traditional Societies." In *Current Topics in Anthropology: Theory, Method, and Content*. Module 35. Reading, Mass.: Addison-Wesley.

Han Kangxin and Qifeng Pan. 1985. "Anyang Yinxu zhongxiaomu rengude yanjiu." In *Anyang Yinxu Tougu Yanjiu* (50–53). Beijing: Wenwu Press.

Han Rubin. 1993. "Recent Archeological Metallurgical Achievements at the University of Science and Technology Beijing." Paper presented at the Chinese Archaeology Enters the 21st Century International Conference, Beijing, May 29.

Harada Masayuki. 1995. *Dogu* [Clay figurines]. Nippon no Bijutsu Series No. 345. Tokyo: Shibundo.

———. 1999. "Dogu: Jomon bunka no naka de hagukumare shuen to tomo ni shomet-sushita dainino dogu" [Figurines: The tools of the second category which flourished and disappeared with Jomon culture]. In T. Kobayashi, ed., *Saishin Jomon-gaku no Sekai* [Latest in the world of Jomon studies] (130–43). Tokyo: Asahi Shimbunsha.

Haraway, Donna J. 1989. *Primate Visions: Gender, Race, and Nature in the World of Modern Science*. New York: Routledge.

———. 1991. *Simians, Cyborgs, and Women: The Reinvention of Nature*. New York: Routledge.

Harlow, Mary. 1997. "Female into Male, Won't Go! Gender and Early Christian Asceticism." In J. Moore and E. Scott, eds., *Invisible People and Processes* (169–77). London: Leicester University Press.

Harunari, H. 1979. "Jomon banki no kongokyoju kitei" [Postmarital residence rules during the Final Jomon]. *Okayama Daigaku Hobungakubu Gakujutsu Kiyo: Shigaku-hen* 40: 25–63.

———. 1986. "Rules of Residence in the Jomon Period, Based on the Analysis of Tooth Extraction." In R. J. Pearson, G. L. Barnes, and K. L. Hutterer, eds., *Windows on the Japanese Past: Studies in Archaeology and Prehistory* (293–310). Ann Arbor: University of Michigan, Center for Japanese Studies.

Hassan, Fekri A. 1985. "Radiocarbon Chronology of Neolithic and Predynastic Sites in Upper Egypt and the Delta." *African Archaeological Review* 3: 95–116.

———. 1988. "The Predynastic of Egypt." *Journal of World Prehistory* 2(2): 135–85.

———. 1993. "Rock Art: Cognitive Schemata and Symbolic Interpretation." In G. Calegari, ed., *L'Arte d l'Ambiente del Sahara prehistorico: Dati e interpretazione*. Milan: Memorie della Societa Italiana di Scienze Naturali e del Museo Civico di Storia Naturale di Milano 26(2): 269–82.

———. 1996. "Grave Goods and Sociopolitical Change in Predynastic Egypt." Unpublished manuscript.

———. 1998. "Toward an Archaeology of Gender in Africa." In S. Kent, ed., *Gender in African Prehistory* (261–78). Walnut Creek, Calif.: AltaMira Press.

Hastorf, Christine A. 1991. "Gender, Space, and Food in Prehistory." In Joan M. Gero and Margaret Conkey, eds., *Engendering Archaeology: Women and Prehistory* (132–59). Oxford: Basil Blackwell.

Hauer, F. R., and G. A. Lamberti. 1996. *Methods in Stream Ecology*. San Diego: Academic Press.

Hawkes, K. 1997. "Hadza Women's Time Allocation, Offspring Provisioning, and the Evolution of Long Postmenopausal Life Spans." *Current Anthropology* 38: 551–77.

Hawkes, K., J. F. O'Connell, and N. G. Burton. 1995. "Hadza Children's Foraging: Juvenile Dependency, Social Arrangements, and Mobility among Hunter-Gatherers." *Current Anthropology* 36: 688–700.

Hayashi, Kensaku. 1977. "Jomon ki no bosei—Dai II bu: Itai no hairetsu, tokuni toihoko" [Mortuary system in the Jomon stage—Part 2: Fundamental features]. *Kokogaku Zasshi* 63(3): 211–46.

Hayden, Brian. 1995. "Pathways to Power: Principles for Creating Socioeconomic Inequalities." In T. Douglas Price and Gary M. Feinman, eds., *Foundations of Social Inequality* (15–86). New York: Plenum Press.

Hayden, Brian, and Aubrey Cannon. 1982. "The Corporate Group as an Archaeological Unit." *Journal of Anthropological Archaeology* 1: 132–58.

———. 1984. *The Structure of Material Systems: Ethnoarchaeology in the Maya Highlands*. SAA Papers No. 1. Washington, D.C.: Society for American Archaeology.

Hays-Gilpin, Kelley, and David S. Whitley, eds. 1998. *Reader in Gender Archaeology*. London: Routledge.

Hegmon, Michelle. 1992. "Archaeological Research on Style." *Annual Review of Anthropology* 21: 517–36.

———. 1995. *The Social Dynamics of Pottery Style in the Early Puebloan Southwest*. Crow Canyon Archaeological Center Occasional Paper No. 5. Cortez, Colo.: Crow Canyon Archaeological Center.

Hegmon, Michelle, Scott G. Ortman, and Jeannette L. Mobley-Tanaka. 1997. "Women, Men, and the Organization of Space in Southwestern Prehistory." Paper presented at the Gender Research in the American Southwest Conference, School for American Research, Santa Fe, New Mexico.

Heidensohn, F. M. 1995. *Women and Crime*. 2nd ed. New York: New York University Press.

Herdt, Gilbert, ed. 1994. *Third Sex, Third Gender: Beyond Sexual Dimorphism in Culture and History*. Cambridge: MIT Press.

Hewitt, R. L. 1986. "Structure, Meaning and Ritual in the Narratives of the Southern San." *Quellen zur Khoisan-Forschung* 2. Hamburg: Helmut Buske Verlag.

Hewlett, B. 1991. *Intimate Fathers*. Ann Arbor: University of Michigan Press.

Higham, Charles, and A. Kijngam, eds. 1984. "Prehistoric Investigations in Northeast Thailand." *British Archaeological Reports* 231 (1–3).

Higham, Charles, and Bernard Maloney. 1989. "Coastal Adaptation, Sedentism, and Domestication: A Model for Socio-Economic Intensification in Prehistoric Southeast Asia." In D. R. Harris and G. C. Hillman, eds., *Foraging and Farming: The Evolution of Plants Exploitation* (650–66). London: Hyman.

Higham, Charles, and Rachanie Thosarat. 1994. *Khok Phanom Di: Prehistoric Adaptation to the World's Richest Habitat*. Fort Worth, Tex.: Harcourt Brace College Publishers.

———. 1998. *Prehistoric Thailand, from First Settlement to Sukhothai*. London: Thames and Hudson.

Hill, A. 1995. "Faunal and Environmental Change in the Neogene of East Africa: Evidence from the Tugen Hills Sequence, Baringo District, Kenya." In E. S. Vrba, G. H. Denton, T. C. Partridge, and L. H. Burckle, eds., *Paleoclimate and Evolution with Emphasis on Human Origins* (178–96). New Haven, Conn.: Yale University Press.

Hill, K., and K. Hawkes. 1983. "Neotropical Hunting among the Ache of Eastern Paraguay." In R. Hames and W. Vickers, eds., *Adaptive Responses of Native Amazonians* (139–88). New York: Academic Press.

Hillenbrand, Robert. 1982. "La Dolce Vita in Early Islamic Syria: The Evidence of Later Umayyad Palaces." *Art History* 5: 1–35.

Hillier, Bill, and Julienne Hanson. 1984. *The Social Logic of Space*. Cambridge: Cambridge University Press.

Hiltbeitel, A., and Barbara Miller, eds. 1998. *Hair in Asian Cultures, Context and Change*. Albany: State University of New York Press.

Hirth, Kenneth. 1993. "The Household as an Analytic Unit: Problems in Method and Theory." In R. S. Santley and K. G. Hirth, eds., *Prehispanic Domestic Units in Western Mesoamerica: Studies of the Household, Compound, and Residence* (21–36). Boca Raton, Fla.: CRC Press.

Hladik, C., A. Hladick, O. Linares, H. Pagezy, S. Semple, and M. Hadley. 1993. *Tropical Forests, People, and Food: Biocultural Interactions and Applications to Development*. Paris: UNESCO and Parthenon.

Hodder, Ian. 1982a. *Symbolism in Action*. Cambridge: Cambridge University Press.
———. 1982b. "Theoretical Archaeology: A Reactionary View." In Ian Hodder, ed., *Symbolic and Structural Archaeology*. Cambridge: Cambridge University Press.
Holland, Thomas. 1989. "Fertility in the Prehistoric Midwest: A Critique of Unifactoral Models." *American Antiquity* 54: 614–25.
Hollimon, Sandra E. 1997. "The Third Gender in Native California: Two-Spirit Undertakers among the Chumash and Their Neighbors." In Cheryl Claassen and Rosemary Joyce, eds., *Women in Prehistory: North America and Mesoamerica* (173–88). Philadelphia: University of Pennsylvania Press.
Holmes, D. L., and R. F. Friedman. 1994. "Survey and Test Excavations in the Badari Region." *Proceedings of the Prehistoric Society* 60: 105–42.
Holmes, K., and R. Whitehouse. 1998. "Anthropomorphic Figurines and the Construction of Gender in Neolithic and Copper Age Italy." In R. D. Whitehouse, ed., *Gender and Italian Archaeology: Challenging the Stereotypes* (95–126). London: Accordia Research Institute and Institute of Archaeology.
Horne, Lee. 1982. "The Household Space." In Richard R. Wilk and William L. Rathje, eds., *Archaeology of the Household: Building a Prehistory of Domestic Life*, American Behavioral Scientist 25 (6): 677–85.
Hotchkiss, Valerie R. 1996. *Clothes Make the Man: Female Cross Dressing in Medieval Europe*. New York: Garland.
Hou Chia Chuang. 1965. Volume 3. Anyang, Henan, People's Republic of China: Institute of History and Philology Sinica Press.
How, M. W. 1970. *The Mountain Bushmen of Basutoland*. Pretoria: Van Schaik.
Howard, Catherine. 1991. "Fragments of the Heavens: Feathers as Ornaments among the Waiwai." In Ruben Reina and Kenneth Kensinger, eds., *Gift of Birds* (50–69). Philadelphia: University of Pennsylvania Museum.
Howell, F. C., and F. Bourliere, eds. 1963. *African Ecology and Human Evolution*. Chicago: Aldine.
Hrdy, S. B. 1999. *Mother Nature: A History of Mothers, Infants, and Natural Selection*. New York: Pantheon Books.
Hu Houxuan. 1970. *Jiaguxue Shangshi Luncong Chuji* [Preliminary study of bone inscriptions on Shang history], Vol. 2: "Yinren Jibing Kao" [Research on illness among the Yin people], p. 8; "Yindai Fenjian Zhidu Kao" [Research on the feudal system of the Yin dynasty], pp. 2–4. Vol. 1: "Yindai Hunyin Jiazu Zongfa shengyu Zhidukao" [Research on marriage, clans and *zongfa* systems of the Yin dynasty], pp. 1–35. Hong Kong: Wenyoutang Bookstore.
Huang Ranwei. 1995. *Yizhou Shiliao Lunji* [Discussion of the historical records of Yin and Zhou periods]. Hong Kong: Joint Publishing.
Hubbard, Ruth. 1990. *The Politics of Women's Biology*. New Brunswick: Rutgers University Press.
Hummel, Susanne, and Bernd Herrmann, eds. 1994. *Ancient DNA*. New York: Springer-Verlag.
Humphreys, R. S. 1991. *Islamic History*. Princeton, N.J.: Princeton University Press.
Hutton, Ronald. 1997. "The Neolithic Great Goddess: A Study in Modern Tradition." *Antiquity* 71: 91–99.
Ikawa-Smith, F. 1980. "Current Issues in Japanese Archaeology." *American Scientist* 68(2): 134–45.
———. 1982. "Co-Traditions in Japanese Archaeology." *World Archaeology* 13: 296–309.
———. 1990. "L'idéologie de l'homogénéité culturelle dans l'archéologie préhistorique japonnaise." *Anthropologie et Société* 14(3): 51–76.
———. 1995. "The Jomon, the Ainu, and the Okinawans: The Changing Politics of Ethnic Identity in Japanese Archaeology." In D. J. Dicks, ed., *Communicating with Japan: Images Past, Present, and Future* (43–56). Montreal: Concordia University.

————. 1999. "Construction of National Identity and Origins in East Asia: A Comparative Perspective." *Antiquity* 73: 626–29.

————. 2000. "Younger Dryas, Radiocarbon Calibration, and the Beginning and Adoption of Pottery Use in Eastern Asia." Paper presented at the Frywell Symposium, 65th Annual Meeting of the Society for American Archaeology, Philadelphia, April 8.

Ikawa-Smith, F., and Junko Habu. 1998. "Women in Japanese Archaeology." Paper presented at the Indo-Pacific Prehistory Association meeting, Kuala Lumpur, July.

Imamura Keiji. 1996. *Prehistoric Japan: New Perspectives on Insular East Asia.* Honolulu: University of Hawaii Press.

Isaac, G. L., ed. 1977. *Olorgesailie: Archaeological Studies of a Middle Pleistocene Lake Basin in Kenya.* Chicago: University of Chicago Press.

Ishida Eiichiro, Namio Egami, Masao Oka, and Ichiro Yawata. 1949. "Nihon minzoku-Nihon bunka no genryu to Nihon kokka no keisei" [Origins of the Japanese people and culture and the formation of the Japanese state]. *Minzokugaku Kenkyu* 13(3). (whole issue)

————. 1958. *Nihonminzoku no Kigen* [Origins of the Japanese people]. Tokyo: Heibonsha.

Ivanchik, A. I. 1996. *Kimmeriitsy.* Moscow: Russian Academy of Sciences.

Jacobs, Sue-Ellen, Wesley Thomas, and Sabine Lang, eds. 1997. *Two-Spirit People.* Urbana: University of Illinois Press.

Jacobson, Esther. 1995. *The Art of the Scythians: The Interpenetration of Cultures at the Edge of the Hellenic World.* Leiden: E. J. Brill.

Janson, Anthony F. 1985. "The Convex Mirror as Vanitas Symbol." *Source: Notes in the History of Art* 4(2/3): 51–54.

Johnson, Allen, and Timothy Earle. 1991. *The Evolution of Human Societies.* Stanford, Calif.: Stanford University Press.

Johnson, R. T., H. Rabinowitz, and P. Sieff. 1959. *Rock Paintings of the South-West Cape.* Cape Town: Nasionale Boekhandel.

Joseishi Sogo Kenkyukai [Association for the Research into History of Women], ed. 1989. *Nippon Joseishi* [History of women in Japan]. Vol. 1. Tokyo: University of Tokyo Press.

————. 1990. *Nippon Josei Seikatsushi* [History of women's life in Japan]. Tokyo: University of Tokyo Press.

Joulian, F. 1986. *Pan Faber: Bibliographie Selective a Propos des Evidences d'outils chez les Singes Superieurs, problematiques anthropologiques.* Memoire de DEA, 3e cycle. Paris: Universite de Paris I.

Joyce, Rosemary A. 1986. "Gender, Role and Status in Middle Formative Mesoamerica: Implications of Burials from La Venta, Tabasco, Mexico." Paper presented at the Fourth Texas Symposium: Olmec, Izapa and Maya. Latin American Studies Program, University of Texas, Austin.

————. 1992. "Innovation, Communication and the Archaeological Record: A Reassessment of Middle Formative Honduras." *Journal of the Steward Anthropological Society* 20 (1–2): 235–56.

————. 1993. "Women's Work: Images of Production and Reproduction in Pre-Hispanic Southern Central America." *Current Anthropology* 34: 255–74.

————. 1996a. "The Construction of Gender in Classic Mayan Monuments." In R. Wright, ed., *Gender and Archaeology* (167–95). Philadelphia: University of Pennsylvania Press.

————. 1996b. "Social Dynamics of Exchange: Changing Patterns in the Honduran Archaeological Record." In Carl Henrik Langebaek and Felipe Cardenas-Arroyo, eds., *Chieftains, Power and Trade: Regional Interaction in the Intermediate Area of the Americas* (31–46). Bogota: Universidad de los Andes, Departamento de Antropología.

————. 1999. "Social Dimensions of Preclassic Burials." In David C. Grove and Rosemary A. Joyce, eds., *Ritual Behavior, Social Identity, and Cosmology in Pre-Classic Mesoamerica* (15–47). Washington, D.C.: Dumbarton Oaks.

———. 2000a. *Gender and Power in Prehispanic Mesoamerica.* Austin: University of Texas Press.

———. 2000b. "Girling the Girl and Boying the Boy: The Production of Adulthood in Ancient Mesoamerica." *World Archaeology* 31(3): 473–83.

Joyce, Rosemary A., and David C. Grove. 1999. "Asking New Questions about the Mesoamerican Preclassic." In David C. Grove and Rosemary A. Joyce, eds., *Ritual Behavior, Social Identity, and Cosmology in Pre-Classic Mesoamerica* (1–14). Washington, D.C.: Dumbarton Oaks.

Junker, Laura L. 1990. "Long-Distance Trade and the Development of Socio-Political Complexity in Philippine Chiefdoms of the First Millennium to Mid-Second Millennium A.D." Ph.D. diss., University of Michigan.

———. 1993a. "Archaeological Excavations at the 12th–16th Century Settlement of Tanjay, Negros Oriental: The Burial Evidence for Social-Status Symbolism, Head-Taking and Inter-Polity Raiding." *Philippine Quarterly of Culture and Society* 21: 39–82.

———. 1993b. "Craft Goods Specialization and Prestige Goods Exchange in Philippine Chiefdoms of the Fifteenth and Sixteenth Centuries." *Asian Perspectives* 32: 1–35.

Justice Department. 1998. *Report by the Bureau of Justice Statistics.* Washington, D.C.: Department of Justice.

Kaiser, Werner. 1957. "Zur inneren Chronologie der Naqadakultur." *Archaeologia Geographica* 6: 69–77.

Kanchanakom, Preecha. 1972. "Prehistoric Pictograph and Petroglyph in Thailand." *Journal of Archaeology* 4(2): 220–38.

Kano, T. 1992. *The Last Ape: Pygmy Chimpanzee Behavior and Ecology.* Translated by E.O. Vineberg. Stanford, Calif.: Stanford University Press.

Kaplan, F., ed. 1997. *Queens, Queen Mothers, Priestesses, and Power.* New York: New York Academy of Sciences.

Kappelman, J., T. Plummer, L. Bishop, A. Duncan, and S. Appleton. 1997. "Bovids as Indicators of Plio-Pleistocene Paleoenvironments in East Africa." *Journal of Human Evolution* 32: 299–356.

Karlisch, Sigrun M., Sibyelle Kästner, and Eva-Marie Mertens, eds. 1997. *Vom Knochenmann zur Menschenfrau: Feministische Theorie und archäologische Praxis.* Münster: Agenda Verlag.

Katzenberg, M. Anne, Shelley Saunders, and William Fitzgerald. 1993. "Age Differences in Stable Carbon and Nitrogen Isotope Ratios in a Population of Prehistoric Maize Horticulturists." *American Journal of Physical Anthropology* 90: 267–81.

Kawanabe, H., G. Coulter, and A. C. Roosevelt. 1999. *Ancient Lakes: Cultural and Biological Diversity.* Ghent, Belgium: Kenobi Productions.

Kawarabuki, Ken. 1992. "Ibaraki-ken no dogu" [Clay figurines of Ibaraki prefecture]. *Bulletin of the National Museum of Japanese History* 37: 175–84.

Kehoe, Alice. 1998. "Appropriate Terms." *SAA Bulletin* 16: 2.

Kelly, R. L. 1995. *The Foraging Spectrum: Diversity in Hunter-Gatherer Lifeways.* Washington, D.C.: Smithsonian Institution.

Kemp, B. J. 1989. *Ancient Egypt. Anatomy of a Civilization.* London: Routledge.

Kenk, Roman. 1986. *Grabfunde der Skythenzeit aus Tuva, Sud-Sibirien.* Munich: C. H. Beck.

Kensinger, Kenneth. 1991. "Feathers Make Us Beautiful: The Meaning of Cashinahua Feather Headdresses." In Ruben Reina and Kenneth Kensinger, eds., *The Gift of Birds* (40–49). Philadelphia: University of Pennsylvania Museum.

Kent, Susan. 1998. *Gender in African Prehistory.* Walnut Creek, Calif.: AltaMira Press.

Kessler, S. 1998. *Lessons from the Intersexed.* New Brunswick, N.J.: Rutgers University Press.

Kessler, Suzanne J., and Wendy McKenna. 1978. *Gender: An Ethnomethodological Approach.* New York: John Wiley & Sons.

Kidder, J. Edward, Jr. 1957. *The Jomon Pottery of Japan*. Ascona, Switzerland: Artibus Asiae.

————. 1959. *Japan before Buddhism*. New York: Praeger.

————. 1966. *Japan before Buddhism*. Rev. ed. New York: Praeger.

King, Dave. 1981. "Gender Confusions: Psychological and Psychiatric Conceptions of Transvestism and Transsexualism." In Kenneth Plummer, ed., *The Making of the Modern Homosexual* (155–83). London: Hutchinson.

Kingdon, J. 1997. *The Kingdon Field Guide to African Mammals*. San Diego: Academic Press.

Kingston, J. D., B. D. Marino, and A. Hill. 1994. "Isotopic Evidence for Neogene Hominid Paleoenvironments in the Kenya Rift Valley." *Science* 264: 955–59.

Kinsey, W. G., ed. 1997. *New World Primates: Ecology, Evolution, and Behavior*. New York: Aldine.

Klein, Richard G. 1999. *The Human Career: Human Biological and Cultural Origins*. Chicago: University of Chicago Press.

Kobayashi Tatsuo. 1977. "Jomon sekai no nakano dogu" [Clay figurines the Jomon world]. In T. Kobayashi and M. Kamei, eds., *Dogu Haniwa* [Jomon clay figurines and Haniwa] (45–53). Nippon Toji Zenshu 3. Tokyo: Chuokoronsha.

————. 1986. "Trends in Administrative Salvage Archaeology." In R. J. Pearson, G. L. Barnes, and K. L. Hutterer, eds., *Windows on the Japanese Past: Studies in Archaeology and Prehistory* (491–96). Ann Arbor: University of Michigan, Center for Japanese Studies.

————. 1993. "Regional Organization in the Jomon Period." *Arctic Anthropology* 29(1): 82–95.

————. 2000. *Jomonjin Tsuikyu* [In pursuit of the Jomon people]. Tokyo: Nippon Kensaishinbunsha.

Kohl, Philip, and Clare Fawcett, eds. 1995. *Nationalism, Politics, and the Practise of Archaeology*. Cambridge: Cambridge University Press.

Komarova, M. N. 1952. *Tomskii Mogil'nik, Pamyatnik istorii drevnikh plemen lesnoi polosy zapadnoi Sibiri: Materialy i issledovaniya po arkheologii SSSR* 24 [Archaeology of the USSR].

Komoto Masayuki. 1975. "Yayoi jidai no shakai" [The Yayoi society]. In Sahara Makoto and Kanaseki Hiroshi, eds., *Inasaku no Hajimari* [The beginning of the rice agriculture] (87–98). *Kodaishi Hakkutsu* Series, Vol. 4. Tokyo: Kodansha.

Kramer, Carol. 1982. "Ethnographic Households and Archaeological Interpretation." In Richard R. Wilk and William L. Rathje, eds., *Archaeology of the Household: Building a Prehistory of Domestic Life*. *American Behavioral Scientist* 25(6): 663–75.

Kramer, Patricia. 1998. "The Costs of Human Locomotion: Maternal Investment in Child Transport." *American Journal of Physical Anthropologists* 107: 71–85.

Kristeva, J. 1991. *Strangers to Ourselves*. Translated by Leon S. Roudiez. New York: Columbia University Press.

Kubarev, V. D. 1987. *Kurgany Ulandryka*. Novosibirsk: Nauka.

————. 1991. *Kurgany Yustyda*. Novosibirsk: Nauka.

Kunstadter, Peter, E. C. Chapman, and Sanga Sabhasri, eds. 1978. *Farmer in the Forest*. Honolulu: University of Hawaii Press.

Lamphere, Louise. 1993. "The Domestic Space of Women and the Public World of Men: The Strengths and Limitations of an Anthropological Dichotomy." In C. B. Brettell and C. F. Sargent, eds., *Gender in Cross-Cultural Perspective* (67–77). Englewood Cliffs, N.J.: Prentice Hall.

Lanfranchi, R., and B. Clist. 1991. *Aux origines de l'Afrique centrale*. Libreville: Centres Culturels Francais d'Afrique Central and Centre International des Civilizations Bantu.

Lanfranchi, R., and D. Schwartz. 1990. *Paysage Quaternaires de l'Afrique Central Atlantique*. Paris: l'Orstom.

Lang, Sabine. 1997. "Various Kinds of Two-Spirit People: Gender Variance and Homosexuality in Native American Communities." In S. E. Jacobs, W. Thomas, and S. Lang, eds., *Two-Spirit People* (100–18). Urbana: University of Illinois Press.

Langlois, Rene. 1987. "Le visage de la Dame au Vix." In J. P. Mohen, ed., *Trésors de Princes Celtes* (212–17). Galeries nationales du Grand Palais. Paris: Editions de la Réunion de musées nationeaux.

Lattimore, Owen. 1940. *Inner Asian Frontiers of China*. London: Oxford University Press.

Lavezaris, Guido de, et al. 1567. "Letter to Felipe II from the Royal Officials." In E. Blair and J. Robinson, eds., *The Philippine Islands,* vol. 34 (1906), pp. 212–14. Cleveland: Arthur H. Clark.

Leacock, Eleanor, and Richard Lee, eds. 1987. *Politics and History in Ban Societies*. Cambridge: Cambridge University Press.

Lee, R. B. 1979. *The !Kung San: Men, Women, and Work*. Cambridge: Cambridge University Press.

Lee, R. B., and R. Daly, eds. 1999. *The Cambridge Encyclopedia of Hunters and Gatherers*. Cambridge: Cambridge University Press.

Lee, Richard B., and Irvin De Vore, eds. 1968. *Man the Hunter*. Chicago, New York: Aldine.

Lee, Yun Kuen. 1996. "Material Representations of Status in the Dian Culture." *Bulletin of the Indo-Pacific Prehistory Association* 14: 216–25.

Lee-Thorpe, Julia A., N. J. Van der Merwa, and C. K. Brain. 1994. "Diet of 'Australopithecus robustus' at Swartkraus from Stable Carbon Isotopic Analysis." *Journal of Human Evolution* 27(4): 361–72.

Lei Congyun. 1996. "Neolithic Sites of Religious Significance." In J. Rawson, ed., *Mysteries of Ancient China* (219–224). New York: George Brazillier.

Lenssen-Erz, T. 1997. "The Third Gender: Human Related Patterns of Activity in the Rock Paintings of the Brandberg, Namibia." Paper presented at Khoisan Identities and Cultural Heritage. Cape Town.

Lepowsky, M. 1983. "Sudest Island and the Lovisade Archipelago in Massim Exchange." In J. W. Leach and E. R. Leach, eds., *The Kula* (467–502). Cambridge: Cambridge University Press.

Lesure, Richard. 1997. "Figurines and Social Identities in Early Sedentary Societies of Coastal Chiapas, Mexico." In Cheryl Claassen and Rosemary A. Joyce, eds., *Women in Prehistory: North America and Mesoamerica* (227–48). Philadelphia: University of Pennsylvania Press.

Lewis, I. M. 1984. "What Is a Shaman?" In M. Hoppal, ed., *Shamanism in Eurasia*. Gottingen: Herodot.

Lewis-Williams, J. D. 1981. *Believing and Seeing: Symbolic Meanings in Southern San Rock Painting*. London: Academic Press.

———. 1983. *The Rock Art of Southern Africa*. Cambridge: Cambridge University Press.

———. 1986. "Cognitive and Optical Illusions in San Rock Art Research." *Current Anthropology* 27: 171–78.

Lewis-Williams, J. D., and T. A. Dowson. 1988. "Signs of All Times: Entoptic Phenomena in Upper Paleolithic Art." *Current Anthropology* 29(2): 201–45.

———. 1989. *Images of Power: Understanding Bushman Rock Art*. Johannesburg: Southern Book Publishers.

Lewis-Williams, J. D., and J. N. Loubser. 1986. "Deceptive Appearances: A Critique of Southern African Rock Art Studies." In F. Wendorf and A. E. Close, eds., *Advances in World Archaeology,* pp. 233–89. New York: Academic Press.

Liang Ssu-yung. 1976. *Houchiachuang*. Vol. 8, No. 3, of Chungkuo Kaoku paokaochi [Reports of Chinese Archaeology], Li Chi, ed. Taipei: Institute of History and Philology, Academia Sinica Press.

Li Chi. 1959. "Chihsing talei chich'i wenshih yenpien" [Eight types of hairpins and the evolution of their decorative patterns]. *Bulletin of the Institute of History and Philology*, no. 30 (pt. 1): 1–69.

———. 1977. *Anyang*. Seattle: University of Washington Press.

Linduff, Katheryn M. 1996. "Art and Identity: The Chinese and Their 'Significant Others' in the Shang." In Michael Gervers and Wayne Schlepp, eds., *Cultural Contact, History and Ethnicity in Inner Asia* (12–48). Toronto: Toronto Studies in Central and Inner Asia, Joint Centre for Asia Pacific Studies.

———.1998. "The Emergence and Demise of Bronze-Producing Cultures." In Victor H. Mair, ed., *The Bronze and Early Iron Age Peoples of Eastern Central Asia*, vol. 2 (619–43). Washington, D.C.: The Institute for the Study of Man.

Linnekin, Joyce 1990. *Sacred Queens and Women of Consequence*. Ann Arbor: University of Michigan Press.

Lin Yun. 1986. "A Reexamination of the Relationship between Bronzes of the Shang and of the Northern Zone." In K.C. Chang, ed., *Studies of Shang Archaeology* (237–73). New Haven, Conn.: Yale University Press.

Lloyd, L. 1911. *Specimens of Bushmen Folklore*. London: Allen.

Liu, Zhengyu. 1982. *Yinzhou sidai de Zhongguo Shehui* [Chinese society during the Yin and Zhou periods]. Beijing: Sanlian Bookstore.

Locsin-Nava, Ma. Cecilia. 1996. "Teresa Magbanua: Woman Warrior." *Review of Women's Studies* (5–6): 60–65.

Lo Porto, F. G. 1972. "La tomba neolitica con idolo in pietra di Arnesano (Lecce)." *Rivista di Scienze Preistoriche* 27: 358–72.

Lovejoy, C. O. 1981. "The Origin of Man." *Science* 211: 341–50.

Lovett, J. C., and S. K. Wasser, eds. 1993. *Biogeography and Ecology of the Rain Forests of Eastern Africa*. Cambridge: Cambridge University Press.

Lowenthal, David. 1985. *The Past Is a Foreign Country*. Cambridge: Cambridge University Press.

LPARI (Liaoning Province Archaeology Research Institute). 1986. "Brief Report on the Excavation of the 'Goddess Temple' and the Stone Graves of the Hongshan Culture at Niuheliang in Liaoning Province." *Wenwu* 8: 1–17.

Lurie, Nancy O. 1953. "Winnebago Berdache." *American Anthropologist* 55(5): 708–12.

Lyons, D. 1989. "Men's Houses, Women's Spaces: The Spatial Ordering of Households in Doulo, North Cameroon." In S. MacEachern, D. J. W. Archer, and R. D. Gavin, eds., *Households and Communities* (28–34). Proceedings of the 21st Annual Conference of the Archaeological Association of the University of Calgary. Calgary: University of Calgary.

Maggs, T. M. O'C. 1971 "Microdistribution of Some Typologically Linked Rock Paintings from the Western Cape." In *Proceedings Sixieme Congres PanAfricain de Prehistoire*, ed H. J. Hugot, pp. 218–20. Dakar.

Makabe Yoshiko. 1962. "Shutsudo jinkotsu no seibetsu yori mita Kofun Jidai shakai no ichikousatsu" [An observation on the Kofun Period society, as seen from sex identification of skeletal remains]. *Okayama Shigaku* [Journal of History and Geography] 12: 37–55.

———. 1985. "Genshi kodai ni miru seisa to bosei" [Gender and motherhood in the ancient period]. In Haruoko Wakita, ed., *Bosei o tou* [Exploring motherhood] (43–78). Kyoto: Jinbunshoin.

———. 1987. "Kokogakukara mita joseino shigoto to bunka" [Archaeological perspective on women's work and culture]. In Koichi Mori, ed., *Josei no Chikara* [Women's power] (17–66). Nippon no Kodai, Vol. 12. Tokyo: Chuokoronsha.

———. 1990. "Josei jinbutsu haniwa shutsugen no haikei" [The background for the appearance of haniwa figures representing females]. *Bulletin of the Kobe Josji Daigaku (Bungakubu)* 24L: 1–22.

———. 1992a. "Josei to kokogaku" [Women and archaeology]. *Kokogaku Janaru* [Archaeologicl Journal] 346: 1.

————. 1992b. "Kofun ni okeru dansei futari gasso" [Male double burials]. *Shinjodaishi-gaku* [Journal of History] 6: 19–41.

————. 1996. "Konin no kokogaku" [The archaeology of marriage]. In Hotsuka Hatsushige et al., eds., *Kokogaku ni yoru Nippon no Rekishi* [Japanese history through archaeology] (113–22). Tokyo: Yuzankaku.

Maley, J. 1995. "The Climatic and Vegetational History of the Equatorial Regions of Africa during the Upper Quaternary." In T. Shaw, P. Sinclair, B. Andah, and A. Okpoko, eds., *The Archaeology of Africa: Food, Metals, and Towns* (43–52). New York: Routledge.

Man, E. H. 1883. "On the Aboriginal Inhabitants of the Andaman Islands." *Journal of the Anthropological Institute of Great Britain and Ireland* 12: 69–175, 327–434.

————. 1885. "On the Andaman Islands, and Their Inhabitants." *Journal of the Anthropological Institute of Great Britain and Ireland* 14: 253–72.

Manhire, Tony, John Parkington, and William S. S. van Rijssen. 1983. "A Distributional Approach to the Interpretation of Rock Art in the South-western Cape." In *Goodwin Series*, pp. 29–33.

Manhire, Tony, John E. Parkington, and Royden Yates. 1985. "Nets and Fully Recurved Bows: Rock Paintings and Hunting Methods in the Western Cape, South Africa." *World Archaeology* 17:161–64

Manson, J. H. 1997. "Primate Consortships: A Critical Review." *Current Anthropology* 38 (3): 353–74.

Mansur, M. E. 1986. *Microscopie due Materiel Lithique Prehistorique: Traces d'Utilization, Alterations naturelles, Accidentelles, et Technologiques.* Cahiers du Quaternaire No. 9. Bordeaux: Centre Nacional de Recherche Scientifique.

Maringer, John. 1974. "Clay Figurines of the Jomon Period: A Contribution to the History of Ancient Religion in Japan." *History of Religion* 14(2): 128–39.

Marks, J. 1992. "Chromosomal Evolution in Primates." In S. Jones, R. Martin, and D. Pilbeam, eds., *Cambridge Encyclopedia of Human Evolution* (298–302). Cambridge: Cambridge University Press.

Marshall, L. 1976. *The !Kung of Nyae Nyae.* Cambridge: Harvard University Press.

Marshall, Yvonne. 1989. "The House in Northwest Coast, Nuu-Chah-Nulth, Society: The Material Structure of Political Action." In S. MacEachern, D. J. W. Archer, and R. D. Gavin, eds., *Households and Communities* (15–21). Proceedings of the 21st Annual Conference of the Archaeological Association of the University of Calgary. Calgary: University of Calgary.

Martin, M. K., and B. Voorhies. 1975. *Female of the Species.* New York: Columbia University Press.

Martynov, Anatoly. 1991. *The Ancient Art of Northern Asia.* Urbana: University of Illinois Press.

Matson, R. G. 1996. "Households as Economic Organization: A Comparison between Large Houses on the Northwest Coast and in the Southwest." In G. Coupland and E. B. Banning, eds., *People Who Live in Big Houses: Archaeological Perspectives on Large Domestic Structures* (107–20). Madison, Wis.: Prehistory Press.

Matsui Akira. 1996. "Archaeological Investigations of Anadromous Salmonids Fishing in Japan." *World Archaeology* 27(3): 444–60.

Mazar, B., and M. Ben-Dov. N.d. "Finds from the Archaeological Excavations Near the Temple Mount." Unpublished manuscript.

McCafferty, Sharisse D., and Geoffrey G. McCafferty. 1991. "Spinning and Weaving as Female Gender Identity in Post-Classic Mexico." In Janet Catherine Berlo, Margot Schevill, and Edward B. Dwyer, eds., *Textile Traditions of Mesoamerica and the Andes: An Anthology* (19–44). New York: Garland.

————. 1994. "Engendering Tomb 7 at Monte Alban: Respinning an Old Yarn." *Current Anthropology* 35(2): 143–66.

McCall, D. F. 1970. "Wolf Courts Girl: The Equivalence of Hunting and Mating in Bushman Thought." *Ohio University Papers in International Studies, Africa Series,* 7.

McGrew, W. C., L. F. Marchant, and T. Nishida. 1996. *Great Ape Societies.* Cambridge: Cambridge University Press.

McNetting, Robert. 1982. "Some Home Truths on Household Size and Wealth." *American Behavioral Scientist* 25(6): 641–62.

Mead, Margaret. [1935] 1963. *Sex and Temperament in Three Primitive Societies.* New York: William Morrow.

———. [1949] 1975. *Male and Female: A Study of the Sexes in a Changing World.* New York: William Morrow.

Meldem, Dejah. 1995. "Botanical Remains at Yutopian." Unpublished report.

Meskell, Lynn. 1995. "Goddesses, Gimbutas, and 'New Age' Archaeology." *Antiquity* 69: 74–86.

———. 1998. "Running the Gamut: Gender, Girls and Goddesses." *American Journal of Archaeology* 102: 181–85.

Mills, Barbara J., and Patricia L. Crown, eds. 1995. *Ceramic Production in the American Southwest.* Tucson: University of Arizona Press.

Milton, K. 1987. "Primate Diets and Gut Morphology: Implications for Human Evolution. In Marvin Harris and E. R. Ross, eds., *Food and Evolution* (93–115). Philadelphia: Temple University Press.

Minnis, Paul E. 1985. *Social Adaptation to Food Stress: A Prehistoric Southwestern Example.* Chicago: University of Chicago Press.

Miracle, Preston, Kari Brandt, Debbie Gold, Seung-og Kim, Jeff Miller, and Uma Swamy. 1991. "Two Burials from Santo Nino Church, Cebu City, Philippines." *Philippine Quarterly of Culture and Society* 19: 37–80.

Mitani, M., L. J. Tutin, E. A. Williamson, M. Fernandez, and G. McPherson, eds. 1994. "Floral Lists from Five Study Sites of Apes in the African Tropical Forests." *Tropics* 3: 247–348.

Mizuno Masayoshi. 1964. "Dogu saishiki no fukugen" [Reconstruction of the figurine ritual]. *Shinano* 26(4): 298–312.

Monahan, J. 1998. *Report on Violence among the Mentally Ill.* Boston: American Medical Association, Archives of General Psychiatry.

Monkhon Kamnuenket, N. 1992. *Ban Prasat, an Archaeological Site.* Bangkok: Fine Arts Department.

Moore, Henrietta. 1988. *Feminism and Anthropology.* Cambridge: Polity Press.

Moore, Jenny, and Eleanor Scott, eds. 1997. *Invisible People and Processes: Writing Gender and Childhood into European Archaeology.* London: Leicester University Press.

Morant, G. M. 1935. "A Study of Pre-Dynastic Egyptian Skulls from Badari Based on Measurements Taken by Miss B. N. Stoessiger and Professor D. E. Derry." *Biometrika* 27: 293–308.

Morbeck, M. E., A. Galloway, and A. L. Zihlman, eds. 1997. *The Evolving Female.* Princeton, N.J.: Princeton University Press.

Morga, Antonio de. 1609. "Relation of the Philippine Islands and of Their Natives, Antiquity, Customs, and Government." In M. Garcia, ed., *Reading in Philippine Prehistory* (1979), pp. 266–306. Manila: Filipiana Book Guild.

Morris, B. 1982. *Economy, Affinity and Inter-cultural Pressure: Notes around Hill Pandaram Group Structure* (man) N.S. 17:3, pp. 452–61.

Morter, J., and J. Robb. 1998. "Space, Gender and Architecture in the Southern Italian Neolithic." In R. D. Whitehouse, ed., *Gender and Italian Archaeology: Challenging the Stereotypes* (83–94). London: Accordia Research Institute and Institute of Archaeology.

Moss, R. P. 1968. *The Soil Resources of Tropical Africa: A Symposium of the African Studies Association of the United Kingdom.* Cambridge: Cambridge University Press.

Munn, Nancy. 1986. *The Fame of Gawa.* Durham, N.C.: Duke University Press.

Munson, Marit K. 2000. "Sex, Gender, and Status: Human Images from the Classic Mimbres." *American Antiquity* 65(12): 127–43.

Murdock, George B. 1949. *Our Primitive Contemporaries*. New York: Macmillan.

Murdock, G. P., and C. Provost. 1973. "Factors in the Division of Labour by Sex: A Cross-Cultural Analysis." *Ethnology* 12: 203–25.

Musil, A. 1907. *Kusejr 'Amra I–II*. Vienna: K. K. Hof und Staatsdruckerei.

Na Nakorn Phanom, Somchai, et al. 1979. *Prehistoric Rock Paintings in Thailand*. Bangkok: Fine Art Department.

Nagamine Mitsukazu. 1986. "Clay Figurines and Jomon Society." In R. J. Pearson, G. L. Barnes, and K. L. Hutterer, eds., *Windows on the Japanese Past: Studies in Archaeology and Prehistory* (255–65). Ann Arbor: University of Michigan, Center for Japanese Studies.

Nagy, B. L. B. 1998. "Age, Activity, and Musculoskeletal Stress Markers." Paper presented at the annual meeting of the American Association of Physical Anthropologists.

Nakamura Toshio and Seiichiro Tsuji. 1999. "Aomori-ken Higashitsugaru-gun Kanita-cho Odai Yamamoto I iseki shutsuto no dokihen ni fuchakushita biryo tankabutsu no kasokuki ^{14}C nendai" [Accelerator mass spectrometry dates of the minute carbon adhesions on potsherds recovered from the Odai Yamamoto I site, Kanita-cho, Higashitsugarou-gun, Amori prefecture]. In Odai Yamamot I Site Excavation Team, ed., *Odai Yamamoto I Iseki no Kokogaku-teki Chosa* [Archaeological research at the Odai Yamamoto I site] (107–11). Tokyo: Kokugakuin University, Department of Archaeology, Odai Yamamoto I Site Excavation Team.

Napintu, Sarapol. 1988. *Ban Lum Kao*. Bangkok: Rongpin Kan Satsana.

National Museum of Japanese History, ed. 1992. "Dogu to sono joho" [Clay figurines ("dogu") and related information]. *Bulletin of the National Museum of Japanese History* 37 (entire issue).

Nelson, Margaret C. 1999. *Mimbres during the Twelfth Century: Abandonment, Continuity, and Reorganization*. Tucson: University of Arizona Press.

Nelson, Sarah Milledge. 1990. "The Neolithic of Northeastern China and Korea." *Antiquity* 64: 234–48.

———. 1991. "The Goddess Temple and the Status of Women at Niuheliang, China." In D. Walde and N. Willows, eds., *The Archaeology of Gender* (302–8). Proceedings of the 22nd Annual Chacmool Conference, Calgary, Alberta, Canada.

———. 1993. "Gender Hierarchy and the Queens of Silla." In Barbara Diane Miller, ed., *Sex and Gender Hierarchies* (297–315). Cambridge: Cambridge University Press.

———. 1995. "Introduction." In *The Archaeology of Northeast China beyond the Great Wall* (1–18). London: Routledge.

———. 1996a. "Ideology and the Formation of Early China in the Northeast." In H. J. Claessen and J. G. Oosten, eds., *The Ideology of the Early State* (153–69). Leiden: E. J. Brill.

———. 1996b. "Ritualized Pigs and the Origins of Complex Society: Hypotheses Regarding the Hongshan Culture." *Early China* 20: 1–16.

———. 1997. *Gender in Archaeology: Analyzing Power and Prestige*. Walnut Creek, Calif. : AltaMira Press.

———. 1998. "Pigs in the Hongshan Culture." In *Ancestors for the Pigs* (99–108). Philadelphia: MASCA Press.

Nelson, Sarah M., and Alice B. Kehoe, eds. 1990. *Powers of Observation: Alternative Views in Archeology*. Archeological Papers of the American Anthropological Association No. 2. Washington, D.C.: American Anthropological Association.

Netting, Robert McC. 1982. "Some Home Truths on Household Size and Wealth." *American Behavioral Scientist* 25(6): 641–42.

Nishimura Masao. 1992. "Long Distance Trade and the Development of Complex Societies in the Prehistory of the Central Philippines: The Cebu Central Settlement Case." Ph.D. diss., University of Michigan.

Nishino Yukiko. 1990. "Kodai josei seikatsushi no kozo" [The structure of the historical study of women in ancient Japan]. In Joseishi Sougou Kenkyukai, ed., *Nippon Josei Seikatsushi* [History of women's life in Japan] (1–33). Tokyo: University of Tokyo Press.

Noguchi Yoshimaro. 1974. "Dogu no kenkyushi" [The history of figurine research]. In Teruya Esaka and Yoshimaro Noguchi, eds., *Dogu Geijutsu to Shinko* [Clay figurine art and belief systems] (91–98). Tokyo: Kodansha.

Nordström, Haus-Aki. 1996. "The Nubian A-Group: Ranking Funerary Remains." *Norwegian Archaeological Review.*

Noto Takeshi. 1983. "Dogu" [Clay figurines]. In S. Kato, T. Kobayashi, and T. Fujimoto, eds., *Jomon Bunka no Kenkyu* [Studies in Jomon culture], Vol. 9 (74–85). Tokyo: Yuzankaku.

Nuñez Regueiro, Victor. 1998. *Arqueología, Historia y Antropología de los Sitios de Alamito.* Tucumán: Ediciones Intedea.

Oba [Tanigawa] Iwao. 1926. "Dogu ni kansuru ni san no kosatsu" [A few observations on clay figurines]. *Kokugakuin Zasshi* 32(5): 48–57.

Obayashi Taryo. 1990. *Higashi to Nishi, Umi to Yama: Nippon no Bunka Ryoiki* [East and west, the sea and the mountains: Culture area of Japan]. Tokyo: Shogakukan.

———. 1991. *Hoppo no Minzoku to Bunka* [Northern peoples and their cultures]. Tokyo: Yamakawa Shuppan.

Ogasawara Yoshihiko. 1990. "Kokka keiseiki no josei" [Women at the time of state formation]. In Joseishi Sougou Kenkyukai [Association for the Research into History of Women], ed., *Nippon Josei Seikatsushi* [History of women's life in Japan] (35–67). Tokyo: University of Tokyo Press.

Ohno Nobutaro. 1910. "Dogu no keishiki bunrui ni tsuite" [On classification of clay figurines]. *Tokyo Jinruigakkai Zasshi* 26(296): 54–60.

Oka Masao. 1956. "Nihon minzokubunka no keisei" [Formation of the culture of the Japanese people]. In K. Kodama et al., eds., *Zusetsu Nippon Bunkashi Taikei* (106–16). Tokyo: Shogakkan.

Ono Miyoko. 1984. *Dogu no Chishiki* [Clay figurines]. Tokyo: Tokyo Bijutsu.

Orpen, J.M. 1974. "The Social Influence of Change in Hunting Technique among the Central Kalahari San." *African Study Monographs* 549–62.

O'Shea, J. 1984. *Mortuary Variability: An Archaeological Investigation.* New York: Academic Press.

Parkington, J. E. 1989. "Interpreting Paintings without a Commentary: Meaning and Motive, Content and Composition in the Rock Art of the Western Cape, South Africa." *Antiquity* 63: 13–26.

———. 1996. "What Is an Eland? N'ao and the Politics of Age and Sex in the Paintings of the Western Cape." In P. Skotnes, ed., *Miscast: Negotiating the Presence of the Bushmen*, pp. 281–89 Cape Town: University of Cape Town Press.

———. in prep. *Elands Bay Cave: a View on the Past.*

Peralta, Jesus, and L. A. Salazar. 1974. *Pre-Spanish Manila: A Reconstruction of the Pre-History of Manila.* Manila: National Historical Commission.

Perzigian, Anthony, Patricia Tench, and Donna Braun. 1984. "Prehistoric Health in the Ohio River Valley." In Mark Cohen and George Armelagos, eds., *Paleopathology at the Origins of Agriculture* (347–66). Orlando: Academic Press.

Petrie, W. M. Flinders. 1900. "Sequences in Prehistoric Remains." *Journal of the Anthropological Institute* 29: 295–301.

Petrie, W. M. Flinders, and J. Quibell. 1896. *Naqada and Ballas.* London: British School of Archaeology in Egypt.

Phillipson, D. 1994. *African Archaeology.* Cambridge: Cambridge University Press.

Pierce, Leslie P. 1993. *The Imperial Harem. Women and Sovereignty in the Ottoman Empire.* New York: Oxford University Press.

Pigafetta, Antonio. 1524. "Pigafetta's Account (from First Voyage around the World)." In F. L. Jocano, ed., *The Philippines at the Spanish Contact* (1975) (44–80). Manila: MCS Enterprises.

Pluciennik, M. 1988. "Historical, Geographical and Anthropological Imaginations: Early Ceramics in Southern Italy." In P. Blinkhorn and C. Cumberpatch, eds., *Not So Much a Pot, More a Way of Life: Current Approaches to Artefact Analysis in Archaeology* (37–56). Oxbow Monograph 83. Oxford: Oxford University Press.

———. 1994. "The Mesolithic-Neolithic Transition in Southern Italy." Ph.D. diss., University of Sheffield.

———. 1998. "Representations of Gender in Prehistoric Southern Italy." In R. D. Whitehouse, ed., *Gender and Italian Archaeology: Challenging the Stereotypes* (57–82). London: Accordia Research Institute and Institute of Archaeology.

Plummer, T. W., and L. C. Bishop. 1994. "Hominid Paleoecology at Olduvai Gorge, Tanzania as Indicated by Antelope Remains." *Journal of Human Evolution* 27: 47–75.

Pollock, Susan. 1991. "Women in a Men's World: Images of Sumerian Women." In J. Gero and M. Conkey, eds., *Engendering Archaeology: Women and Prehistory* (366–87). Oxford: Basil Blackwell.

Polosmak, N. V. 1991. "Un nouveau kourgane a 'tomb gelee' de l'Altai (rapport preliminaire)." *Arts Asiatiques* 46: 5–12.

———. 1994. "The Ak-Alakh 'Frozen Grave' Barrow." *Ancient Civilizations from Scythia to Siberia* 1(3): 346–54.

———. 1998. "The Burial of a Noble Pazyryk Woman." *Ancient Civilizations from Scythia to Siberia* 5(2): 125–63.

Pookajorn, Surin. 1984. *The Hoabinhian of Mainland Southeast Asia: New Data from the Recent Thai Excavation in the Ban Kao Area.* Thai Khadi Research Institute No. 16. Bangkok: Thammasat University.

Popkin, Barry M. 1980. "Time Allocation of the Mother and Child Nutrition." *Ecology of Food and Nutrition* 9: 1–14.

Postma, Antoon. 1991. "Laguna Copper-Plate Inscription: A Valuable Philippine Document." *Bulletin of the Indo-Pacific Prehistory Association* 11: 160–71.

Potter, James. 1998. "Communal Ritual and Faunal Remains: An Example from the Delores Anasazi." *Journal of Field Archaeology* 24 (3): 353–364.

Prance, G. T., ed. 1982. *Biological Diversification in the Tropics.* New York: Columbia University Press.

Quindoza-Santiago, Lilia. 1996. "Roots of Feminist Thought in the Philippines." *Review of Women's Studies* 5–6: 159–72.

Quinn, Naomi. 1991. "The Cultural Basis of Metaphor." In J. Fernandez, ed., *Beyond Metaphor: The Theory of Tropes in Anthropology* (56–93). Stanford, Calif.: Stanford University Press.

Quirke, S. 1992. *Ancient Egyptian Religion.* London: British Museum.

Rachman, Ali M. A. 1991. "Social Intergration and Energy Utilization: An Analysis of the Kubu Terasing of Indonesia and the Temuan Orang Asli of Malaysia." In A. Terry Rambo and Kathleen Gillogly, eds., *Profiles in Cultural Evolution.* Anthropological Papers No. 85. Ann Arbor, University of Michigan, Museum of Anthropology.

Radcliffe-Brown, A. A. 1922. *The Andaman Islanders.* Cambridge: Cambridge University Press.

Radina, F. 1992. "Una statuetta neolitica da Canne." In *Atti della XXVII Riunione Scientifica dell'Istituto Italiano di Preistoria e Protostoria, Firenze 1989* (455–63). Firenze.

Rafael, Vicente. 1988. *Contracting Colonialism: Translation and Christian Conversion in Tagalog Society under Early Spanish Rule.* Manila: Ateneo de Manila University Press.

Rai, Navin. 1990. *Living in Lean-To: Philippine Negrito Foragers in Transition.* Anthropological Papers No. 80. Ann Arbor: University of Michigan, Museum of Anthropology.

Rainey, Froelich. 1947. "The Whale Men of Tigara." *Anthropological Papers of the Museum of Natural History* 41(2): 231–483.

Rapoport, Amos. 1990. "Systems of Activities and Systems of Settings." In Susan Kent, ed., *Domestic Architecture and the Use of Space: An Interdisciplinary Cross-Cultural Study* (9–20). Cambridge: Cambridge University Press.

Redclift, Nanneke. 1985. "The Contested Domain: Gender, Accumulation and the Labour Process." In Nanneke Redclift and Enzo Mingione, eds., *Beyond Employment: Household, Gender and Subsistence* (92–125). New York: Basil Blackwell.

Reed, K. E. 1997. "Early Hominid Evolution and Ecological Change through the African Plio-Pleistocene." *Journal of Human Evolution* 32: 289–322.

Reid, Anthony. 1988. *Southeast Asia in the Age of Commerce, 1450–1680: The Lands below the Winds.* New Haven, Conn.: Yale University Press.

Reiter, Rayna, ed. 1975. *Toward an Anthropology of Women.* New York: Monthly Review Press.

Renmin Ribao. 1988. "Another Important Discovery of the Chinese Northern Cultural Relics—Neolithic Casting Mold Unearthed in Inner Mongolia." January 10.

Reynolds, J. D., and P. H. Harvey. 1994. "Sexual Selection and the Evolution of Sex Differences." In R. V. Short and E. Balaban, eds., *The Differences between the Sexes* (53–70). Cambridge: Cambridge University Press.

Richards, M., H. Côrte-Real, P. Forster, V. Macaulay, H. Wilkinson-Herbots, A. Demaine, S. Papiha, R. Hedges, H.-J. Bandelt, and B. Sykes. 1996. "Paleolithic and Neolithic Lineages in the European Mitochondrial Gene Pool." *American Journal of Human Genetics* 59: 185–203.

Robb, J. 1994a. "Burial and Social Reproduction in the Peninsular Italian Neolithic." *Journal of Mediterranean Archaeology* 7: 27–71.

———. 1994b. "Gender Contradictions, Moral Coalitions, and Inequality in Prehistoric Italy." *Journal of European Archaeology* 2: 20–49.

Robben, A. C. G. M. 1989. "Habits of the Home: Spatial Hegemony and the Structuration of House and Society in Brazil." *American Anthropologist* 91: 570–88.

Roler, Kathy, and Barbara L. Stark. N.d. "Recognizing Poor Households in the Archaeological Record: A Case Study from South-Central Veracruz, Mexico." Unpublished paper.

Rolle, Renata. 1989. *The World of the Scythians.* Berkeley and Los Angeles: University of California Press.

Roosevelt, A. C. 1998. "Ancient and Modern Hunter-Gatherers of Lowland South America: An Evolutionary Problem." In W. Balee, ed., *Advances in Historical Ecology* (190–212). New York: Columbia University Press.

Roosevelt, A. C., M. Lima da Costa, C. Lopes Machado, M. Michab, N. Mercier, H. Valladas, J. Feathers, W. Barnett, M. Imazio da Silveira, A. Henderson, J. Slilva, B. Chernoff, D. S. Reese, J. A. Holman, N. Toth, and K. Schick. 1996. "Paleoindian Cave Dwellers in the Amazon: The Peopling of the Americas." *Science* 272: 373–84.

Rosaldo, Michelle Zimbalist. 1974. "Women, Culture and Society: A Theoretical Overview." In Michelle Zimbalist Rosaldo and Louise Lamphere, eds., *Women, Culture and Society* (17–42). Stanford, Calif.: Stanford University Press.

———. 1980. "The Use and Misuse of Anthropology: Reflections on Feminism and Cross-Cultural Understanding." *Signs* 5(3): 389–414.

Rosaldo, Michelle Zimbalist, and Louise Lamphere, eds. 1974. *Women, Culture and Society.* Stanford, Calif.: Stanford University Press.

Roscoe, Will. 1988. "We'wha and Klah: The American Indian Berdache as Artist and Priest." *American Indian Quarterly* 12(2): 127–50.

———. 1994. "How to Become a Berdache: Toward a Unified Analysis of Gender Diversity." In Gilbert Herdt, ed., *Third Sex, Third Gender: Beyond Sexual Dimorphism in Culture and History* (329–72). Cambridge: MIT Press.

————. 1998a. *The Zuni Man-Woman*. Albuquerque: University of New Mexico Press.

————. 1998b. *Changing Ones: Third and Fourth Genders in Native North America*. New York: St. Martin's Press.

Rose, G. 1993. *Feminism and Geography*. Cambridge: Polity Press.

Roseberry, William. 1988. "Political Economy." *Annual Review of Anthropology* 17: 161–85.

Rosen-Ayalon, M. 1975. "The Contribution of Local Elements to Umayyad Art." *Eretz-Israel* 12: 194–99.

Rosenblatt, J. S., and C. T. Snowdon. 1996. *Parental Care: Evolution, Mechanisms, and Adaptive Significance*. San Diego: Academic Press.

Rossen, Jack. 1998. "Archaeobotanical Remains from the Yutopian Site, Argentina (1996 and 1998 Field Seasons)." Unpublished report.

Rubinson, Karen S. 1975. "Herodotus and the Scythians." *Expedition* 17(4): 16–20.

————. 1989. "Between East and West: Lands of the Nomads." Paper presented at the Ancient Traditions: Culture and Shamanism in Central Asia and the Americas conference, Denver.

Rudenko, Sergei I. 1970. *Frozen Tombs of Siberia*. Berkeley and Los Angeles: University of California Press.

Sahagún, Bernardino de. 1951. *Florentine Codex: General History of the Things of New Spain, Book 2—The Ceremonies*. Translated by Arthur J. O. Anderson and Charles E. Dibble. Monographs of the School of American Research, No. 14, Part 3. Santa Fe: School of American Research and the University of Utah Press.

————. 1969. *Florentine Codex: General History of the Things of New Spain, Book 6—Rhetoric and Moral Philosophy*. Translated by Arthur J. O. Anderson and Charles E. Dibble. Monographs of the School of American Research, No. 14, Part 7. Santa Fe: School of American Research and the University of Utah Press.

Sahlins, Marshall. 1972. *Stone Age Economics*. Chicago: Aldine.

Saladin d'Anglure, Bernard. 1994. "From Foetus to Shaman: The Construction of an Inuit Third Gender Sex." In A. Mills and R. Slobodin, eds., *American Rebirth: Reincarnation Belief Among North American Indians and Inuit* (82–106). Toronto: University of Toronto Press.

Salazar, Zeus. 1996. "The *Babaylan* in Philippine History (Translated from the Pilipino by P. D. Tapales)." In *Women's Role in Philippine History: Selected Essays* (209–22). Quezon City: University of the Philippines Press.

Sanday, Peggy Reeves. 1981. *Female Power and Male Dominance: On the Origins of Sexual Inequality*. Cambridge: Cambridge University Press.

Sangvichien, Sood. 1974. "Prehistoric Rock Painting." In Amarat Kantisit, ed., *Adit* [The past] (275–78). Bangkok: Pikkanet Press.

Sarkar, S. J. 1974. "Socio-Economic Aspects of Onge Fishing." *Anthropos* 69(3/4): 568–89.

Sarno, L. 1993. *Song from the Forest: My Life among the Ba-Benhelle Pygmies*. New York: Penguin Books.

Sasaki Komei. 1997. *Nippon Bunka no Taju-kozo: Ajia-teki Shiya kara Nippon Bunka o Saiko suru* [Multilayered structure of Japanese culture: A reconsideration of Japanese culture from an Asian perspective]. Tokyo: Shokakukan.

Scarre, Christopher, and Brian M. Fagan. 1997. *Ancient Civilizations*. New York: Longman.

Scattolin, M. Cristina. 1990. "Dos Asentamientos Formativos al Pie del Aconquija: El Sitio Loma Alta, Catamarca, Argentina." *Gaceta Arqueológica Andina* 5(17): 85–100.

Schafer, H. 1974. *Principles of Egyptian Art*. Oxford: Clarendon Press.

Schapera, Isaac. 1930. *The Khoisan Peoples of South Africa: Bushmen and Hottentots*. London: G. Routledge and K. Paul.

————. 1933. *The Early Cape Hottentots*, described in the writings of Olfert Dapper (1668), Willem ten Rhyne (1686) and Johannes Bulielmus de Grevenbroek (1695), the original texts with translations into English by I. Schapera and B. Farrington, edited by I. Schapera. Cape Town: The Van Riebeeck Society.

Schele, L., and D. Freidel. 1990. *A Forest of Kings: The Untold Story of the Ancient Maya.* New York: William Morrow.

Schlanger, Sarah H., and Richard H. Wilshusen. 1993. "Local Abandonments and Regional Conditions in the North American Southwest." In Catherine M. Cameron and Steve A. Tomka, eds., *Abandonment of Settlements and Regions: Ethnoarchaeological and Archaeological Approaches* (85–98). New York: Cambridge University Press.

Schlumberger, Daniel. 1946–48. "Deux fresques Omeyyades." *Syria* 25: 86–102.

Scholes, R. J., and B. H. Walker. 1993. *An African Savanna: Synthesis of the Nylsvley Study.* Cambridge: Cambridge University Press.

Sciulli, Paul. 1998. "Evolution of the Dentition in Prehistoric Ohio Valley Native Americans: II. Morphology of the Deciduous Dentition." *American Journal of Physical Anthropology* 106: 189–205.

Scott, William H. 1982. "Filipino Class Structure in the Sixteenth Century." In W. Scott, ed., *Cracks in the Parchment Curtain* (96–126). Quezon City: New Day Publishers.

————. 1984. "Linguistics and Palaeography." In W. Scott, ed., *Prehispanic Source Materials for the Study of Philippine History* (33–62). Quezon City: New Day Publishers.

————. 1994. *Barangay: Sixteenth-Century Philippine Culture and Society.* Quezon City: Ateneo de Manila University Press.

Service, Elman. 1975. *Origins of the State and Civilization: The Process of Political Evolution.* New York: W. W. Norton.

Shinto Koichi. 1999. "Jomon bunka no hikari wa mimami Kyushu kara" [Jomon culture starts from southern Kyushu]. In T. Kobayashi, ed., *Saishin Jomon-gaku no Sekai* [Latest in the world of Jomon studies] (112–20). Tokyo: Asahi Shimbunsha.

Shirai Mitsutaro. 1886. "Kaizuka yori ideshi dogu no ko" [On clay figurines recovered from shell middens]. *Tokyo Jinruigakkai Hokoku* [Reports of the Anthropological Society of Tokyo] 1(2): 26–29.

Shoocongdej, Rasmi. 1996. *Forager Mobility Organization in Seasonal Tropical Environments: A View from Lang Kamnan Cave, Western Thailand.* Ann Arbor: University of Michigan Press.

Shtier, Ann B. 1996. *Graduate Women's Studies: Visions and Realities: Papers Arising from a Conference Held at York University May 1995.* North York, Ont.: Inanna Publications and Education.

Sikes, N. E., and R. Potts. 1999. "Early Pleistocene Habitat in Member 1 Olorgesailie Based on Paleosol Stable Isotopes." *Journal of Human Evolution* 37:721–46.

Silberbauer, G. 1981. *Hunter and Habitat in the Central Kalahari Desert.* Cambridge: Cambridge University Press.

Sillen, Andrew, and Patricia Smith. 1983. "Sr/Ca Ratios Reveal Weaning Age in a Skeletal Population." *American Journal of Physical Anthropology* 60: 253–54.

Silverblatt, Irene. 1988. "Women in States." *Annual Review of Anthropology* 17: 427–60.

Skeates, R. 1994. "Burial, Context and Gender in Neolithic South-Eastern Italy." *Journal of European Archaeology* 2: 199–214.

Skotnes, Pippa, ed. 1996. *Miscast: Negotiation the Presence of the Bushmen.* Cape Town, South Africa: University of Cape Town Press.

————. 1991. "Is There Life after Trance?" *De Arte* 44: 16–24.

Slobodkin, L. B. 1968. "Toward a Predictive Theory of Evolution." In R. C. Lewontin, ed., *Population, Biology and Evolution* (187–205). Syracuse, N.Y.: Syracuse University Press.

Small, Meredith F. 1993. *Female Choices: Sexual Behavior of Female Primates.* Ithaca, N.Y.: Cornell University Press.

Smith, Shelley. 1984. "Gender Definition and Material Remains: Predynastic Egypt as a Test Case." M.A. thesis, Washington State University.

Smole, W. 1976. *The Yanoama Indians: A Cultural Geography.* Austin: University of Texas Press.

Snyder, M. C., and M. Tadesse. 1995. *African Women and Development: A History.* Johannesburg: University of Witwatersrand Press.

Sogo Joseishi Kenkyukai [Association for the Integrated Study of Women's History]. 1993. *Nippon Josei no Reikishi—Onna no Hataraki* [History of Japanese women—Women's work]. Tokyo: Kadokawashoten.

Solomon, A. 1992. "Gender, Representation and Power in San Ethnography and Rock Art." *Journal of Anthropological Archaeology* 11:291–329.

————. 1994. "Ethic Women: A Study in Variability in San Art." In *Contested Images: Diversity in Southern African Rock Art Research,* ed. T. A. Dowson and J. D. Lewis-Williams, pp. 331–72. Johannesburg: Witwatersrand University Press.

————. 1996. "Rock Art Incorporated: An Archaeological and Interdisciplinary Study of Certain Human Figures in San art." Unpublished Ph.D. dissertation, Department of Archaeology, University of Cape Town.

Sorensen, Per. 1974. "Prehistoric Iron Implements from Thailand." *Asian Perspectives* 16: 134–73.

————. 1988. *Archaeological Excavations in Thailand: Surface Finds and Minor Excavations.* London: Curzon.

Sorensen, Per, and Tove Hatting. 1967. *Archaeological Excavations in Thailand. Vol I: Ban Kao.* Copenhagen: Munkgaard.

Sourdel, J., and J. Sourdel. 1967. "Châteaux omeyyades de Syrie." *Revue des Études Islamiques* 39: 1–52.

Spector, J. 1983. "Male/Female Task Differentiation among the Hidatsa: Toward the Development of an Archaeological Approach to the Study of Gender." In P. Albers and B. Medicine, eds., *The Hidden Half* (77–99). Washington, D.C.: University Press of America.

Spector, Janet. 1993. *What This Awl Means: Feminist Archaeology at a Wahpeton Dakota Village.* St. Paul: Minnesota Historical Society.

Spector, Janet, and Mary Whelan. 1989. "Incorporating Gender into Archaeology Courses." In Sandra Morgan, ed., *Gender and Anthropology: Critical Reviews for Research and Teaching* (65–94). Washington, D.C.: American Anthropological Association.

Spencer, L. M. 1997. "Dietary Adaptations of Plio-Pleistocene Bovidae: Implications for Hominid Habitat Use." *Journal of Human Evolution* 32: 201–28.

Spielmann, Katherine A., ed. 1998. *Migration and Reorganization: The Pueblo IV Period in the American Southwest.* Anthropological Research Papers No. 51, Arizona State University, Tempe.

Spindler, Konrad. 1983. *Die Frühen Kelten.* Stuttgart: Reclam.

Splendeur des Sassanides. 1993. Brussels: Musées Royaux d'Art et d'Histoire.

Sponheimer, M., and J. Lee-Thorp. 1999. "Isotopic Evidence for the Diet of an Early Hominid, *Australopithecus africanus.*" *Science* 282: 386–390.

Srisuchat, Amara. 1989. *Rock Art in Kanchanaburi.* Bangkok: Chumnum Sahakon Kankaset.

————. 1990. *Rock Art at Khao Plara, Uthai Thai.* Bangkok: Chumnum Sahakon Kankaset.

————. 1991. *Rock Art: A Shadow of Thailand's Past.* Bangkok: Amarin Printing.

Stark, Barbara L., and Barbara Ann Hall. 1993. "Hierarchical Social Differentiation among Late to Terminal Classic Residential Locations in Mixtequilla, Veracruz, Mexico." In Robert S. Santley and Kenneth G. Hirth, eds., *Prehispanic Domestic Units in Western Mesoamerica* (249–73). Ann Arbor, Mich.: CRC Press.

Stern, Henri. 1946. "Notes sur l'architecture des châteaux omeyyades." *Ars Islamica* 11–12: 72–97.

Stevenson, J. 1995. "Man-the Shaman: Is It the Whole Story? A Feminist Perspective on the San Rock Art of Southern Africa." Unpublished M.A. thesis. Witwatersrand University, Department of Archaeology.

Steward, J., ed. 1946. *The Marginal Tribes: Handbook of South American Indians*. Washington, D.C.: Smithsonian Institution, Bureau of American Ethnology.

Stone, Glenn Davis, M. Priscilla Johnson-Stone, and Robert McNetting. 1984. "Household Variability and Inequality in Kofyar Subsistence and Inequality." *Journal of Anthropological Research* 40: 90–108.

Strathern, M. 1988. *The Gender of the Gift*. Berkeley and Los Angeles: University of California Press.

————. 1993. "Making Incomplete." In V. Broch-Due, I. Rudie, and T. Bleie, eds., *Carved Flesh, Cast Selves: Gendered Symbols and Social Practices* (41–51). Oxford: Berg.

Striccoli, R. 1980. "Il complesso ergologico e oggetti vari di Grotta Pacelli." In *Atti del II Convegno sulla Preistoria e Protostoria della Daunia* (83–112). San Severo: Archaeo Club d'Italia.

Strömberg, Agneta. 1993. *Male or Female: A Methodological Study of Grave Gifts as Sex-Indicators in Iron Age Burials from Athens*. Jonsered: Paul Aströms Förlag.

Sugihara Sosuke and Mitsunori Tozawa. 1965. "Ibaraki-gen Tatsuki site" [Shell mounds of the late and latest periods in Jomon age at Tstsugi, Ibaragi prefecture]. *Kokogaku Shukan* 3(2): 35–72.

Sullivan, Thelma. 1982. "Tlazolteotl-Ixcuina: The Great Spinner and Weaver." In Elizabeth Boone, ed., *The Art and Iconography of Late Post-Classic Central Mexico* (7–35). Washington, D.C.: Dumbarton Oaks.

Sun Miao. 1987. *Xiashang Shigao* [Historical records of Xia and Shang]. Beijing: Wenwu Press.

Sun Shoudao. 1984. "On the Hongshan Culture Jade Dragon at Sanxingtala." *Wenwu* 6: 7–10.

Sun Shoudao and Guo Dashun. 1984. "On the Primitive Civilization of the Liao River Basin and the Origin of Dragons." *Wenwu* 6: 11–20.

————. 1986. "Discovery and Study of the 'Goddess Head Sculpture' of the Hongshan Culture at Niuheliang." *Wenwu* 8: 18–24.

Supakijwilekakarn, Pibul. 1990. *Study on Prehistoric Painting at Khao Deang, Tambon Maehalab, Amphoe Si Swat and Tam Ta Duang, Tambon Chong Sa Dao, Amphoe Muang, Changwat Kanchanaburi*. Bangkok: Silpakorn University, Faculty of Archaeology.

Takahashi Mitsuko et al. 1998. "Toyama Sakuramachi iseki shutsudo kuri itai no DNA kaiseki" [DNA analysis of chetnet remains from the Sakuramachi site, Toyama prefecture]. In *Abstracts of the Papers Presented at the 15th Meeting of the Japan Society for Scientific Studies of Cultural Property* (58–59). Chiba: Archaeological Laboratory, Chiba University.

Takamure Itsue. 1938. *Bokeisei no Kenkyu* [Study of matrilineal system]. Tokyo: Koseikaku. Reprinted as Vol. 1 of the *Collected Works of Takamure Itsue* (Tokyo: Rironsha, 1966).

————. 1953. *Shoseikon no Kenkyu* [Study of matrilocal marriage]. Tokyo: Kodansha. Reprinted as Vols. 2 and 3 of the *Collected Works of Takamure Itsue* (Tokyo: Rironsha, 1966).

————. 1965. *Hi no Kuni no Wonna no Nikki* [Diary of a woman from the land of fire]. In *Collected Works of Takamure Itsue*, Vol. 10. Tokyo: Rironsha.

Taniguchi Yasuhiro. 1999. "Yuragu 'Jomon Bunka' of wakugumi" [Challenges to the framework of "Jomon culture"]. *Shiroi Kuni no Uta*, no. 520: 20–27.

Tarragó, Myriam N., and M. Cristina Scattolin. 1999. "La Problematica del Período Formativo en el Valle de Santa María." *Actas XII Congreso Nacional de Arqueología Argentina, La Plata, Argentina* 1: 142–53.

Tayles, N. G. 1998. *The People of Khok Phanom Di*. Research report. London: Society of Antiquaries.

Tenazas, Rose C. 1968. "A Report on the Archaeology of the Locsin-University of San Carlos Excavations in Pila, Laguna." Privately circulated.

Teng Shuping. 1997. "A Theory of the Three Origins of Jade Culture in Ancient China." In Rosemary E. Scott, ed., *Chinese Jades* (27–36). Colloquies on Art and Archaeology in Asia No. 18. London: Percival David Foundation of Chinese Art.

Terasawa Tomoko. 2000. "Kenryoku to josei" [Power and women]. In H. Tsude and M. Sahara, eds., *Kodaishi no Ronten 2: Onna to Otoko, Ie to Mura* [Issues in ancient history 2: Women and men, household and village] (235–76). Tokyo: Shogakkan.

Thomas, E.W. 1950. *Bushman Stories*. Cape Town: Oxford University Press

Thomas, M. F. 1975. *Tropical Geomorphology: A Study of Weathering and Landform Development in Warm Climates*. London: Macmillan.

Tiger, L. and R. Fox. 1971. *The Imperial Animal*. New York: Holt, Rinehart and Winston.

Tilley, C. 1994. *A Phenomenology of Landscape*. Oxford: Berg.

Tinè, S. 1983. *Passo di Corvo e la civiltà neolitica del Tavoliere*. Genova: Sagep.

Tinè, V. 1996. "Favella." In V. Tinè, ed., *Forme e tempi della neolitizzazione in Italia meridionale e in Sicilia: Atti del seminario internazionale, Rossano 29 aprile–2 maggio 1994* (423–25). Rossano: Instituto Regionale per le Antichità Calabresi e Bizantine and Instituto Italiano Archeologia Sperimentale.

Tonkinson, Robert. 1991. "Ideology and Domination in Aboriginal Australia: A Western Desert Test Case." In Tim Ingold, David Riches, and James Woodburn, eds., *Hunter-Gatherer 2: Property, Power, and Ideology*, pp. 150–64. new York: Berg.

Tooby, J., and I. DeVore. 1987. "The Reconstruction of Hominid Behavioral Evolution through Strategic Modeling. In W. Kinzey, ed., *The Evolution of Human Behavior: Primate Models* (183–237). Albany: State University of New York Press.

Torii Ryuzo. 1922. "Nihon sekki jidai minshu no joshin shinko" [The goddess belief among the people of the Japanese Stone Age]. *Jinruigaku Zasshi* 37(11): 371–83.

Torii Ryuzo and Kimiko Torii. 1904. "Etudes Archeologique et Ethnologique—Populations Primitive de la Mongolie Orientale." *Journal of the College of Science, Imperial University of Tokyo* 36: art. 4.

Tricart, J. 1973. *The Landforms of the Humid Tropics: Forests and Savannas*. Translated by C. J. Kiewiet de Jonge. New York: St. Martin's Press.

Troy, Lana. 1986. *Patterns of Queenship in Ancient Egyptian Myth and History*. Boreas 14. Uppsala: Acta Universitatis Upsaliensis.

———. 1994. "The First Time: Homology and Complementarity as Structural Forces in Ancient Egyptian Cosmology." *Cosmos* 10(1): 3–51.

Tsude Hiroshi. 1982. "Genshi doki to josei—Yayoi jidai no seibetsu bungyo to konin kyoju kitei" [Ancient pottery and women—Division of labor by gender and post–marital rules of residence during the Yayoi period]. In Jeoseishi Sogo Kenkyukai, ed., *Nippon Joseishi* [History of Women in Japan], Vol. 1 (1–42). Tokyo: University of Tokyo Press.

Tsude Hiroshi and Sahara, Makoto, eds. 2000. *Kodaishi no Ronten 2: Onna to Otoko, Ie to Mura* [Issues in ancient history 2: Women and men, household and village]. Tokyo: Shogakkan.

Turnbull, C. 1981. "Mbuti Womanhood." In F. Dahlberg, ed., *Woman the Gatherer* (205–20). New Haven, Conn.: Yale University Press.

———. 1983. *The Mbuti Pygmies: Change and Adaptation*. New York: Holt, Rinehart and Winston.

Turner, Terence. 1980. "The Social Skin." In J. Cherfas and R. Lewin, eds., *Not Work Alone* (112–40). Beverly Hills, Calif.: Sage Publications.

Ucko, Peter. 1968. "Ethnography and Archaeological Interpretation of Funerary Remains." *World Archaeology* 1(29): 262–80.

Vallibhotama, Srisak. 1993. "Nature and Rituals in the 12-Month Cycle: A Case Study of the 6th Month's Ritual." In *Man and Nature: A Cross-Cultural Perspective* (153–64). Bangkok: Chulalongkorn University Press.

Vandiver, Pamela, and Joan Gero. In press. "Preliminary Technical Analysis of Scoria and Other Materials from a Living Floor Context at Yutopian, Argentina. Appendix to Gero and Scattolin, 'Hacia la Comprensión de la Jerarquización: Un Estudio desde Yutopian,

Valle de Cajón.' " *Actas y Memorias del XI Congreso Nacional de Arqueología, Mendoza, Argentina.*

Varien, Mark. 1999. *Sedentism and Mobility in a Social Landscape.* Tucson: University of Arizona Press.

Vinnecombe, Patricia. 1976. *People of the Eland: Rock Paintings of the Drakensberg Bushmen as a Reflection of Their Life and Thought.* Pietermaritzburg: University of Natal Press.

Vitelli, K. D. 1993. "Power to the Potters: Comments on Perlès' 'Systems of Exchange and Organization of Production in Neolithic Greece' " *Journal of Mediterranean Archaeology* 6(2): 247–57.

———. 1995. "Pots, Potters, and the Shaping of Greek Neolithic Society." In W. Barnett and J. Hoopes, eds., *The Emergence of Pottery: Technology and Innovation in Ancient Societies* (55–63). Washington, D.C.: Smithsonian Institution Press.

Vrba, Elisabeth. 1995. "The Fossil Record of African Antelopes (Mammalia, Bovidae) in Relation to Human Evolution." In E. S. Vrba, G. H. Denton, T. C. Partridge, and L. H. Buckle, eds., *Paleoclimate and Evolution with Emphasis on Human Origins* (385–424). New Haven, Conn.: Yale University Press.

Wadley, L. 1998. "The Invisible Meat Providers: Southern African Hunter-Gatherer Spatial Patterning and the Archaeological Record." In S. Kent, ed., *Gender in African Prehistory* (69–82). Walnut Creek, Calif.: AltaMira.

Wadley, Lyn, ed. 1997. *Our Gendered Past: Archaeological Studies of Gender in Southern Africa.* Johannesburg: University of Witwatersrand Press.

Wajima Seiichi. 1948. "Genshi shuraku no kosei" [The organization and composition of prehistoric settlements]. In Tokyo Daigaku Rekishigaku Kenkyukai, ed., *Nihon Rekishigaku Koza* [Lectures in Japanese history] (1–32). Tokyo: Gakusei Shobo.

Walker, Phillip L., and Della Collins Cook. 1998. "Brief Communication: Gender and Sex: Vive la difference!" *American Journal of Physical Anthropology* 106: 255–59.

Wang Tao. 1999. "The Important Archaeological Discoveries: 1991–1995." In Roderick Whitfield and Wang Tao, eds., *Exploring China's Past* (228–245). London: Saffron Books.

Wang Ying. 1999. "The Carved Bone Artifacts at Anyang: Indicators of Gender and Status." Ph.D. diss., University of Pittsburgh.

Washburn, S. L., and I. DeVore. 1961. "Social Behavior of Baboons and Early Man." In S.L. Washburn, ed., *Social Life of Early Man* (91–105). Chicago: Aldine.

Wason, Paul K. 1994. *The Archaeology of Rank.* Cambridge: Cambridge University Press.

Watanabe Hitoshi. 1968. "Subsistence and Ecology of Northern Food Gatherers, with Special Reference to the Ainu." In R. Lee and I. DeVore, eds., *Man and Hunter* (69–77). Chicago: Aldine.

———. 1972. *The Ainu Ecosystem: Environment and Group Structure.* Tokyo: University of Tokyo Press.

———. 1997. "Jomon doju to joshin shinko—Minzokushi teki joho no kokogaku e no taikeiteki enyo ni kansuru kenkyu (I)" [Jomon clay figurines and the goddess cult—An ethnoarchaeological study, part 1]. *Bulletin of the National Museum of Ethnology* 22(4): 829–973.

———. 1998. "Jomon doju to joshin shinko—Minzokushi teki joho no kokogaku e no taikeiteki enyo ni kansuru kenkyu (II)" [Jomon clay figurines and the goddess cult—An ethnoarchaeological study, part 2]. *Bulletin of the National Museum of Ethnology* 23(1): 129–251.

———. 1999. "Jomon doju to joshin shinko—Minzokushi teki joho no kokogaku e no taikeiteki enyo ni kansuru kenkyu (3)" [Jomon clay figurines and the goddess cult—An ethnoarchaeological study, part 3]. *Bulletin of the National Museum of Ethnology* 24(2): 291–460.

Watson, Patty Jo, and Mary Kennedy. 1991. "The Development of Horticulture in the Eastern Woodlands of North America: Women's Role." In Joan Gero and Margaret

Conkey, eds., *Engendering Archaeology: Women and Prehistory* (255–75). New York: Blackwell.

Weiner, Annette. 1976. *Women of Value, Men of Renown: New Perspectives in Trobriand Exchange.* Austin: University of Texas Press.

Weismantel, M. J. 1989. "Making Breakfast and Raising Babies: The Zumbagua Household as Constituted Process." In R. R. Wilk, ed., *The Household Economy: Reconsidering the Domestic Mode of Production* (55–72). Boulder, Colo.: Westview Press.

Wheatley, Paul. 1972. *Pivot of the Four Corners.* Edinburgh: Edinburgh University Press.

Wheelwright, Julie. 1989. *Amazons and Military Maids.* London: Pandora.

Whitam, Frederick L., and Robin M. Mathy. 1986. *Male Homosexuality in Four Cultures.* New York: Praeger.

White, F. 1983. *The Vegetation of Africa: A Descriptive Memoir to Accompany the UNESCO AETFAT UNSO Vegetation Map of Africa, 1981.* Paris: UNESCO Natural Resources Research.

White, Joyce C. 1997. "A Brief Note on New Dates for the Ban Chiang Cultural Tradition." *Bulletin of the Indo-Pacific Prehistory Association* 16: 103–6.

Whitehead, Harriet. 1981. "The Bow and the Burden Strap: A New Look at Institutionalized Homosexuality in Native North America." In Sherry B. Ortner and Harriet Whitehead, eds., *Sexual Meanings: The Cultural Construction of Gender and Sexuality* (80–115). Cambridge: Cambridge University Press.

Whitehouse, R. D. 1984. "Social Organisation in the Neolithic of Southern Italy." In W. Waldren, R. Chapman, J. Lewthwaite, and R.-C. Kennard, eds., *The Deya Conference of Prehistory* (iv) (1109–33). British Archaeological Reports International Series 229. Oxford: Oxford University Press.

———. 1992a. "Tools the Manmaker: The Cultural Construction of Gender in Italian Prehistory." *Accordia Research Papers* 3: 41–53.

———. 1992b. *Underground Religion: Cult and Culture in Prehistoric Italy.* London: Accordia Research Centre.

———, ed. 1998. *Gender and Italian Archaeology: Challenging the Stereotypes.* London: Accordia Research Institute and Institute of Archaeology.

Whittle, Stephen. 1996. "Gender Fucking or Fucking Gender? Current Cultural Contributions to Theories of Gender Blending." In Richard Ekins and Dave King, eds., *Blending Genders: Social Aspects of Cross-Dressing and Sex-Changing* (196–214). New York: Routledge.

Wilk, R. 1988. "Maya Household Organization: Evidence and Analogies." In R. Wilk and W. Ashmore, eds., *Household and Community in the Mesoamerican Past* (135–52). Albuquerque: University of New Mexico Press.

———. 1989. "Decision Making and Resource Flows within the Household: Beyond the Black Box." In Richard R. Wilk, ed., *The Household Economy: Reconsidering the Domestic Mode of Production* (23–52). Boulder, Colo.: Westview Press.

———. 1990. "The Built Environment and Consumer Decisions." In Susan Kent, ed., *Domestic Architecture and the Use of Space*, pp. 34–42. London: Cambridge University Press.

———. 1991. *Household Ecology: Economic Change and Domestic Life among the Kekchi Maya in Belize.* Tucson: University of Arizona Press.

Wilk, Richard R., and Robert McC. Netting. 1984. "Households: Changing Forms and Functions." In R. McC. Netting, R. Wilk, and E. J. Arnold, eds., *Households: Comparative and Historical Studies of the Domestic Group* (1–28). Berkeley: University of California Press.

Wilk, Richard R., and William L. Rathje. 1982. "Household Archaeology." In Richard R. Wilk and William L. Rathje, eds., *Archaeology of the Household: Building a Prehistory of Domestic Life. American Behavioral Scientist* 25 (b): (617–39).

Wilkinson, R. H. 1992. *Reading Egyptian Art.* London: Thames and Hudson.

Wilson, E. O. 1978 *On Human Nature*. Cambridge, Mass.: Harvard University Press.

WoldeGabriel, G., T. D. White, G. Suwa, P. Renne, J. de Heinzelin, W. K. Hart, and G. Helken. 1994. "Ecological and Temporal Placement of Early Pliocene Hominids at Aramis, Ethiopia." *Nature* 371: 330–33.

Wolters, O. W. 1982. *History, Culture, and Region in Southeast Asian Perspectives*. Singapore: Institute of Southeast Asian Studies.

Wongthes, Suchit. 1994. *The Thais Were Always Here in Southeast Asia*. Bangkok: Ruen Kaew Press.

Woodhouse, Annie. 1989. *Fantastic Women: Sex, Gender and Transvestism*. New Brunswick, N.J.: Rutgers University Press.

Wrangham, Richard, and Dale Peterson. 1996, *Demonic Males: Apes and the Origins of Human Violence*. New York: Houghton Mifflin.

Wright, Henry T. 1984. "Pre-State Political Formations." In T. Earle, ed., *On the Evolution of Complex Societies: Essays in Honor of Harry Hoijer 1982* (41–77). Malibu, Calif.: Undena Publications.

Wright, Lori, and Henry Schwarcz. 1998. "Breastfeeding and Weaning in Prehistory." *American Journal of Physical Anthropology* 106: 1–8.

Wright, Rita P. 1991. "Women's Labor and Pottery Production in Prehistory." In Joan M. Gero and Margaret W. Conkey, eds., *Engendering Archaeology: Women and Prehistory* (194–223). Cambridge, Mass.: Basil Blackwell.

———. 1996. "Technology, Gender and Class: Worlds of Difference in Ur III Mesopotamia." In R. Wright, ed., *Gender and Archaeology* (79–110). Philadelphia: University of Pennsylvania Press.

Wu, K. C. 1982. *The Chinese Heritage*. New York: Crown Publishers.

Wust, I. 1994. "The Eastern Bororo from an Archaeological Perspective." In A. C. Roosevelt, ed., *Amazonian Indians from Prehistory to the Present* (315–42). Tucson: University of Arizona Press.

Wylie, Alison. 1992. "Feminist Theories of Social Power: Some Implications for a Processual Archaeology." *Norwegian Archaeology Review* 25(1): 51–67.

Yablonsky, Leonid. 1995. "The Material Culture of the Saka and Historical Reconstruction." In Jeannine Davis-Kimball et al., eds., *Nomads of the Early Iron Age* (201–39). Berkeley, Calif.: Zinat Press.

Yamani, Mai, ed. 1996. *Feminism and Islam*. Berkshire: Ithaca Press.

Yang Shengnan. 1983. "Puci Suojian Zhuhoudui Shangwangshi de Shengshu Guanxi" [*Shengshu* relations between the Shang royal house and the vassals as revealed in the oracle bone inscriptions]. In Hu Houxuan, ed., *Jiaguwen yu Yinshangshi* (134–35). Shanghai: Shanghai Guji Press.

Yang Xiaoneng. 1988. Beijing: Tai Dao Publishing.

Yates, R., J. Golson, and M. Hall. 1985. "Trance Performance: The Rock Art of Boontjieskloof and Sevilla." *South African Archaeological Bulletin* 40:70–89.

Yates, R., and R. Jerardino. 1996. "A Fortuitous Fall: Early Rock Paintings from the West Coast of South Africa." *South African Journal of Science* 92: 110.

Yinxu de faxian yu yanjiu. 1994. Beijing: Institute of Archaeology.

Yinxu Fuhaomu. 1980. Beijing: Wenwu Press.

Yoneda, Konosuke. 1884. *Dogu* [Clay figurines]. Kokogaku Library No. 21. Tokyo: Nyu Saiensusha.

You-Di, Chin. 1974. "Prehistoric Rock Painting." In Amarat Kantisit, ed., *Adit* [The past] (114–38). Bangkok: Pikkanet Press.

Zhongyuan Wenwu. 1986. 3: 14–23.

Zihlman, A. 1996. "Reconstructions Reconsidered: Chimpanzee Models and Human Evolution." In W. C. McGrew, L. F. Marchant, and T. Nishida, eds., *Great Ape Societies* (293–304). Cambridge: Cambridge University Press.

Index

Abba, 189
Abydos cemetery, 52
Ache, 362, 367
Adena, 230, 231
ADNA analysis, 241, 243, 253, 255
affective space, 10, 36–37
Africa: herder/farmer in, 94–95; hunter-gatherer displacement in, 94–95; hunter-gatherer in, 93–94; hunting/sex, relationship between, 97–99. *See also* San; San, hunting by
Agta, 182, 185, 188–89
Ahura Mazda, 304
Aisne-Marne, 255
Al Alakh 3, 69–70
Alaska, 156–57, 243
Alawniyeh cemetery, 52
Albertson, Donald, 228
Alcina, Ignacio, 310, 313
Algonquin language, 159
Allan, Sarah, 79
Altayan burial, 70, 72
Amaterasu, 325
Amazonian Indian, 86–87, 160–61, 362, 364, 365, 367
American Indian. *See* Native American
Anahita, 304
Andaman Islands, 120–21; burials on, 178–79; division of labor on, 176, 181–82; exhumation on, 179; gender distinction on, 183–84; Hava Beel Cave on, 181–82; in-

sular structure of, 180; midden at, constitution of, 173; position of woman in, 183–85; ritual on, 176, 178, 183–84; sex role on, 184; status, as age related on, 173
Andaman Islands, Chauldari shell midden: bone tools from, 177–79; shell artifacts from, 174–77; stone tools from, 179–81
Andaman Islands study: background of, 173–74; discussion of findings, 182–85; gendered bone use evidence in, 177–78; gendered shell use evidence in, 175, 177; hunting evidence in, 178, 182; symbolism of *Polymesoda* shell, 176
Andean community, 129–30, 131, 166
androcentrism: in archaeology, 15; in contemporary culture, 3, 4
anemia, 208, 213, 228, 231
Angelino, Henry, 248
Angkor, 222
animal remains, in grave, 219
anthropomorphic figurine: in Arnesano tomb, 28, *30;* at desert palace, 297, 300, 302; at Dongshanzui, 75; as gender study source, 6; in Grotto di Cala Seizzo, 28, *29;* jade, 257, *258–59;* in Meso-America, 89–90, 257, *258–59;* in predynastic Egypt, 11, 52–55, *53,* 63; settlement, 10, 32, 33, 352; in Sicily, 33; tattooed, *59–60. See also* Italy, Neolithic, gender study, of figurine; Jomon period, figurine of

413

About the Contributors

Bettina Arnold is an associate professor in the Department of Anthropology at the University of Wisconsin, Milwaukee. Her area of expertise is early Iron Age Europe, but she has participated in archaeological projects ranging from the Middle Bronze Age through the Roman period. She is the director of a long-term, collaborative research project in southwestern Germany that combines conventional analysis of burial data dating to the Late Hallstatt period with the analysis of ancient DNA in order to reconstruct aspects of social organization (for more information, see <http://www.uwm.edu/~7Ebarnold/>). Her research interests include European prehistory generally, Celtic Europe, the archaeology of gender, mortuary analysis, material culture as a system of communication, and ethical issues in archaeology, including the use and abuse of the past for political purposes.

Elisabeth A. Bacus (Ph.D., University of Michigan) is a lecturer in the archaeology of Southeast Asia at the Institute of Archaeology, University College, London (UCL). Prior to joining UCL in 1997, she held a University of California President's Postdoctoral Fellowship in the Department of Anthropology at the University of California, Berkeley. She has been conducting archaeological research in Southeast Asia, specifically in the Philippines, since 1986. In addition to continuing her research on issues of political economy in first- to mid-second-millennium A.D. Visayan polities, she is currently involved in two interrelated projects in Bali, Indonesia: *Biocomplexity: Emergence of Cooperation from Human-Environmental Interactions* (headed by Stephen Lansing, University of Arizona) and *Transformations in the Political and Economic Landscapes of South-Central Bali during the First Millennium A.D.: An*

Archaeological Investigation of Early Balinese States (with I. Wayan Ardika, Universitas Udayana, and John Schoenfelder, University of California, Los Angeles). Her recent publications include *Complex Polities in the Ancient Tropical World* (edited with L. Lucero).

Cheryl Claassen is currently interested in the sociology of archaeology after twenty years of working in the positivist paradigm working on shells and humans in the Archaic period of the Eastern United States. She has a Ph.D. from Harvard University (1982) and has edited three volumes on archaeology and gender as well as three on shell. In the last several years she has engaged in several ethnographic projects.

Zarine Cooper (Ph.D. archaeology, Deccan College, Poona University) has research interests in prehistoric adaptation patterns in Southeast Asia, ethnoarchaeology, central Indian folktales, coastal adaptations in the Andaman and Nicobar Islands, and memorial traditions among the tribes of India. Since the 1980s, she has given lectures and conducted courses at the Australian National University, Canberra; at Cambridge, England; and at Dresden, Germany. Since 1992, she has been a reviewer of research proposals to the anthropology program of the National Science Foundation, Washington, D.C. She received a Homi Bhabha Fellowship (1984) for research on archaeological and ethnographic investigations in the Andaman islands and a grant from the Smithsonian Institution, Washington, D.C., to study the W. L. Abbott Ethnographic Collections from the Andaman and Nicobar Islands (1986). In 1989, she was granted a Young Scientist's Fellowship by the Indian Department of Science and Technology for further archaeological research in the Andamans.

Joan M. Gero teaches anthropology at American University in Washington, D.C. She focuses her field research on gender and power issues in prehistory, especially in the Andean regions of Argentina and Peru, and has directed excavations at early administrative centers as well as at domestic household complexes in the Andes. She writes about the origins of state-level society, feminist interpretations of prehistory, and the sociopolitics of doing archaeology and is interested in the epistemology of archaeological knowledge, especially in Paleo-Indian studies. Her many publications include the popular book *Engendering Archaeology: Women and Prehistory* (with Margaret Conkey). Presently, she serves as senior North American representative to the World Archaeological Congress and hopes that the many readers of this volume will join the World Archaeology Congress (<http://www.wac.uct.ac.za>) and attend the Congress in 2003.

Donna Glowacki (M.A., University of Missouri, Columbia) is a graduate student working on her Ph.D. at Arizona State University in Tempe. She is also an associate researcher at Crow Canyon Archaeological Center, a not-for-profit education and research institution in Cortez, Colorado. Most of her archaeological research has been carried out in the Mesa Verde region in the American Southwest, but she has also worked on archaeological sites in the Midwest. Her research interests include Southwest prehistory, ceramic production, and exchange, social relations, and migration.

Fekri A. Hassan is Petrie Professor of Archaeology, Institute of Archaeology, University College London. His principal topical interests deal with the cultural dynamics of state formation in Ancient Egypt. He has attempted to elucidate the role of gender in the early religious and political developments in previous studies of rock art as well as the attributes of earliest Egyptian goddesses.

C. F. W. Higham has been the Foundation Professor of Anthropology at the University of Otago, New Zealand, since 1968. He read archaeology at Cambridge University and has been conducting excavations in Southeast Asia for the past 30 years. His publications include *Archaeology of Mainland Southeast Asia, Bronze Age of Southeast Asia,* and *Prehistoric Thailand* (coauthored with Rachanie Thosarat). His current research involves excavations in Thailand and Cambodia to illuminate the origins of the civilization of Angkor. He has been a research affiliate of the University of Pennsylvania, visiting professor at the University of London, and a fellow of St. John's College, Cambridge. He is a fellow of the British Academy and a regular visitor to Britain, where he has given the Academy's Mortimer Wheeler Lecture, but he enjoys nothing more than returning to Southeast Asia to continue excavating.

Fumiko Ikawa-Smith was born in Kobe, Japan, and was educated at Tsuda College, Tokyo (B.A.'53, English), Radcliffe College (A.M.'58, Anthropology) and Harvard University (Ph.D.'74, Anthropology). She has been affiliated with McGill University, Montreal, since 1968, where she is professor of anthropology, specializing in prehistoric archaeology of East Asia. She served twice as the president of the Japan Studies Association of Canada (1988–90, 1999–2000).

Rosemary Joyce is an anthropologist and archaeologist currently engaged in archaeological fieldwork in the Ulua River valley in northern Honduras. At the University of California, Berkeley, she teaches courses in archaeological method and theory, museum studies, the archaeology of Central America and the Maya, household archaeology, and (with Ruth Tringham and Meg Conkey) the poetics of place and time. She also participates in the Multimedia Authoring Center for Instruction in Anthropology (MACTIA). She is the former director of the Phoebe Apperson Hearst Museum of Anthropology at Berkeley and former assistant director and curator at the Peabody Museum, Harvard University, where she taught anthropology from 1985 to 1994. Her publications center on the intersection of materiality and identity and include *Gender and Power in Prehispanic Mesoamerica, Beyond Kinship: Social and Material Reproduction in House Societies* (with Susan D. Gillespie), *Social Patterns in Pre-Classic Mesoamerica* (with David C. Grove), *Women in Prehistory: North America and Mesoamerica* (with Cheryl Claassen), and *Cerro Palenque: Power and Identity on the Maya Periphery.*

Katheryn M. Linduff is a professor of art, history, and archaeology specializing in the study of early China and inner Asia at the University of Pittsburgh. She is interested in the rise of complex society and especially in the interplay of ethnic, cultural, and gender identity with economic and political diversity and change in antiquity. Recent publications include *The Emergence of Metallurgy in China* (2000) and *Ancient Bronzes of the Eastern Eurasian Steppes* (1997, with Emma C. Bunker, Trudy Kawami, and Wu En). She is currently in charge of a regional settlement survey in eastern Inner Mongolia and conducting research for a second volume on metallurgy, this one on the region between the Yennesi and the Yellow Rivers.

Margaret Nelson is professor of anthropology at Arizona State University. Her research interests include land use among small-scale agriculturalists, technological organization, and issues of gender equity. She is author of *Mimbres during the Twelfth Century: Abandonment, Continuity, and Reorganization* (University of Arizona Press, 1999) and co-editor with S. Nelson and A. Wylie of "Equity Issues for Women in Archaeology" (Archeological Papers of the American Anthropological Association). Nelson worked as a research assistant to Brian Hayden in 1979 on the Coxoh Ethnoarchaeology Project, when the data for her paper in this volume were collected.

Sarah Milledge Nelson (Ph.D., University of Michigan) is John Evans Professor of Archaeology at the University of Denver. She does most of her archaeology in China and Korea and has long had an interest in gender and archaeology. Three of her recent books are *Gender in Archaeology: Analyzing Power and Prestige, The Archaeology of Northeast China,* and *The Archaeology of Korea.*

John Parkington is a professor of archaeology at the University of Cape Town, where he has taught since 1966. His research has focused on the lives of precolonial hunter-gatherers and herders in the Cape region of South Africa. He has recorded rock paintings and excavated shell middens and other sites extending back some 250,000 years. His publications include several on paleo-environmental reconstruction, the significance of rock art in the lives of pre-colonial stone age hunters and gatherers, and changing settlement histories.

A. C. Roosevelt (B.A., Stanford University; Ph.D., Columbia University) is the curator of archaeology at the Field Museum and a professor of anthropology at the University of Illinois, Chicago. She is interested in human ecology and evolution. The National Science Foundation, the National Endowment for the Humanities, and the MacArthur Foundation have funded her research. In the 1970s, she investigated prehistoric agriculture and demography in the Orinoco, Venezuela. She directed geoarchaeological research at the mouth of the Amazon in Brazil in the 1980s and researched early human sites in the Republic of Congo and the Central African Republic in the late 1990s. Her publications include *Moundbuilders of the Amazon, Amazonian Indians from Prehistory to the Present,* and *The Excavations of Corozal,* in addition to articles in *Science* and *Nature.* Roosevelt is vice chair of the American Academy of Arts and Sciences Midwest Council, consulting editor for *Latin American Antiquity,* trustee of Science Service, and an adviser to Human Relations Area Files.

Myriam Rosen-Ayalon is Leo A. Mayer Professor of Islamic Art and Archaeology at the Hebrew University of Jerusalem, where she held the position of head of the Institute of Asian and African Studies from 1989 to 1992. She has conducted fieldwork in Susa, Iran, and in Khirbat al-Minya, Ramla, and Ashkelon, Israel. She has held many academic appointments, including at Princeton University, the Sorbonne, and the University of Kiel, Germany. She has served as an adviser to the Musée du Louvre, Paris, and the Israel Museum, Jerusalem, and organized the 1987 International Conference on Islamic Jewelry in conjunction with the Israel Museum. Her publications include *La Céramique Musulmane de Suse* (1974), *The Early Islamic Monuments of al-Haram al-Sharif, Jerusalem* (1989), and *Art et Archéologie Islamiques en Palestine* (in press).

Karen Rubinson is a research associate in the Department of Anthropology, Barnard College, where she directs the Project for Archaeological Exchange. Her primary research areas are the Caucasus and Central Asia, where she has focused on many kinds of cultural interaction, particularly as expressed through archaeological and art historical materials. She received her Ph.D. from the Department of Art History and Archaeology, Columbia University.

M. Cristina Scattolin received her degree in archaeology from the Universidad Nacional de La Plata (UNLP), Argentina. She has held the position of associate researcher at the National Council of Research (CONICET) since 1991 and of associate professor of the Facultad de Ciencias Naturales y Museo, UNLP, since October 1995. Her areas of interest include the archaeology of early village societies and South Andean archaeology, especially of northwestern Argentina. She has been conducting excavations in the Aconquija Range in Catamarca for 20 years to contribute to the knowledge of formative societies of the first millenium A.D. Since 1985, she has been affiliated at the Museo Etnográfico of the University of Buenos Aires. Her articles include "Dos asentamientos formativos al pie del Aconquija: El sitio Loma Alta in Gaceta Arqueológica Andina" (1990) and "Santa María durante el Primer Milenio A.D.—Tierra Baldía?" published in *Årstryck, Journal of Etnografiska Museet i Göteborg* (2000).

Rasmi Shoocongdej is an assistant professor of archaeology in the Department of Archaeology, Silpakorn University, Bangkok, Thailand. She was educated at the Silpakorn University (B.A.) and the University of Michigan (M.A. and Ph.D.). Her geographic specialization is in Southeast Asia, especially Thailand. Her broader theoretical interests cover many areas, including hunter-gatherer mobility organization, late- to post-Pleistocene adaptation, cave archaeology, archaeology and education in developing countries, and politics and archaeology. She has conducted the archaeological project in western, northwestern, and central Thailand.

Annette Smith lives outside of Las Vegas and is currently an anthropology master's student at the University of Nevada, Las Vegas. She is also a teaching assistant and analyzes Virgin Anasazi artifacts in the Far West Pueblo laboratory at UNLV. Focusing on archaeology of the Southwest and Great Basin, her research concentrates on the frontier or periphery interactions of the various prehistoric peoples in Southern Nevada.

Shelley J. Smith (B.A. Anthropology, Pennsylvania State University 1975; M.A. Anthropology, Washington State University, 1984) is a branch chief in the Bureau of Land Management's Utah State Office, overseeing programs in planning, wilderness, recreation, and cultural resources. She has worked in the federal service for twenty years, much of it as an archaeologist. Her professional focus has been archaeology education, and she initiated and directed the Project Archaeology: Intrigue of the Past archaeology education program. She recently co-edited *The Archaeology Education Handbook: Sharing the Past with Kids* (AltaMira Press 2000) and served for three years as vice-chair of the Society for American Archaeology's Public Education Committee.

Ruth D. Whitehouse is a reader in archaeology at the Institute of Archaeology, University College London. She is a prehistoric archaeologist who specializes in the prehistory of Italy and the western Mediterranean. For many years, she has been involved in excavations and field survey projects in Italy and Menorca. Her research interests include archaeological theory and religion/ritual in prehistory. In recent years, she has become interested in the archaeology of gender, which is now one of her main research areas. Recent publications include an edited volume, *Gender and Italian Archaeology,* which introduces approaches to gender studies to her traditional research field—prehistoric Italy—where they had previously received little attention.